Modern Papua New Guinea

MODERN PAPUA NEW GUINEA

Edited by
Laura Zimmer-Tamakoshi

Library of Congress Cataloging-in-Publication Data

Modern Papua New Guinea / edited by Laura Zimmer-Tamakoshi
        p.   cm.
     Includes bibliographical references and index.
     ISBN 0-943549-51-5 (alk. paper)   0-943549-57-4 (pb: alk. paper)
     1. Papua New Guinea.   I. Zimmer-Tamakoshi, Laura, 1944–
DU740.M62   1998
995.3—dc21   97-50223
                                                              CIP

Published by Thomas Jefferson University Press at Truman State University in
Kirksville, Missouri 63501 USA, (800) 916-6802 (*http://tjup.truman.edu/*).

Contents

Laura Zimmer-Tamakoshi

INTRODUCTION

𝒫APUA NEW GUINEA IS A COUNTRY of great diversity. With over seven
hundred languages, as many cultures, diverse physical types, and a
landmass encompassing coral reef, mangrove swamp, rain forest,
mountain ranges, and extensive river systems, Papua New Guinea has
long attracted the interest of scientists and others seeking to understand or control some part of its rich diversity. Today, with a changed
political structure, involvement in the global economy, a diverse
national and expatriate community, and the exposure of its peoples to
new ideas and values through interactions with other Papua New
Guineans and foreigners, Papua New Guinea is even more multilingual,
multicultural, multiracial, and socially complex than a century ago
when European explorers, missionaries, traders, and colonizers began
arriving in significant numbers on New Guinea's shores.

To get a taste of this diversity, one need only visit Jackson Airport in
the nation's capital of Port Moresby. There, in the international arrivals
area, one sees expatriate children and the children of mixed-race marriages and elite Papua New Guineans arriving home from school in
Australia, wearing western fashions, and speaking a mixture of English,
Tok Pisin, Motu, or *Tok Ples.*[1] As children leave the airport in their parents' air-conditioned cars and head for the comfort of European-style
homes, less affluent youth stare openly, their expressionless faces

---

[1] *Tok Pisin* is a widely used form of Pidgin English. *Motu* is a trade language commonly
spoken in Papua. *Tok Ples* is the *Tok Pisin* expression for 'native language'.

I

masking whatever feelings they have about the differences between their own and the students' lifestyles. In the domestic terminals, individuals from all parts of Papua New Guinea crowd into lines for planes taking them back to their home areas or to jobs in other towns or remote government and mission outstations. Women dressed in colorful *laplaps* and *meri* blouses and carrying small children and heavy *bilums* jostle for place with women in high heels and men carrying briefcases.[2] Those who come to see the travelers off may follow the departing passengers to the gate to give last-minute instructions to attend to this or that matter back in the village. Or, they may chance to meet an old schoolmate or former work partner and engage in gossip or enlivened discussion of the latest gold find.

Discovering order in this diversity is not easy. Part of the difficulty lies in the different histories of contact and involvement with the outside world which affected the regions and peoples of Papua New Guinea in different ways, and part of it lies in the varied responses of individuals and discrete cultural groupings to similar forces for change. At the University of Papua New Guinea, for example, students coming from the more remote and more recently contacted areas of the country and who are the first of their particular societies to attend school sit beside students whose parents were among the first graduates of the university. At the same time, although early contact gave certain advantages to groups living on the coast, some of the longest-contacted groups are among the more culturally conservative, while in the more recently contacted highlands are some of the brashest, most westernized businessmen in the country.

Given the complexity of modern Papua New Guinea, the reader should view this book of readings as an attempt to bring some perspective and understanding into Papua New Guinea's varied social scene and the challenging political and economic realities of a recently independent Third World country. Unlike most such books, many of the readings also focus on issues of more personal concern to Papua New Guineans—such as AIDS, domestic violence, and the restructuring of the education system to fit the needs of a primarily rural population. To assist the reader who has little knowledge of Papua New Guinea or its peoples, the remainder of this introduction includes a brief history of

---

[2] *Laplaps* are pieces of cloth which women and sometimes men wear as ankle or knee-length skirts or loincloths. *Meri* blouses are loosely gathered smocks which come down over women's *laplaps*. *Bilums* are net bags used as carryalls by women throughout much of Papua New Guinea.

Papua New Guinea's colonization and emergence as an independent nation state in 1975, a discussion of the papers in this reader, a table of significant dates in the development of modern Papua New Guinea, and suggestions for further reading. More suggested readings are referred to in the part overviews.

The original idea for *Modern Papua New Guinea* arose as a result of a course (with the same title) the editor put together and taught at the University of Papua New Guinea in the late 1980s. Lacking a text, the editor relied on photocopies of relevant journal articles and chapters from published books for classroom materials but set about soliciting contributors for a proposed reader. This volume, then, is geared towards upper division and graduate level courses on Papua New Guinea or the contemporary Pacific. It is also useful for specialists in Third World development who do not know much about Papua New Guinea, and as a reference work for Papua New Guinean specialists.

THE COLONIAL PERIOD

Papua New Guinea is the creation of Australian colonialism and Papua New Guinean nationalism. This section focuses on the first while the following section looks at the contributions of Papua New Guineans to the making of an independent and unified Papua New Guinea state. In 1828, the Dutch claimed the western half of the island of New Guinea as part of their empire in southeast Asia. It was not until much later, however, when other Europeans and Australians had begun to take more than a passing interest in the eastern half of the island and its outer archipelagoes, that the Dutch announced the interior boundary of their claim as a straight line along the 141st meridian, from the eastern shore of Humboldt Bay in the north to the mouth of the Bensbach River in the south.

Prior to the 1880s, Australian interest in New Guinea was primarily economic, with labor recruiters visiting the islands in search of men to work on the Queensland sugar plantations and pearlers, traders, and *bêche-de-mer* fishermen operating in the Torres Strait and the island-strewn waters to the east of the main island. In the late 1870s and early 1880s, however, many persons in Britain's Australian colonies—particularly those living in Queensland—were alarmed by the growing German presence in the northeastern portion of New Guinea and various proposals were put forth for Britain to acquire the eastern half of New Guinea along with the islands of New Britain, New Ireland, and the Solomons to protect Australian economic interests and to provide a barrier against invasion from foreign powers. At first, Britain was reluctant to extend its holdings in the Western Pacific, and in 1883 the Queensland Colonial Government took it upon itself to annex all of New Guinea east of the Dutch border in the name of the Crown. Although the Queensland annexation was not ratified by the British government, it did bring the New Guinea question to a head. When a German protectorate was proclaimed over the northeastern section of the island in October 1884, the British Government moved quickly to protect Australian interests, establishing a protectorate over the southern shores of New Guinea in November 1884 and extending its claims even further in December of the same year to include the northern shores of Papua and the adjacent D'Entrecasteaux Islands. In 1888, the Protectorate of British New Guinea became the Crown Colony of British New Guinea, and in 1906—five years after Australian Independence—came under Australian control as the Territory of Papua.

Until the Second World War, the two halves of eastern New Guinea were administered separately, at first by Britain (1884–1906) and Germany (1884–1914) and then by Australia, both in Papua (1906–1942) and New Guinea (1914–1942). From the beginning, German New Guinea was administered for the economic benefit of privately owned German businesses. Thousands of New Guinean men and boys were employed as cheap labor on German-owned cocoa and copra plantations. Even after 1899, when the German government took control of the colony from the New Guinea company of Berlin, administrative policy focused on pacification by force and the opening up of new labor recruiting grounds. Such education as the New Guineans received was left primarily in the hands of missionaries.

On 17 September 1914, Australia took possession of the German colony—a move that was later formalized when the League of Nations gave Australia a mandate to administer New Guinea in the interests of the indigenous inhabitants. Like the Germans before them, however, Australian policy was to make the territory of New Guinea pay for itself and to make it an attractive and safe venture for Australian businessmen. After the First World War, German plantations were expropriated and given to ex-servicemen. Throughout the time period between the two world wars, labor recruiters, prospectors, missionaries, and government patrols pushed inland, discovering the populous Wahgi Valley in 1933 and bringing much of the interior under at least nominal control. On the eve of the Second World War, New Guinea had a flourishing economy based on gold mining and plantations. Few New Guineans, however, could be said to have benefited much from Australia's stewardship, in spite of the novel experiences gained as wash boys, plantation labor, and workers in the gold mines.

It was otherwise in Papua, where more paternalistic British and Australian administrations were less inclined to foster such naked exploitation of the local peoples. Altogether, there was less violence in the extension of government control in Papua and numerous acts were passed preventing large-scale alienation of customary land and excessive abuse of native workers. Nonetheless, although according to official government policy Papuans were to be encouraged to take part in the economic development of the region, it was expected that Australians would be the owners and managers while Papuans would be the unskilled labor. In any event, the economy was stagnant, few Australians made their fortunes in Papua, and, lacking sufficient funds, the administration left the education of Papuans in the hands of overburdened missionaries. In 1942, Papua was far less developed than New Guinea and many Papuans were as frustrated as their Australian masters over the virtual absence of economic opportunities.

On 23 January 1942, Japanese troops captured Rabaul Harbor and from there spread out to occupy the north coast of New Guinea and many of the offshore islands. Pushing southward to within forty-eight kilometers of Port Moresby in September 1942, the Japanese invasion posed a serious threat to Australia's security. It also brought about widespread destruction in New Guinea as Australian and American forces spent the remainder of the war engaged in fierce battles on land, sea, and in the air to get the Japanese out of New Guinea. For their part, while some Papua New Guineans welcomed the Japanese as 'liberators', many directly assisted the Allied troops as soldiers, laborers, and stretcher bearers while others looked after and hid pilots who had crash-landed behind Japanese lines. In the aftermath of war, there was a change in attitudes in both Papua New Guineans and Australians towards their former relationships. Having seen the vulnerability of Australians at war and having fought beside them as equals, few Papua New Guineans were willing to return to the old inequality. Indebted to Papua New Guineans for their assistance during the war, many former Australian soldiers called for a 'new deal' for Papua New Guinea, one which put Papua New Guineans first and expatriates second. This change in attitudes was matched by a change in Australia's international role in New Guinea. In 1942, the two territories were combined under a single military administration headquartered in Port Moresby. After the war the joint administration of Papua and New Guinea was taken over by civilian authorities and in December 1946 this union was given international sanction when the United Nations gave Australia trusteeship over the new Trust Territory of Papua New Guinea.

According to the terms of the United Nations agreement Australia was to prepare Papua New Guinea for self-government and independence, and to promote—in the meantime—the economic, social, and physical well-being and advancement of Papua New Guineans. The immediate response of the Australian government was to increase its annual grant to Papua New Guinea over fiftyfold. Compensation was paid out alike to villagers and expatriate plantation owners for war damages. A newly created Education Department built the first government primary and secondary schools. Papua New Guinean men were trained as carpenters, plumbers, and mechanics to help in the work of postwar reconstruction. Providing basic health care to all Papua New Guineans became an administrative priority as did the training of Papua New Guinean health workers for hospitals and village aid posts. And the Department of Agriculture took on the task of raising the efficiency of subsistence farming and assisting the villagers to become cash farmers.

Begun with high hopes, the new deal for Papua New Guinea was only a limited success. Government schools did not meet the needs of villagers and many village cooperatives failed due to a lack of business and management skills and, all too frequently, a lack of cooperation among the participants. In the 1950s, the government continued to promote improvements in health, education, and agriculture, but economic policy shifted away from encouraging village-based development projects to favoring private Australian enterprise as a means of developing the territory and its resources. Similarly, although the government encouraged the establishment of local government councils, it was widely believed that for many years to come Papua New Guineans would be unable to play an important role in the overall administration of the territory. In the 1950s few Papua New Guineans had either the necessary education or opportunity to disprove this assessment of their capabilities, but in the 1960s a changing world and the ambitions of a small but growing number of Papua New Guinean activists demanded the end of gradualism and the beginning of self-determination.

SELF-GOVERNMENT AND INDEPENDENCE

In 1962, a select committee of the territory's Legislative Council, made up of four Australians and two Papua New Guineans, recommended the formation of a House of Assembly in which Papua New Guineans would be in the majority. Shortly before the committee submitted its report, a United Nations Visiting Mission recommended a similar move although the Visiting Mission wanted no special electorates for nonindigenous groups, a provision which was rejected by the colonial administration as impractical in the absence of a sufficient number of well-educated and experienced Papua New Guinean candidates.

In 1964, when the first House of Assembly met, it was composed of twenty-six expatriates and thirty-eight Papua New Guineans. In general, the Papua New Guinean members were poorly educated and ill equipped to carry out their responsibilities as national leaders. By 1968, however, the second House of Assembly was manned by younger and better-educated Papua New Guineans who were able to articulate the concerns of all Papua New Guineans and to confront (or cooperate with) their Australian colleagues on issues of national importance and self-determination.

One such new member was Michael Somare, a former public servant who had successfully contested the East Sepik regional electorate. Ardently pro–self-government, Somare was highly vocal in his agreement with the 1968 United Nations Visiting Mission that immediate steps should be taken to bring Papua New Guinea closer to independence but sided with the Australian government (as well as many Papua New Guineans) on the need to promote economic self-reliance first if independence was to have any real meaning. In 1972, Somare was reelected to the House of Assembly where, as Pangu Party leader and head of the National Coalition Government, he presided as Chief Minister. In December of 1972, Somare announced his Eight Point Plan—a set of national goals calling for increased localization and economic self-reliance, equality of opportunity for all Papua New Guineans regardless of sex, and decentralization. With self-government on the horizon, secessionist movements arose in Papua, New Britain, Bougainville, and elsewhere as regions with different colonial histories and patterns of economic development feared for their particular interests under a centralized government dominated by Papua New Guineans from other regions. Crises such as that which erupted in Bougainville—over the alienation of land for the new copper mine and the importation of thousands of non-Bougainvilleans to work at the mine—precip-

decentralization and, after independence, the institution of provincial governments.

In December 1973, Papua New Guinea became self-governing. Although little had been done to implement the goals of the Eight Point Plan and Papua New Guinea was far from economically self-sufficient, Australia was facing economic problems of its own and was committed to getting out of Papua New Guinea as quickly as it could decently do so. It remained for Somare and other Papua New Guinean leaders to negotiate a reasonable aid package from Australia in order that government services could continue during the transition from self-government to independence and long after. It was also necessary to delay the acquisition of power as long as possible to avoid confusion and fear among government workers and the population at large.

Whatever doubts Papua New Guineans may have had about their ability to stand on their own, on 15 September 1975 Papua New Guinea became an independent country. In the years following independence, Papua New Guinea and its citizens have faced numerous and difficult challenges. As many of the chapters in this reader show, not all of the challenges have been met. This is understandable given the speed with which change is taking place and the fragmented nature of Papua New Guinean society. Moreover, in the absence of universal literacy and an expanded education-media system, which would bring useful and timely information to the more remote rural areas as well as the more accessible and better educated segments of the population, it is not always possible for Papua New Guineans to accurately assess the probable consequences of their own and others' actions.

THE PAPERS

The aim of this reader is to describe some of the changes and challenges now facing Papua New Guinea. The organization of the chapters into four parts—The State and National Identity, Economic Development, The New Society, and The People's Welfare—is intended to introduce readers to some of the major forces for change before getting into particular problem areas in the final section. Clearly, however, the important issues and developments in modern Papua New Guinea are interrelated, and a course instructor may wish to have students explore the chapters' interconnections differently than the order in which I have presented them in this text. Someone interested in the topic of women and gender relations, for example, will want to read as a set the chapters by Laura Zimmer-Tamakoshi, Martha Macintyre, and Jeanette Dickerson-Putman in part 3, The New Society, along with the chapters by Lawrence Hammar and Christine Bradley in part 4, The People's Welfare. All five authors look at the changing conditions and lifestyles of Papua New Guinean women and men, although Hammar's and Bradley's foci are more specifically on the especially virulent outcomes of women's unequal involvement in the development of their country—prostitution, AIDS/STDs, and an upsurge in wife-beating—hence their inclusion in part 4, The People's Welfare.

A central theme of most of the chapters is challenges facing the state. For example, the chapters by Peter Larmour and Norrie Mac-Queen in The State and National Identity, Oscar Kurer in Economic Development, and Sinclair Dinnen in The People's Welfare all raise important questions concerning the state's effectiveness in meeting the challenges of political disunity, the absence of a monopoly of physical force, a weak and inefficient bureaucracy, citizens' demands for accelerated economic growth and patronage, legal pluralism, increasing violence, corruption, and the need for a foreign policy that is both viable and conducive to Papua New Guinea's further development. Going into greater detail on one aspect of Papua New Guinea's foreign policy, David King in The State and National Identity gives us an in-depth account of Papua New Guinea's uneasy relations with neighboring Indonesia and her ambivalence about the influx of West Irian refugees and border-crossers into Papua New Guinea. Other challenges to be met by both the state and ordinary citizens are the destruction of the environment and the loss of valuable land and water supplies as a result of poorly planned mining operations, the need for conservation and proper management of wildlife and forest areas, and the issue of customary land and the state. Sound development policies may help to preserve Papua New Guinea's rich environment for future generations, but, as Colin Filer's paper in Economic Development and two of the papers in The People's Welfare demonstrate (the papers by Hughes and Sullivan, and King and Hughes), there are many pressures—demographic, economic, social, political, cultural, and individual ignorance and greed—which threaten to destroy this vision. Filer goes further by highlighting 'the very limited *scale of cooperation* which has always been characteristic of Melanesian society' as the biggest obstacle to Papua New Guinea's even achieving the 'development' which everyone wants, much less sustainable development. Still other challenges—also examined in The People's Welfare—lie in the area of health and education.

In his chapter, Lawrence Hammar illuminates processes by which prostitution and STDs/AIDS now flourish throughout Papua New Guinea. His analysis is gendered in that he links gendered economic, social, and legal inequalities to 'women's exchanging sex for money and goods casually and institutionally because they do not have access to the means of production equal to men's'. Hammar concludes that '[i]f prostitution is caused by men's biologically greater sex drive, then not much can be done about it, but if prostitution is a contradiction social in origin and perpetuation, then it can be unraveled and made unnecessary', as can sexually transmitted diseases.

Looking at the Papua New Guinea school system, Michael Crossley reviews past and present education policies and raises the sensitive topic of whether or not all Papua New Guinean students should be taught an academic curriculum. While an earlier generation of national teachers and leaders were in favor of an academic model, today's elite are more inclined to support a dual curriculum. As Michael Monsell-Davis suggests in his chapter, however, most parents would probably not be in favor of such a move, desiring as they do that their children's education result in prestigious and well-paid jobs in town. Responding further to the question of universal high school education, Monsell-Davis outlines the constraints facing unemployed school leavers when they try to use their education in their home areas and concludes that Papua New Guinea needs to expand education and promote rural development in ways that will attract and make good use of the nation's graduates.

Of prime importance to any state is the need to promote a sense of unity among its people. One area of cultural engineering that has great potential for accomplishing this by propagating national symbols and pride is media, including the visual arts, television, radio, music, and theater. Even expatriates are moved, for example, by local television coverage of the prime minister's plane—Kumul One—as it arrives in some foreign country and the prime minister himself receives the red carpet treatment. Nonetheless, as Pamela Rosi shows in her chapter in The State and National Identity, the modern artist is not only a 'cultural creator' but also a professional who must earn a living and balance his or her obligations and commitments in two conflicting worlds—the world of museums, collectors, and tourists, and the world of *wantoks* (T.P., members of the same language group) and personal relations.

A second focus of many of the writings in this collection is on change. With increasing mobility, occupational specialization, income differences, and opportunities for greater self-expression and new social groupings, the diversity that was a hallmark of Papua New Guinea societies in precolonial times has taken on new dimensions and meanings. In my chapter on Papua New Guinean women in town, in The New Society, I show how the role of urban homemaker is evolving differently among different segments of urban society. Among low-income families, for example, the role of homemaker is vital to family well-being as well as personally more satisfying and secure than the very different roles played by unemployed housewives in higher-income families and working wives. The distinctions I make in my title, between homemakers, housewives, and household managers, reflect differences in the experiences of women in terms of their household labor input, involvement in household decision making, and their relations with their husbands, families, and larger community.

Also in The New Society, Martha Macintyre's analysis of the causes of persistent gender inequality in Papua New Guinea gives special attention to the sentimental nationalism of urban elite males who idealize the lives of village women and fail to see that 'harking back to a utopian "traditionalism"' is unfair to both rural and urban females who, in common with one another, continue to suffer economic, social, cultural, and political oppression. Although the Papua New Guinea Constitution grants equality of status to women, the rhetoric of equality between the sexes 'disguises informal but systematic discrimination against women in education and employment'. Rather significantly, in the more than twenty years since independence there have been only three female members of National Parliament and very few women in high-status government jobs. While gender inequality is striking in Papua New Guinea, not all victims of 'development' and change are female. As Jeanette Dickerson-Putman shows in her chapter, Bena Bena men's experience of development has varied as older men have lost their social control over younger men (and women) and younger generations have been confronted with an unstable, unsatisfying social situation marked with deep inequalities among men as well as between men and women.

A third chapter which examines inequality of another sort is David King's spatial analysis of socioeconomic differentiation in urban areas of Papua New Guinea, in The New Society. Supporting the view that there is no fully developed class structure in Papua New Guinea, King demonstrates that in spite of a high correlation between house type, education, activity (e.g. wage earning, unemployed), and occupational category, income differences between high-cost, low-cost, and informal housing areas are not great and dependency and unemployment rates vary within only a limited range. Put simply, while high-cost housing areas contain the wealthiest people in the city only a small proportion can really be described as rich and many such households are homes to less prosperous relatives who join the household labor pool. Implicit in all the chapters is choice: the choices being made by Papua New Guineans as they make use of changing circumstances and opportunities and the difficult choices facing the state and its agencies in their efforts to manage and assist in the development of an energetic and diverse population. Other choices arise from Papua New Guinea's rich natural environment which is threatened by mining and timber projects yet offers Papua New Guineans the tantalizing possibility of sustained economic growth and independence. In Fred Olson and Tim Kan's chapter on the fisheries of Papua New Guinea, in Economic Development, they make the point that Papua New Guinea's seas are highly productive, yet few local decision makers seem to appreciate that fact or the potential for the country's fishery sector to contribute to national nutrition and economic development. As a result, every year, Papua New Guinea imports many millions of dollars worth of canned mackerel, fish that could be supplied by an expanded local fishing and canning industry.

SOME DATES IN THE DEVELOPMENT OF MODERN PNG SOCIETY

1828   Dutch make formal claim to western New Guinea.

1847   Marist mission established on Woodlark Island.

1871   London Missionary Society's New Guinea mission established in Torres Strait Islands.

1875   Interior boundary of Dutch claim set at 141st meridian. Wesleyan Methodist mission founded on Duke of York Island.

1879   Captain Eduard Hernsheim, German trader, sets up business in Gazelle Peninsula of New Britain.

1882   Sacred Heart Mission established in east New Britain.

1883 Queensland annexes eastern New Guinea in the name of Britain, a move soon repudiated by Britain.

1884 Partition of eastern New Guinea between Germany and Britain. The first Papuans graduate from the London Missionary Society pastors' training school in Port Moresby.

1885 Sacred Heart Mission founded on Yule Island, northwest of Port Moresby.

1886 Lutheran missions established in Finschhafen and Bogadjim in German New Guinea.

1888 British New Guinea becomes a Crown Colony of Britain.
Gold discovered on Sudest Island.

1891 Methodist Mission Society begins operations in the D'Entrecasteaux Islands, the Trobriands and the Louisiades.
Anglican missionaries begin work in the area of the northeast coast of German New Guinea.

1896 Society of the Divine Word establishes its first station on the north coast of German New Guinea.

1901 Australian independence.

1906 Australia takes over the administration of the Territory of Papua (formerly British New Guinea).

1910 Work begins on the Lakekamu goldfield.

1914 Australian military occupation of German New Guinea.

1921 German New Guinea becomes a mandated territory of Australia.

1926 Start of Edie Creek gold rush.

1930 Exploration of the central highlands begun by Michael Dwyer and Michael Leahy.

1932   Dredging begins on the Bulolo goldfields.

1933   Penetration of the Wahgi Valley by Australian Patrol Officer James Taylor and gold prospectors Mick, Dan, and James Leahy.

1942   Japanese invade Papua New Guinea.

1945   Japanese surrender.

1961   Western New Guinea (formerly Dutch New Guinea) invaded by Indonesians.

1964   Discovery of large deposits of copper on Bougainville Island. Election of indigenous leaders for the First House of Assembly.

1966   First National Census.
        Fauna (Protection and Control) Act passed.
        National Parks and Gardens Act passed.

1968   Discovery of gold at Ok Tedi.
        Election for the Second House of Assembly.

1971   Second National Census.
        National Parks Act passed.

1972   Election for the Third House of Assembly.
        Michael Somare announces Eight Point Plan.

1973   National Broadcasting Commission established.
        Papua New Guinea becomes self-governing.

1975   Papua New Guinea becomes independent.
        Former Chief Minister Michael Somare becomes prime minister.
        National Council of Women established and first national women's convention held.

1976   Bougainville agreement.

1977   Organic Law on Provincial Government passed.
        First election for National Parliament.
        Michael Somare retains his position as prime minister in the
            general election.

1978   Environmental Planning Act passed.
        Environmental Contaminants Act passed.
        Conservation Areas Act passed.

1979   International Trade in Endangered Species of Wild Flora and
            Fauna Act passed.

1980   Third National Census.
        Julius Chan becomes the country's second prime minister in a
            vote of no confidence in Michael Somare.

1981   PNG Foreign Policy White Paper released.

1982   National Parks Act passed.
        Michael Somare returns as prime minister.

1985   Paias Wingti becomes new prime minister in vote of no confi-
            dence in Michael Somare.

1987   Barnett Commission convened to examine forestry industry.
        Paias Wingti maintains his position as prime minister in the
            general election.
        Fiji coup.
        Treaty of Mutual Respect, Friendship, and Cooperation with
            Indonesia.

1988   Rabbie Namaliu takes over as prime minister in vote of no con-
            fidence against Paias Wingti.

1989   State of Emergency declared on Bougainville.

1990   Fourth National Census.

1992   Paias Wingti elected as prime minister in general elections.

1993   Wingti reelected in election subsequently deemed unconstitu-
        tional.

1994   Deputy Prime Minister Julius Chan replaces Paias Wingti as
        prime minister.
        Chan organizes Bougainville peace conference but cease-fire is
        short-lived.

1995   Human rights abuses committed by Indonesian armed forces
        against indigenous West Papuans living near the Freeport
        mine in Irian Jaya.

1997   Chan steps aside after nine days of national unrest and Papua
        New Guinea armed forces rebellion over his unpopular
        decision to bring foreign mercenaries into the ongoing
        conflicts at Bougainville.
        Papua New Guinea's Mining and Petroleum Minister, John
        Giheno, named acting prime minister, to replace Sir Julius
        Chan. Bill Skate, former governor of Port Moresby, becomes
        prime minister.

SUGGESTED READINGS

Ambrose, D., Chappell, D. A., Tarte, S., and Wesley-Smith, T., 1996. 'Melanesia in review: international issues and events, 1995', *The Contemporary Pacific,* 8(2):418–442.

Campbell, I. C., 1989. *A History of the Pacific Islands.* Berkeley: University of California Press.

Chappell, D. A., Henningham, S., Lal, B. V., and Wesley-Smith, T., 1995. 'Melanesia in review: issues and events, 1994', *The Contemporary Pacific,* 7(2):355–378.

Chowning, A., 1973. *Introduction to the Peoples and Cultures of Melanesia.* California: Cummings.

Crocombe, R., and Crocombe, M., 1982. *Polynesian Missions in Melanesia: From Samoa, Cook Islands and Tonga to Papua New Guinea and New Caledonia.* Suva: University of the South Pacific.

Dorney, S., 1990. *Papua New Guinea: People, Politics and History Since 1975.* Milsons Point, NSW: Random House Australia Pty Ltd.

Griffin, J., Nelson, H., and Firth, S., 1979. *Papua New Guinea: A Political History.* Richmond, Victoria: Heinemann Educational Australia Pty. Ltd.

Langmore, D., 1989. *Missionary Lives: Papua, 1874–1914.* Honolulu: University of Hawaii Press.

Schieffelin, E. L., and Crittenden, R., eds., 1991. *Like People You See in a Dream.* Stanford: Stanford University Press.

Turner, M., 1990. *Papua New Guinea: The Challenge of Independence.* Victoria, Australia: Penguin Books.

Part One

THE STATE AND NATIONAL IDENTITY

$\mathcal{B}$EFORE EUROPEAN COLONIALISM, people living on the island of New Guinea were organized into many thousands of independent political groupings, some created by individual 'Big Men' and 'Great Men,' others led by powerful chiefs (Berndt and Lawrence, eds., 1971; Godelier 1986; Sahlins 1963; Strathern 1971). Jealously guarding their autonomy, these groups were linked in loose, yet extensive, networks of trade, marriage, and exchange. These horizontal power structures are still important power bases for contemporary Papua New Guinean politicians at both the level of village politics and national parliament (Standish 1992, 1993; Wolfers and Regan 1988). What is different in contemporary politics is that national politicians must make decisions affecting an entire nation rather than simply serving the needs of their particular constituencies, and being suited to national leadership roles requires that one be a part of an educated elite that is developing interests of its own that are often in opposition to the interests of more ordinary citizens. A case in point is the lack of 'grassroots' sympathy for elite sexual politics and elite women's efforts to be elected to prominent positions in the Papua New Guinea government (Zimmer-Tamakoshi 1993); another is the beginning of a hereditary class system based on differences in 'education, training, qualifications for jobs, business success, financial position, and the capacity to raise financial support in the community' (Brown 1988:102). While yet multiethnic in character, Papua New Guinea's elite leadership does operate on the basis of 'wide personal contacts from school, university, and friendships outside

their tribe and district' (Brown 1988: 103), and there is increasing inter-
marriage between persons of different ethnic backgrounds who meet at
such national institutions as the University of Papua New Guinea or
the National Arts School (Rosi and Zimmer-Tamakoshi 1993). The
development of vertical power and the distancing of high-level leaders
from the peoples who have put them into office is an important element in Papua New Guinea's national identity crisis. Few villagers and
townspeople see themselves as Papua New Guineans first and members
of particular groups second. This is readily apparent in the reemergence
of tribal fighting in the Highlands (Strathern 1993) and the resistance
of Papua New Guineans to the judgments of imposed legal systems
(Gordon and Meggitt 1985). Underlying this crisis is a growing frustration and disillusion with national politicians' and leaders' roles in
making it easy for outsiders to exploit the country's resources. Further
dividing Papua New Guineans, historical and regional differences have
meant that some parts of the country have disproportionate influence
and economic power while other parts suffer low levels of education,
health care, development opportunities, and national impact (Dorney
1990; Griffin *et al.* 1979). The chapters that follow look at some of the
consequences of these disunities for the state along with nationalism
and foreign policy issues. The most recent threats to the state have been
the furor over former Prime Minister Julius Chan's decision to bring
mercenaries into the Bougainville debacle, a furor fed by Papua New
Guinea Armed Forces leaders that resulted in nine days of military and
civilian unrest and the stepping down of Chan in late March of 1997
(Radio Australia, Wednesday 26 and Thursday 27 March 1997; international news reports on the crisis are accessed on the World Wide Web:
http://coombs.anu.edu.au/SpecialProj/PNG/WWWVL-PNG.html), and bribery allegations against Prime Minister Bill Skate (*Sydney Morning Herald,*
Friday 28 November 1997).

SUGGESTED READINGS

Berndt, R., and Lawrence, P., eds., 1971. *Politics in New Guinea: Traditional and in the Context of Change—Some Anthropological Perspectives.* Nedlands: University of Western Australia Press.

Brown, P., 1988. 'New men and big men: emerging social stratification in the third world, a case study from the New Guinea highlands', *Ethnology,* 87-106.

Dorney, S., 1990. *Papua New Guinea: People, Politics, and History since 1975.* Sydney: Random House Australia Pty. Ltd.

Godelier, M., 1986 (orig. French 1982). *The Making of Great Men: Male Domination and Power Among the New Guinea Baruya.* London: Cambridge University Press.

Gordon, R., and Meggitt, M., 1985. *Law and Order in the New Guinea Highlands.* Hanover: University Press of New England.

Griffin, J., Nelson, H., and Firth, S., 1979. *Papua New Guinea: A Political History.* Richmond, Victoria: Heinemann Educational Australia Pty. Ltd.

Rosi, P., and Zimmer-Tamakoshi, L., 1993. 'Love and marriage among the educated elite in Port Moresby', in R. Marksbury, ed., *The Business of Marriage: Transformations in Oceanic Matrimony.* University of Pittsburgh Press, pp. 175-204.

Sahlins, M.D., 1963. 'Poor man, rich man, big-man, chief: political types in Melanesia and Polynesia', *Comparative Studies in Society and History,* 5:285-303.

Standish, W.A., 1992. 'Simbu paths to power: political change and cultural continuity in the Papua New Guinea highlands' unpublished doctoral dissertation, Australian National University.

———, 1993. 'Papua New Guinea in 1992: challenges for the state', *Asian Survey,* Feb.: 211-217.

Strathern, A., 1971. *The Rope of Moka: Big Men and Ceremonial Exchange in Mount Hagen, New Guinea.* Cambridge University Press.

———, 1993. 'Violence and Political Change in Papua New Guinea', *Pacific Studies,* 16(4):41-60.

Wolfers, E., and Regan, A., 1988. *The Electoral Process in Papua New Guinea: A Handbook of Issues and Options.* Boroko: Institute of Applied Social and Economic Research.

Zimmer-Tamakoshi, L., 1993. 'Nationalism and sexuality in Papua New Guinea', *Pacific Studies,* 16(4):61-97.

Peter Larmour

STATE AND SOCIETY IN PAPUA NEW GUINEA

Iғ THE STATE IS CONSIDERED to be a centralised, bureaucratic structure of government, then it is a fairly recent introduction in Papua New Guinea. Traditional Papua New Guinea political systems were small and stateless (Langness 1972; Chowning 1977). Order within them was maintained by a mixture of self-help, reciprocity, gossip, shaming, and supernatural sanctions (Taylor 1982). Responsibility for maintaining order was much more widely dispersed among various institutions and the adult population than it was in more specialised 'stateful' societies (Southall 1968). Unlike some parts of Polynesia, there was no process of indigenous state formation to be interrupted by colonial rule (Spriggs 1988). The colonial powers—Germany and Australia—defeated or enlisted local leaders but did not inherit an existing centralised, bureaucratic structure of government.

The introduction of the state was not simply a matter of running up a flag. Colonial rule took several decades to establish itself in Papua New Guinea (Wolfers 1975). At its edges, state officials (*kiaps*) often ruled in personal and violent, rather than bureaucratic, ways. The Highlands were only incorporated in the 1930s and 1940s.

By the end of the 1940s the public service still only numbered about a thousand people (Dwivedi 1986). By independence it had grown to about fifty thousand (Turner 1990). It grew a little in the late 1970s, then contracted in the early 1980s. It now consists of about 150 different agencies. The largest of these are the 24 national and 19 provincial departments (Simpson and McKillop 1994), but the telephone directory lists a variety of other agencies, including a Narcotics Bureau, a Rubber Board, and a Sheriff (Posts and Telecommunications Corporation 1994). In comparison with other developing and industrial societies, the Papua New Guinea public service seems quite modest in size (table 1). At about one-third of GDP, its public expenditure, however, is more like an industrial than a developing economy.

Table 1
Public employment and expenditures (percent)

	Public sector employment (percent of population)	Central government expenditure (percent of GDP)
Papua New Guinea	2.2	33
Developing economy average	3.7	28
Industrial economy average	9.0	34

Source: Larmour, P., 1992. 'States and Societies in the South Pacific', *Pacific Studies*, 15(1):99–121.

Nevertheless, there is now widespread dissatisfaction with the performance and appropriateness of the public service in Papua New Guinea. Explaining current attempts to reform the system of provincial government, Axline (1993:5) identified a 'crisis of governance' where people accused the government of 'mismanagement, waste, inefficiency, corruption, disruptive political conflict, overgovernment and neglect'. A recent Public Service Rationalisation Task Force drew similar damning conclusions, noting:

> a deterioration in a sense of nationalism within the public service of the 'one nation one public service' concept;
>
> compartmentalisation and fragmentation of departments rather than a sense of belonging to a larger public service;
>
> envy and rivalry between departments at both provincial and national levels;
>
> a politicisation of the public service to the point that advancement was a political decision rather than a professional one which results in an undermining of responsible managers;
>
> lack of accountability in the financial management of departments so that expenditures were properly allocated and controlled;

legislation which creates overlapping functions for various departments or agencies. (quoted in United Nations Joint Inter-agency Mission to Papua New Guinea on Sustainable Development 1994:20)

IN WHAT WAYS IS PAPUA NEW GUINEA A STATE?

Papua New Guinea is an independent state in the international legal
sense, and is recognised as such by other states. This paper focuses on
the domestic side of Papua New Guinea's 'stateness', while recognising
that the international dimensions of its 'stateness' do give the government domestic leverage. For example, the unlikelihood that other
states will recognise Bougainville's claims to independence gives the
Papua New Guinea government great advantage in its negotiations to
end the rebellion.

Tilly (1975) argues that from the history of European states, an
organisation controlling the population in a particular territory counts
as a state if:

it is differentiated from other organisations operating in the same territory;

it is autonomous;

it is centralised;

its divisions are formally coordinated with one another.

Each of these is a matter of degree, and following Nettl (1968), it is
probably better to talk of degrees of 'stateness' than to make sharp distinctions between states and non-states.

Differentiation

In Papua New Guinea's precolonial stateless societies big men, elders,
and chiefs performed a number of functions. Governing activity was
not sharply differentiated from economic or cultural activity. Governing activity is characteristically more differentiated in states; nevertheless lines are hard to draw. Are schools and the media, for example, part
of the state or not? Even if privately owned, they are subject to regulation of what they can teach and broadcast. In Papua New Guinea,
apparently non-state institutions like clans and tribes are supported by
laws that prohibit the alienation of customary land. The Papua New
Guinea government has shares in at least thirty-one public enterprises
which straddle the line between state and economy. Its holdings range

from 16.6 percent (Stettin Bay Lumber Company) to 100 percent (Live-stock Development Corporation), and include holdings of from 19 to 25 percent of five large mining projects (*Economic Insights* 1994). Voluntary organisations such as the Red Cross, which runs the blood transfusion service, are closely integrated with state hospitals.

Even private business organisations depend on legislation and the courts to constitute and defend themselves, and depend on tax breaks or subsidies to survive.

Autonomy

In many ways, independence reduced the autonomy of the Papua New Guinea state from the society it governed. National elections and the introduction of ministerial government made departments formally responsible to a locally elected legislature. The legal basis of the colonial state had been acts of the Australian parliament. Instead the independence constitution was said to be homegrown—drafted by a committee of Papua New Guineans after widespread popular consultation and adopted by the Papua New Guinea parliament acting as a constitutional convention. The Constitutional Planning Committee was very conscious of the need to bring the state closer to society. It recommended a system of decentralisation to provincial governments on the grounds that it would, among other things, allow greater participation by local leaders and make government services 'more accessible' (Papua New Guinea, Constitutional Planning Committee 1974: 10–12). The recommendation was resisted by politicians and public servants until Bougainville leaders successfully threatened to set up an independent state of their own (Republic of the North Solomons). Localisation has made the bureaucracy more representative of society. At independence, 13 percent of public service posts were held by noncitizens, falling to 6 percent in 1984 (Goodman *et al.* 1985), and 3 percent in 1990 (Turner 1990). The state extracts an increasing percentage of its revenue from local sources, while the proportion of its budget funded from Australia has fallen from 60 percent in 1973 to 13 percent in 1993 (Callick and Tait 1993).

Centralisation

Centralisation and decentralisation have been a persistent issue since the late 1970s when the government's promise of a system of provincial government for Bougainville was generalised to all nineteen provinces. National public servants carrying out provincial functions were regrouped into departments, responsible through a secretary to the Provincial Executive Council, chosen by premiers from elected provincial assemblies. There were persistent complaints that decentralisation had not gone far enough, and local governments had been disempowered by the creation of provincial assemblies. There were squabbles between national and provincial politicians, particularly because the latter now controlled the funds that delivered visible services like schools and clinics to rural voters.

National political hostility to provincial government culminated in the creation of the Bipartisan Select Committee which recommended in 1993 that elected provincial assemblies be replaced by authorities consisting of national Members of Parliament (MPs) and local government councillors (Simpson and McKillop 1994). Though resisted by provincial leaders (some of whom threatened secession), legislation embodying these recommendations was drafted by a Constitutional Review Commission, and passed by the national parliament in June 1995.

Coordination

The links between the 150 agencies of the Papua New Guinea government and the capacity to act in concert are often weak. Several kinds of links have been addressed by governments since independence: links between elected politicians and appointed public servants, horizontal links between agencies, and vertical links between headquarters and local officials.

The links between elected ministers and appointed public servants have been constitutionally awkward. A Supreme Court case involving the minister for police and the police commissioner (who refused the minister's direction to provide him with information) found that ministers' constitutional responsibility did not, of itself, give them powers of direction or control over departments (though these powers could be found elsewhere; see Ghai and Hegarty 1982). The court also found that the cabinet could hire and fire department heads at will. Between 1984 and 1986 the government moved to increase ministerial control over the public service by reducing the authority of the independent Public Service Commission and giving hiring and firing power to politically appointed departmental heads.

The second link, sideways between agencies, has been addressed through reforms to the budget process. Typically, most public expenditure is determined by existing commitments: salaries for staff already employed and maintenance of facilities already constructed. Beginning with the National Public Expenditure Plan in 1977, however, the government has made a series of attempts to direct new commitments and additional revenues toward planned objectives. Currently about 18 percent of its expenditure comes within a Public Investment Program that funds projects aimed at increasing economic growth and rural employment (Simpson and McKillop 1994).

The vertical link is between the planners and policy makers at the tops of departments and the desk and field officers at lower levels. The introduction of provincial government, for example, has made it possible to strengthen horizontal links between different agencies of government at provincial level, but it has also weakened the vertical links between field officers and specialist departments in Port Moresby. This persistent tension between horizontal coordination among agencies and vertical links between headquarters and field officers is most recently addressed in the Constitutional Review Commission's proposals to strengthen the role of the district manager to whom district specialists would report (*Economic Insights* 1994).

To summarize its degrees of 'stateness', Papua New Guinea does quite well on Tilly's first criterion of differentiation, though the line between state and non-state is necessarily blurred. Its autonomy, Tilly's second criterion, has probably declined since independence. Its degree of centralisation remains sharply contested, not least by the secessionists in Bougainville who are demanding to be treated as a special case regardless of the fate of provincial governments elsewhere in the country. Finally, it is weak on coordination, in spite of a series of attempts to better link ministers, officials, and departments in the budget process, headquarters, and field. It probably shares these problems of coordination, however, with most modern states.

Generally, Papua New Guinea's domestic 'stateness' is not a fixed entity—it may rise in one dimension while falling in another. Papua New Guinea's experience also suggests a tension between Tilly's third and fourth criteria: decentralisation may be a way of achieving better coordination at provincial or local level.

WEAK AND STRONG STATES AND SOCIETIES

What is the character of the relationship between the state and the rest of society in Papua New Guinea? Recent writing on the breakdown of law and order in Papua New Guinea characterises the state as 'weak'

(Standish 1994; Dinnen 1994). Migdal (1988) defines state strength in terms of the ability of state elites to impose their preferences on the rest of society and measures it in three ways:

(1) popular compliance with legislation

(2) popular participation in state-run institutions

(3) legitimacy accorded by the population to state elites.

Treating the list as a scorecard, Papua New Guinea does well on participation (measured, for example, by turnout for elections), but less well on compliance and legitimacy.

The strength of society, on the other hand, is measured by 'the resistance posed by chiefs, landlords, bosses, rich peasants, clan leaders, *za'im, effendis, aghas, caciques,* and *kulaks* (for convenience "strongmen") through their various social organisations' (Migdal 1988:33).

Land tenure systems play an important role in Migdal's argument: the ability to impose statutory law over customary tenure is one measure of the relative strength of states vis-à-vis the societies they nominally govern. If so, the Papua New Guinea state is pretty weak. Ninety-seven percent of the land in Papua New Guinea is held under customary tenure, though there have been several very limited attempts to introduce customary land registration. Also, the government has made a number of ad hoc compensation payments to traditional claimants for land the state already owned (Fingleton 1981), and it continues to come under pressure to increase payments for vulnerable sites, such as telecommunications repeater stations. The state's legal rights to subsurface minerals are also under challenge (Donigi 1994).

The four possible combinations of state and society, with Migdal's examples, are shown in table 2. In which cell should Papua New Guinea fall? If its state is weak, then the choice is between II and IV, and the issue is the degree of social control exercised by organisations such as clans, tribes, and linguistic and ethnic groups. Here we can only speculate, but it may be that these social controls are stronger at the very local level, in rural rather than urban areas, or in some parts of the country rather than others. But Migdal's argument is important in drawing attention to the character of Papua New Guinea society as well as the character of the state: it is the combination of the two that determines the difference between a diffused system of power and anarchy.

Table 2
State–society relations

	Strong state	Weak state
Strong society	I (no example)	II diffused (Sierra Leone)
Weak society	III pyramidal (France, Israel)	IV anarchical (China 1939–45, Mexico 1910–20)

Source: Migdal, J., 1988. *Strong Societies and Weak States,* Princeton University Press, New Jersey.

The sharp antagonism that Migdal draws between state and society, however, may miss the role of the state in creating and sustaining social organisations like clans, tribes, and ethnic groups. Customary land tenure in Papua New Guinea, for example, is sustained by legal prohibitions on land alienation. Historians of the 'invention of tradition' have noted how tribes and chiefs are often at least partly the constructions of colonial policy (Hobsbawm and Ranger 1983), while writing on governance sees the state acting through and with non-state actors in achieving social order (Kooieman and van Vliet 1993).

THE STATE IN PAPUA NEW GUINEA

Theories about the role of the state in Papua New Guinea are not simply academic. They are used by reformers to urge changes in structure and staffing, and reflect or amplify popular opinion which in turn affects the way people respond to state initiatives. Thus in the 1970s, the arguments of the dependency theory, which saw state officials as *compradors* and the state itself as a 'transmission belt' for foreign exploitation, echoed and justified the populist economic nationalism of the time. In the 1980s, theories proposed by neoclassical economists typically argued from first principles for a reduced role for the state, but they also reflected, and gained plausibility from, popular hostility to apparently wasteful and ineffective bureaucracies. More recent concern with what Weber (1983:11) called the state's 'monopoly of the legitimate use of violence' reflects widespread popular concern with crime and violence.

A desire for a unitary, well-managed, and depoliticised system of government is expressed in the reports of the rationalisation task force and the Bipartisan Committee. Yet Papua New Guinea's indigenous political traditions are clearly stateless, and Papua New Guinea is currently incompletely 'stateful'. To the extent that the state is weak, outcomes will depend on the character of Papua New Guinea society.

Though the state has been discussed in terms of organisation and strength, the concept of the state has moral and evaluative overtones. It is hard to talk about the state in Papua New Guinea without implying that there should be some impersonal authority standing above politics and acting in the public interest. Yet in writing about state traditions Dyson (1980) argues that the idea of the state as an absolute, impersonal authority acting in the public interest is specific to Western Europe and does not travel well, even to the United Kingdom and the United States, let alone Papua New Guinea. Dyson suggests that liberal Anglo-Saxon societies with political traditions that are suspicious of government interference are, to that extent, stateless. The idea of the state thus partly constitutes a state: if state officials and their clients do not believe in it, the state becomes simply a cluster of organisations.

REFERENCES

Axline, W., 1993. *Governance in Papua New Guinea: Approaches to Institutional Reform,* INA Discussion Paper 58, INA, Port Moresby.

Callick, R., and Tait, M., eds., 1993. *The Papua New Guinea Handbook.* Canberra: National Centre for Development Studies, The Australian National University.

Chowning, A., 1977. *An Introduction to the Peoples and Cultures of Melanesia.* Menlo Park, California: Cummings.

Dinnen, S., 1994. 'Public order in Papua New Guinea—problems and prospects', in A. Thompson (ed.), *Papua New Guinea: Issues for Australian security planners.* Canberra: Australian Defence Studies Centre, Australian Defence Force Academy, 99–117.

Donigi, P., 1994. *Indigenous or Aboriginal Rights to Property: A Papua New Guinea Perspective.* Utrecht: International Books.

Dwivedi, O. P., 1986. 'Growth of the public service in Papua New Guinea', in O. P. Dwivedi and N. Paulias, eds., *The Public Service of Papua New Guinea.* Boroko: Administrative College, pp. 72–89.

Dyson, K., 1980. *The State Tradition in Western Europe.* New York: Oxford University Press.

Economic Insights, 1994. *Papua New Guinea: The role of Government in Economic Development,* International Development Issues Paper 33. Canberra: Australian Agency for International Development.

Fingleton, J., 1981. 'Policy making on lands', in J. Ballard, ed., *Policy Making in a New State: Papua New Guinea 1972–77.* St. Lucia: University of Queensland Press, pp. 212–237.

Ghai, Y., and Hegarty, D., 1982. 'Ministerial and bureaucratic power in Papua New Guinea: aspects of the Bouraga/Dutton dispute', in P. Sack, ed., *Pacific Constitutions, Proceedings of the Canberra Law Workshop.* Canberra: Research School of Social Sciences, The Australian National University, pp. 247–56.

Goodman, R., Lepani, C., and Morawetz, D., 1985. *The Economy of Papua New Guinea: An independent review.* Canberra: Development Studies Centre, The Australian National University.

Hobsbawm, E. J., and Ranger, T., eds., 1983. *The Invention of Tradition.* Cambridge and New York: Cambridge University Press.

Kooieman, J., and van Vliet, M., 1993. 'Governance and public administration', in J. Kooieman and M. van Vliet, eds., *Managing Public Organisations: Lessons from contemporary European experience.* London: Sage Publications, pp. 58–72.

Langness, L., 1972. 'Political organisation', in P. Ryan, ed., *Encyclopedia of Papua and New Guinea,* vol. 2. Clayton: Melbourne University Press, pp. 922–935.

Larmour, P., 1992. 'States and societies in the South Pacific', *Pacific Studies,* 15(1):99–121.

Migdal, J., 1988. *Strong Societies and Weak States: State-society relations and state capabilities in the Third World.* Princeton, New Jersey: Princeton University Press.

Nettl, J., 1968. 'The state as a conceptual variable', *World Politics,* 20:559–592.

Papua New Guinea, Constitutional Planning Committee, 1974. *Final Report,* Constitutional Planning Committee, Port Moresby.

Posts and Telecommunications Corporation, 1994. *Papua New Guinea Telephone Directory,* Posts and Telecommunications Corporation, Boroko.

Simpson, G., and McKillop, R., 1994. *Public Administration, Planning and Budgeting in Papua New Guinea.* Canberra: Australian Agency for International Development.

Southall, A., 1968. 'Stateless society', in D. Sills, ed., *International Encyclopedia of the Social Sciences.* New York: Collier Macmillan and Free Press, pp. 157–167.

Spriggs, M., 1988. 'The Hawaiian transformation of ancestral Polynesian society: conceptualising chiefly states', in J. Gledhill and B. Bender, eds., *State and Society: The Emergence and Development of Social Hierarchy and Political Centralisation.* London: Unwin Hyman, pp. 57–73.

Standish, B., 1994. 'Papua New Guinea: the search for security in a weak state' in A. Thompson, ed., *Papua New Guinea: Issues for Australian security planners.* Canberra:Australian Defence Studies Centre, Australian Defence Force Academy, pp. 51–88.

Taylor, M., 1982. *Community, Anarchy and Liberty.* Cambridge: Cambridge University Press.

Tilly, C., ed., 1975. *The Formation of States in Western Europe.* Princeton, New Jersey: Princeton University Press.

Turner, M., 1990. *Papua New Guinea: The Challenge of Independence.* Ringwood, Victoria: Penguin Books.

United Nations Joint Inter-agency Mission to Papua New Guinea on Sustainable Development, 1994. *Yumi Wakain.* Port Moresby: United Nations Development Programme.

Weber, M., 1983. 'Politics as vocation', in D. Held *et al.,* eds., *States and Societies.* Oxford: Martin Robertson, pp. 111–112.

Wolfers, E., 1975. *Race Relations and Colonial Rule in Papua New Guinea.* Brookvale: Australia and New Zealand Book Company.

Pamela Rosi

CULTURAL CREATOR OR NEW *BISNISMAN*
Conflicts of Being a Contemporary Artist in Papua New Guinea

The role of art in my country must now be twofold: on the one hand, art must be a genuine expression of the personality of the artist and his cosmos.... On the other hand, art should be an instrument of synthesis in the process of national integration.

M. T. Somare

For the contemporary artist John Mann, art is a pure commercial activity. It is a means to an end—a way of making a living.

Patrick Matbob

JN PAPUA NEW GUINEA'S developing society, contemporary artists of all categories play a significant role as creators of culture and adjudicators of cultural values. Constitutional lawyer and former Minister of Justice Bernard Narokobi, has written that new artists, who work in new styles and media, are 'national treasures' because they express Papua New Guineans' 'longing to be new, yet rooted in our rich and ancient past' (1990:21). National leaders, including Michael Somare, Albert Maori Kiki, Paulius Matane, and Rabbie Namaliu, have therefore encouraged government support for the arts in order to build a rich and distinctive national identity and further national integration.

Despite official support for the arts, including the establishment of a National Arts School (NAS), the position of the contemporary artist remains problematic, for these artists are faced with recurrent problems that stress their lives and hinder the attainment of professional success (Rosi 1994). As Ulli Beier has underscored, in contrast to his or her traditional counterpart, the modern urban artist is an 'outsider' in contemporary society (Beier 1977). Consequently, today, only a few young Papua New Guineans—nearly all of whom are men (Rosi 1995)—are willing to invest their education in such a precarious occupation as making 'art'.

This chapter has two purposes: to discuss the socioeconomic and cultural dilemmas now confronting the contemporary artist in PNG's modernizing society, and to suggest some actions that can be taken to improve the art market and draw public attention to the role of the modern artist in the development of national culture.[1] To provide comparison and context, discussion begins by briefly describing the significance of art and artists in traditional society and the factors which have led to the emergence of modern art and new art institutions in the years before and after independence in 1975.

ART AND ARTISTS IN TRADITIONAL SOCIETY

In the small-scale societies of traditional Melanesia, the production of art has an ancient heritage (Newton, Gathercole and Kaeppler 1979). Existing in many forms and media created by a variety of techniques, these plastic forms and designs were integral to all aspects of traditional village life (Firth 1936; Strathern and Strathern 1971; Tuzin 1980). They were associated with sacred cults and life cycle rituals (Bowden 1983; Gell 1975; Lincoln 1986; Thomas 1995), activities of trade and warfare (Gerbrands 1967a; Malinowski 1922), and elaborate systems of body decoration (Strathern and Strathern 1971; O'Hanlon 1989). Also, as researchers have shown, aesthetic forms manifested power (Clay 1986; Errington 1974; Forge 1962) and gave meaning to the existential questions of life and one's place in the cosmos (Gell 1975; Schieffelin 1963; Williams 1940).

Moreover, in these traditional societies everyone participated in some way in artistic activities, learning from childhood to recognize and identify with particular tribal or clan configurations (Beier and Kiki 1970; Crawford 1981; Forge 1970). Nevertheless, trained specialists

[1] Analysis is based on research carried out at the NAS in 1986 with the support of NSF Grant BNS 8515528 and a travelling fellowship from Bryn Mawr College, and ongoing communication with national artists, NAS staff, and administrators. Artist and major informant Larry Santana visited the U.S.A. in 1989.

also existed (Gerbrands 1967b; Mead and Kernot 1983), and gender differentiation meant that men and women worked in both separate and linked spheres of creativity (Teilhet 1983; McKenzie 1991). But within these boundaries, men and women artists worked in tune with the value systems of their respective communities, although the traditional artist worked within a 'confined aesthetic framework' and his individuality was expressed within its boundaries (Beier 1976). With the impact of colonialism, 'missionization', and modernization, the sociocultural contexts which supported traditional art have been gradually destroyed or changed to reflect new relations of land, labour, and loyalty. Today, therefore, traditional artists work largely for museums, collectors, and tourists (May 1975). Two important exceptions are: traditional *bilas* (decoration), which continues to be used in village contexts for both old and new purposes (Berman 1990); and the *Malangan* funerary sculpture of Northern New Ireland, described by Susan Kuchler (1992).

THE EMERGENCE OF URBAN ARTISTS AND CONTEMPORARY ART

In contrast to traditional art, which evolved for millennia in a multitude of village environments, contemporary PNG art developed in the urban setting of Port Moresby and announced its arrival with a modern artistic event. On 29 February 1969, Timothy Akis, an illiterate villager from Madang Province, exhibited forty drawings at the University of Papua New Guinea. The press hailed him as a 'possible genius' and labelled him the territory's first indigenous contemporary artist (*S. Pacific Post,* 28 February 1969). The exhibition was, moreover, a cultural and financial success (Beier 1974), creating the precedent for many others which followed. The 'discovery' of Akis and the creation of contemporary art are, however, events embedded in a wider historical context affected by such factors as: new ways of seeing the world; the move towards political independence creating colonial concern for the revitalization of indigenous culture; and the fortuitous presence of expatriate artists and teachers who were anxious to promote local grassroots art and pressure the government to establish new art institutions to introduce native artists to modern artistic techniques and media (Rosi 1994).

The impact of colonialism has affected all aspects of traditional life, including ways of seeing. In traditional communities children unconsciously absorbed the underlying principles of local artistic conventions,

Timothy Akis. Photograph courtesy of Tom Craig, Creative Arts Centre.

which then determined what they would 'see' in two and three dimensions (Forge 1970). With culture contact, however, these local conventions have been modified because migration, urbanization, and education have introduced people to new ideas, experiences, and modes of pictorial representation (Baker 1980; Ison 1975, 1976; Walker 1978; Frost and Walker 1983).

Throughout the colonial period the Australian administration ignored the teaching of art and culture to nationals, regarding them as unimportant to primary education (Swatridge 1985; Smith 1975). However, in the 1960s when it became evident that independence would become an immediate reality, swift efforts were made to expand secondary and tertiary education and revise school syllabi to contain a new Papua New Guinean content and stir national consciousness (Weeks and Guthrie 1985). With this change in policy, a new contingent of expatriate teachers dedicated to the creation of national culture began to enter the country. Two of these people, Georgina Beier and Tom Craig, were instrumental in the development of PNG contemporary art (Rosi 1994).

Georgina Beier and her husband, Ulli, arrived at the University of Papua New Guinea in 1967.[2] Interested in discovering indigenous aesthetic talent, Georgina opened her studio to nationals—especially migrants—seeking art instruction (Beier 1974). Paying these people small sums of money for their first work, she was responsible for getting them to persevere in their creative efforts to express their own ideas and develop their own styles. Her most successful students were the painter Kauage and the welder-sculptor Ruki Fame. After they had perfected their techniques, she then arranged for them to have well-publicized exhibitions to sell their work at prices directed largely to expatriates and the new Papua New Guinean elite. Because of her connections in the international art world, Beier also made it possible for these new village artists to exhibit overseas, thereby gaining international recognition for themselves and Papua New Guinea (Beier 1974).

To continue its development, however, contemporary art required stable institutional support. With independence on the horizon, the minister of education decided, in 1972, to establish the Creative Arts Centre to support and train individuals with artistic talent who could contribute to the growth of national culture.[3] Given a small budget, Tom Craig, the head of Visual Arts at the newly established Goroka

---

[2] Ulli had taught at the University of Ibaden. In Africa, he had been deeply involved in promoting African art, literature, and history. He was the founder and editor of the leading literature journal *Black Orpheus*. With his wife, Georgina—a well-known artist—he had sponsored and organized a series of workshops in Oshogbo in 1961–1962, which produced a controversial school of grassroots painters known as the 'Oshogbo School'. At UPNG, Ulli Beier taught a course on creative writing, which produced the first generation of PNG poets and playwrights. From 1974 to 1978, he was the first director of the Institute of Papua New Guinea Studies in Boroko.

Teachers' College, was appointed the Creative Arts Centre's first director (Rosi 1994). An innovative teacher, Craig believed that to encourage creativity students should be taught informally and encouraged to work cooperatively. Also, to raise funds for the school and the students, the centre regularly staged exhibitions and was involved in commissioned work—often for national projects—from all over PNG and abroad (The National Arts School 1984).

In 1974, a large grant from Australia enabled the centre to expand its facilities and increase the number of its students, staff, and programs. Further changes occurred in 1976, when the centre became the National Arts School (NAS) following the board of governors' decision to introduce academic diplomas to satisfy the nation's requirements for qualified professionals. Nevertheless, associations with village artists were maintained, for they came to the NAS as artists-in-residence and exhibited regularly at the school.[4]

Following independence, strong leadership and an adequate budget enabled the NAS to continue its development of contemporary art. To further government policies to promote national culture, NAS artists began to travel regularly at home and abroad. In 1976, Jakupa Ako became the first Papua New Guinean to have a solo exhibition in Australia, and in 1981 he was honoured by Queen Elizabeth of England with an O.B.E. (Order of the British Empire) for his contribution to national art. In Port Moresby, the NAS also carried out an exhibition schedule of more than ten shows a year. According to Tom Craig, who was school director until 1983, public demand for the new imagery was

---

[3] Although both men and women were encouraged to apply to the Centre, very few women have become professional artists. Gender has also influenced the choice of artistic media. Following tradition, only men work as contemporary painters and sculptors. Women generally elect to work in textiles, but men work in this area also.

[4] Other village artists were supposed to have been recruited through the Provincial Cultural Centres, but this did not happen. Since the deaths of Akis, Cecil King Wunge, and Jakupa Ako, the only village artists still exhibiting nationally are Kauage, John Mann, Ruki Fame, and Benny Moore. But in the late 1980s, a small number of Kuage's relatives and countrymen—Apa Hugo (his adopted son), John Siune (his brother-in-law), and Oscar Towa and Gigs Wena (both from Simbu Province)—have adopted his characteristic style and are selling their flamboyant images to Port Moresby tourists outside hotels and other street venues.

In addition to producing the always popular bird of paradise motifs, these young artists are also documenting critical local events, including the Bougainville civil war, environmental pollution, and urban crime and violence. As noted by Susan Cochrane (1997:57), Gigs Wena is being assisted by his sister. But, although this young woman is herself a graduate of the Faculty of Creative Arts, she has chosen not to produce paintings in her own name. This information suggests that the cultural constraints which impede PNG women from working as independent artists continue to operate (Rosi 1995).

Tom Craig makes Jakupa the janitor an artist, by Jakupa Ako, 1983. Courtesy of Tom Craig.

high, and at most shows all the exhibited works were sold to local
patrons (Craig personal communication 1989).

With increased professionalism, NAS artists also became involved in significant projects in the applied arts, particularly architectural embellishments for the new buildings being constructed in the capital to further national development and the display of national identity. These commissions included facades for the Development Bank at Waigani, the PNG Banking Corporation in Port Moresby, and the extensive iconographic program for the exterior and interior of the new monumental Parliament House. This huge undertaking required the establishment of a production workshop, employing a team of contemporary artists, NAS students and staff, and traditional carvers drawn from all over the nation (Briggs 1989; Rosi 1991).

Papua New Guinea Parliament House.

The completion of the Parliament House, in 1984, marked the most significant contribution of the NAS and its artists to the production of national artistic culture. Yet, it also signalled the government's downward spiral of support for contemporary art in the task of creating national sentiments and symbols: at the parliament's glittering opening ceremonies, not a single member of the production team was invited in recognition of their services (Brennan, pers. comm. 1989);

furthermore, the Manpower Act of 1985 gave priority in nation build-ing to the development of the country's natural resources. Conse-quently, the Department of Education ordered the NAS to reduce its expenditure and justify its existence as an independent institution.

By 1986, the effects of budget cuts were clearly apparent—school supplies were at a premium, exhibitions were being cancelled, and stu-dents, staff, and artists were becoming increasingly alienated by what they perceived as a lack of official support for their work. In 1987 and 1988, as the national fiscal crisis deepened, funding for art exhibitions was eliminated and positions for staff ending their contracts were fro-zen. Successive administrative reorganisations also paralysed leader-ship as the NAS was moved in rapid succession between the Departments of Culture and Tourism, Aviation, and the new National Tourist Corporation. At the end of 1989, the government decided to affiliate the school with the University of Papua New Guinea. Then, after only six weeks, it was reassigned to the Tourist Corporation. Frus-trated students went on strike, placarding signs to a national TV audi-ence saying, 'we feel like a football being kicked around', 'no art for money', 'public servants without pay' (Hand 1990). Further public pro-test pressured the government to reverse its position and, in April 1990, the NAS was affiliated officially to the University of Papua New Guinea as the Faculty of Creative Arts.

This controversial decision to amalgamate with the University of Papua New Guinea has, however, neither automatically revitalized the new department, nor has it brought increased economic support for PNG artists. Instead, the escalating expenses of the ten-year-long civil war in Bougainville, the devaluation of the kina, and other government revenue problems have forced the university to face its own budget crisis—where its priorities are with 'the hard sciences'. As a result, few arts students are interested in becoming professional painters or sculp-tors because, as they point out, these occupations are becoming increasingly precarious. The reasons for this predicament and the prob-lems which confront contemporary artists in PNG's modernizing soci-ety are numerous.

ECONOMIC, SOCIAL, AND CULTURAL PROBLEMS OF THE CONTEMPORARY ARTIST

In 1988, the well-known Pacific writer Albert Wendt stated at the Waigani Seminar on the State of the Arts in the Pacific that, in compar-ison to other artists in Oceania, the contemporary Papua New Guinean artist holds a favourable position in society (*Post-Courier* 6 September 1988). As just discussed, the PNG government has supported the development of modern art by maintaining a National Arts School and, until its affiliation with the university, funded an exhibition program to help sell the work of national artists. To ensure attendance at these shows, the former school sent out nearly four hundred invitations for each opening reception to individuals in government, business, education, and the arts all over the country. During the 1970s and 1980s, prices for displayed works ranged from K50 to K3,000. Since these amounts are substantial by local standards, many Papua New Guineans believe that being a modern artist can be a profitable occupation (Brash and Shimauchi 1986).

In reality, the contemporary artist is faced with economic, social, and cultural problems not encountered by his or her traditional counterpart. While traditional artists were integrated closely into their respective societies, producing objects that were needed and respected by their particular groups, the modern artist creates within a cash economy and depends on others to help him sell his work. Often this is to expatriates who may or may not buy his art (Beier 1976). Socially, moreover, the individual and professional needs of the modern artist often compete with obligations demanded by kin, which results in frustration and often deep personal distress (Rosi and Zimmer-Tamakoshi 1993). Because of these conflicts, a number of artists have simply moved on to do different things. Others, instead, try to hold down jobs while exhibiting their work sporadically; and a lucky few manage to pursue a career of teaching while also maintaining a schedule of exhibitions. Very few artists, however, are successful enough to maintain themselves solely from the sale of their artwork. They often fall on hard times and turn for help to relatives and friends.

ECONOMIC DEPENDENCY

In Papua New Guinea few specialized art shops, studios, or popular markets exist where, as in Africa, artists come to sell their work to the public (Jules-Rosette 1984; Szombati-Fabian 1976). In Port Moresby, several village artists, including Kauage, Ruki Fame, and Henry Vileka, have tried to run their own workshops, but these have failed. Only John Mann, one of PNG's remaining village artists, has made a successful business selling his drawings to tourists who visit the Madang Cultural Centre (Matbob 1987). For the most part, therefore, contemporary artists sell their work in two ways: from special commissions, or through exhibitions sponsored and organized by special patrons, particularly the former National Arts School, the Arts Council of Port Moresby, the PNG Orchid Society, and occasional venues at local hotels.

As a consequence of independence, urban growth, and rapid modernization, contemporary artists now receive a variety of commissions from government, business, churches, and private individuals wanting imagery which portrays aspects of national life. For example, Martin Morubububa has painted a colourful series of murals for the Port Moresby Hospital, he has decorated stalls at the new Gordon's Market at Boroko, and with a team of NAS students, he has executed other murals at the University of Papua New Guinea. But such assignments are irregular, depending upon the availability of funding. With severe financial restraints now affecting national and provincial budgets, artists can no longer expect to be engaged in substantial architectural projects, such as the building of the national Parliament House at Waigani. Furthermore, with fewer and smaller commissions available, artists will be in competition with one another and it will be much more difficult for newcomers to win recognition and establish themselves. Art students are well aware of the hard realities of this economic situation. The majority are therefore studying for diplomas in graphic or textile design since these fields offer promising commercial opportunities. Unfortunately, the civil war in Bougainville has now disrupted the operation of Tiare Designs in Arawa—a firm which has employed several NAS graduates. Moreover, the very few students who are working in fine arts hope to become teachers and most plan to enrol at the Goroka Teachers' College.

Urban art exhibitions are colourful spectacles that merge culture and economics. As former prime minister Michael Somare has stated, 'art must be a genuine expression of the personality of the artist and his cosmos' (Somare 1974). However, in contemporary PNG society, the modern artist is not just a 'cultural creator', but must work in the capitalist system to earn a living and invest profits judiciously. From this perspective, according to Patrick Matbob, making art is also 'the art of making money' (Matbob 1987).

However, the strategic use of the exhibition as a vehicle to promote and sell modern art leaves the artist in a position of double dependency: a sponsor must provide a suitable venue and underwrite the necessary costs of publicity and an opening reception, and buyers are difficult to secure. As noted previously, since prices for contemporary art are very high by indigenous standards, the market is directed primarily to resident expatriates and the new Papua New Guinea elite. With increasing numbers of expatriates leaving the country in response to government policies of indigenization and the high rate of crime and lawlessness, this market is shrinking perceptibly. While some members of the elite are acquiring new art forms to embellish their offices and homes and to display national pride and identity, most prefer to invest in other symbols of modern prestige, particularly cars, or, most recently, television sets.

In addition to these problems of dependency, artists are faced with further financial problems. They must have sufficient funds to buy supplies, and they have to restrict social obligations to utilize available time and money to produce a large body of work. This is no easy matter, and it may take more than a year. During my residence at the National Arts School in 1986, all the foregoing problems were noticeable. For example, John Mann's show was cancelled by the administration and did not occur until one year later. Also, despite the usual publicity, attendance at other school exhibitions was light. According to informants, in the days of the Creative Arts Centre or in the period right after independence, these events were crowded and sales were brisk. In 1986, however, only about half of the pieces displayed at Jakupa's exhibition were sold, and numbers were considerably less for a show of Gickmai Kundun's sculpture.

Moreover, another well-known artist was forced to cancel his scheduled show at the school. He was experiencing financial difficulties but, in addition, he had been evicted from his house because his landlord had failed to pay rent to the Housing Commission. With no other public accommodations available, he and his wife were living apart with different relatives, and he had nowhere to paint. Like other artists, he therefore worked at night, because during the day he was employed on projects subcontracted to him by the school's production workshop.

Financially insecure and working long hours, these 'night' artists may also stress their health with a heavy consumption of *buai* (betel nut chewing), cigarettes, and black coffee taken to sustain their energy. Four years ago, a young artist, who was then working full-time as a graphic designer, wrote to say that in trying to prepare for an exhibition scheduled in Australia, and to make extra money for his children's school fees by working on outside projects, he had developed severe heart palpitations and had collapsed at work. These problems with stress at work are compounded if—as frequently is the case—the demands of being an artist conflict with the social obligations of kinship and other alliance relationships. This *wantok* system—as it is named in Papua New Guinea—is, according to Bernard Narokobi, the mainstay of 'the Melanesian Way' (1980:49). Traditionally, it maintained the structure of village life and, in new urban environments, it continues to be the primary mechanism for establishing networks of supportive relationships (Levine and Levine 1979; Strathern and Strathern 1975). The obligations incurred through the *wantok* system can, however, place a considerable strain on individual resources and so become a potential source for ill will, violence, and deep fears of sorcery.

MANAGING THE *WANTOK* SYSTEM

Because contemporary artists require the resources of an urban environment to produce and sell art, most now live in Port Moresby. Like the majority of the city's population, they are migrants and live in areas where they are among *wantoks,* or in housing provided by employers. Like other newcomers, they want to maintain ties to their original communities, and they do this by visiting, sending back remittances, or investing in village business ventures, such as tradestores or growing coffee. To maintain cordial relationships with their village kin, they are also expected to host visitors in town and support newcomers who come to the capital looking for employment (Levine and Levine 1979). The problem which all artists inevitably face thus becomes how to balance the continual demands of the *wantok* system with the needs of their own work production and economic investments.

Writing in 1974 about the experiences of PNG's first modern artists, Georgina Beier has indicated that while creative success brought material rewards, new wealth also produced incumbencies and psychological distress. For example, Kauage was able to buy a house and acquire sufficient brideprice for two wives—an extraordinary accomplishment by PNG standards—but, as Beier describes (1974:15):

> To be in possession of a house brings liabilities. It will be impossible for him to refuse accommodation to wantoks ... [and he will] become responsible for housing some of the homeless bachelors of his village. He is already responsible for a large proportion of Chimbu drunks.... Europeans have commented that Kauage is frittering away his money ... but as a successful town dweller, Kauage is expected to share his wealth with his countrymen.... He is meeting his social obligations.

In her other commentaries about the lives of contemporary artists, Beier also points to the pressures which *wantoks* can exert on new art

businesses, causing them to fail. In 1972, Henry Vileka, a young Highlander she had trained in textile design, set up Hara Hara Prints. With
rising national sentiments, fabrics with indigenous designs were in
great demand in the capital. However, Vileka and his partners dis-
trusted one another and the workshop collapsed. Beier also documents
the fears which artists experience if they believe they are under the sor-
ceries of kin. Indeed, these fears may even be expressed in an artist's
work. In 1976, Jakupa produced a painting entitled *Wari long hai bilong
mi,* showing how he paid a 'magician' to remove pieces of coloured
glass from his eyes put there by jealous relatives (Solander Gallery
1976). Jakupa and other School artists were also convinced that the
sudden deaths of Akis and Cecil Wunge in 1984 were the outcome of
sorcery. As Jakupa informed me, 'tradestores, coffee, and other *bisnis*
can bring plenty trouble' (personal communication 1986).[5]

In 1986, the *wantok* system operated to help and to hinder artists.
On the positive side, two technicians at the NAS, who could not pay
their utility bills, simply moved in temporarily with their relatives until
this situation was remedied. For other artists, however, relatives created
a variety of burdens. One NAS teacher had his house filled with *wantoks*
for four months and he had no time or space to paint; two other artists
were intending to contribute the proceeds of their forthcoming exhibitions to village ceremonies held during the Christmas vacation to
maintain village ties and prestige; and a talented designer, about to be
sent abroad to represent PNG in an arts festival, arranged for a friend to
represent her in a press photograph because she wanted to prevent her
relatives from knowing about her success. This trip had no financial
rewards, but her relatives would believe otherwise and so make overtures for money. These requests would be difficult and untimely
because she was hoping to reopen a business that had failed.

At the time of this research, another young artist was also experiencing harassment from his in-laws over the question of brideprice.
Demanding K1,500 (US $1,600), they arrived at his house each pay
period to take half of his earnings. Fearful of violence and afraid they
would take away his wife and children, he was considering leaving his
job in an advertising firm and returning to his relatives in another town
(Rosi and Zimmer-Tamakoshi 1993). In sudden, desperate crisis, however, *wantoks* can become the source of survival. In 1988, Larry Santana,

[5] Jakupa's unexpected death from malaria, which occurred during a visit to his village
in November 1997, was also attributed to sorcery by some of his friends in Port Moresby.
As one of them informed me by telephone, Jakupa was well when he left town, but he was
also anxious about problems creating friction back in Goroka.

Wari long hai bilong mi. Painting by Jakupa Ako, 1976.

a graphic artist, suddenly lost his job and his house when his employer went bankrupt. With nowhere to go, he moved his family to the six-mile squatter dump to be with his wife's relatives. Here, they helped him to construct a dwelling with debris scavenged from the dump. Unable to find work for a year, Larry has symbolically recorded the tribulations of his existence in a self-portrait entitled *Struggle and Pain at the Six-Mile Dump.* He describes the imagery as follows:

> This is an image of myself and the little settlement house which I built. My hands hold my brush. Tears and blood are in my eyes—signs of my suffering. The silhouette of the people in the back are my in-laws coming from the dump where they have collected scraps of food and material waste from the city. The background carving represents the traditional culture we have lost. The wash of red is the pain of living in the city.... The blue below shows my little kids playing around the house in the dirt. This is the struggle and pain that I face when I have no job and have run out of money. I can't stand it. Life is not worth living, but I have my family to care for.... How can I live with only a few kina? I see the kids sick. It is such a struggle to keep us all together. I feel so down, and I can't paint when these problems come to my mind. As you can see, my sketch is not too neatly done. But it is a painting with feeling from my heart—to let the world know what is happening to artists like myself as we struggle to survive on the garbage dump. (tape received August 1989)

PROBLEMS OF ALIENATION AND IDENTITY

Observing the frustrations of modern artists in the Third World, the Beiers have argued that feelings of alienation stem from their 'outsider' position in society. While traditional artists were integrated into the community, expressing its values and identity, modern artists now labour alone to produce images made primarily for strangers. Consequently, although the contemporary artist is now free to experiment with new forms, he pays the price in being cut off from his own group—thus experiencing loneliness, depression, and great personal struggle (G. Beier 1977; U. Beier 1976).

Although the Beiers correctly conclude that contemporary Papua New Guinean artists sell their work to expatriates and that the majority of their countrymen are unfamiliar with their work and its meaning, it should also be recognized that modern artists execute many commissions for public display in Papua New Guinea, and that they have expressed great pride in their ability to sell their work to expatriates and to represent their nation abroad in art exhibitions (Rosi 1994). Thus, as

Struggle and Pain at the Six-Mile Dump. Painting by Larry Santana, 1989. Courtesy of the author.

this discussion has emphasized, the feelings of alienation experienced by artists result primarily from culture clash—of having to move and mediate between two conflicting worlds. In this respect, contemporary artists are no different from many other Papua New Guineans who are also struggling with the impact of changing traditions and the forces of modernization.

In recent years, however, artists and art students have become increasingly disillusioned by what they consider the growing government indifference to their role in society. In the optimistic days of the Creative Arts Centre, PNG's first contemporary artists believed they were contributing in an important way to the growth of national culture. Now, in the wake of sharp cuts to institutional budgets, few local exhibitions, and lack of ministerial support, artists feel that they are being gradually abandoned by the source that helped bring them into being. Although established artists doggedly continue their struggle to exhibit and sell their work (Rosi 1994)—even displaying their artworks on the street (Cochrane 1995)—most art students are electing to study commercial arts in the hope of finding jobs in the communications industry after graduation.

If this trend continues, the new Faculty of Creative Arts may have difficulty in attracting creative young people willing to carry on the traditions of contemporary art established by the first generation of village artists at the Creative Arts Centre. In 1988, the National Arts School graduated twenty-six students—awarding diplomas in Music, Fine Arts, Textiles, Graphic Design, and Photography. Eleven two-year certificates were also granted in music. Last year, the Faculty of Creative Arts graduated just three students. This discussion now concludes by suggesting some actions to improve the contemporary art market and to attract wider public attention to the presence and importance of modern art in national life.

CONCLUSIONS: BUILDING THE MARKET TO EXPRESS CULTURE

Four fundamental problems currently undermine the professional well-being of modern PNG artists: limited possibilities for selling their work in Papua New Guinea; lack of public appreciation for their art, including the issue of authenticity; difficulties in managing earnings and new businesses; and absence of overseas markets. The following addresses each of these problems in turn.

First, given the lack of specialized art shops, studios, or popular markets regularly selling new contemporary art, government agencies and the National Cultural Council must make further efforts to help artists secure new venues to sell their art. Appropriate facilities would be in large hotels, travel lodges, and shops in cultural centres which attract tourists and business people. Other locations would be the National Museum or the Parliament House as these sites draw many visitors. To attract wider audiences, artists must also diversify their works and prices, while still maintaining quality. For example, more prints and posters should be available for sale since these items are inexpensive and portable. In addition, distinctive cards and calendars could also be produced from modern images and designs.[6]

Secondly, to sell new art to the public, appreciation must exist regarding its aesthetics, meaning, and cultural authenticity; that is, people need to know more about new Papua New Guinean artists and their work, and to think of this as being truly Papua New Guinean and worth attention. Art educators and administrators must ensure that children visit exhibitions and are taught about the work of PNG's contemporary artists in their expressive art classes.[7] National television can also run programs on the arts, and new videos can be produced for wide public viewing. Moreover, museums, libraries, cultural Centres, and PNG embassies and missions abroad should make further efforts to display works of modern artists.[8] Art administrators at the University of Papua New Guinea and the National Cultural Council should also exert more pressure on government officials and the elite to attend exhibition openings because their presence gives prestige to the national importance of new art forms.

Third, to help artists manage their businesses, the National Cultural Council or the new business sector of the university should regu-

[6] In the past, students at Sogeri National High have produced cards illustrating village life and legends, which were sold in the UPNG Bookshop and other stores in Port Moresby. In 1980, the NAS also produced a calendar featuring works by contemporary artists. In 1990, Larry Santana designed a series of Christmas cards and notes with his paintings for Independence Books. These sold well, and Santana designed a full range of greeting cards for 1991.

[7] Although exhibitions at the NAS are announced in the press and on the radio, in 1986 only one class from the International High School came to see Jakupa's exhibition. There were no visits from national schools or Sogeri National High School for other shows occurring during the period of research. Moreover, during visits to Aiyura and Passam National High Schools, students appeared largely unaware of the names and works of PNG's modern artists.

[8] The National Museum and Art Gallery has a collection of the early works of contemporary artists. However, this is not on permanent display because the space is needed for visiting exhibitions (personal communication, Saroi Eoi 1986). Hugh Stevenson donated his personal collection of works to the University of Papua New Guinea in 1985. Part of this collection was included in an exhibition entitled *Luk Luk Gen* (Cochrane-Simons and Stevenson 1990) which toured Australia and New Zealand through 1991.

larly conduct workshops to teach market strategies and how to deal with *wantoks*. Without this guidance, artists will continually lack the resources to acquire supplies and materials.[9]

Finally, although it will require professional expertise and government efforts to secure funding, attempts should be made to develop the contemporary art market overseas. Through skilful management and interest generated by museums, aboriginal art has achieved considerable success in Australia. Moreover, in 1988, a striking exhibition of modern aboriginal paintings and sculpture was presented at the Asian Institute in New York which, in turn, helped to stimulate considerable critical interest and gallery traffic in aboriginal art in New York (Myers 1989; 1995). Although modern PNG artists can also produce powerful aesthetic forms, they cannot achieve international recognition without successfully marketing their art with the aid of official backing and the interest produced by scholarly publications.

Unfortunately, in Papua New Guinea, the national government manifests an inconsistent policy toward the social value of art. Although officials declare that expressive arts are a vital resource for achieving national integration and the emergence of national identity, current manpower policies give top priority to development of the nation's natural resources and regard the need for artists to be inconsequential. As a result, the government considers art as little more than 'art for art's sake'—i.e., decoration, and not something essential for furthering modernization. Instead of being 'national treasures', contemporary artists are, as Martin Morububuna reports, fighting to survive:

> [F]inally, I and the other artists are still struggling through the ignorances of the politicians and I hope that one day the NCC will recognize what we are.... They talk about culture but finances and common understanding is not there. We are lost, we don't know where we fit in. Top or bottom—I can't say anything.... (letter, 1988)

The lack of government recognition for contemporary artists and their work has been the target of media criticism by Loujaya Dunar, a 1986 National Arts School graduate and one of Papua New Guinea's few art reporters. As she described in the *Post-Courier* in September 1989, Jakupa—the only PNG artist to have been honoured with an O.B.E.—

---

[9] In October 1986, the Marketing Office of the National Cultural Council sponsored the first National Handicrafts Workshop in Lae. Very useful sessions were organized dealing with the problems of establishing and maintaining arts and handicraft businesses. Business and professional practices are also subjects of discussion in NAS courses.

resided in a 'dingy little room' at the National Arts School, and received no living allowance for being an 'artist in residence' (Dunar 1989). Furthermore, Kauage and Ruki Fame, whose work has been presented to foreign dignitaries as official state gifts, still lived and worked in squatter settlements.

The working conditions for Larry Santana, the young graphic artist referred to earlier, also continue to be precarious. Although he managed to move out of the squatter settlement at the six-mile dump in 1993, he now lives with his family in a one-bedroom apartment which, during the day, also serves as the office for his new small desktop publishing business. The cost for this small space is K400 (about U.S. $400). This is a large sum to obtain each month from his business. Indeed, as he told me recently, the family could not survive without the supplemental income his wife makes baby-sitting the young children of several working women neighbours. Life for Santana and his wife therefore continues to be a struggle to pay their rent and to feed and educate their three children. In 1994, to compound Santana's difficulties, a fire destroyed all his possessions—including the paintings he was preparing to display in an exhibition sponsored by the National Museum (personal communication).

This disjuncture between the ideal role of artists as cultural creators—where art is valued above money (Hand 1990)—and the everyday reality of being *bisnismen,* produces personal frustration and conflict. From the artists' perspective, the Papua New Guinean government has failed to recognize the artists' service to the nation and, despite continual promises of support, has abandoned them to the forces of the 'market'. Yet, most artists, like Larry Santana, are resilient. He has now begun a new series of paintings, entitled 'Risen from the Ashes', and he has recently completed commissions to paint large murals for the new ANZAC memorial and recently renovated and enlarged the national airport at Port Moresby. The money will help Santana pay this year's school fees and buy supplies needed for his business and artwork.

It should also be noted that, although trying to survive as a professional artist in Papua New Guinea is a precarious enterprise, the work of these men (and some women) is beginning to receive critical attention from scholars and museums in Germany, Australia, and the United States (Dissanayake 1988; Raabe 1992, 1995; Cochrane 1997; Cochrane-Simons and Stevenson 1990; Rosi 1987, 1991, 1994, 1995; Thomas 1995). The appearance of permanent collections of contemporary Papua New Guinean art in these countries, together with travelling exhibitions, and scholarly criticism, helps to publicize these new art forms and to give them legitimacy as hybrid dynamic art forms reflective of the cultures they image, and challenge (Cochrane-Simons and Stevenson 1990; Rosi 1994; Thomas 1995).

Another important recent milestone has been the publication of the new journal *Art and Asia Pacific* because, as with the 1995 special issue on *Pacific Art Now,* the journal serves as a regular forum to bring the forms and meanings of Papua New Guinea's art to a global audience. This will raise the national consciousness and pride of Papua New Guinean artists, but it will also be good for their art business. As Chia (1996) has recently underscored, 'art' is not the autonomous activity of specially trained individuals, but the total situation of art making which occurs in a social context mediated and influenced by special institutions and cultural attitudes.

REFERENCES

Baker, C., 1980. *The Innocent Artists; Student Art from Papua New Guinea*. Poole: Blanford Press.

Beier, G., 1974. *Modern Images from Niugini*. Queensland: Jacaranda Press.

Beier, U., 1976. *The Position of the Artist in a Changing Society*. Discussion Paper No. 15. Boroko: Institute of Papua New Guinea Studies.

Beier, U., and Kiki, A. M., 1970. *Hohao: The Uneasy Survival of an Art Form in the Papuan Gulf*. Melbourne: Thomas Nelson.

Berman, M., 1990. 'What is contemporary Melanesian Art?', in *Luk Luk Gen: Contemporary Art from Papua New Guinea*. Sydney: Rainforest Publishing, pp. 59–63.

Bowden, R., 1983. *Yena: Art and Ceremony in Sepik Society*. Oxford: Pitt Rivers Museum.

———, 1992. 'Art, architecture, and collective representations in a New Guinea society', in J. Coote and A. Shelton, eds., *Anthropology Art and Aesthetics*. Oxford: Clarendon Press, pp. 67–94.

Brash, E., and Shimanchi, R., 1986. 'Ruki Fame, artist, welder', in E. Brash and R. Shimanchi, eds., *Faces and Voices of Papua New Guinea: A National Family Album*. Bathurst: Robert Brown and Associates.

Briggs, M., 1989. *Parliament House Papua New Guinea*. Port Moresby: Independent Books.

Chia, J., 1996. 'Trouble at hand: Singapore women artists', in D. Dysart and H. Fink, eds., *Asian Women Artists*. Roseville East, NSW, Australia: Craftsman House, pp. 8–15.

Clay, B., 1987. 'A line of Tatania', in L. Lincoln, ed., *Assemblage of Spirits: Idea and Image in a Melanesian Ritual*. Ithaca: Cornell University Press, pp. 63–73.

Cochrane, S., 1995. 'Art in the contemporary Pacific', *Art and Asia Pacific* 2(4):50–56.

———, 1997. *Contemporary Art in Papua New Guinea*. Craftsman House.

Cochrane-Simons, S., and Stevenson, H., eds., 1990. *Luk Luk Gen! Look Again! Contemporary Art from Papua New Guinea*. Perc Tucker Regional Gallery. Townsville, Queensland, Australia.

Crawford, A., 1981. *Aida: Life and Ceremony of the Gogodala*. Bathurst: Robert Brown and Associates.

Dissanayake, E., 1988. 'Coming of age in Papua New Guinea', *Art in America*, 3:45–47.

Dunar, L., 1989. '"The Academic" and grass-roots artists', *Post-Courier*, 13 September, p. 20.

Errington, F., 1974. *Karavar: Masks and Power in a Melanesian Ritual*. Ithaca: Cornell University Press.

Firth, R., 1936. *Art and Life in New Guinea*. London: The Studio, Ltd.

Forge, A., 1962. 'Paint—a magical substance', *Palette*, 9:9–16.

———, 1970. 'Learning to see in New Guinea', in P. Mayer, ed., *Socialization: The Approach from Social Anthropology*. ASA Monographs No. 3. London: Tavistock, pp. 269–291.

Frost, R., and Walker, M., eds., 1983. *Arts and Education Seminar: Recommendations and Proceedings*. Department of Education, Papua New Guinea.

Gell, A., 1975. *Metamorphosis of the Cassowaries: Umeda Society, Language, and Ritual*. London School of Economics, Monograph on Social Anthropology No. 51. New Jersey: Athlone Press.

Gerbrands, A., 1967a. *The Asmat of New Guinea. The Journal of Michael C. Rockefeller*. New York: Museum of Primitive Art.

———, 1967b. *Wow-ipits: Art in Context*. Series in EthnAesthetics: Field Report No. 3. The Hague: Mouton Publishers.

Hand, D. B., 1990. 'Shall we degrade the study of art?', *The Times of Papua New Guinea*, 8 March, p. 10.

Ison, B., 1975. *Asimba: A Collection of Designs by Young Artists from Sogeri Senior High School*. Port Moresby: Hebamo Press.

———, 1976. 'Art development at Sogeri High School'. *Gigibori* 3(1):5–11.

Jules-Rosette, B., 1984. *The Messages of Tourist Art: An African Semiotic System in Comparative Perspective*. New York: Plenum Press.

Kuchler, S., 1992. 'Making skins: Malangan and the idiom of kinship in Northern New Ireland', in J. Coote and A. Shelton, eds., *Anthropology, Art, and Aesthetics*. Oxford: Clarendon Press, pp. 94–113.

Levine, H., and Levine, M., 1979. *Urbanization in Papua New Guinea: A Study of Ambivalent Townsmen*. Cambridge University Press.

Lincoln, L., ed., 1987. *Assemblage of Spirits: Idea and Image in New Ireland*. The Minneapolis Institute of Art: George Braziller.

MacKenzie, M., 1991. *Androgynous Objects: String Bags and Gender in Central New Guinea*. Melbourne: Harwood Academic Publishers.

Malinowski, B., 1922 (1961). *Argonauts of the Western Pacific*. New York: Dutton.

Matbob, P., 1987. 'The art of making money', *The Times of Papua New Guinea*, 2-8 July, p. 17.

May, R., 1975. 'Tourism and the artifact industry in Papua New Guinea', in B. Finney and K. A. Watson, eds., *A New Kind of Sugar: Tourism in the Pacific*. Honolulu: East-West centre.

Mead, S., and Kernot, B., eds., 1983. *Art and Artists of Oceania*. New Zealand: Dunmore Press.

Mount, M., 1974. *African Art: The Years since 1920*. Bloomington: University of Indiana Press.

Myers, F., 1989. 'Truth, beauty and Pintupi painting', *Visual Anthropology*, 2:163–195.

———, 1995. 'Representing culture: the production of discourse(s) for aboriginal acrylic paintings', in G. Marcus and F. Myers, eds., *The Traffic in Culture*. Berkeley: University of California Press, pp. 55–95.

Narokobi, B., 1980. *The Melanesian Way*. Boroko: Institute of Papua New Guinea Studies.

———, 1990. 'Transformations in art and society', in S. Cochrane-Simons and H. Stevenson, eds., *Luk Luk Gen: Contemporary Art from Papua New Guinea*. Sydney: Rainforest Publishing Company, pp. 17–21.

The National Arts School, 1984. *The Arts Applied*. Catalogue for an Exhibition of Commissioned Works Undertaken by the National Arts School August 24–September 13.

Newman, J., 1984. 'Parliament House', *Paradise* 49, November, pp. 5–9.

O'Hanlon, M., 1989. *Reading the Skin: Adornment, Display and Society among the Wahgi.* London: The British Museum Publications.

Post-Courier, 1988. 'Pacific cultures need to fight for survival', 6 September, p. 2.

Raabe, E., 1992. 'Collecting contemporary art at the Museum für Volkerkunde, Frankfurt, a.M., Germany', *Pacific Arts,* 5:14–18.

———, 1995. 'Modernism or folk art?', *Art and Asia Pacific,* 2:4:96–103.

Rosi, P., 1987. *Contemporary Art of Papua New Guinea.* Exhibition Catalogue. Monmouth College, New Jersey, November 20–December 23.

———, 1991a. 'Papua New Guinea's new Parliament House: a contested national symbol', *The Contemporary Pacific,* 3(2):289–323.

———, 1991b. 'Larry Santana', *Paradise,* 87:31–34.

———, 1994. 'Bung Wantaim: The Role of the National Arts School in Creating National Culture and Identity in Papua New Guinea', unpublished doctoral dissertation, Bryn Mawr College, PA.

———, 1995. '*O Meri Wantok* (My Countrywoman): images of indigenous women in the contemporary arts of Papua New Guinea'. Paper presented to the ASAO Meetings, Kona, HI.

Rosi, P., and Zimmer-Tamakoshi, L., 1993. 'Love and marriage among the urban elite in Port Moresby', in R. Marksbury, ed., *The Business of Marriage: Transformations in Oceanic Matrimony.* ASAO Monograph Series No. 14. Pittsburgh: University of Pittsburgh Press, pp. 175–204.

Schieffelin, E. L., 1976. *The Sorrow of the Lonely and the Burning of the Dancers.* New York: St. Martin's Press.

Smith, G., 1975. *Education in Papua New Guinea.* Melbourne: Melbourne University Press.

Solander Gallery, 1976. *Jakupa.* Exhibition Catalogue with introduction by Tom Craig. Boroko: Creative Arts Centre.

Somare, M., 1974. 'Forward', in S. M. Mead, ed., *Exploring the Visual Art of Oceania.* Honolulu: The University Press of Hawaii, pp. xiii–xviii.

Strathern, A., and Strathern, M., 1975. *Self-Decoration in Mount Hagen.* Toronto: University of Toronto Press.

Swatridge, C., 1985. *Delivering the Goods: Education as Cargo in Papua New Guinea.* Manchester University Press.

Szombati-Fabian, I., and J., 1976. 'Art, history, and society: popular painting in Shaba, Zaire', *Studies in the Anthropology of Visual Communication,* 3(1):1–23.

Teilhet, J., 1983. 'The role of women artists in Polynesia and Melanesia', in S. M. Mead and B. Kernot, eds., *Art and Artists of Oceania.* The Dunmore Press, pp. 45–56.

Thomas, N., 1995. *Oceanic Art.* London: Thames and Hudson.

Tuzin, D., 1980. *The Voice of the Tambaran: Truth and Illusion in Ilahita Arapesh Religion.* Berkeley: University of California Press.

Walker, M., 1978. 'A developing style of the arts in Papua New Guinea'. Paper presented at INSEA 23rd World Congress held in Adelaide, 15 August.

Weeks, S., and Guthrie, G., 1984. 'Papua New Guinea', in R. M. Thomas and T. N. Postlethwaite, eds., *Schooling in the Pacific Islands.* New York: Pergamon Press.

Williams, R. E., 1940. *Drama of Orokolo.* London: Oxford University Press.

Norrie MacQueen

NATIONAL IDENTITY AND THE INTERNATIONAL SYSTEM
The Search for a Foreign Policy

THE QUESTION OF NATIONAL FOREIGN POLICY has been regarded with ambivalence by successive governments in Papua New Guinea since independence in 1975. In this they have shared an attitude common to many ex-colonial territories in the first years of statehood. On one hand, the formulation of basic objectives and the regulation of interactions with other international actors, whether states or organisations, are recognized as obvious indicators of national independence. On the other hand, though, the process of foreign policy-making frequently illuminates the limitations of the very sovereignty which it is supposed to confirm. The new state is required to act in an international system already established according to rules which it has had no influence in formulating. Its diplomatic voice is, moreover, likely to be faint through lack of both experience and resources, compared with other, longer established players.

In the face of these disadvantages new states tend to adopt particular strategies to increase the impact of their foreign policies. A strong regional focus is attractive as it offers at least the impression of significant national influence. The favoured vehicles of diplomacy will often be multilateral rather than bilateral as activism in intergovernmental organisations (IGOs) is much less demanding of scarce economic and human resources than an equivalent range of bilateral interactions. Additionally, the collective nature of institutional diplomacy can have a greater tangible impact on an otherwise indifferent international system than unilateral initiatives on the part of a single, weakly resourced state.

The development of Papua New Guinea's foreign policy provides a fairly typical illustration of these problems and devices. PNG has, however, faced some specific difficulties in the utilisation of these strategies. Both geography and culture have, firstly, confused the country's regional identity within Asia-Pacific and, secondly, somewhat undermined a clear commitment to collective activity.

From the pre-independence period attempts were made to establish guiding principles for the formulation and conduct of external relations. Until the early 1980s foreign policy was notionally based on the principle of 'universalism'. This formulation was expressed in the rather anodyne slogan of 'friends to all and enemies to none'. The concept of universalism emerged during the period of self-government from early 1974 until independence in September 1975 and the hand of a nervous Australian administration can be seen in its combination of high-flown principle and commonplace practicality. It was, supposedly, proposed as an alternative to the more common Third World stance of the period, nonalignment. The diplomatically radical posture of nonaligned 'neutralism' in the mid-1970s was not to the taste of a Canberra government anxious to install a pro-western orientation in the new state's external relations from the outset. In the event, the highly individualistic and nonideological nature of Papua New Guinea's political culture—and its strong missionary-influenced religious underpinning—militated against any significant flirtation with either Moscow or Beijing. Emblematically, perhaps, membership in the Non-Aligned Movement came only in the early 1990s when the whole concept had lost its original diplomatic piquancy.

Regardless of PNG's attitude to nonalignment, it was soon evident that a vague and general notion like universalism was an unsatisfactory substitute for a practical framework for policy-making, planning, and formulation. Universalism could too easily become a means of evading foreign policy rather than a model for its successful conduct.

In 1981 a white paper was published which attempted a systematic analysis of PNG's place in the world, and which sought to provide guidelines for a more effective national foreign policy (*Papua New Guinea Foreign Affairs Review*, 1(4), January 1982). The new approach, which emerged largely from a consultancy conducted by an Australian academic, saw universalism superseded by 'active and selective engagement'. This involved the concentration of the limited economic and manpower resources at the disposal of the Department of Foreign Affairs on selected targets (whether other states or IGOs) of particular importance to the national interest. The main significance of the white paper lay in its acknowledgment that foreign policy does not just happen but is made as the result of a process. It was also a valuable pointer to how the process could be efficiently conducted (King 1985:273–281). Most important, perhaps, was its emphasis on the opportunities provided by an active regional—as opposed to a blandly global—focus for Port Moresby's foreign policy. It could not, however, do very much about PNG's geographical position or the competing historical and cultural bases from which the foreign policy process had to begin.

Papua New Guinea occupies a position on the Asia-Pacific interface which bridges the established regional subsystems of southeast Asia on one side and the island south Pacific on the other. Complicating the situation further is PNG's location in the south of this geographical nexus. This location, combined with the country's particular colonial history, places it firmly in Australia's geopolitical orbit. The interplay between the differing and often competing claims of this trilateral identity has been an enduring characteristic of Papua New Guinea's external relations since 1975 (MacQueen 1989b:530–541).

To the west, the southeast Asian region has represented both threat and opportunity. The colonial division of the island of New Guinea meant that PNG inherited an extended and virtually unmanageable frontier with Indonesia. Jakarta had acquired the former territory of Dutch New Guinea (now the province of Irian Jaya) by a combination of military adventuring and diplomatic manoeuvring in the 1960s. Subsequently, relations between PNG and Indonesia were punctuated by recurrent crises on the border as the Indonesian army attempted to contain the separatist struggle in Irian Jaya (May 1982:85–159). Tensions were particularly high in the first half of the 1980s as fighting in the border region led to a massive influx of refugees to PNG, although the separatist struggle has continued sporadically into the late 1990s.

The Indonesian domination of Irian Jaya, along with its invasion of East Timor which came within months of PNG's independence in 1975, inevitably gave rise to fears of an expansionist neighbour bent on the domination of a 'mega-archipelago' from Sumatra to the Trobriand Islands. These fears were not allayed by Indonesia's transmigration program which moved settlers from the over-populated central islands of

Java and Bali into Irian Jaya. The changing ethnic composition of Irian Jaya (and the alienation of customary land which came with it) tended to confirm Melanesian suspicions on both sides of the border of a deliberate policy of 'Asianization' by Jakarta.

Successive governments in Port Moresby have had to balance the widespread public sympathy for the plight of the Melanesians in Irian Jaya with the realistic acceptance of the permanence of Indonesian rule there. In the later 1980s, however, something of a virtue of necessity was made over the enforced special relationship with Jakarta. The southeast Asian region was seen by an influential group of economic planners in PNG as a possible escape route from continuing dependency on Australia. The relationship with Indonesia might, it was suggested, provide a vehicle for PNG's closer association with the other states to the west, in particular those of the Association of Southeast Asian Nations (ASEAN).

Paias Wingti, the country's third prime minister since independence, whose first term in office began in November 1985, was particularly anxious to restructure Papua New Guinea's postcolonial relationship with Australia and therefore particularly interested in the ASEAN option. To this end he took a much more active approach to relationships with southeast Asia than had his predecessors, a policy with the ultimate objective of ASEAN membership. In 1986 a Treaty of Mutual Respect, Friendship, and Cooperation was signed with Indonesia, which contributed to a general easing of border relations (Wolfers 1988:177–182). The following year PNG was admitted to the ASEAN Treaty of Amity and Cooperation, which fixed a preferential relationship with the organisation short of actual membership. This, however, was as far as southeast Asia seemed willing to go in according regional status to PNG. ASEAN has always been highly exclusive in its approach to membership and Papua New Guinea, regardless of its self-perception, is not perceived by the ASEAN states as a regional partner either economically or culturally. Papua New Guinea's role in southeast Asia is, therefore, likely to remain that of peripheral trading partner, at least in the medium-term.

Despite the frustration of Wingti's ASEAN ambitions, the rapprochement with Indonesia has been fairly well maintained even in the face of continuing separatist activity in Irian Jaya. It is probably the case that public opinion (so far as it exists at this stage of development in PNG's political culture) has gradually come to terms with Indonesia's rule in Irian Jaya and is less inclined than in the past to see it as a threat to the existence of Papua New Guinea itself. More broadly, however, developments in external relations to the Asian west, both with and through Indonesia, have done little to resolve the issue of regional identity for PNG.

To what extent might PNG's eastern geographic axis provide an answer to this problem of regional identity? It is within this Pacific islands region that PNG would most often be placed in the perceptions of foreigners and citizens alike. Yet there are many grounds for challenging this categorisation. For one thing Papua New Guinea is not, geographically speaking, an island nation. As we have seen, it shares a land-mass of continental proportions with a major southeast Asian state. PNG's population of over three million is of an entirely different order from those of even the larger Pacific island countries such as Solomon Islands and Fiji.

Table 1
Papua New Guinea and Island Neighbours Compared

	Population [in thousands]	Land Area [in sq. kms.]	Sea Area [in millions of sq. kms.]
PNG	3,060.6	462,243	3,120
Fiji	646.5	18,272	1,290
Solomons	235.0	2,755	1,340
W. Samoa	156.0	2,935	120
Vanuatu	119.9	11,880	680

Additionally, PNG's economic resources, actual and potential, are different in kind and quantity from those of the island states further east in the south Pacific. These discrepancies pose particular dilemmas for Papua New Guinea's foreign policy. While Port Moresby is presented with the possibility of a leadership role in the southwest Pacific region, attempts to assume such a position can be (and have been) regarded with suspicion by island governments apprehensive of a push for regional hegemony by PNG.

Different administrations in Port Moresby have responded to this problem in different ways. In 1980 Michael Somare, PNG's first prime minister who was then in opposition, fiercely criticized his successor's, Sir Julius Chan's, decision to intervene in Vanuatu's independence crisis.

In so doing, Somare aligned himself with his friend and fellow 'father of Pacific independence' Fijian Prime Minister Ratu Sir Kamisese Mara. The dispatch of a military force to Vanuatu in order to guarantee the transfer of power to the government of Father Walter Lini was a domestic triumph for the Chan government, constituting as it did a successful act of anticolonial and pan-Melanesian solidarity. But the rest of the Pacific island states were less happy with this projection of PNG's military capability, and Somare appeared to sympathize with their misgivings (MacQueen 1988:245–247). Somare's political apprenticeship had been served at a time when the southwest Pacific barely existed as an independent region, and his identification tended naturally to be with the region as a whole rather than with the sub-regions which came into being as decolonization progressed, whether Melanesian, Polynesian, or Micronesian. His concern to avoid misperceptions of PNG's intentions in foreign policy among the island states had been expressed right from independence and continued throughout his career.

In contrast, Paias Wingti demonstrated his frustration with what he saw as the obstructive caution of the Polynesians (and by implication the inappropriateness of the broader south Pacific as a unit of regional cooperation) by focusing on the Melanesian sub-region. The main impetus for this came in 1986 and 1987 with a deterioration in the situation in the French territory of New Caledonia. Like Vanuatu before it, New Caledonia raised a triad of highly sensitive issues: French colonialism, Melanesian ethnic identity, and the evident absence of pan-Pacific solidarity on the part of the Polynesian states. The Melanesian Spearhead Group, which emerged as an ad hoc caucus in 1986, was formalized as a sub-regional IGO by the signing of Agreed Principles for Cooperation between PNG, Vanuatu, and Solomon Islands in early 1988.

No inconsistency was acknowledged between this sub-regionalism and the Wingti government's parallel ambition for the creation of a strong 'Single Regional Organisation' combining the principal regional IGO, the South Pacific Forum, and the older colonial-inspired South Pacific Commission. For Wingti, pan-Melanesianism provided an alternative string to the southeast Asian bow in the attempt to redirect PNG foreign policy away from the former metropole, Australia. With the return of Somare in 1988 as foreign minister in the Namaliu government, however, the larger region again became the focus of Port Moresby's Pacific diplomacy.

Central to PNG's problems of regional identity is the link, both current and historical, with Australia. Relations between Port Moresby and Canberra are unique in a number of ways. They differ from those of other European ex-metropoles with their former tropical colonies in that the postimperial relationship is one between two neighbouring states preoccupied with many of the same issues in their regional international relations. Independence for Papua New Guinea did not come as the result of any particularly sharp or protracted anticolonial struggle. The process was, if anything, initiated by the coloniser rather than the colonized and involved an essentially amicable transfer of power. The postcolonial relationship was, at least for the first decade, characterized by continued large-scale financial assistance from Canberra which amounted to about one third of PNG's annual budgetary requirements. Perhaps, however, this was not the most satisfactory form of relationship. Continued economic dependency, along with a perception of Australia as a dominant and domineering regional power contributed to a *ex post facto* anticolonialism which, ironically, had barely existed during the period of actual colonial rule. This attitude found expression in criticisms of Australia's supposedly overbearing role in the region in relation to such things as the 1985 nuclear free zone treaty and its pressure on the post-1987 regime in Fiji. Simultaneously Canberra was accused of lack of commitment in the campaign against French colonial and nuclear policies and abuses by the American tuna fishing fleet of the islands' two-hundred-mile economic zones.

More practically, budgetary dependence on Australian aid has made the country extremely vulnerable to the vicissitudes of the metropolitan economy. The extent of this vulnerability was illustrated in mid-1986 when, in response to a major liquidity crisis at home, Canberra unilaterally cut the annual subvention to PNG by some A$10 million. This represented a default on the part of Australia on the third postindependence five-year aid agreement which had been negotiated less than a year previously (Saffu 1987:271–272).

It was against this background that the Wingti government set about the redefinition of the relationship with the former metropole. One part of this redefinition involved, as we have seen, the opening of alternative economic and diplomatic channels to southeast Asia in the west and to the other Melanesian states to the east. Another part concerned the reformulation of the Australian relationship itself. In December 1987 Prime Ministers Wingti and Hawke signed a Joint

Declaration of Principles (JDP) in Canberra which redrew the postcolonial association in terms more appropriate to PNG's emerging identity as an independent international actor. Aid was de-emphasized in favour of an expanded and more balanced trading relationship. And, for the first time in the postindependence period, Australia committed itself to the possibility of joint action in the event of external threats to Papua New Guinea's security.

The Joint Declaration of Principles was hailed as a major step forward in the assertion of a distinct and independent PNG foreign policy. Objectively it was. What was less clear, however, was whether the redefinition of relationships embodied in the Joint Declaration of Principles would have been feasible had it not coincided with changes in the direction of Australia's own foreign and defence policy. The progressive introduction of superpower competition into the southwest Pacific in the 1980s and the instability generated by the provocative French presence combined to force a re-examination of regional relationships in Canberra itself. This diplomatic stock-taking was accelerated after 1987 by a new realisation in Australia of the limits of its regional influence, starkly illustrated by developments surrounding the coup in Fiji that year. The result was a generally more responsive and sensitive approach to bilateral relations with the independent Pacific states, and the Joint Declaration of Principles must be seen in this context as well as that of a newly assertive Papua New Guinean foreign policy.

This question of initiative goes to the centre of the problem of PNG's foreign policy effort. How far does PNG (or any small state) initiate its own foreign policy and how far does it merely react to the diplomatic *force majeure* of larger regional actors? The southeast Asian axis of PNG's diplomacy can certainly be interpreted in this light. The 'opening' to the ASEAN states appears to have been regulated by the Asians themselves, particularly Indonesia, in their own best interests. Border cooperation is at least as important to Indonesia as it is to Papua New Guinea. More broadly, the economic opportunities offered by PNG's natural resources have attracted considerable attention within ASEAN, especially from Malaysia and Singapore. While PNG's full membership in the Association might be too high an investment in the exploitation of these opportunities, a 'special relationship' may be regarded by the ASEAN states as a worthwhile concession, offering them access without entanglement.

Foreign policy activism on the part of Papua New Guinea therefore is not in itself proof of greater independence of international action.

'Active and selective engagement' has often involved the selection and active cultivation of actors which have sought to adjust their own policies towards Papua New Guinea for their own self-interests.

A further question mark was placed over PNG's freedom of foreign policy manoeuvre in the later 1980s by the sudden importation of superpower competition to the southwest Pacific. Papua New Guinea's fundamentally pro-western orientation was deeply rooted in both political culture and economic structure. Serious negotiations for the establishment of a Soviet diplomatic mission only began on the eve of the disintegration of the Soviet Union itself. But the generally light-handed approach of the United States towards PNG perhaps depended less on these domestic factors than on changing systemic pressures in the region. The cold war came late to the south Pacific and, happily, was over before it demanded any decisive response from the foreign policies of the region's states. In other words, Port Moresby's capacity to formulate and sustain a truly autonomous global foreign policy was not tested in the years of bipolarity and has yet to be fully confirmed.

Yet, however much the problems of geographical location and an inchoate political culture may have prevented the pursuit of a streamlined foreign policy, the consequences for PNG's national interests have not so far been serious. Conditions within the Asia-Pacific area have not as yet placed any exceptional strain on Papua New Guinea's diplomatic capacity.

Threats do exist. The border relationship with Indonesia still has the potential to create considerable regional insecurity. While the management of the frontier *per se* may not provoke problems, the larger issues of Indonesian separatism and the associated pressures for democratisation appear to be mounting rather than lessening in the later 1990s and could come to confound Jakarta's border relations at all points. Meanwhile, the continued presence of France, especially where actively opposed as in New Caledonia and increasingly in Polynesia, is also a possible source of problems. And, while it is unlikely that the Bougainville tragedy with its potential for territorial dispute and military incursion will yet lead to transnational conflict, it is not inconceivable. Certainly, relations with the Solomon Islands deteriorated sharply in the early 1990s as PNG Defence Force incursions into the territory of the latter led to heated protests—although things improved after the signing of a treaty of understanding in September 1995. Despite periodic setbacks, the Indonesian relationship has been generally more stable since the 1986 Treaty of Friendship. Appropriately,

Paias Wingti worked to consolidate the new relationship when he
returned to power in mid-1992, although border problems have persisted. Developments in France's domestic politics appear to have
averted an entangling anticolonial struggle in New Caledonia, at least
in the medium term. The region's 'French problem', however, also
involves the nuclear issue, and PNG was at the forefront of the diplomatic campaign against Paris during the testing program of 1995. But
the cold war is no more, and Australia's apprehensions of the mid-
1980s about a possible Libyan intrusion in the region had passed by the
end of the decade, as Tripoli's general interventionist enthusiasm
waned.

In short, the stability of the environment within which PNG formulates its foreign policy seems reasonably assured into the next century. The passing of the ideological backwash of the cold war saw the
emergence of a more functional tone in Port Moresby's external relations, a development facilitated by the replacement of the Melanesian
nationalist Wingti by the more business-minded Sir Julius Chan in
August 1994.

Beyond this general consideration of systemic environment, however, other challenges remain. The continued convergence of PNG's
policy objectives with those of its larger neighbours—which has given
an impression of successful activism to its diplomacy—cannot be guaranteed. The Bougainville secession crisis exposed the limits of PNG's
freedom of foreign policy manoeuvre by highlighting the extent of
Port Moresby's continued dependency on Australia. The degree to
which Australia sees its own interests being served in meeting these
requirements is unclear. If in this—or indeed in any other significant
area—the foreign policy objectives of PNG finally begin to diverge significantly from those of its larger neighbours, the projection of a distinct national identity might quickly run into the sand. The buoyancy
of Port Moresby's mechanisms of foreign policy formulation and
implementation has yet to be tested in other than essentially calm
waters.

REFERENCES AND SUGGESTED READINGS

Australia, Parliament of the Commonwealth Joint Committee on Foreign Affairs, Defence and Trade (Report) 1991. *Australia's Relations with Papua New Guinea*. Canberra: Senate Publishing and Printing Unit.

Australian Foreign Affairs Record, June 1975. ('Universalism').

———, November–December 1987. ('Joint Declaration of Principles').

Babbage, Ross, 1987. 'Australia and the defence of Papua New Guinea, *Australian Outlook*, 41(2):87–94.

Dorney, Sean, 1990. *Papua New Guinea: People Politics and History since 1975*. Sydney: Random House.

Downs, Ian, 1980. *The Australian Trusteeship: Papua New Guinea 1947–75*. Canberra: Australian Government Publishing Service.

King, Peter, 1985. 'The foreign policy white paper of 1981: a critique', in Peter King *et al.*, eds., *From Rhetoric to Reality* (Papers from the 15th Waigani Seminar). Port Moresby: University of Papua New Guinea Press, pp. 272–281.

MacQueen, N., 1988. 'Beyond *Tok Win*: the Papua New Guinea intervention in Vanuatu, 1980', *Pacific Affairs*, 61(2):235–252.

———, 1989. 'Sharpening the spearhead: subregionalism in Melanesia', *Pacific Studies*, 12(2):33–52.

———, 1989b. 'Papua New Guinea's relations with Australia and Indonesia: diplomacy on the Asia-Pacific interface', *Asian Survey*, 24(5):530–541.

———, 1991. 'New directions for Papua New Guinea's foreign policy', *Pacific Review*, 4(2):102–173.

———, 1993. 'An infinite capacity to muddle through? a security audit for Papua New Guinea', *Journal of Commonwealth and Comparative Politics*, 21(2):133–154.

May, R. J., ed., 1986. *Between Two Nations: The Indonesia-Papua New Guinea Border and West Papua Nationalism*. Bathurst NSW: Robert Brown & Associates.

Neemia, Uentabo Fakaofo, 1986. *Cooperation and Conflict: Costs, Benefits and National Interests in Pacific Regional Cooperation*. Suva: Institute of Pacific Studies of the University of the South Pacific.

Papua New Guinea Foreign Affairs Review, January 1982. (White Paper).

Saffu, Yaw, 1987. 'Papua New Guinea in 1986', *Asian Survey*, 27(2):264–273.

Standish, Bill, 1984. *Melanesian Neighbours*. Canberra: Legislative Research Service Department of the Parliamentary Library Basic Paper No. 9.

Turner, Mark, 1990. *Papua New Guinea: The Challenge of Independence*. Melbourne: Penguin.

Wolfers, Edward P., ed., 1988. *Beyond the Border*. Port Moresby and Suva: University of Papua New Guinea Press and University of the South Pacific Institute of Pacific Studies.

David King

REFUGEES AND BORDER CROSSERS ON THE PAPUA NEW GUINEA–INDONESIA BORDER

$\mathcal{B}$ETWEEN 1994 AND 1996 landowners from villages along the Ok Tedi
and Fly rivers in Western Province took Broken Hill Proprietary to court
in Melbourne, demanding compensation for pollution of the rivers
totalling US$4 billion. While the case was settled out of court in 1996
for no more compensation than had originally been offered, the landowners were successful in reopening investigation of an appropriate
tailings dam. The media portrayed the case as a type of David-and-Goliath struggle of environmental activism. It certainly was such a struggle,
but no mention was ever made of the thousands of refugees and displaced people living in the worst-affected parts of the river system. For
the Yonggom people along the most heavily polluted parts of the Ok
Tedi River, the presence of 4,000 refugees (Kirsch 1993:60) in their villages and camps west of the river has created land pressure and introduced an element of politicisation among people who harbour and
support an active guerilla army. While the court case was initiated by
the leaders from over a hundred villages, representing over 30,000 people, the main leaders in the case were from Yonggom communities. The
issue of the refugees and displaced persons in the Ok Tedi area is a social
and political time bomb that will probably bring about further conflict
and activism during the remaining life of the mine, whether or not
Broken Hill Proprietary cleans up its environmental act.

THE BORDERS

The arbitrary boundaries drawn by foreigners have left problems as serious as many of the social changes that they, the foreigners, introduced. The first boundary to be fixed in Melanesia was the 141st line of longitude that divided New Guinea in half; Britain and the Netherlands agreed on that line in 1848. The island had originally been claimed by Ortiz de Retes for Spain in 1545. The Dutch claimed the western end in 1606, although they did not establish any settlement on the island until 1828, when they made an agreement with the sultan of Tidore in the Moluccas that he should control West New Guinea on their behalf. There was never any practical control, except intermittent trading expeditions, but this deal with the sultan was used by the Indonesians to justify their claim to West New Guinea as part of the historical sultanate of Tidore, which had subsequently been absorbed into the Republic of Indonesia.

The other boundaries of Papua and New Guinea were drawn just as arbitrarily. In 1884 Britain and Germany divided East New Guinea with three straight lines joining coordinates of latitude and longitude from a rock in the Solomon Sea to a point on the 141st meridian. It is on Papua New Guinea's western side that it has its longest land border and its biggest problem. The Dutch in 1848 defined it as the 141st longitude, but no one made any concerted effort to demarcate it before 1960 (Van der Veur 1966). The Tugeri invasions of British Papua in the 1890s prompted a definition of the southern part of the border, especially on the coast (Verrier 1986). For easy demarcation the mouth of the Bensbach River was selected as the southernmost boundary point. This in not actually on the 141st longitude, but subsequent negotiations on the border allowed the straight line from Bensbach River to follow the thalweg of the River Fly once it bisected the river. This forms a bulge on the border, protruding into the west New Guinea side. From the northern edge of the Fly bulge, the border follows the 141st longitude. The Fly bulge is the only natural feature used by the border, which runs for over 700 kilometres through rain forest, swamp, hills, and the mountains of the central cordillera.

Much of the strike of the land, hills, mountains, and types of vegetation is east-west. Trade routes between people in the border area were both east-west and north-south. For people who wished to expand into contiguous areas of similar resources, the direction was east or west. Thus many cultural and linguistic groups are divided by the border. Farming and hunting land is distributed on either side of this imaginary line. The border totally disregarded the people who lived in its vicinity, and they in turn have disregarded the border (Pula, Jackson *et al.* 1984). In fact, many people in the interior near the border region were not even contacted by the governments that had divided them until the late 1950s and early 1960s (Hyndman 1979). Before the Second World War, both Dutch and Australian development of New Guinea was extremely limited, and in the remote border areas, virtually nonexistent.

REALIGNMENT AND INDEPENDENCE

The ease with which the Japanese displaced the colonial powers in southeast Asia intensified independence moves in diverse directions. The Indonesian nationalists, led by Sukarno, Yamin, and Hatta, planned an extended postwar state (Osborne 1985). The Indonesians were thwarted when the Dutch returned in 1945 and four years of independence struggle ensued. At the same time as the Indonesians were planning for independence, the Dutch and a few educated Melanesians in Netherlands New Guinea also began to formulate ideas of an independent nation of West Papua, which they named Iryan (a Biak word meaning a steamy mountainous land). The Indonesians subsequently altered this to the acronym Irian, meaning 'follow the Indonesian Republic in its struggle against the Netherlands' (Osborne 1985). The Indonesian independence slogan *Merdeka* (freedom) was also taken up by the West Papuan nationalists in their initial anti-colonial struggle against the Dutch. During the 1950s the Organisasi Papua Merdeka (OPM) was formulated in opposition to Dutch colonialism and then transferred its attention to the subsequent Indonesian invaders (Nyamekye and Premdas 1979).

As the Dutch were being pushed out of Indonesia they began rapid development of West New Guinea. They used Indonesians as middle class administrators, but also, with the missionaries, pushed the development of an indigenous Melanesian middle class. This group particularly strove for an independent Irian, and subsequently took the struggle into the jungle alongside the rural people.

For the West Papuans, Dutch development in the 1950s was positive. In the border area the Dutch were bringing change and development, as missions and administrative posts were extended into very remote parts of the island. Some parts of Kiunga District in the northern Western Province of Papua New Guinea were actively administered by Netherlands New Guinea. During this period it is estimated that there was a significant drift of border dwellers westward from the Australian to the Dutch territory (Pula, Jackson, *et al.* 1984).

INDONESIAN TAKEOVER

Before the Second World War multinational companies involved in resource exploitation in West New Guinea were less than enthusiastic about the liberal development of the territory, and associated policies of protecting the rights of the indigenous population. Oil companies, particularly, favoured Indonesian government of West New Guinea. The strength of communism in Indonesia worried the U.S.A., and thus Australia, so that global policy in relation to Indonesia was one of appeasement. Tapol (1983) claims that Indonesia, backed by multinational companies, was primarily concerned with gaining control of West New Guinea's rich mineral resources and extensive, sparsely populated land.

Thus when Indonesia pressed its claims and Sukarno made 'recovery' of Irian Jaya a nationalist issue, the rights and aspirations of 800,000 Melanesians were considered less important than Indonesian stability. The U.S.A. accepted the inevitability of Indonesian rule as early as 1961, while the Dutch opted for United Nations control until planned independence. In 1961 the West Papuans elected a national New Guinea Council and raised the West Papuan flag. Eight months later the Indonesians invaded and remained to assist the United Nations administration. This initial invasion triggered the first small waves of migration eastward into Papua and New Guinea.

A plebiscite of all West Papuans was held in 1969 called the Act of Free Choice (or the Act of No Choice by most West Papuans). Under the scrutiny of Indonesian troops, but outside the control of the U.N., the vote went in favour of joining Indonesia. At this point a far greater number of people voted with their feet by leaving West Papua for Papua New Guinea (Osborne 1985). In taking over the country Indonesia destabilized the West Papuan population.

DESTABILIZATION

Destabilization need not necessarily have occurred, despite a military invasion. The Indonesians exacerbated destabilization in three main areas of their dealings with West Papuans: oppression, exploitation of resources, and transmigration.

Oppression

Oppression and atrocities are recorded by Tapol and published in its bulletins, while several other writers have also independently recorded infringements of human rights (International Commission of Jurists 1983; Osborne 1985; R. May 1986; Nyamekye and Premdas 1979; Research Institute of Oppressed Peoples 1985; Sharp 1977; Smith, Trompf, and Clements 1985; Smith and Hewison 1986; Verrier 1986). Oppression takes the form of killings, torture, beatings, imprisonment, rape, destruction of churches and villages, and the wholesale slaughter of pigs. While much of this oppression is aimed generally at the population, opposition politicians and OPM members have been killed, executed, or imprisoned. There have been a number of uprisings in West Papua since the Indonesian invasion, all of which have been put down and followed by village burning, murders, rapes, and imprisonment. Heavy military force is employed by the Indonesians, including air attacks and bombing raids on villages.

After the abortive OPM/West Papuan uprising of 1984, military action was stepped up. Other forms of oppression involve racial, religious, and cultural persecution. Indonesia being predominantly Muslim, West Papuans find their pig herds are attacked and their churches and non-Christian sacred sites attacked or defiled. The Indonesians also speak to and treat West Papuans as inferior to themselves, claiming that they are there to civilize them. Tapol (1983) provides numerous accounts from reporters, film makers, missionaries, West Papuan individuals, and even the Indonesians themselves of overt racism and cultural genocide.

Resource Exploitation

Three main areas of resource exploitation are minerals, agricultural land, and timber. Land is obtained from local landowners by fraud, expropriation, or sale for low prices. Some land is identified for the transmigration scheme, but a great deal of expropriated land is taken by informal or unofficial transmigrants, and soldiers and administrators who have taken land in order to retire or settle in Irian Jaya. Javanese and West Papuan notions of land ownership are significantly different. West Papuans generally have no desire to sell any of their land. Most societies are shifting cultivators whose land needs are extensive. Despite the hot, wet climate, much of the land is not of high fertility. Losing this land to expropriation, the shifting cultivators are either forced onto increasingly marginal lands, or they must become absorbed into the Javanese homestead or transmigrant system. Furthermore, the land is frequently communally owned, with different rights pertaining to different clans and families, and to different spiritual and cultural entities. Thus the removal of the land from the people or the people from the land is itself cultural genocide.

Trees and forests have the same significance as land. The sale of trees and forests goes against cultural responsibility. Expropriation of forests and land causes enormous difficulties in Papua New Guinea, where the extent of such operations is small and compensation usually generous. However, loggers are ruthlessly exploiting West Papuan forests, paying very little for logs and using forced labour in localized deforestation programs (Tapol 1983, Osborne 1985). This is not restricted to West Papua. Forests throughout southeast Asia and the Pacific are being mined by ruthless prospectors, while local landowners in other places have opposed the logging companies.

West Papua has become an exporter of raw materials (Tapol 1983:33–34). Most of the export wealth comes from oil and gas, copper and prawns. There are several oil companies. Petromer Trend was producing 170,000 barrels a day from its Sorong oil well. Initially the company employed large numbers of West Papuans, but they were gradually phased out in favour of Indonesians. The same happened at the Manokowari well and has been repeated as new concessions have been opened up. Transmigrants have been moved into the vicinity of the oilfields to provide a stable labour force. The policy of Pertamina, the national oil company, is to avoid employing Melanesians in the oil industry.

In strong contrast to the experience at both of Papua New Guinea's copper mines on Bougainville and at Ok Tedi, the Freeport Mine at Mount Ertzberg in West Papua employed few local people (150 West Papuans out of a 731 work force), paid them extremely low wages, paid no compensation or royalties for the land and its resources, forcibly removed local people, and shot or imprisoned protesters. Land was alienated from the local Amungme people in exchange for the promise of education, health, and employment opportunities. Few examples of these ever transpired (Aditjondro 1986).

Apart from these instances of cynical exploitation there is generally little local development of West Papuan land. If local people stand in the way of any resource exploitation they are dealt with harshly. The general attitude from the Indonesians is that the land and the resources are for the benefit of the nation, and no payment is needed for people who wastefully occupy vast areas of unused land.

Transmigration

Estimates of the numbers of people involved in transmigration to West Papua vary enormously. For the Indonesians it probably represents too little, while for the West Papuans it is certainly too much. Of more significance than any argument about the numbers is the impact of the idea of transmigration on the West Papuans. The transmigrants represent a threat of cultural suffocation, continued expropriation of land, increased racism, and numerical domination of West Papua by Muslim Javanese.

Transmigration has been going on throughout this century. The main territories receiving these transmigrants are in Sumatra, Kalimantan, Sulawesi, Maluku, and Irian Jaya, although the capacity of Irian Jaya is listed as being very small in comparison to other destinations (Maris 1982; Oey 1982). After 1965 a further function of transmigration was to increase food production and to suppress inflation. In tackling the food supply problem, transmigration has been more effective in extending the amount of land under cultivation than in reducing the population of Java, as the total national transmigration scheme has moved fewer people out of Java than have been added to its population by natural increase.

The only existing transmigration blocks near to the Papua New Guinea border have introduced small numbers of people and alienated relatively little land. Transmigrants are only a minority of the total migration stream. Estimates (Sharp 1977; Tapol 1983; Arndt 1986; R. May 1986; Aditjondro 1986) suggest that up to 400,000 Indonesians had already been added to the 800,000 West Papuans by the mid-1980s. The official Indonesian total of 10,000 transmigrants to Irian Jaya does not include large numbers of spontaneous migrants, government, and industrial workers, although it should be noted that most of these migrants have moved to Sorong and the Birds Head rather than close to the border. The National Plan, Repelita 4, targeted alienation by 1989 of 1.5 to 3.2 million hectares for transmigrants, industry, cash cropping, roads, and logging (Hastings 1986).

The only transmigrant area close to Kiunga District in Papua New Guinea is that around Mindiptana on the edge of the Yonggom (Muyu) territory. Arndt's map (1986) lists most of these blocks as having been surveyed, but judged to be unsuitable. However, the fear of alienation must be seen as a reality and a contributing factor in the OPM involvement of these people and their subsequent flight into Papua New Guinea.

INDONESIAN OPPRESSION AND THE OPM

Indonesian authorities refer to the OPM as 'Wild Terrorist Gangs' (GPL), but rarely do they have the opportunity to engage them in battle. Thus the response to OPM raids is usually air attacks on and destruction of the nearest rural community, sometimes causing considerable loss of life. The OPM is unable to take on the Indonesian forces, but undoubtedly plays a powerful role in sustaining anti-Indonesian propaganda, especially in the remoter parts of the country. The total active membership of the OPM is probably only 300 to 400 and is particularly effective along the border, providing safe retreat into Papua New Guinea. The weapons of the OPM are few and old, and are supplemented by spears, axes, and bows and arrows. There is little support for the organization from outside countries, including Papua New Guinea, and it is split by factions. Yet despite these limitations it has been able to organize a number of simultaneous uprisings and protests. After thirty-five years of opposition it remains weak and yet as determined as ever in the face of Indonesia's massive armed forces.

It is largely because of Indonesian oppression that people have moved and it is for the same reason that they justify refugee status, and may be afforded residential rights. The policies that Indonesia has pursued in West Papua have destabilized the indigenous population, creating violent opposition and violent reaction. These same policies have in some cases displaced West Papuan populations; in other instances they have created a climate of fear and unease about the future. Even if the Indonesians have no intention of obliterating the rights and cultures of the West Papuan people, the fact that the West Papuans believe that to be the case is a destabilizing factor that has contributed to their flight, turning them into refugees.

BORDER PROBLEMS

Fourteen marker posts have been placed along the 700-kilometre border. There are no natural barriers along the border, and nearly all of it is thickly forested. In an unstable situation it lends itself perfectly to all types of cross-border movement including armed incursions. The Indonesians believe that the Papua New Guineans supply and support the OPM, so cross-border raids are common, and a number of Papua New Guinean villages have been attacked. However, the two governments have made strenuous efforts to avoid incidents and confrontations, with border agreements having been made between Papua New Guinea and Indonesia in 1979, 1984, and 1989.

BORDER CROSSING
There are three types of cross-border movements:

1. General patterns of movements that might be defined as customary or traditional.

2. Movement trends towards towns and developments.

3. Political events and the resulting flow of refugees with the likelihood of repetition in the future.

Rural mobility
Throughout the border area the societies that are adjacent to the border or actually divided by it are highly mobile, shifting cultivators and hunter-gatherers. Pula and Jackson's (1984) survey of the Western Province border area listed extensive cross-border connections. Whereas Papua New Guinea recognizes communal ownership of land as a form of land tenure, Indonesia places greater emphasis on individual or family ownership. For the Yonggom, Mindiptana or Kiunga are simply alternative central places at either side of their group territory. The border agreement permits cross-border trade of 'traditional' goods, but for people who have always traded with their neighbours, the arresting of that trade into 'traditional' items only is restrictive and anti-developmental. The trade pattern that existed in precontact times has been substituted in modern times with steel axes for stone, and rice for sago. The border agreement precluded the continuance of such a trade. During the 1990s an effective 'no-go area' has been created on the Indonesian side of the border, tacitly supported by the government of PNG.

For the Yonggom, part of the normal patterns of society were trade across the whole territory, marriage into distant clans, and the consequent rights to land use in a number of areas. When people take up the right to farm an area, they must necessarily relocate their settlements to the site of the new gardens. Now the place in which an individual is born assumes a new significance which would previously have been less important.

Schoorl's description of the Yonggom (or Muyu) in the 1950s shows the mobility and trading movement of the people. Journeys out to modern centres such as Merauke and later Mindiptana were frequent. Similarly people developed a general pattern of going 'walkabout' at holiday time. It is also interesting that he lists their population in 1953 as 12,223 with the comment that only a small portion of them lived on the Australian side of the border. Pula and Jackson (1984) state that there were 1,400 Yonggom people in Papua New Guinea in 1953, which increased slowly to 2,519 in 1983. This situation has now significantly altered. It is likely that the majority of the Yonggom now live in Papua New Guinea. Two reasons for the distribution change are greater recent development on the Papua New Guinean side and political events in West Papua that have acted as a push.

DEVELOPMENT AT OK TEDI

During the 1950s the Yonggom especially were drifting westward as vigorous development took place under the last colonial gasp of the Dutch. The missions were also active, especially the Catholics through the Order of the Sacred Heart (Smith and Hewison 1986). Some areas of the Australian territory were even administered by the Dutch (Van der Veur 1966). Between Kiunga and the Star Mountains there was spontaneous relocation and building of villages amongst the Ningerum and Awin people, as the first road began to be constructed north from Kiunga in the 1970s. Subsequently rubber was introduced as the first village cash crop into the area.

With the discovery of the massive copper deposit on Mount Fubilan, the likelihood of mining development created an axis of concentration along the route between Kiunga, the port on the River Fly, and Tabubil the embryonic mining camp. Village relocation involved many more people than drift to the towns, but in Kiunga, especially, there appeared a number of village-based squatter settlements, called corners in Western Province. Surveys carried out in 1979 (King 1983), before mining began and in 1983 after the initial construction period, showed that these settlements contained a large part of the population of Kiunga, and that they represented urban bases for virtually every group of villages in the territories of the Awin, Ningerum, Yonggom, and Suki (within Papua New Guinea). The populations of these corners were not fixed. There were a few semi-permanent families represented in each of them, but most of the houses provided accommodation for the large floating population. Many people, especially in 1979, regularly commuted between Kiunga and their villages. In this way people were in position to take advantage of job opportunities as they arose.

By 1983 dramatic changes had taken place in the whole North Fly area as the mine construction had begun, the road had been built as far as Tabubil, and massive construction camps housed several thousand workers. Meanwhile, villages in the surrounding rural areas had been deserted and rubber plantations neglected. In the Star Mountains there was a cross-border move from West Papua to Kombit, while the village of Kawentigin moved into Papua New Guinea, then continued to shift eastward toward Tabubil. Once the mine began at Ok Tedi, large numbers of Ningerum people moved into squatter settlements on the edge of Tabubil. The authorities moved them out, relocating many in the corners of Kiunga from which they had started out. They have since extended their settlement pattern as far north as their land will reach and have established a large village at Ok Ma camp number eleven, which gives them access to the road that leads into Tabubil.

Within Kiunga in particular there are significant numbers of people who were born in West Papua. People have been drifting across the border, other than as refugees, finding accommodation in Kiunga through the use of kinship networks, and finding jobs. They are also a reasonably educated group so that they have been able to merge into Papua New Guinean society. The numbers of border crossers are not dramatic, but as people have drifted into villages and towns along the 700-kilometre border, the number probably runs into a couple of thousand people.

As far as the governments of both Papua New Guinea and Indonesia are concerned, the drift across the border, even if it flows only one way, should not constitute a problem because the numbers involved are so small. If development along the border were equal on both sides, any exchange of populations would probably balance.

REFUGEES

As a consequence of Indonesian policies and the West Papuan response in the form of uprisings and support for the OPM, West Papuans have been fleeing into Papua New Guinea to escape retribution for acts of opposition, to escape from army attacks, or to escape general oppression. The OPM with its small numbers has not maintained a consistent level of opposition, but has concentrated activity into periods of greater intensity. Following each of these active periods has been an Indonesian reaction and a consequent movement of refugees.

R. May (1986) claims that by the end of 1968 1,200 refugees had entered Papua New Guinea, followed by a trickle throughout the 1970s. Nyamekye and Premdas (1979) claim that 10,000 refugees had entered by 1979. The Indonesians have attempted to curtail border movements to prevent the establishment of a sizeable West Papuan community in Papua New Guinea. For Papua New Guinea the early refugees represented a problem in its relations with Indonesia. Generally, however, the individuals were absorbed easily enough and were granted permissive residence on the condition of refraining from anti-Indonesian action. By the late 1970s the border area was quiet. The OPM was split by rival factions although this appears to have had little effect on Indonesian attitudes.

During the 1980s the OPM reorganised itself and began a more vigorous campaign that sought a great deal more publicity for its cause. The culmination of its campaign was the raising of the West Papuan flag in Jayapura on 13 February 1984. This was followed by a number of similar flag raisings in towns and administrative stations throughout West Papua. The OPM followed this up with raids on Indonesian posts and patrols. Subsequently, the Indonesians reacted with a 'clean sweep' campaign that started out of Jayapura and gradually spread throughout the rural areas along the border. This followed the usual pattern of attacks on villages, including killings, beatings, murder, rape, and burning. In the Yonggom area air and army attacks shot up the villages of Woropko, Tinika, and Ninati (International Commission of Jurists 1985).

There thus began a series of waves of refugee migrations that continued throughout 1984. The first wave consisted of mainly middle-class people from Jayapura, who had been directly involved in opposition. By March, 320 had arrived in Vanimo, followed by a steady trickle of village dwellers: 437 to Vanimo; 320 to Kamberatoro, with a further 300 heading there; 1,000 heading for Green River from Ubrul; and up to 1,000 more from Waris and Arso heading towards Imonda and Bewani. The largest wave of refugees came across the Western Province part of the border. The movement was gradual and into remote areas, so that the size of the flight only gradually dawned on the national government. By August 1984 9,000 refugees had entered Papua New Guinea, and by the end of the year the number peaked at about 12,000.

The largest single group were Yonggom people who had moved a relatively short distance into Papua New Guinean Yonggom-speaking areas. The Indonesians estimated that 5,000 out of the 8,500 population of Mindiptana sub-district, and 4,400 out of the 6,100 population of Waropko sub-district had left (Smith and Hewison 1986). The whole village of Ninati had left, while Woropko, Tinika, Kawangtet, Kangewot, Yeteteam, Amuan, Upetjetko, Kamanget, and Wangatkimbi were severely depopulated. The major receiving villages in Kiunga District were Dome, Niakombin, Atkamba, Iogi, Komopkin, Kungim, and Bankim. In the north the main camps were at Blackwater Creek, outside Vanimo, Amanas, and Green River (Brunton 1984).

Subsequently there was some relocation between these camps, but during mid-1984 the Papua New Guinea government simply ignored them. There were allegations that the government was attempting to starve the refugees back to West Papua, and a number of deaths occurred through disease and malnutrition. It represented the largest refugee migration that Papua New Guinea had experienced and was a strain on limited resources. The government ultimately sought the assistance of the United Nations High Commission for Refugees (UNHCR). A legal political furor erupted when Papua New Guinea defined refugees as illegal border crossers and began to repatriate some of them, until the Indonesians began to shoot repatriated OPM activists.

Some of the refugees, especially amongst the Yonggom, came across well prepared and quite casually. Wholesale Indonesian action in their area had not occurred. It seems likely that the OPM themselves encouraged the people to leave, possibly to give the OPM a clear fighting zone or more likely to draw international attention to their cause. Many of the refugees claimed that they were fleeing from both the Indonesians and the OPM.

The UNHCR took over the administration of the refugee camps and continues in this role. The OPM also continued to use the camps as a supply base and rest area. Consequently the refugees in the North Fly were moved away from the Yonggom-speaking areas along the border and relocated in the East Awin camp at Iowara, well inside Papua New Guinea in the flat empty jungle between the Fly and Strickland Rivers. Despite the fact that the Awin had largely deserted this swampy remote area in relocating to the roadside, they are unenthusiastic about refugees taking their land. There have consequently been compensation claims and demands for the return of the land to the Awin landowners. These actions have limited potential economic development at the Iowara camp, maintaining its 2,000 to 3,000 inhabitants in a position of dependency.

Some voluntary repatriation took place to West Papua, and people were moved out of the Blackwater Camp at Vanimo and relocated at Iowara. Semi-permanence seems to have come to the East Awin camp as services and facilities steadily improved. The recommendations of government and law have continued to legitimize the refugees. The International Commission of Jurists (1985) recommended UNHCR administration, no repatriation against the will of the individual, permissive residence for the refugees in Papua New Guinea, nondiscrimination against refugees, and the ratification by the government of Papua New Guinea of the Refugee Conventions and Protocol.

By the end of 1988 just under 3,000 refugees were housed in the UNHCR camp at Iowara, of whom at least 1,000 were Yonggom. A further 4,000 refugees remained in the Yonggom border villages of Dome, Iogi, Kungim, Timkwi, and Kuyu. These camps were officially closed down and the occupants were encouraged to move to the East Awin camp. Thus no services or food are provided to these 4,000 people who refuse to be administered by a United Nations agency. They hold the United Nations responsible for the loss of their sovereignty. To gain better access to Kiunga they concentrated into Dome and neighbouring villages, on the Ok Tedi River, swelling the population of the Dome alone to 1,500. Thus the refugees, including members of the OPM, concentrated along the most polluted parts of the river, adding to pressure on resources, but deriving no benefit from the mining company.

During the 1990s there has been some dispersal away from the Dome concentration, with a number of new camps being established further down the Ok Tedi and adjacent to the Fly River, south of Albertis junction. Reports from villages along both the Ok Tedi and Fly rivers suggest that the Indonesian army has effectively established a 'no-go zone' on its side of the border, such that villagers are no longer willing to cross the border. This effectively traps the refugees and OPM members inside PNG. As these people refuse to be administered by the United Nations, they are best described as displaced persons, rather than as officially recognized refugees. Thus they continue to face hardship in exile, while at the same time having a stake in the impact of an environmentally disastrous mine through their kin relations.

CONCLUSION

There are two different forces behind the movements of border residents: 'natural' and 'political'. The former movement is primarily an economic migration. The latter movement is politically motivated; crossing the border for political safety or security. Papua New Guinea generally takes an anti-OPM stance, and certainly does nothing to support that movement in arms or finance, while criticizing Indonesia only mildly and occasionally. The U.S.A./Australian policy of not upsetting the Indonesians will reinforce Indonesian exploitation of West Papua and their suppression of all forms of opposition. At the moment, there is no optimism for the West Papuans in their own land. They must adapt to Indonesian assimilation, resist, or flee. It is likely that different parts of West Papuan society will differ in their response. In that event it is almost certain that Indonesian reaction will prompt renewed flight by some into Papua New Guinea. In the event of a major uprising a much greater influx may take place in the future.

Papua New Guinea's role can only be to accept such an influx. But the country cannot do it without continued UNHCR help. In the meantime the country must deal with the impact of refugees on local Papua New Guinean groups. In the North Fly River region the refugees and displaced persons have introduced a new political element that does not exist at any other mine site in the country. Their anger and activism will continue to influence opposition to the mine while the more passive U.N.-administered refugees at Iowara prompt a response from the hitherto passive Awin, on whose land these people are housed, fed, and serviced, while at the other side of their territory they share the polluted banks of the Ok Tedi with their Yonggom neighbours. The refugees, and especially the displaced persons on the west bank of the Ok Tedi, are a political time bomb in an unstable political environment.

REFERENCES

Aditjondro, G., 1986. 'Transmigration in Irian Jaya: issues, targets and alternative approaches.' Waigani Seminar, UPNG.

Anonymous. Undated. 'Nationalism in West Papua New Guinea: from millenarianism to armed struggle.' ASEAN.

Arndt, H., 1986. 'Transmigration in Irian Jaya', in May, R., ed., *Between Two Nations: The Indonesia-Papua New Guinea Border and West Papua Nationalism*. Bathurst: Robert Brown.

Brunton, B., 1984. 'Refugees, human rights and Irian Jaya: a critique of policy.' Conference on Papua New Guinea and Australia: Papua New Guinea Perspectives. A.N.U. Australian Foundation for the peoples of the Pacific.

Chapman, M., and Prothero, M., 1985, eds., *Circulation in Population Movement: Substance and Concepts from the Melanesian Case*. London: Routledge & Kegan Paul.

Department of Foreign Affairs (Australia), 1975. Agreement between Australia and Indonesia concerning certain boundaries between Papua New Guinea and Indonesia (Jakarta 12 February 1973). Canberra: Australian Government.

Eiso, D., 1986. *Impact of Mining on the Economic Development of Papua New Guinea: The Case of Bougainville Copper and Ok Tedi*. Port Moresby: Kumah Enterprises.

Filer C., Ilave T., Jackson R., and Townsend P., 1984. *Progress and Impact of the Ok Tedi Project*. Report 2. Port Moresby: Institute of Applied Social and Economic Research.

Government of Papua New Guinea, 1969. 'Statement on crossing of the border of West Irianese.' Port Moresby: Papua New Guinea House of Assembly.

Hastings, P., 1986. 'Prospects: a state of mind', in May R., ed., *Between Two Nations: The Indonesia Papua New Guinea Border and West Papua Nationalism*. Bathurst: Robert Brown.

Herlihy, J., 1986. 'Border development: a political necessity again', May R., ed., *Between Two Nations: The Indonesia Papua New Guinea Border and West Papua Nationalism*. Bathurst: Robert Brown.

Hyndman, D., 1979. *Wopkaimin Subsistence: Cultural Ecology in the New Guinea Highland Fringe*. Ph.D. thesis. University of Queensland.

International Commission of Jurists, 1985. Status of border crossers from Irian Jaya to Papua New Guinea. Sydney: Australian Section of International Commission of Jurists.

Jackson, R., 1977. *Kiunga Development Study*. Port Moresby: Department of Finance.

———, 1982. *Ok Tedi: the Pot of Gold*. Port Moresby: University of Papua New Guinea.

———, Emerson C., and Welsch R., 1980. *Impact of the Ok Tedi project: a Report Prepared for the Department of Minerals and Energy*. Port Moresby: Department of Minerals and Energy.

———, and Ilave T., 1983. *Progress and Impact of the Ok Tedi Project*. Report No. 1. Port Moresby: Institute of Applied Social and Economic Research.

Jones, B., 1980. 'Consuming society: food and illness among the Faiwol', unpublished doctoral dissertation, University of Virginia.

King, D., ed., 1980. *Kiunga Fieldwork Report*. Geography Department Student Research Paper No. 4. Port Moresby: University of Papua New Guinea.

———, 1983. *Kiunga Re-visited*. Port Moresby: Institute of Applied Social and Economic Research.

Kirsch, S., 1993. *The Yonggom People of the Ok Tedi and Moian Census Divisions*. Ok-Fly Social Monitoring Program Report No. 5. Prepared for OTML, Unisearch, Port Moresby.

Maris, R., 1982. 'Regional development and transmigration in Indonesia'. ASEAN countries seminar on regional development planning. Jakarta: UN Centre for Regional Development.

May, R., 1986. 'East of the border: Irian Jaya and the border in Papua New Guinea's domestic and foreign politics', in May R., ed., *Between Two Nations: The Indonesia Papua New Guinea Border and West Papua Nationalism*. Bathurst: Robert Brown, pp. 85–160.

Ministry of Public Works (Indonesia), 1983. Screening (phase 2) studies of transmigration settlement development in Irian Jaya (Group K): final report. Jakarta: Government of the Republic of Indonesia.

Morren, G., 1986. *Miyanmin: Human Ecology of a Papua New Guinea Society*. Ann Arbor: UMI Research Press.

Nyamekye, K., and Premdas, R., 1979. Colonial origins of the Organisasi Papua Merdeka (OPM) of the Free Papua Movement. Discussion Paper No. 1. Port Moresby: Institute of Papua New Guinea Studies.

——, 1979. *Papua New Guinea-Indonesia Border: Papua New Guinean Perceptions, Internal Pressures and Policies*. Port Moresby: Institute of Papua New Guinea Studies.

Oey, M., 1982. 'The transmigration program in Indonesia', in Jones, G., and Richter, H., eds., *Population Resettlement programs in South East Asia*. Monograph No. 30. Canberra: ANU Development Studies Centre.

Osborne, R., 1986. 'OPM and the quest for West Papuan unity', in May R., ed., *Between Two Nations: The Indonesia Papua New Guinea Border and West Papua Nationalism*. Bathurst: Robert Brown, pp. 49–64.

——, 1985. *Indonesia's Secret War: The Guerilla Struggle in Irian Jaya*. Sydney: Allen and Unwin.

Pintz, W., 1984. *Ok Tedi: Evolution of a Third World Mining Project*. London: Mining Journal Books.

Prescott, J. R. V., 1986. 'Problems of international boundaries with particular reference to the boundary between Indonesia and Papua New Guinea', in May R., ed., *Between Two Nations: The Indonesia Papua New Guinea Border and West Papua Nationalism*. Bathurst: Robert Brown, pp. 1–17.

Pula, A., Jackson, R., Butuna, E., and Tapari, B., 1984. Population survey of the border census divisions of Western Province: a report prepared for the department of foreign affairs and trade. Port Moresby: Institute of Applied Social and Economic Research.

Research Institute of Oppressed Peoples, 1985. *Tragedy of the Papuans and the International Political Order*. Amsterdam: Research Institute of Oppressed Peoples.

Royal Australian Survey Corps, 1966. *Gazetteer; New Guinea Border Zone: Papua New Guinea-West Irian between Longitudes 140 East and 142*. Canberra: Division of National Mapping.

Rumbiak, M., 1985. 'Nimboran migration to Jayapura, Irian Jaya,' in M. Chapman and P. Morrison, eds., special Issue of *Pacific Viewpoint*, 26(1).

Schoorl, J. W., 1959. *Kultuur en Kultuurveranderingen in Het Moejoe-Gebied*. Den Haag: J. N. Voorhoeve.

Sharp, N., 1977. *Rule of the Sword: The Story of West Irian*. Malmsbury: Kibble/Arena.

Smith, A., 1984. 'What's going on in Jayapura?' Port Moresby: National Broadcasting Commission, ACE program.

Smith, A., Trompf, G., and Clements, K., 1985. *Flight into Limbo: Refugees in Papua New Guinea*. Religious Society of Friends.

Smith, A., and Hewison, K., 1985. '1984: the year OPM pulled the plug on Indonesia-Papua New Guinea relations.'

——, 1986. '1984: refugees, holiday camps and deaths', in May R., ed., *Between Two Nations: The Indonesia Papua New Guinea Border and West Papua Nationalism*. Bathurst: Robert Brown, pp. 200–217.

Smith, B., 1984. 'Reviewing the Papua New Guinea-Indonesia border agreement.' Port Moresby: National Broadcasting Commission, Ace program.

Stewart, J., 1982. *Customs and Culture of the Aekyom, Upper Fly, Papua New Guinea.* Rumginae, Western Province.

Suvero, H. di. Melanesian response to Imperial Indonesia: West Papua/ Irian Jaya reexamined. Australian Universities Law Schools Association.

Swadling, P., 1983. 'How long have people been in the Ok Tedi impact region?' Port Moresby: Papua New Guinea National Museum.

Tapol, 1983. *West Papua: The Obliteration of a People.* London: Tapol.

Tsamenyi, M., 1983. *West Irianese Border Crossers: Some Preliminary Observations.* Port Moresby: Law Faculty, University of Papua New Guinea.

Tsamenyi, M., 1984. 'Papua New Guinea and the West Irianese border crossers'. 39th AUSLA Conference, St. Lucia.

Verrier, J., 1986. 'Origins of the border problem and the border story to 1969', in May R., ed., *Between Two Nations: The Indonesia Papua New Guinea Border and West Papua Nationalism.* Bathurst: Robert Brown, pp. 18–48.

Veur, P. W. Van der, 1966. *Search for New Guinea's Boundaries: From Torres Strait to the Pacific.* Canberra: ANU Press.

——, 1962. 'West New Guinea: Irian Barat or Papua Barat'. Address to the New Guinea Society, Canberra.

Welsch, R., 1982. 'Experience of illness among the Ningerum of Papua New Guinea', unpublished docotral dissertation, University of Washington.

Zeipi, P., 1986. 'Ethics of the border: a critique of what happened, what next.' 1986 Waigani Seminar. University of Papua New Guinea.

Zelinsky, W., 1971. 'The hypothesis of the mobility transition,' *Geographical Review,* 61.

Part Two

ECONOMIC DEVELOPMENT

*T*HE UNEVEN PACE AND DISTRIBUTION of economic development in Papua New Guinea is an ongoing challenge facing Papua New Guinea's leaders. Everyone wants 'development' be it a road, a mine, or better ways of marketing agricultural production to fast-growing towns and cities. Writing in the 1960s and 1970s, when cash cropping was the 'road' to wealth throughout Papua New Guinea, anthropologists described the early success stories of the 'big men of business', entrepreneurs who organized coffee or cocoa plantations using traditional ties to get land and labor (Epstein 1968; Finney 1973; Salisbury 1970). Subsequent accounts have focused more on development's negative effects, such as the environmental destruction associated with large gold mines (Hyndman 1994) and unregulated commercial logging (Barlow and Winduo 1997), increased economic and social inequality (cf. MacWilliam 1993; Thompson and MacWilliam 1992), and economic individualism and the ascendancy of short-term private ends over public interests (Errington and Gewertz 1993). Why people want development requires more than a simple answer. One reason, however, lies in the dynamic and demanding traditional exchange systems that siphon income from development to be used in creating and recreating extensive series of reciprocities linking village and town, and rich and poor. In the highlands society where I do most of my research, inequality in jobs and income makes it difficult for Gende men and women to maintain their exchange relations in good order. Many young people, without lucrative employment in town or at home, disappoint their elders with meagre returns on past investments in their upbringing and education and suffer the consequences of receiving inadequate bride-price help and land rights from older clan members who favor shifting their alliances to more successful migrants (Zimmer 1990). Even successful migrants suffer the constant demands of 'reciprocity', as they are expected to give more and more often, and achieving a balance sometimes seems well-nigh impossible (Monsell-Davis 1993). The Gende, however, took some of the sting out of their aggressive exchange relations by creating a parallel exchange system based on gambling and the redistribution of mostly small (but sometimes very large) amounts of cash from those who have to those who don't (Zimmer 1986). Relations between the sexes have also been affected by inequality, with men more likely to participate in and benefit from the cash economy than women. Again, some Papua New Guineans have found ingenious ways to compensate for these sorts of imbalance. Many Daulo and other highlands women participate in the *wok meri* movement, a kind of revolving bank account in which market women pool earnings and take turns using the accumulated cash to invest in large projects, owned by the women and used to show men how they might fruitfully use their larger incomes (Sexton 1986). While 'communitarian' solutions often work, in some instances they impede development and the fair distribution of profits as well as threaten traditional culture. David Lea (1996:50–51; see also Filer, this volume) argues that landowner associations formed in the early years of the Bougainville mine froze social power and material wealth in the personal holdings of a few instead of allowing it to devolve throughout a larger social pool according to indigenous social customs. As the following chapters show, Papua New Guinea has a rich potential, but wise investment of that wealth at the national level and fair distribution at the local level is crucial to continued social and political well-being.

SUGGESTED READINGS

Barlow, K., and Winduo, S., 1997. 'Introduction', in K. Barlow and S. Winduo, eds., *Logging the Southwestern Pacific: Perspectives from Papua New Guinea, Solomon Islands, and Vanuatu,* special issue, *The Contemporary Pacific,* 9(1):1–24.

Epstein, T. S., 1968. *Capitalism, Primitive and Modern: Some Aspects of Tolai Economic Growth.* Canberra: Australian National University Press.

Errington, F., and Gewertz, D., 1993. 'The triumph of capitalism in East New Britain? A contemporary Papua New Guinean rhetoric of motives', *Oceania,* 64(1):1–17.

Finney, B. F., 1973. *Big Men and Business: Entrepreneurship and Economic Growth in the New Guinea Highlands.* Canberra: Australian National University Press.

Hyndman, D. C., 1994. *Ancestral Rain Forests and the Mountain of Gold: Indigenous Peoples and Mining in New Guinea.* Boulder: Westview Press.

Lea, D. R., 1996. 'Communitarian challenges to the liberal state: Fiji, Quebec, and Bougainville', *South Pacific: Journal of Philosophy and Culture,* 1:46–58.

MacWilliam, S., 1993. 'The politics of privatisation: the case of the Coffee Industry Corporation in Papua New Guinea', *Australian Journal of Political Science,* 28:481–498.

Monsell-Davis, M. 1993. 'Urban exchange: safety-net or disincentive? *Wantoks* and relatives in the urban Pacific', *Canberra Anthropology,* 16(2):45–66.

Salisbury, R. F., 1970. *Vunamami: Economic Transformations in a Traditional Society.* Berkeley: University of California Press.

Sexton, L., 1986. *Mothers of Money, Daughters of Coffee: The Wok Meri Movement.* Ann Arbor, Michigan: University of Michigan Press.

Thompson, H., and MacWilliams, S., 1992. *The Political Economy of Papua New Guinea.* Manilla, Philippines: Journal of Contemporary Asia Publishers.

Zimmer, L., 1986. 'Card-playing among the Gende: a system for keeping money and social relationships alive', *Oceania,* 56:245–63.

Zimmer, L., 1990. 'Conflict and violence in Gende society: older persons as victims, trouble-makers and perpetrators', *Pacific Studies,* 13(3):205–224.

Oskar Kurer

POLITICS AND ECONOMIC DEVELOPMENT

*T*HIS CHAPTER ANALYZES THE EFFECT of salient political forces on economic development in Papua New Guinea (PNG). The relationship is going to be interpreted in the light of African experience. It is argued that a number of political forces operating in PNG have close parallels in Africa,[1] and that PNG is in danger of replicating the main elements of African development. This may result in the African malaise: low rates of economic growth in the agricultural and industrial sector of the economy, and dismally low levels of performance in a public sector that is riddled with corruption.

Some important events began to unravel in Africa shortly before independence. One of the main promises of independence was material betterment of the populace, an expectation nurtured by the local politicians themselves. These promises were easily fulfilled for the elite.[2] However, to fulfill the promises to the populace at large constituted a major political problem. Since people expected material betterment, successful performance in this respect largely legitimised political power in the eyes of their constituents. Failure to perform

[1] More precisely, the focus is on sub-Saharan Africa.

[2] For our purposes, members of the elite are those individuals with access to state power either directly through the control of the legislature and/or administration or indirectly through their ability to influence those who have this power. Since substantial businesses are usually not simply exploiting market forces but using monopoly power acquired through political influence, many owners of private enterprises are part of the elite in our sense.

meant a loss of legitimacy and ultimately threatened the position of the politicians. In reaction to these demands (coupled sometimes with ideological convictions), rulers in Africa resorted to three courses of action: accelerated development, economic nationalism, and systematic patronage. The pursuit of these aims, together with measures enriching the elite of the country, are largely responsible for choking off economic growth.[3]

A certain set of ideas and beliefs helped to speed these events along on their path. The expectations about the benefits accruing from the departure of the colonialists may well have existed independently of the promises of politicians. Furthermore, development economists claimed 'to have solved the problems of the origins and nature of poverty and to be able to provide formulas which could ensure its eradication' (Fieldhouse 1986:85). Policies of accelerated development were advocated throughout that profession without considering the nature of the political and social environment; economic nationalism was widely thought to be essential for economic development; and systematic patronage and corruption were considered by some as a method of allocating resources hardly detrimental to economic growth, or even beneficial for it (Leff 1964; Nye 1967).

It would be simplistic to blame political processes for all economic ills. The social upheaval associated with a large-scale transformation of society would strain any social and political system. For example, the growth-retarding law and order problems could hardly have been avoided. But even here political factors play a role: how effectively these problems are dealt with depends in part on the state of the body politic.

There are fundamental differences between PNG and African societies. Perhaps one of the most important is the weakness of the state in PNG. Local tribal warfare did not generally re-emerge after independence on a substantial scale. Nowhere was the state proved to be capable of enforcing contracts between landowners and outsiders, or even with the state itself![4] The weakness of the state may well aggravate the problems which are discussed below.

---

[3] The focus here is on internal problems to development and neglects external factors. However, by now there is widespread agreement that internal constraints have indeed been central in arresting growth.

[4] The most dramatic example of this failure is obviously the Bougainville crisis.

THE POLITICAL SETTING COMPARED

A statement by Nkrumah illustrates the expectations kindled by African politicians: 'If we get self-government, we'll transform the Gold Coast into a paradise in ten years' (quoted from Fieldhouse 1986:90). Nkrumah was by no means alone in promising substantial material betterment.[5] Similar expectations were nurtured in PNG. Kiki for one held out to his constituents the promise of education, hospitals, economic development, shipping services, water supply, and roads (Kiki 1968:173–74). Voters in Africa and PNG responded by supporting those politicians promising and providing material benefits. In PNG, many 'of the voters' expectations of their Members of Parliament (MPs) appear to be geared toward "distributive" politics. In most parts of the country voters do expect some return of delivery of goods from their MPs' (Hegarty 1983:15). If re-election is the issue, all of the studies of the 1977 election highlight the question uppermost in voters' minds: 'What has he done for us?' (*ibid.* 15).

The politicians expected to benefit, too. In the 1977 elections in PNG, for example, politicians often argued that being 'in government' enhanced their chances of access to patronage and spoils (Hegarty 1983:15). Such measures as the abolition of the dual salary scale[6] were among the 'serious grievances' which united 'all political conscious people' (Kiki 1968:92,149). This of course meant increasing the salaries of the indigenous civil servants, not lowering those of the foreigners. There were expectations of taking over expatriate businesses, particularly in the plantation sector.

The scene was set: everybody expected a massive increase in their standard of living after independence, all provided by the government.[7] Many of these expectations were, and still are, clearly unrealistic.[8]

After independence, the elite in Africa as well as in PNG found themselves in the enviable position of having access to the resources of the state to draw on for their own benefit. However, at the same time,

---

[5] In 1964 Tanzania's planners drew up a fifteen-year plan, aiming at doubling per capita income in this period, self-sufficiency in manpower except for the most highly skilled occupations, and increasing life expectancy from thirty-five to fifty years (Ake 1979).

[6] According to which expatriate labour was paid at a higher rate than national labour.

[7] The type of promises made are identical to those of African politicians at the time of independence (*Post* 1963:284–328).

[8] Kepsy Ekaimu, in a letter to the editor, agrees 'with Mr Ramoi when he says that PNG has enough wealth to make every Papua New Guinean rich' (*Post-Courier*, Friday, 3 November, 1989, p. 10).

they were in the unenviable situation of having to attempt to satisfy the demands they had helped to nurture.[9] Since the satisfaction of these demands largely legitimised their rule, they could neglect them only at the peril of losing office. The policies pursued to satisfy these expectations can by summarised as systematic patronage, economic nationalism, and accelerated development.

PATRONAGE AND CORRUPTION

In a context where political allegiance is largely determined by the material benefits provided by the politicians, 'pork-barrel' policies and benefits to individual supporters then become the most important means to remain in power. Whereas pork-barrel policies are a legal means to gain political support if they are approved by regular parliamentary procedures, benefits to individuals tend to involve corruption, since benefits to individuals are only seen as a remuneration for political support if they go beyond what is allocated through regular bureaucratic procedures.[10] A political system, therefore, where political support is exchanged directly for material benefits provides a fertile breeding ground for corruption.

What was once described as the 'infantile sickness' of African independence has ended as a 'chronic malady' (Amuwo 1986:287). In President Mobutu's words:

> [E]verything is for sale, anything can be bought in our country…[H]e who holds the slightest cover of public authority, uses it illegally to acquire money, goods, prestige, or to avoid all kinds of obligation…. Thus the right to be heard by a public servant, to register one's children in school or to obtain their report cards at the end of the year, to obtain medical care, a seat on an airplane, an important permit, a diploma—and I could go on—are all subject to this tax which, though invisible, is known and expected by all. (quoted from Gould 1980:49)

The situation in PNG is still far removed from that of the most corrupt African states. There are hardly any visible signs of low-level civil servants who impose illegal charges for state services. Health orderlies and rural hospitals do not impose illegal fees on their patients, a pass-

---

[9] A typical expression of this pressure: 'You must choose a leader who will bring development, a man who will bring goods and services to the community, builds roads and develop[s] your area' (Letter to the Editor, *Post-Courier,* Friday, Sept. 15, 1989, p. 10).

[10] Corruption, as usually defined, involves breaking established laws, rules, and procedures.

port is issued and extended following regular procedures, and teachers are not known to distribute grades according to the amounts of bribes they receive. In other words, the lower echelons of the administrative services are so far largely free from corruption. Those services upon which the common man relies are (if available at all), available on bureaucratic principles.

The situation seems to be different at higher levels of the administration, both in the provincial and national government. Misappropriation of government funds is common. There is hardly a report coming from the auditor general's office where substantial irregularities are not discovered, both nationally[11] and in the provinces. Dorney quotes an accountant's report where the following qualification was added: 'I have prepared the financial statements—bearing in mind that much source documentation was unobtainable—from the books and records.... I express no opinion on whether they present a true and fair view of the position... and no warranty of accuracy or reliability is given'(1990, 170). Not surprisingly, such a situation fosters misappropriation of funds, one of the main reasons for the frequent suspension of provincial governments.

Observers agree that political corruption on the national level has become increasingly common. A leading judge describes it as a 'growing problem' (*Post-Courier,* Tuesday, 29 September 1989); one elder statesman believes that corruption has affected 'most leaders in the national, provincial, local government, community government and many tribal, clan, and family village leaders' (*Times,* 19–25 October 1989, p. 12); and another claims that 'if you know the right consultant you can buy your way through NIDA,[12] you can even buy political patronage and bypass the system' (*Post-Courier,* Friday, 10 November 1989, p. 3).

Again, as in Africa, corruption does not seem to undermine political support, as long as it is seen as benefiting the constituents. A recent prominent example of such practices involved the then minister of forestry,

---

[11] Much of the 1987 budget deficit was attributed to 'lack of revenue collection capacity...and numerous irregularities, misappropriations and at times outright theft of funds.... Among them were: Supplies and services obtained without quotations; private vehicles hired without approval; large advances unacquitted and unaccounted; failure to obtain replacements for dishonored cheques; funds defrauded through overpayments; equipment bought but not used or maintained' (*Post-Courier,* 2 November 1989, p. 1). The situation in the provinces is even worse (*Times,* 23–29 November 1989, pp. 1, 3).

[12] The National Investment Development Agency was in charge of regulating foreign investment.

who allocated logging rights to a company in which he had a major interest, and which conspired to defraud the state. These practices did not undermine his political support.

PNG does, however, have functioning institutions which combat corruption. Hence we do find leading politicians resigning from Parliament because of investigations under the leadership code,[13] and politicians are sentenced for corruption.[14] Such cases, which involve some of the most powerful political figures, will provide a major test of strength for these institutions.

One of the main problems in African countries is the allocation of positions in government service according to patronage criteria. This has serious implications either when persons are appointed who are blatantly incompetent, or when jobs are created without economic or administrative justification. As to PNG, some observers believe that 'public service appointments at the national level have been largely free of nepotism and inappropriate political influence' (Goodman 1985:194). There is little information available on the appointment procedures in the provinces.

As Hyden has pointed out, one of the most outstanding features of the patronage approach to politics is 'the ability of individual politicians to command resources for their respective communities though official policies made no mention of such allocation' (1983:42). The power of patronage of national politicians, however, was seriously limited in PNG by the decentralised structure of the government, where the provinces monopolise most of the patronage possibilities. To counteract the falling influence of the national MPs the national government introduced the so-called slush-funds.[15] Parliamentarians receive money in order to pursue development projects in their constituencies.[16] This avowedly is one of the means to increase the power of patronage of MPs in legal ways. Even so, much of the money seems to be used irregularly.[17]

---

[13] Gabriel Ramoi resigned from parliament probably in a bid to avoid a trial under the Leadership Code (*Post-Courier*, 26 September 1990, p. 3; 27 September 1990, p. 2).

[14] A former Wingti government transport minister, Roy Yaki, who has been sentenced to two years' hard labor for misappropriation, is one example (*Post-Courier*, 2 August 1990, p. 1).

[15] National Development Fund; since 1990, Electoral Development Program.

[16] Additional money is also distributed: 'Amounts ranging from K15,000 to K60,000 were released to some MPs in 1989 (*Post-Courier*, 26 October 1989, p. 3; *Times*, 26 October, 1 November 1989, p. 2).

[17] At one stage, the chief ombudsman found that there 'are 60 to 90 substantial cases that require immediate and thorough investigations under the Leadership Code', many of them apparently related to the National Development Fund (*Post-Courier*, 14 December 1990, p. 1).

ECONOMIC NATIONALISM

Economic nationalism in Africa aimed at transfering ownership and control of the means of production to nationals (or sometimes more specifically a particular group of nationals), and limit external transactions. The measures invariably benefited the elite by providing them with assets and privileges, and additional power of patronage. Far from promoting the welfare of the bulk of the population, they were often detrimental to their welfare. Nationalism therefore not only concealed inequality, but aggravated it.

In PNG, nationalist arguments were wholeheartedly espoused in the influential Faber report. The main policy aim, according to the authors, was the redistribution of income from expatriates to nationals by rapidly localising employment in government and private industry as well as the ownership of the means of production (Overseas Development Group 1973:4,12,14,62). Growth, the authors assumed, could be left to itself, and would continue at a rate of 7 to 9 percent a year at constant prices (*ibid.*, 18). These views closely correspond to the Eight Point Plan, perhaps the most important policy document of PNG, which grew out of the Faber report. The first of these eight points aims at a 'rapid increase in the proportion of the economy under the control of Papua New Guinean individuals and groups and in the proportion of personal and property income that goes to Papua New Guineans' (Central Planning Office 1974:x).

In both Africa and PNG, nationalist ideas were used to justify the localisation of the civil service at a very rapid rate.[18] The shortage of qualified local manpower meant that rapid localisation could only be achieved by such ploys as upgrading civil servants, introducing crash courses, and lowering entry requirements. Moreover, as a result of the decline of training and of rapid promotion, there was little opportunity to instil a particular civil service ethos and an allegiance to the new state. The allegiance of civil servants continued to belong to traditional groups. In Africa, this meant in practice that 'the bureaucracy does not function primarily in accordance with a rational-legal code.... On the contrary, administrative action is determined in large measure by personal ties and obligations and is characterised by preferential treatment of friends and relatives' (Tordoff 1984:127; also Roberts 1982:47). These problems were aggravated by the massive expansion of the civil service which went on simultaneously: not only were middle- and high-level

[18] For Tanzania see Mutahaba 1975:203; for the Ivory Coast see Young 1983:198–200.

positions localised, but many more positions were created as a result of
expanding government activities.

Localisation in PNG proceeded rapidly. In 1976, 13.5 percent of all
public servants were expatriates, mainly in middle- and high-level positions. By 1985, this ratio had fallen to 5.7 percent. Over this period,
more than 350 positions were localised each year (McGavin 1986:26).
To put this figure in perspective, one has to keep in mind that higher
education was virtually nonexistent in PNG until the late 1960s. The
two universities[19] began turning out students in the early 1970s, producing each year an average of 337 graduates with bachelor degrees and
another 116 holders of assorted diplomas and certificates between 1976
and 1982 (UPNG 1983; 1982; Unitech 1985). Taking this into account,
the rapidity of localisation was substantial indeed. To what degree
localisation has affected administrative performance is difficult to
assess. According to some observers, 'capacity for planning and
management has varied widely among individual departments' (Goodman *et al.* 1985:195). It seems that many have lost the capacity for
innovation and to respond imaginatively to challenges, and some have
been allowed to stagnate and become an obstacle to progress (*Ibid.*,
195).[20] The frequent suspension of provincial governments suggests
that the situation there is worse.

Economic nationalism in Africa and PNG was directed against
groups who settled only recently in particular communities, and
against foreign capital. There is little doubt that the policy was and is
carried by a groundswell of popular support.[21]

The most prominent casualties of economic nationalism in Africa
were the Asian community in East Africa and the Lebanese in West
Africa. They constituted the economically most advanced part of the
population, which might have taken the lead in the development of
the country. They were endowed with the necessary attitudes, skills,
and capital to set a process of capital accumulation in motion. In
restricting the scope of their activity, the nascent states largely elimi-

[19] The University of Papua New Guinea in Port Moresby and the Papua New Guinea
University of Technology (Unitech) in Lae.

[20] Some hard data is available from a study on the teaching of mathematics in primary
schools, which shows that the entrants into a particular teacher's college were equipped
with arithmetical skills inferior to grade 5 children in Australia, that during teacher's
training little arithmetic was taught (the focus is on teaching it), and tests of teachers and
pupils at grade 6 level showed similar results (Lancy 1983:178–181).

[21] A recent example is the controversy surrounding the Kutubu oil field (*Post-Courier*,
20–27 July 1990).

nated the prospect of rapid economic transformation by the indigenous private sector. The local population could hardly be expected to
replace such groups in the short term.

In PNG, late settler communities were insignificant at the time of
independence in terms of numbers as well as in terms of their economic impact. The two main groups were the Chinese community,
mainly located in Rabaul, and the Australian settlers operating in the
plantation sector of the economy. The Chinese community shifted the
centre of their activity from retail trade to other areas, but little is
known about emigration and investment patterns.

The Australian settler community was affected by the Plantation
Redistribution Scheme introduced in 1975. It was to pave the way for
greater participation by nationals in the estate sector and to alleviate
local land shortages where land had been alienated. It stipulated the
compulsory acquisition of plantations at an artificially low price
(Goodman 1985:121). There can be hardly any doubt that this is one of
the factors which led to a decline in output of this sector of the economy (*ibid.*, 86).[22]

The same nationalistic arguments are used against foreign capital.
In Africa, foreign capital was increasingly exposed to restrictions,
threats of nationalisation and indigenisation. This contributed to a low
rate of reinvestment, added to capital outflow, and restricted new
investment to projects with an exceedingly high return which compen-
sated for the high country risk.[23] PNG followed a similar course. The
scope for foreign investment began to be restricted (World Bank
1978:72). Some foreign capital is welcome in principle, but any specific
foreign investment proposal requires an agreement involving a long
and tortuous process of negotiation with the PNG government. 'The
bureaucracy... is indecisive and slow to respond.... [I]t is both expensive and difficult for new investors to obtain the necessary approvals to
establish a project' (Goodman 1985:206). PNG seems to have
approached the stage where foreign capital is only investing in ventures
with very high expected rates of return.

A common trend in both Africa and PNG is the emergence of what
Schatz called 'nurture capitalism' (Schatz 1977:3–4). One of the characteristics of nurture capitalism is a system of programs and policies to
assist and stimulate locally owned businesses. Typical programs

---

[22] See also MacWilliam's chapter in this volume.
[23] The risk not inherent in a project itself but emanating from the social and political
environment of a country.

include preferential access to credit, the exclusion of foreign or foreign-owned companies from some sectors of the economy, and the creation of industrial estates and other business extension programs. Credit programs turned out to be very expensive and ineffective everywhere, partly as a result of inefficient and corrupt administration (Schatz 1977:chap. 13). The granting of monopolies to local producers and the creation of industrial estates tended to be costly and ineffective exercises, and business extension services have been unsuccessful (*ibid.*:chaps. 9–11). The relationship between the failure of nurture capitalism and administrative inefficiency is worth stressing: an incompetent, politicised, and corrupt administration is hardly likely to make a success of any scheme, including nurture capitalism.

Attempts at nurture capitalism have been made in PNG, in particular through credit schemes. A credit scheme for small businesses, though well managed, has been expensive and has had little impact (Kurer 1988). One for large businesses seems to have been a major and expensive disaster. The disaster notwithstanding, there is great pressure at present to reactivate the scheme. Provincial government attempts at nurture capitalism resulted in a series of expensive failures.[24]

POLICIES OF ACCELERATED DEVELOPMENT

After the time of independence, it was widely felt that the burden of development should be borne by the state. There were two main factors which made this decision inevitable. First of all, policies of nationalism denied a major role to late settlers or foreign capital. Secondly, despite the ambitious development aims of the first development plans, local entrepreneurship was too underdeveloped to take on a leading role. Thus, the only instrument available to achieve rapid growth was the state.

The rapid expansion of the parastatal sector was therefore inevitable. It satisfied the desire for national control of the means of production, and for economic growth. In addition, it provided a convenient extension of the patronage system and increased the scope for the elite to enrich itself. The growth of the parastatal sector therefore occurred even in countries pursuing allegedly laissez-faire policies (Killick 1985:57). The performance of the parastatal companies in Africa has, as a rule, been thoroughly unsatisfactory. They have tended to

[24] Milne Bay: *Post-Courier*, 17 October 1989, p. 3; Morobe: 17 November 1989, p. 1, and 8 November 1989, p. 12.

under-utilise their capacity, be overmanned, unable to finance invest-ments, and have become a drain on public finances.[25] Hyden found that the 'causes of the poor performance of public enterprises tend almost uniformly to be of four types: (1) politicisation of decisions and the decision-making structures; (2) corruption; (3) shortage of man-power; and (4) lack of control' (1985:100).

In 1981, the central government of Papua New Guinea had a con-trolling interest in fifty-one companies either directly or through the government-owned Development Bank and the Investment Corpora-tion (Trevilcock 1982:4). These companies provided employment for between 20,000 and 22,000 full-time employees (*ibid.*, 43). Of these public enterprises it is known that ten were operating profitably, and thirteen unprofitably (*ibid.*, 61). To complete the picture, the operation of the business arm of each province has to be taken into account. From what little is known, their record is even worse.[26] PNG has faithfully replicated African development: it has acquired a substantial and badly managed parastatal sector (accounting for approximately 10 percent of total formal employment), suffering at least from two of Hyden's dis-eases: lack of financial control and politicisation.

Policies of accelerated development in Africa included substantial welfare provisions. The 'basic needs' school in development economics argued that such things as provision of basic health and education con-stitute an important element of economic development, and the human capital school held that they increased human capital, thereby accelerating economic growth. To the politician, their pursuit was dic-tated by the demands of the electorate, particularly for education serv-ices.[27] Despite popular pressure, PNG has not followed this trend. The number of public servants only increased from 49,700 in 1977 to 52,696

[25] They have been largely unprofitable, despite the monopoly power they often enjoy. Killick's (1983) survey confirms the World Bank's findings that they 'do not pay taxes. Most of their investment costs are covered by transfers; in some cases their cash surplus is less than their depreciation; and in a few instances cash flow does not even cover running costs' (World Bank 1981: 38; see also Young 1982:39;163;169;176, and Killick 1978:chap. 9).

[26] Fly River Provincial Government: *Post-Courier,* Friday, 20 October 1989, p. 2; San-daun and Manus, *Times,* 23–29 November 1989, p. 3.

[27] The provision of these welfare services put an increasing burden on government spending. In Africa, governments 'ended up with a rapidly expanding social service sec-tor, first characterised by large-scale investment in facilities and subsequently by over-whelming recurrent expenditures' (Hyden 1983:3). As a result, the gap between government revenue and expenditure quickly grew out of hand. This phenomenon af-fected all African countries irrespective of ideological pretension to different degrees (*ibid.*, 3). Such expansion partly explains the massive growth of the civil service.

in 1985, remaining a stable 27.1 percent of the work force (McGavin 1986:16). Government expenditure as a proportion of GDP in fact declined from 41.6 percent in 1980 to 37 percent in 1987, albeit as a result of the relative decline in capital expenditure (Blyth 1988:9–10). Government expenditure on social services, unlike the situation in Africa, has been kept under control.

SOCIAL CONSEQUENCES

As a consequence of institutionalised corruption, patronage, and failed policy initiatives to provide the expected material improvement, two institutions which put a brake on some of the excesses of government activities came under attack: the media and the judiciary.

Not surprisingly, the constant criticism by an independent media is not popular among politicians, and in Africa media became either controlled by the government directly, or they fell under the sway of an increasingly rigid censorship (e.g., *Index for Censorship* 1988). The process of suppressing independent voices may again be able to exploit nationalist feelings if the media are owned by foreigners or minorities. Similar arguments to control the media are heard in PNG. The press is frequently under attack, and a former government did prepare measures to restrict its independence at the time it fell from office. A recent proposal to nationalise the media came from the trade and industry minister, only to be repudiated by the prime minister the following day (*Post-Courier,* 27 August 1990, p. 1; 29 August, p. 2).

The second institution which came increasingly into the firing line was the judiciary. The abolition of the separation of powers (often weak to begin with), had the dual advantage of ridding the politicians, administrators, and the business community of the risk of punishment for their misdeeds, and of extending the scope for patronage and corruption. An independent judiciary therefore is a rarity in Africa (Berg-Schlosser 1984:129). Again, the situation is different in PNG; there have been no efforts to undermine the independence of the judiciary.

ECONOMIC CONSEQUENCES

How do these policies affect the public sector? Social programs, inefficiency in administration, and the large-scale misuse of government funds all result in massive government spending. The drain of resources by the parastatal sector exacerbates the situation. Acute financial problems are the result.

Government expenditures can either be financed by domestic taxation, by foreign borrowing or aid, or by printing money. Borrowing from abroad will bring temporary respite, until repayments begin to add up.[28] At that stage, foreign exchange shortages occur, often leading to restrictions on the convertibility of the domestic currency. Devaluations may be resisted for a time to avoid upsetting vocal urban groups. Ultimately, however, devaluation is unavoidable, and a period of exchange rate instability, often coupled with exchange rate regulations, is ushered in. Exchange rate regulations, in turn, have a tendency to increase corruption, as selling exchange rate licenses is a particularly lucrative activity. They also tend to affect negatively the already inefficient parastatal sector, which becomes starved for imported spare parts and materials. Printing money also brings only temporary respite at the cost of high and accelerating inflation, followed by exchange rate instability.

Exchange rate instability, high and varying rates of inflation, corruption, and rapidly changing legislation and regulations resulting from nationalistic policies all have the same effect: the future becomes more uncertain. As the level of uncertainty increases, the rate of investment will inevitably fall, as only those projects are executed which have an expected return high enough to cover the increased risk factor. Lastly, corruption and red tape impose transaction costs on private producers and parastatals, whose efficiency declines in proportion to the amount of time and money spent in dealing with government administration and government regulation. This will be reflected in a distorted price structure, and in a fall of competitiveness on international markets.

As competitiveness falls and the risk to domestic investment increases, investment abroad becomes relatively more attractive. Nationals and foreigners alike begin to reduce domestic investment. Savings, instead of being invested domestically, are transferred abroad: capital flight becomes common. The ensuing stagnation in the private sector calls for even more government activity. This, in turn, must be financed, and as domestic savings flee the country, borrowing from abroad increases even further. Typically, we find members of the elite active at both ends: borrowing from abroad to pursue a set of discred-

---

[28] From 1970 to 1979 public debt of sub-Saharan African countries increased from US$3,438.2 to US$17,490.8 million (World Bank 1981).

ited policies and transferring their own savings abroad. The lack of investment inevitably leads to a stagnating private sector.

Up to the late 1980s this spectre was a far cry from being a reality in PNG. Government expenditures were indeed relatively large but have been kept under control. In addition, there was no indication of rapid growth of the parastatal sector. The external public debt had increased substantially,[29] but it remained at a manageable level of 38 percent of GDP in 1988, with a debt service ratio of 16.5 percent of export earnings (World Bank 1990:224). The value of the currency had been stable since independence in terms of moderately strong world currencies up to the Bougainville crisis.[30] The exchange rate was not kept artificially high but followed the market value reasonably well. Lastly, PNG had avoided the trap of taxing agricultural exports extensively.

Since the late 1980s the situation has deteriorated. The Kina has come under threat and had to be devalued. The government budget deficit reached the unsustainable level of 4.5 percent of GDP in 1994 (World Bank 1996a:248), and for the first time the government had to ask for financial support from international lending agencies. Still, foreign public indebtedness remained relatively stable,[31] and the revenue from mineral resources is in principle sufficient to service the foreign debt.

Most importantly, however, PNG's major problem remained unresolved: the rate of growth of the economy was less than population growth. Overall, the standard of living of PNG residents has not increased since independence.[32] This was not perceived as a political problem since it was possible to redistribute wealth and income from foreign residents to nationals, and it may well be that the standard of living of PNG nationals improved.[33] However, such a redistribution obviously cannot go on forever. Any future improvement in the standard of living of Papua New Guineans can only be achieved by economic growth.

Even mineral booms will not significantly improve the situation. A mineral boom will certainly lead to some economic growth in the mineral sector. It will also supply resources to service the external debt and provide substantial revenue for the government. However, there is no

[29] From US$338 million in 1977 to US$1,269 million in 1988 (World Bank 1977:154; 1990:224).

[30] US$ and UK£.

[31] US$1,622 million in 1994 or 32 percent of GDP.

[32] Based on the figures provided by Blyth 1988:46.

[33] There are no recent PNG statistics available.

guarantee that growth in the mineral sector of the economy will greatly stimulate growth in the other sectors of the economy. On the contrary, the impact on the industrial sector will probably be small, and it may even be negative for the agricultural sector (mainly by moving the terms of trade against agriculture). However, these latter sectors are crucial for the development of the PNG economy. Agriculture will remain the major employer for a long time to come, and the industrial sector should become an important employer in the future. In addition, if these sectors do not develop, and mineral resources are exhausted, PNG will not be better off than it is now.

Mineral booms will therefore not solve PNG's development problems. This brings us immediately back to the political issues involved. A mineral boom increases the ability of the elite to increase their salaries and perks and their income derived from corruption. However, it will not lead the masses of the people to be satisfied with their lot. The agriculturalists, who will gain little directly, if anything at all, will continue to demand material betterment through provisions by the government. The political pressures to engage in policies of nationalism, accelerated development, and patronage are unlikely to abate. Pressure on the press and on the judiciary may well increase in order to remove the barriers to unbridled patronage and corruption, and to avoid criticism for failed policy measures. Thus the spectre emerges as a real possibility for PNG's future.

An African example illustrates what might occur. The Nigerian oil boom resulted firstly in the impoverishment of the agricultural sector. Secondly, the carefully nurtured local capitalists did little to expand production during the upsurge of the economy, but looked to government coffers as a predominant source of income, a state of affairs Schatz has christened 'pirate capitalism' (Schatz 1984:55). And lastly, as Fieldhouse put it, 'The supreme irony of Nigerian economic development…is that, despite the flow of oil wealth, by 1982 the country was more heavily burdened by debt than at any previous time' (1986:159).

CONCLUSION

It has been argued that unrealistic expectations about material progress on the part of the elite and the population at large created political pressures which led African nations to pursue policies of nationalism, accelerated development, corruption, and patronage to a degree that they undermined vital state institutions and the economy. The same political pressures operate in PNG but have been contained much more than in Africa. The disruption of vital institutions and the economy is substantially less advanced in PNG. Whether PNG will recreate the African malaise is still an open question. It will depend to a large degree upon whether the elite can contain their own ambition, withstand the pressure of the electorate, and keep policies of accelerated development, nationalism, corruption, and patronage (which will undoubtedly be pursued in the future) at a level that still allows for substantial economic growth.

REFERENCES

Ake, C., 1979. 'Ideology and objective conditions', in J. D. Barkan and J. J. Okumu, eds., *Politics and Public Policy in Kenya and Tanzania*. New York: Praeger.

Al-Teraifi, A. A., 1973. 'Localisation policies and programs in the Sudan', *Journal of Administration Overseas*, 12(2):125-135.

Amuwo, K., 1986. 'Military-inspired anti-bureaucratic corruption campaigns: an appraisal of Niger's experience', *Journal of Modern African Studies*, 24(2):285-301.

Baguma, R., 1975. 'Inefficiency, irresponsiveness and irresponsibility in the public service: is Mwongozo to blame?', *African Review*, 5(2):195-200.

Balogun, M. J., 1983. *Public Administration in Nigeria. A Developmental Approach*. London: Macmillan.

Berg-Schlosser, D., 1984. 'African political systems. typology and performance', *Comparative Political Studies*, 17(1):121-151.

Biersteker, T. J., 1987. *Multinationals, the State, and Control of the Nigerian Economy*. Princeton: Princeton University Press.

Blyth, C. B., 1988. *Government Expenditure in Papua New Guinea*. Port Moresby: Institute of National Affairs.

Central Planning Office, Government of Papua New Guinea, 1974. *Strategies for Nationhood*. Port Moresby: Government Printer.

————, 1976. *National Development Strategy*. Port Moresby: Government Printer

Dorney, S., 1990. *Papua New Guinea. People, Politics and History since 1975*. Sydney: Random House.

Fieldhouse, D. K., 1986. *Black Africa. 1945-80: Economic Decolonization and Arrested Development*. London: Allen & Unwin.

Gellner, E., 1983. *Nations and Nationalism*. Oxford: Basil Blackwell.

Goodman, R., Lepani, C., and Morawetz, D., 1985. *The Economy of Papua New Guinea. An Independent Review*. Canberra: Development Studies Centre, Australian National University.

Gould, D. J., 1980. *Bureaucratic Corruption and Underdevelopment in the Third World*. New York: Pergamon.

Hegarty, D., 1983. *Electoral Politics in Papua New Guinea. Studies on the 1977 National Elections*. Port Moresby: University of Papua New Guinea.

Hirschman, D., 1981. 'Development or underdevelopment administration? A further 'deadlock', *Development and Change*, 12(3):459-479.

Hyden, G., 1983. *No shortcuts to Progress: Administration and Development in Africa*. London: Heinemann.

Kiki, A. M., 1968. *Ten Thousand Years in a Lifetime. A New Guinea Autobiography.* Melbourne: F.W. Cheshire.

Killick, T., 1978. *Development Economics in Action.* London: Heinemann.

———, 1983. 'Role of public sector in the industrialization of African developing countries', *Industry and Development,* 7:57–88.

Kurer, O., 1988. *The Credit Guarantee Scheme in PNG. An evaluation. Report to the Economic Policy Unit, Department of Finance and Planning.* Port Moresby: Department of Finance and Planning.

Lancy, D. F., 1983. *Cross-Cultural Studies in Cognition and Mathematics.* New York: Academic Press.

Leff, N., 1964. 'Economic development through bureaucratic corruption', *American Behavioral Scientist,* 8(3):8–14.

Leys, C., 1975. *Underdevelopment in Kenya. The political Economy of Neo-Colonialism. 1964–1971.* London: Heinemann.

Lungu, G. F., 1980. 'Africanization and the merit principle in the Zambian public service', *Journal of Overseas Administration,* 19(2):88–99.

Martin, R., 1985. 'Re-thinking 'law and development', *Journal of Modern African Studies,* 23(1):133–137.

McGavin, P. A., 1986. *The Labour Market in Papua New Guinea. A Survey and Analysis.* Port Moresby: Institute of National Affairs.

McKillop, R. F., 1974. *The Agricultural Extension Service in Papua New Guinea.* Port Moresby: Department of Agriculture, Livestock and Fisheries.

Mukandala, R. S., 1983. 'Bureaucracy and socialism in Tanzania: the case of the civil service', *African Review,* 10(1):1–21.

Mutahaba, G., 1975. 'The effects of changes in the Tanzania public service system upon administrative productivity 1961–72', *African Review,* 5(2):201–207.

———, 1982. 'The human resources factor in African public administration: a review', *African Review,* 9(1):32–58.

Nye, J. S., 1967. 'Corruption and political development: a cost-benefit analysis', *American Political Science Review,* 61(2):417–427.

Overseas Development Group, 1973. *A Report on Development Strategies for Papua New Guinea (Faber report).* Washington, D.C.: International Bank for Reconstruction and Development.

Post, K. W. J., 1973. *The Nigerian Federal Election of 1959.* Oxford: Oxford University Press.

Rimmer, D., 1984. *The Economics of West Africa.* London: Weidenfeld & Nicholson.

Roberts, H., 1982. 'The Algerian bureaucracy', *Review of African Political Economy,* 24:39–54.

Rweyamamy, A. H., 1975. 'The predicament of managers of public enterprises in Tanzania', *African Affairs,* 5(2):119–126.

Schatz, S. P., 1977. *Nigerian Capitalism.* Berkeley: University of California Press.

———, 1984. 'Pirate capitalism and the inert economy of Nigeria', *Journal of Modern African Studies,* 22(1):45–57.

Tordoff, W., 1984. *Government and Politics in Africa.* London: Macmillan.

Trebilcock, M. J., 1982. *Public Enterprises in Papua New Guinea.* Port Moresby: Institute of National Affairs.

Unitech (Papua New Guinea University of Technology), 1985. *List of Graduates, Diplomates and Certificate Holders.* Lae: Unitech.

UPNG (University of Papua New Guinea), 1982. *List of Graduates, 1970–1982.* Port Moresby: UPNG.

———, 1983. *List of Diplomates, 1970–1982.* Port Moresby: UPNG.

Wellings, P., 1983. 'Making a fast buck: capital leakage and the public accounts of Lesotho', *African Affairs,* 82(329):495–507.

World Bank, 1978. *Papua New Guinea. Its Economic Situation and Prospects for Development.* Washington, D.C.: World Bank.

————, 1979. *World Development Report 1977.* Washington, D.C.: World Bank.

————, 1981. *Accelerated Development in sub-Saharan Africa. An Agenda for Action.* Washington, D.C.: World Bank.

————, 1990. *World Development Report 1990.* Washington, D.C.: World Bank.

————, 1996a. *World Development Report 1996.* Washington, D.C.: World Bank.

————, 1996b. *World Debt Tables 1996.* Washington, D.C.: World Bank.

Young, C., 1982. *Ideology and Development in Africa.* New Haven: Yale University Press.

Acknowledgments

Helpful comments to earlier versions of this work were received from Herb Thompson, Murdoch University, and Peter Carroll, QUT.

Scott MacWilliam

PLANTATIONS AND SMALLHOLDER AGRICULTURE

$\mathcal{A}$N ESPECIALLY PROMINENT FEATURE of agriculture in PNG is the widespread presence of households occupying smallholdings, most of which are less than one hectare in size. Comprising at least 85 percent of the national population of about 3.6 million, smallholders utilise by far the largest proportion of the cultivated land area and produce most of the marketed crops, for export and local consumption. The importance of smallholdings is further enhanced because these also are sites for the production of substantial amounts of nonmarketed foodstuffs and other items for immediate consumption by households.[1]

By comparison, plantations and estates, which range from twenty to over one thousand hectares in size, occupy a much smaller proportion of land on a country-wide basis. Although invariably having greater yields per hectare than smallholdings, the large holdings produce significantly less in total output, while in the late 1980s employing fewer than 70,000 people (NSO 1990b). Since the closure of most plantations in the North Solomons, where a major revolt continues,

[1] Immediate has a particular, if little examined, significance for household production in PNG. The significance arises because the staple food crops grown on smallholdings generally cannot be stored for more than a few days. Harvesting of root crops including sweet potatoes takes place continuously, as long as seasonal conditions permit, and these are consumed shortly after harvesting. There is no substantial production of cereal crops which can be gathered and stored: imported white rice is the major grain crop consumed by households in many areas.

wage employment on large holdings has declined even further. With a few exceptions, large holdings are further limited in their role, almost entirely being used to produce crops for international markets. Such crops are consumed in small quantities, if at all, by the bulk of the local rural or urban population.

Because the sight of households labouring upon smallholdings is such a prominent one, it can appear that the welfare of the majority of the people is determined principally by the productivity of those who work in 'their gardens'. Further, there are often romantic but nevertheless misguided efforts to suggest that such work represents a continuing tradition, an 'original way of life', which is only 'now being affected by the modern sector' (UNDP 1994:146). The importance of the romance of smallholdings in contemporary PNG is directly related to the fact that their role has changed substantially over the last decade and a half.

Of declining importance for the national balance of payments, as mineral and energy exports rapidly expand, agriculture—especially in the form of households occupying smallholdings—is increasingly performing the role of a sponge, utilised to soak up rapidly increasing numbers of unemployed and underemployed. Politicians and other state officials regularly enthuse about measures which promote 'village life' as the preferred alternative to social disorder. In so doing, the indigenous leaders of the independent nation-state sound remarkably like the late colonial officials who also promoted the virtues of rural existence, and emphasised the need to strengthen smallholder agriculture in order to restrain the formation of a landless proletariat.

However, the superficial similarity in the pronouncements of contemporary indigenes and earlier Australians should not confuse the important differences in the place of agriculture between the first thirty years after the Second World War and the most recent period, that is, since the early 1980s. Further, while the differences appear to coincide roughly with the shift from colonial to postcolonial, they are not primarily explicable by this shift. As has been shown elsewhere, initially the colonial administration supervised a scheme of smallholder agriculture which *extended capitalised commercialisation* in the countryside, especially in the highlands, island, and coastal regions which came to constitute the economic spine of the colony (MacWilliam 1988, 1991; Thompson and MacWilliam 1992, esp. chap. 4). The scheme resulted in major increases in the production of export crops (particularly coffee and cocoa), and the consumption of marketed, especially imported, products. Until the mid- to late-1970s, and partly as a conse-

quence of the continued expansion of state-provided services (education, health, roads, and bridges), there were substantial improvements
in living conditions for much of the rural population.

From at least the early 1980s, and in line with global changes which
have affected primarily rural, agricultural and urbanised, industrial
countries alike (Leys 1994), the most rapid improvements stopped and
conditions stagnated, even began to decline. Not only did mining
become of increasing absolute importance for national revenues, particularly after the end of the spectacular coffee boom of 1976–1977, but
a long-term downward trend in prices for the major agricultural
exports negated efforts to retain their relative importance by increasing
export volumes. Put most simply, agriculture became less important in
national calculations, such as the balance of payments. Smallholdings
also ceased to provide the basis for improved living standards for the
bulk of the population, a condition which became even more apparent
in the 1980s and early 1990s drive to restrain and then reduce government expenditure.

But with a rapidly growing population, and only small increases in
wage employment, *the failure to reproduce capitalisation* through the
expanded production and consumption of households only increased
the pressure to construct another role for smallholdings. These have
become increasingly a site for the *relative surplus population*, where the
unemployed and underemployed can be held, and as much as possible
provided with some of the conditions necessary for maintaining or
establishing labour discipline (MacWilliam 1996).

Indeed it is a measure of how much the place of agriculture has
changed in Papua New Guinea over the last decade, that even large
holdings are now being defended not because of their export significance, nor their profitability, but for their wage employment role. In
Papua New Guinea, critics of plantations regularly base their attacks
against large holding agriculture on comparisons which purport to
show the greater productivity and/or cost-effectiveness of plantations
elsewhere (Simmons 1993). Indeed, so prolonged and effective has the
attack become that representatives of large holders now defend their
position not in terms of relative profitability, compared to other forms
of production in PNG, but by eliding the difference between large and
small holders and claiming that 'formal (i.e., cash cropping) agriculture
still provides work at a cheaper cost per job than either mining or manufacturing' (Manning 1994:137). Between 1985 and 1993, when agriculture's share of total exports fell from nearly 36 percent to 10 percent,

and mineral and related exports came to dominate, apparently no better defense could be constructed by the president of the Papua New Guinea Growers' Association, an organisation principally representative of copra and cocoa large holders, than plantation agriculture's role in absorbing rising numbers of unemployed and underemployed. Unfortunately, for the advocates of large holdings, there were no signs of employment increases on large holdings (Overfield, Smith, Kufinale, and Kuimbakal 1993:36): the closure since 1989 of plantations on Bougainville, previously some of the most important in the country, makes such a future development even less likely.

The first part of this chapter sets out a particular conception of household production as capitalist. The conception categorises large and small holding operations as distinct instances, different forms of the subsumption of labour to capital-in-production, or productive, industrial, capital. The explanation here is brief because the argument has been developed at length elsewhere, for the case of Papua New Guinea (Thompson and MacWilliam 1992, esp. introduction and chap. 4) and also for Kenya, in East Africa (Cowen 1982; Cowen 1983; MacWilliam, Desaubin, and Timms 1995; Cowen and MacWilliam 1996, esp. chaps. 4–5). Nevertheless, the importance of the description lies in providing the basis for showing how household production in PNG, as with households in other countries, is determined by accumulation on a global as well as a local scale of reckoning.

In the second part of this chapter, it is shown in greater detail how in PNG the terms of household production have changed over the last decade and a half, and the significance of this change for large and small holdings as well as the national political economy. The account shows that, with the exception of a short period in the 1950s when plantations were established for coffee growing in the Highlands, the rapid postwar expansion of smallholdings initially blocked any continuing spread of large holdings. In the 1960s to early 1970s, a rising tide bearing smallholdings lapped around and threatened the established large holdings. Subsequently, over the last decade and a half, smallholdings have become even more important but for a different reason, their capacity to absorb a *relative surplus population*.

CAPITAL AND SMALLHOLDER PRODUCTION

A description of estate and plantation, large holding, production as capitalist is unlikely to be controversial. The ownership and operation of these large holdings appears to conform to well-established notions of capitalism, such as private property ownership, the employment of wage labour under the surveillance of managerial authority, and the immediate importance of profitability in determining if and how agricultural operations are conducted on a particular piece of land. Regardless of whether the description *capitalist* is embraced or rejected as ideological, with preference instead being given to such notions as private or free enterprise, there would be little disagreement about the conditions which govern large holding operations (private property, wage labour, profitability, etc.). It is the ownership and organisational arrangements of corporate capitalism which preside over most large holding operations, where capitalists at the helm of joint stock companies accumulate means of production according to criteria of profitability.

If the nature of large holding production as a form of industrial capital seems clear-cut, such is not the case with smallholdings. Descriptions of household production have multiplied, with little attempt at theoretical clarification. The predominant description locates households as primarily subsistence producers. The picture has such a strong grip on the popular and academic imagination that it is regarded as unnecessary to describe the form in other than the most superficial terms. Shaw (1985:2), for instance, did not hesitate to assert that the 'largest component of economic activity in (PNG) is subsistence agriculture...' (see also AIDAB 1990:6). But what characterises the activity? 'Subsistence production is defined as that for the household's consumption and includes housing, ceremonial goods, fuel, containers and food fed to animals such as pigs...' (p. 3). More recently, some have expanded the description to encompass change by the simple device of adding an adjective: 'The economy is predominantly of mixed subsistence character...' (AusAID 1996:1).

The problem lies with how household existence is conceived in the prevailing descriptions. Most often it is not constructed in terms which make possible an examination of the social determinants of household production and consumption, but characterised as a trans-historical existence marked principally by occupation-ownership of smallholdings and the seeming independence, or autonomy, of households tilling 'their own soil'. Thus, in most current descriptions of PNG, the relationship between households and capital, including the role of the state, rarely appears.

Only with historically constituted general categories is it possible, for instance, to explain how levels of consumption, levels of labour's subsistence, fluctuate at particular moments for different forms of labour. The necessity of such categories is especially important, including in the case of PNG where there have been few attempts to construct the terms of household experience during the twentieth century in relation to international changes (exceptions include Amarshi, Good, and Mortimer 1979; Fitzpatrick 1980; Donaldson and Good 1988). Yet this experience has been one of increases, then stagnation and reduction in levels of consumption/subsistence. Increases were especially pronounced in the twenty-five years after the Second World War, when much of the country had changes along the lines being experienced elsewhere in the world. Since the late 1970s, although with fluctuations and regional differences, there has been general stagnation, and possibly even decline. The latter changes, too, have occurred in concert with movements in the terms of daily existence in many other places on the earth's surface. Indeed, in most countries of the industrial world real wages have fallen and living standards at least stagnated, if not also declined since the mid-1970s.[2]

Since it is being claimed here that households have living standards which are determined by capitalism, and not by some autonomous capacity to expand or retract production, precisely what is meant by capitalism needs to be specified. In particular, it is important to recognise that incessant accumulation (of capital), one defining characteristic of capitalism as a form of social existence, occurs through different forms of capital. The forms include merchant and industrial capital (Kay 1975). It is necessary to spell out the distinction between these two forms in order to understand major features of household existence in PNG.

Merchant or trading capital is the form which has had the earliest and seemingly most continuous presence in much of the PNG countryside. Whether in the late nineteenth century practice of 'blackbirding', that is, recruiting labour to work in northern Australian canefields, or the twentieth century practice of buying crops and selling internationally manufactured goods in many villages, the trading form of capital

[2] Contrary to Kurer's emphasis (in the previous chapter in this collection) upon postindependence decline in sub-Saharan Africa, it is by now well established that for Kenya at least, there was considerable continuity between the late colonial and early postcolonial period in terms of improving living standards for much of the country's population. The history of the earlier period, and of the decline from the late 1970s until the 1990s, is summarised in MacWilliam, Desaubin, and Timms 1995, where extensive references also are provided to the literature on the subject. It is unlikely that Kenya was alone in following this pattern of initial improvement followed by retraction.

has been omnipresent.[3] Since at least the last century, merchant capital has been the most prominent form by which village life, and therefore household labour on smallholdings, joined accumulation of a global order.

Two features of merchant capital need to be understood so that its possible effects upon rural areas can be considered. The first is that it is unproductive: merchant capital accumulates through exchange, not by producing. In and of itself, merchant capital cannot change the way goods are produced or increase the levels of production. Secondly, the accumulation occurs through unequal exchange. Traders and merchant firms 'buy cheap and sell dear'. 'Buying cheap' means purchasing commodities at prices lower than their value (Kay 1975; Marx 1976).

The value of any commodity is the labour time socially necessary for its production. Where the transaction occurs between smallholders and forms of trading capital, the reproduction of households at existing levels of consumption is continuously threatened by the terms of the (unequal) exchange. Where merchant capital is the dominant form of capital, the effect upon households is invariably widespread impoverishment. Being unequal, in the sense just defined, exchange between households and trading firms acts to continuously drive down the value of the labour power which is employed in family labour processes on smallholdings. Not only is the productive capacity of the labourers separated from their consumption, or needs, as it is in all forms where labour is subjected to capital. Merchant capital also threatens that capacity itself through continuous impoverishment of those whose labour is essential for production to occur.

By and large, households in PNG do not live in the impoverished conditions which characterise rural life in many other countries. If merchant capital is omnipresent in the countryside, and has been so for much of the current century, how have households escaped impoverishment of the especially severe forms found elsewhere? The answer, in brief, is that while trading capital has been prominent, it has not been predominant. To understand why not requires a specification of

[3] Household consumption of purchased goods is extensive and continuous in many areas of rural PNG. In the period following the Second World War, the flow of imported foodstuffs and other products expanded dramatically. Also, households are consumers of domestically manufactured goods, the most prominent of which is beer. While a continuity in the purchase of commodities by households has been established, with many smallholders regularly buying both means of production (tools, vehicles, crop-processing machinery, etc.) and consumption goods (tinned fish, rice, lamps, etc.), there are also substantial fluctuations in line with seasonal cycles and prices for marketed crops.

another form of capital as well as a consideration of relationships between forms of capital and the state, colonial as well as postcolonial.

Industrial capital, capital-in-production, is a particular case of the general condition of capitalist accumulation. In this case, the commodities labour power and other means of production are joined in the process of production, for the production of surplus value. In the best known forms of industrial capital, the capitalist who owns money capital purchases the commodities and joins them in a centralised labour process, such as on a plantation or in a factory. The means of production are acquired as commodities through an exchange which is equal, in the sense that the commodities exchange at their values. Labour power, for instance, exchanges at a value which is equal to the socially necessary labour time to produce that commodity. Unlike merchant capital, which accumulates out of unequal exchange, industrial, productive capital exchanges commodities at value, or equal exchange. It is the process of production, and not terms of (unequal) exchange, that through the circuit of capital-in-production results in commodities of a greater value than the value of the commodities initially purchased at the beginning of the circuit.

Under both merchant and industrial capital, surplus labour time is appropriated, or labour exploited, because its needs, or socially necessary consumption, are separated from, as well as less than, its capacities, or the production which results from the act of labour. However, the terms of exploitation, or the appropriation of surplus labour time, differ. Where the exploitation, or accumulation, by merchant capital necessarily results in labour power exchanging below value or absolute impoverishment, productive capital's necessary effect is 'only' relative impoverishment for the class of labour. That is, where labour is subsumed by industrial capital, impoverishment is relative to the growing concentration of social wealth in the hands of a capitalist class, which accumulates surplus product. Since impoverishment is relative, not absolute, where productive capital is dominant there is the possibility of absolute increases in the value of labour power or living standards, rather than the certainty of absolute impoverishment which accompanies merchant capital.

As noted above, the twentieth-century experience of many areas of rural PNG is one of changes in living standards, the increases after the Second World War being especially pronounced. Instead of facing continuous absolute impoverishment, as would be the case if merchant capital had been predominant, household consumption in PNG after the Second World War has seemed to follow global phases of expansion and stagnation. The critical question to be asked then becomes: have the changes occurred because of household autonomy from capital, or because smallholders are subsumed by capital-in-production?

According to Turner (1990:51), in the period following the Second World War 'farmers have carried out (a) food growing revolution largely on their own'. The claim is advanced to support a radical anti-statist stance, that 'the government' has 'played' almost no part in the 'revolution' (Turner 1990:51). This position supports, even underpins, most descriptions which emphasise that households are largely subsistence producers.

It certainly is clear that households are not subsumed by capital-in-production under the terms which hold for urban workers, even if the latter grow vegetables and flowers to supplement household wage incomes and for relaxation. Three important differences are immediately apparent. The first is that households in rural PNG are in occupation of land under different terms than the workers of urban centres. The second is that the labour processes through which households are employed differ substantially, including in the extent of centralisation, from those of factory and office workers. Thirdly, in the case of smallholders there is no capitalist class registering a continuous presence in surveillance, supervision, and ownership of the means of production. One effect of the three differences is that the competition between capitalists which impacts directly and in myriad daily forms upon urban proletarian existence does not appear to determine rural household living conditions.

If capital-in-production, productive capital, only describes the industrial capital which operates in manufacturing and large holding agriculture, then it is clear that households in rural PNG do not comprise a form of labour subsumed by capital. However, the argument of this chapter rests upon the proposition that (rural household) labour is subsumed in another form. The central elements of that form are: (a) that most households, particularly but not only those in the export crop producing regions of PNG, produce for markets, international and domestic;[4] (b) that the purchase and consumption of food and other

---

[4] Between the 1971 and 1990 censuses, as the extent of monetization of the labour force increased rapidly, the increase was accompanied by two important movements: firstly, into 'cash farming as a form of self-employment', and secondly, from self-employment (i.e. households producing and trading commodities) into unemployment (Millett 1993:9), or the relative surplus population.

goods is extensive; and (c) that the terms of household occupation of land are set principally in the exchange of these commodities, as well as under state-superintended arrangements of landholding (MacWilliam 1988; 1991; Thompson and MacWilliam 1992, introduction and chap. 4).

For Marx the landless proletariat of England became the form of labour subsumed by industrial capital through which the category labour power was formulated. An important quality of the form of labour and the category labour power was that the labourers had been removed from a prior occupation of land and deposited in urban centres as a landless proletariat. However it is important to recognise that subsequent to Marx's formulation, a late nineteenth and twentieth century opposition to landlessness has been of particular importance in setting the contemporary terms of labour's subsumption (Cowen and Shenton 1996). Before the Second World War this opposition was instrumental in restraining the action of capitalists from separating households from land in some British and other colonies (Phillips 1989; MacWilliam 1988, 1991).

While the opposition to landlessness has been important in constructing state policy, a more important determinant of the direction of colonial and postcolonial states has been the global dominance of industrial, productive, capital over trading capital (Kay 1975). In circulating commodities, exporting agricultural crops, and importing manufactured goods for household consumption, merchant firms mainly act as bearers of internationally established values, or prices of production. These values have been established in the labour processes of industrial capital, both in the metropolitan centres and in PNG. Consequently, as a result of the actions of the trading firms, production and consumption in the country have been exposed continuously to calculations of an international order. The calculations were transmitted as well to commodities, such as shells, which acted as mediums of exchange, standards of equivalence, even before a state-backed currency penetrated all commodity relations after the Second World War (Hughes 1978).

Given the importance of merchant capital in conveying the values of commodities, established on circuits of industrial capital, as well as the fact that this form of capital accumulates through unequal exchange, which could have threatened households with impoverishment, state practices have taken on a dual character. Trading firms have been encouraged to extend their reach, including by state provision of roads, bridges, and ports, channelling manufactured goods to a wider population. Consumption of imported goods in many rural and all urban areas has been a prominent feature of postwar PNG (Shaw 1985). But simultaneously, state-imposed price controls and credit restrictions have limited household indebtedness, especially by restraining the capacity of smallholders to exchange land for consumer goods and loans.[5]

From the 1940s, substantial pools of money capital became available internationally. Simultaneously, both in the metropoles and the colonies, state policy was turned toward ensuring that economic growth became the first priority of state action. That is, in PNG as elsewhere a particular idea of development was associated with a *doctrine of development*, specifically that the spontaneous force of capitalism needed to be harnessed to a deliberate intent to develop. Intention was to be effected through the state (Cowen and Shenton 1996). Accordingly, in the colonies where restraining the actions of merchant capitals had been of importance prewar, restraint took second place behind a more contemporary object of state power. Colonial officials, in PNG and elsewhere (Thompson and MacWilliam 1992: chap. 4; Cowen 1982; 1983), became concerned to ensure that household occupation of smallholdings resulted in the expanded production of commodities for international and domestic markets.

Because households had remained attached to land in these colonies, it always was possible that official action which produced increases in household production only would result in increased consumption, or extended leisure hours. If that had been the case, money advanced by metropolitan states and international banks to state branches and to households would not have been money capital, but merely a welfare payment. Further, without landlessness, wages and machine-driven production, some of the most important means of economic coercion which have been exerted against labour to force increases in production, were absent. If the money advanced out of the international pools was to become money capital, it was necessary to formulate schemes of household production which would ensure that

[5] A sign of the continuing power of the long-held concern for landlessness as the possible consequence of household indebtedness is the prevailing barrier to land being used as collateral for loans in rural Papua New Guinea. Of course now the demands for removing the barriers are most often expressed by banks, state officials, and entrepreneurs who advocate 'freeing up the land' for commercial purposes. Rarely do the same advocates of changes to land law recognise that an immediate effect would be a continuing rise in landlessness and social 'disorder' which state policy has been designed to check.

family labour processes not only produced value, but also surplus value. The schemes integrated money capital and means of production so that an expanded mass of (capitalist) commodities, rather than simply more consumption and more leisure, resulted.

In the case of PNG, from the 1950s there was an increasing flow of grants made by the Australian state. Since the 1960s, loans by major international institutions, including the World Bank, the Asian Development Bank, and the European Community, have been particularly significant (MacWilliam 1986; 1996). A range of colonial and postcolonial state branches, including the variously named agriculture departments, commodity boards, and Development Bank/Agbank, have supervised and coordinated households. While the scheme had a footing in the pre–Second-World-War opposition to particular effects of capital, including landlessness and unemployment, its principal features were formed after the global conflict ended. The features included means of keeping the brakes upon merchant and certain forms of industrial capital, especially in large holding agriculture, while expanding household production and consumption of both marketed and nonmarketed produce.

By guaranteeing the payment of interest on international loans, the state has acted to ensure that the flows of money from international sources fulfilled important capitalist criteria. The most obvious was the requirement that commodity production be expanded continuously. The increased output of export crops provides one index. But as well, and less easily recognised, there was an important shift in the items produced for immediate consumption and domestic markets.

AGRICULTURAL PRODUCTION IN PAPUA NEW GUINEA

Large Holdings
The establishment and operation of large holdings which have produced commodities for international markets since the end of the nineteenth century, seems to suggest industrial capital followed a similar trajectory in PNG to that taken in many other parts of the globe: noncapitalist existence was disrupted by the removal of land from previous uses and forms of occupation. Consolidated under freehold and leasehold titles, the land became the subject of concentrated private property rights, with ownership held by either joint stock companies or a stratum of owner-occupiers. In either case, whichever ownership form prevailed, wage workers were employed to grow, harvest, and process

crops destined for international markets. Employment on the plantations and estates was predicated upon the production of surplus value, a portion of which accrued as dividends out of company profits to the capitalists who held shares in the operating firms or as revenue, and expanded consumption, to the owner-occupiers, themselves subject to capital.

Large holdings in PNG also have been conducted subject to particular late-nineteenth- and twentieth-century terms, terms which include an opposition to tendencies of industrial capital. Thus both the German and British/Australian administrations, in the cases of New Guinea and Papua respectively, adopted measures which checked the formation of a landless proletariat. The area of land for alienation by large holders was restricted. Plantation wage workers remained attached to rural households in occupation of smallholdings under a form of tenure which checked the capacity of either trading or industrial capital to acquire ever greater amounts of land (cf. MacWilliam 1988; Fitzpatrick 1980). With the exception of a brief period after the Second World War, when coffee large holdings were established, and several subsequent instances in which a number of tea and oil palm estates were created on leasehold land, state actions have continued to focus upon means of securing household tenure and blocking further consolidation of land. The extent to which household occupation has been secured and re-secured through the state has ensured the formation of a tide bearing ever-expanding households which threatens to flood over the existing large holdings.

In 1986 there were 80,770, 43,648, and 10,271 hectares planted to coconuts, cocoa, and coffee, respectively, on large holdings (NSO 1990a). A further 10,591 hectares carried rubber trees. (The characterisation of the area under oil palm, of around 12,000 hectares in large holdings, should be treated with caution because no figures are provided for the area operated by households whose smallholdings surround the nucleus estates, on which the processing factories operate. Production of palm oil commenced in the early 1970s.) There were 379 large holdings producing copra, 304 cocoa, and a further 271 coffee, with just 49 growing rubber.

Output from the large holdings approximated 65,000 tonnes of copra, 10,500 tonnes of cocoa, and 14,000 tonnes of coffee green bean. Rubber production amounted to nearly 5,000 tonnes, and oil palm, again ostensibly just from large holdings, over 240,000 tonnes.

From the early 1970s until the late 1980s, and with the only pronounced exception being oil palm, large holdings did not expand in
number and area. Employment, too, changed little, with periods of
increase doing little more than returning numbers to the levels hired
before the most recent reduction. Indeed for each of copra and cocoa
there have been major reductions in the numbers of large holdings, the
area under crop and also in output (cf. Bureau of Statistics 1977: table 1,
and NSO 1990a: table 1). Copra production declined from 80,000
tonnes in 1972 to 65,000 tonnes in 1986, while over the same period
the large holding cocoa output almost halved, from 18,700 to 10,500
tonnes. Even a 1980s effort to reverse the output trend for cocoa was
undercut by the long-running revolt in the North Solomons Province,
with many plantations on Bougainville, once the most productive in
the country, marketing little or no crop since the 1988–1989 season.
The commodity price slump of 1989-1990 further weakened large holding production elsewhere in the country for these two crops.

After peaking in 1988-1989 at 18,000 tonnes, plantation output of
cocoa began to decline. Hit further by the major international price
reduction of the late 1980s to early 1990s, and by the after-effects of the
1994 volcanic eruption at Rabaul, by 1994–1995 plantation cocoa production had fallen further to just 8,302 tonnes (Cocoa Board of PNG
1996: table 5).

Coffee has provided a partial exception to these large holding
trends, for at least two reasons. The first is that despite a continuing
decline in the number of estates and plantations, and only a small
increase between 1975 and 1985 in the area planted to crop, output
from these holdings increased, largely due to improvements in productivity per hectare (cf. Bureau of Statistics 1977: table 1, and NSO 1990a:
table 1). Total output from estates and plantations rose from 10,705
tonnes (1975) to 13,359 tonnes (1983) and reached a new peak of over
18,000 tonnes in the early to mid-1990s, as prices recovered from a dramatic slump (Coffee Industry Corporation 1996:14, table 4) and extensive new plantings of bushes came into full production. Secondly, due
to the rapid expansion of a new form of production on consolidated
land, in the 1980s there appeared to be a major increase in the number
of large holdings and a substantial expansion of the area planted to
coffee in the Highlands. The new form, dubbed twenty-hectare
projects, seemed to join features of plantation and household production together (see below). The increased production from the projects
began to appear in large holding output figures by the mid-1980s. The

difference between previously established large holdings and twenty-hectare projects, discussed below, was reflected by 1988–1989 in the Coffee Industry Board's separation of the two forms of production in its official figures. If the project or block expansion is removed from the large holding total, then by the end of the 1980s estates and plantations covered a very similar area, although with a smaller number of holdings, to that planted to coffee in the early 1970s.

Smallholdings

Since the late nineteenth century, at least, households in some parts of what is now PNG have produced commodities for international and domestic markets (Epstein 1968). However, the expansion of household production during the fifty years after the Second World War ended has been especially striking, in terms of the number of households engaged, the areas of the country involved, and increases in output registered. This production has taken three principal forms, only two of which can be adequately quantified at present. The commodity forms are wage workers, export crops, and products for domestic markets.

The first important commodity produced by households was labour power. Since the late nineteenth century, it has been from households that the estates and plantations, mines, and colonial administration recruited workers (Amarshi, Good, and Mortimer 1979; Fitzpatrick 1980). Mostly male, the workers have retained connections to rural households in the areas from which they were recruited and to which they returned when wage employment ended. Where out-migration by wage workers is most pronounced, as in the northern and southern coastal mainland regions, one effect is that rural households have fewer males of working age, with women and children performing much of the labour. Such regions, significantly, became primarily labour reserves in which the production of crops for export and probably also for domestic markets was lowest.

Households in other areas produced crops for export and newly enlarged domestic markets almost from the moment plantations and mines were established nearby. After the Second World War, and most noticeably from the 1960s, smallholders became the major producers of coffee, copra, and cocoa. In each case, smallholder production now exceeds the output from large holdings. For coffee, more than 70 percent of a total output of between 50,000 and 70,000 tonnes comes from households. In the most recent coffee season for which figures are available, that of 1994–1995, smallholdings probably produced around

74 percent of about 58,000 tonnes (Coffee Industry Corporation 1996:14, table 4). Coffee-growing smallholdings probably cover in excess of 50,000 hectares, compared to the 7,000–10,000 hectares of large holdings (see above). Approximately 277,000 households, each cultivating 300 to 700 bushes, grow coffee: that is, at a very conservative estimate, at least 35 percent of all rural households produce the crop (Overfield, Smith, Kufinale, and Kuimbakul 1993:36). In the main smallholder coffee-growing provinces of Chimbu, Eastern, and Western Highlands, the proportion of households growing coffee probably increases to more than 80 percent.

Cocoa production, too, has become dominated by household producers. At least until the 1989 outbreak of revolt in the North Solomons, cocoa-growing in that province had acquired a similar importance for households as coffee in the Highlands. In areas not previously noted for smallholder export crop production, a drive by households to increase their output of copra also became apparent in the late 1970s and the early 1980s (Gerritsen 1985; R. Foster, private communication).

Household production for domestic markets, along with labour power and export crops the third major form of marketed smallholding output, cannot be described adequately in quantitative terms. There is no information of a national character on the subject (Shaw 1985:39; Thompson 1986; 1991), and with the reductions of the last two decades in the capacity of state branches which might collect such information, the situation is unlikely to change in the immediate future. While the claim (noted above) has been made, that households have engaged in a 'food revolution' (Turner 1990:51), there is very little detailed information on the subject. About all that can be said with certainty about country-wide conditions is that households produce nearly all of the vegetables, fruit, and other products which appear in rural and many urban markets.

During the colonial and postcolonial years, all manner of state officials and international advisors have pushed continuously for expanded household production for domestic markets as well as immediate consumption. Further, and especially during the late colonial period, the administration played a major role in coordinating and supervising smallholder production. Apart from restraining warfare, which often destroyed food gardens, supervising and coordinating the building of means of communication, extending health and education services, these officials saw very precise connections between preventing landlessness and unemployment, and the capacity of smallholders to produce marketed crops.

A central element of the connections was the need, under capitalist conditions of accumulation, to reduce the labour-time devoted to producing household consumption. In order to increase the production of surplus value, or change the ratio between surplus product and labour's necessary consumption, the value of labour-power had to be lowered. One way of doing this would have been to allow merchant capital free rein in bearing the products of international manufacturing capital into household consumption. The value of these products was being lowered rapidly in the postwar years by the centralised labour processes of, and competition between, manufacturing capitals. But to allow unrestrained access by trading firms, often in advance of the production of export crops, which were to be the means of purchasing consumer goods, would have necessitated that the gap between consumption and production be bridged through credit. Credit only could have been advanced against land, the major asset held by households. By its own logic, driven by fear of the effects of landlessness, the colonial administration was forced to block the buying and selling of smallholder land and pay attention to changing many forms of smallholder production (for the case of pig production, see Thompson and MacWilliam 1992:138–140). Such action flies against the claims by Turner and others of colonial state inattention to household production for immediately consumed as well as marketed crops.

The changes frequently show up in a manner which makes even more obvious the deficiencies of the prevailing notion of subsistence to describe household production for self-consumption. Consider the following, which appears in a report of a patrol undertaken by Cadet Patrol Officer F. C. Anglin in the Eastern Highlands (Okapa no. 6 of 1963/1964): 'As with other highland areas, a big majority of crops are grown for subsistence purposes. These crops include sweet potato, taro, yam, banana and sugar cane. European type vegetables are also grown in increasing quantities'. Although it is clear from the rest of the report that these 'European type vegetables' were produced regularly for immediate consumption, in this case and in other census districts visited, such produce was never 'traditional' and thus never 'subsistence'.[6] As noted earlier, the concept subsistence itself has a history which is missing from most current accounts of household production.

---

[6] I am indebted to former CPO Anglin's daughter, Ms. T. Anglin, for the use of copies of his patrol reports.

The crops households grew, as well as the land used and the family labour processes by which smallholder production occurred, were a deliberate expression of state practices aimed at expanding all forms of production. New and improved varieties of pigs, chickens, and vegetables were brought to PNG and inserted into household production. Agricultural extension services, begun before the Second World War, conducted experiments to improve strains and then distributed the higher yielding varieties, along with advice for their cultivation.

A major shift in international and domestic conditions from the late 1970s or early 1980s until the present, marks off the later period from the first decades after the war. While there appears to be an economic and political continuity, expressed through the statements of colonial officials and postindependence politicians, in the importance of household occupation of smallholdings, an important break has occurred. Instead of being able to continuously expand consumption, as an expression of labour's subsumption to capital during the postwar global boom, since at least the early 1980s households have been subjected to a prolonged and intense international drive to reduce costs of production, including the value of household labour power.

Because of the rapidity of crop price fluctuations on international markets, and the importance of these prices for households, which produce the bulk of output, since the mid-1970s a range of state practices have been formulated to underpin commodity markets. All postindependence governments have supported commodity price stabilisation schemes (Brogan and Remenyi 1987; Jolly, Beck, and Bodman 1990; Overfield 1991). While the terms of the schemes regularly have been criticised as being overly favourable to large holding owners, the principal object of the schemes was initially to encourage expanded smallholder production and more recently to maintain that production (MacWilliam 1996).

In addition, governments have secured continuing flows of money from international institutions (MacWilliam 1986). In 1986, the Agbank advanced a record PGK 31 million, the bulk of which was for agriculture, with smallholding production being the principal target (Agbank 1986:14). The total amount lent by the Agbank increased again in 1987, to PGK 32.3 million. In both years, the bank 'financed much of its agricultural lending activities with a loan from the World Bank as part of the Third Agricultural Credit Project' (Agbank 1987:7). By 1994, total lending of the newly renamed Rural Development Bank had climbed to PGK 414 million, of which PGK 202 million was for agriculture (Rural Development Bank 1994:34). Further, there was a renewed emphasis upon 'lending for (the) smallholder sector to improve the living standard of (the) rural population' (p. 9). Nearly all the funds employed had been lent by international institutions to the PNG Government, which on-lent the money to the Bank (Rural Development Bank 1994:28).

In the early 1980s, during an intensified drive to raise productivity and lower the value of family labour power, the terms of the previously constructed scheme of smallholder production were subject to increasing pressure. With devolution of agricultural services to provincial governments, at the same time as there were efforts to reduce state expenditures, the capacity of state branches to supervise and coordinate the scheme was reduced. Since these branches had been of particular importance previously in ensuring that increased household production did not lead automatically to expanded consumption, further advances of money capital became dependent upon reforms in the terms of supervision. The reforms became even more important given the growth in lawlessness, including attacks on large holding operations and the agents of merchant firms who purchased crops.

It is in this context, and particularly in the Highlands, that a new form of centralised production, known as twenty-hectare projects, was developed. First begun in the late 1970s, when concern for reductions in the rate of growth of smallholder production was becoming widespread, the projects involved consolidating household land held under customary tenure (Hulme 1983). Banks, principally the Development Bank/Agbank, advanced funds for extending plantings, particularly of coffee and cocoa.

Initially a state institution established to assist the indigenous takeover of former expatriate owned large holdings, the National Plantation Management Agency (NPMA), became the management agency which supervised and coordinated operations on most of the projects. However in the 1980s, private management firms took over operations on the bulk of the twenty-hectare projects. The firms controlled operations and attempted to secure the repayment of loans. The most important of the firms which managed operations on the older-established plantations also ran the majority of the twenty-hectare projects. In 1989, six agencies managed over 60 percent of the 253 Eastern and Western Highlands projects, containing approximately 61 percent, or 3,100 hectares, of the area planted to the projects (private communication). Often against the resistance of smallholders, many of whom became little more than shareholders anticipating a future disbursement of dividends, the management agencies used labour teams and equipment from nearby plantations to operate the projects.

Although the households which had been formed into business groups for the purpose of land consolidation and obtaining advances of money capital from the PNG Agbank continued to live proximate to the project, much of the conduct of operations had been removed from the family labour processes employed on smallholdings. One effect of the efforts to conduct these operations under the criteria of profitability, where Agbank loans had the first claim on revenue raised by crop sales, was that management agencies conducted projects along lines which tried to stop nearby households of project land-owners taking crop from 'their land'. Further centralisation of operations occurred, with ripe fruit transported to central factories rather than being processed on the same location as it was grown.

The major international price downturn of the late 1980s–early 1990s displaced this struggle between management agencies and households over the rate of surplus value production. Instead projects collapsed, along with most management agencies. Indebtedness to the banks, especially the Development Bank/Agbank, increased greatly. The latter institution was forced to restructure its own management operations in an attempt to recoup even a small proportion of the loans advanced. By 1991, the Coffee Industry Board's publications no longer attempted to present statistics for the twenty-hectare 'block' form of production, simply adding output from the few projects still operating into a total large holding figure. The principal remaining lessons from the twenty-hectare projects are the importance of state supervision for this form of production, and that further reform of supervision will be a necessary part of any drive to increase production and productivity in smallholder agriculture.

In the conditions of the last decade, even maintaining smallholder production of export crops has been difficult. Since the last coffee price 'mini-boom' of 1986–1987, household output has been consistently below that year, even up to one-third less at the bottom of the 1989–1991 slump. The subsequent price increases and efforts to strengthen state assistance (MacWilliam 1990, 1993), have brought only a partial recovery (Coffee Industry Corporation 1996:14). For cocoa, new plantings in the early to mid-1980s resulted in a major peak of nearly 30,000 tonnes in 1988–1989 followed by a fluctuating but declining trend. The trend suggests that households have adopted lower levels of maintenance of bushes while prices underwent a major drop. In 1994–1995, smallholder output fell to 18,000 tonnes, a level first attained in 1981–1982 (Cocoa Board of PNG 1996: tables 1–5).

Smallholdings and the Relative Surplus Population

While increasing household production and labour productivity remains important, and is probably occurring although in a step-wise manner, this is currently being supplanted by an even more important role for smallholdings. Papua New Guinea, like nearly every other country in the world, is currently facing 'a crisis of unemployment'. That is, *the rate of increase of unemployment* has accelerated dramatically. To take just one indication of the substantial change, consider the following: that by 2000, approximately 300,000 people will be unemployed, a figure larger than the projected total number of people in wage employment. As well, 'unemployment is growing four times as fast as wage employment' (Millett 1993:10). Concludes Millett: 'Because 85 percent of the problem originates in the rural areas where land and labour markets do not work well, public investment may be required to solve it.... Self-employment, mainly cash farming, offers most scope for income earning opportunities both as to numbers and growth' (1993:10).

Self-employment and cash farming are, of course, euphemisms for smallholder existence. But when this existence is itself increasingly fragile, the scope clearly does not extend to improvements in living standards, and probably does not even suggest maintenance of existing conditions. Instead, what is implicit in this prescription is expanded household occupation of smallholdings at lower (than previous) levels of consumption, with state subsidies provided under conditions which ensure that certain minimum levels of labour discipline and social order are maintained.

Any further extension of smallholdings also raises the important political matter of on which land the households will be located. On Bougainville, this seems to have occurred already by the simple process of occupying plantations left vacant by large holding owners. Elsewhere, continuing plantations are forced to defend their operations by the employment of security guards and the construction of substantial fences.

If in one respect this encroachment seems to parallel the actions of squatters on the Gazelle Peninsula during the 1960s and early 1970s, now the politics of such forms of land redistribution have changed fundamentally. For the owners of nearly all the large holdings are indigenes, either as owner-occupiers or in a corporate form, not the expatriate Australians who were the object of the earlier attacks. These indigenous owners are represented politically in the major parties, as well as in the executives and legislatures at the national and local levels (Thompson and MacWilliam 1992: chaps. 2–3). Any enlargement of the land area occupied by households, whether for the production of agricultural commodities or for absorbing the unemployed, has the potential for not only increasing the more-or-less spontaneous 'tribal fighting' which has become prominent in many rural areas but also for systematic conflict arranged nationally to capture/recapture 'traditional lands'. Such an enlargement of the tussles over land for household occupation, as well as to resolve disputed ownership of large holdings, could become the 'ethnic cleansing' which is so prominent elsewhere, including in Africa.

CONCLUSION

Because household production in the years following the Second World War has been carried on a rising tide of international money capital, changes in conditions which affect flows of money capital to smallholdings are of great importance. As well, sentiments about the nature of state actions, such as the now rampant neo-liberalism, will have significance in settling whether means are found of reforming the state's part in household production. As Millett indicates, further expansion of the scheme would appear to be predicated upon reforms.

Current political conditions within PNG point toward the likelihood of further attempts to renew the scheme of household production. The tendency towards impoverishment of households, as well as revolt, lawlessness, and other forms of more or less spontaneous opposition, continuously threatens governments and drives party opposition. A predictable political response, given the barriers which exist to constructing a project of import-substituting, labour extensive manufacturing which would employ large numbers, already has been to re-emphasise the importance of re-attaching labour to smallholdings (MacWilliam 1996).

Whether re-attachment is principally for political or economic reasons, the availability of land necessarily is a central component of any renewal of household production. At a time when the profitability of many large holdings has been reduced, these have become an easy target. Indeed, it is quite possible that the plantation form of large holdings is about to disappear and a new wave of land redistribution, state-sanctioned or not, will finally obliterate this historic form.

The fact that many of these are owned by wealthy and powerful indigenes, will only intensify the domestic political struggle over the ownership of the large holdings. At the moment the struggle takes a largely inchoate, fragmented form, with attacks against individual plantations and plantation personnel at specific moments (e.g. harvesting, pay-days, etc.). But it is quite possible that in PNG another systematic redistribution of large holdings, of a much more substantial form than occurred in the 1970s, will become an important part of the wider national political agenda. For advocates of such a direction, whether dressed up in the clothes of neo-traditionalism, as a 'back to the land' movement, or not, it is important to recognise that the effect of a further extension of smallholdings would be to extend the subsumption of household labour to capital. Whether this is what the devotees of household existence envisage is, of course, another matter altogether.

REFERENCES

Agriculture Bank of Papua New Guinea (Agbank). *Annual Reports, 1986 and 1987.* Boroko: Agriculture Bank.

Amarshi, A., Good, K., and Mortimer, R., 1979. *Development and Dependency: The Political Economy of Papua New Guinea.* Melbourne: Oxford University Press.

Australian International Development Assistance Bureau (AIDAB), 1990. *Australia's Development Cooperation Program with Papua New Guinea.* Canberra: AGPS.

Australian Agency for International Development (AusAID), 1996. *The Economy of Papua New Guinea, 1996 Report.* International Development Issues No. 46. Canberra: Economic Insights P/L.

Brogan, B., and Remenyi, J., eds., 1987. *Commodity Price Stabilisation in Papua New Guinea – a Work-in-Progress Seminar.* Discussion paper No. 27. Port Moresby: Institute of National Affairs.

Bureau of Statistics, 1977. *Rural Industries 1974-1975.* Port Moresby: Bureau of Statistics.

Cocoa Board of Papua New Guinea, 1996. *Cocoa Statistics of Papua New Guinea.* Madang: Cocoa Board.

Coffee Industry Corporation, 1996. *Industry Affairs Division Coffee Report No. 37.* Goroka: PNG CIC.

Cowen, M. P., 1982. 'The British state and agrarian accumulation in Kenya', in M. Fransmann, ed., *Industry and Accumulation in Africa.* London: Heinemann, pp. 142-169.

Cowen, M. P., 1983. 'The commercialisation of food production in Kenya after 1945', in R. Rotberg, ed., *Imperialism, Colonialism and Hunger: East and Central Africa.* Lexington: D. C. Heath, pp. 199-224.

Cowen, M. P., and MacWilliam, S., 1996. *Indigenous Capital in Kenya: The 'Indian' dimension of debate.* Interkont Books 8. Helsinki: Institute of Development Studies, University of Helsinki.

Cowen, M. P., and Shenton, R., 1996. *Doctrines of Development.* London: Routledge.

Donaldson, M., and Good, K., 1988. *Articulated Agricultural Development: Traditional and Capitalist Agricultures in Papua New Guinea.* Aldershot: Avebury.

Epstein, T. S., 1968. *Capitalism, Primitive and Modern: Some Aspects of Tolai Economic Growth.* East Lansing, Michigan: Michigan State University Press.

Fitzpatrick, P., 1980. *Law and State in Papua New Guinea.* London: Academic Press.

Gerritsen, R., 1985. 'The romance of price elasticities of supply: the case of Milne Bay Copra', *Yagl-Ambu,* 12(4):29-42.

Hughes, I., 1978. 'Good money and bad: inflation and devaluation in the colonial process', *Mankind,* 11(3):308-318.

Hulme, D., 1983. 'Credit, land registration and development: implications of the lease-leaseback scheme', *Melanesian Law Journal,* 11:91-98.

Jolly, L., Beck, A., and Bodman, P. M., 1990. *Commodity Price Stabilisation in Papua New Guinea.* Canberra: AGPS.

Kay, G., 1975. *Development and Underdevelopment: A Marxist Analysis.* London: Macmillan.

Leys, C., 1994. 'Confronting the African tragedy', *New Left Review* 204:33-47.

MacWilliam, S., 1996. '"Just Like Working for the Dole": rural households, export crops, and state subsidies in Papua New Guinea', *The Journal of Peasant Studies* 23(4):40-78.

———, 1993. 'The politics of privatisation: the case of the Coffee Industry Corporation in Papua New Guinea', *Australian Journal of Political Science* 28(3):481-498.

———, 1991. 'Smallholder production, the state and land tenure', in P. Larmour, ed., *Customary Land Tenure: Registration and Decentralisation in Papua New Guinea.* IASER Monograph 29, pp. 9-32.

———, 1990. 'The politics of an agricultural disease in Papua New Guinea', *Journal of Contemporary Asia,* 20(3):291-311.

————, 1988. 'Smallholdings, land law and the politics of land tenure in Papua New Guinea', *The Journal of Peasant Studies*, 16(1):77–109.

————, 1986. 'International capital, indigenous accumulation and the state in Papua New Guinea: the case of the Development Bank', *Capital and Class*, 29:150–181.

————, 1985. 'Against the compatibility thesis: forms of production in Papua New Guinea', *Yagl-Ambu*, 12(4):4–28.

MacWilliam, S., Desaubin, F., and Timms, W., 1995. *Domestic Food Production and Political Conflict in Kenya*. Monograph No. 10. Nedlands: Indian Ocean Centre for Peace Studies, University of Western Australia.

Manning, M., 1994. 'Private sector rural employment', in UNDP *Papers and Proceedings of the National Employment Summit*. Port Moresby: UNDP, pp. 136–145.

Marx, K., 1976. *Capital*. Harmondsworth, Middlesex: Penguin.

Millett, J., 1993. 'The unemployment problem', in J. Millett, ed., *Seminar on Employment, Agriculture and Industrialisation*. Port Moresby: INA/NRI, pp. 9–32.

National Statistical Office, 1990a. *Rural Industries 1986*. Port Moresby: NSO.

National Statistical Office, 1990b. *Rural Industries 1988 (preliminary)*. Port Moresby: NSO.

Overfield, D., 1991. *Coffee Price Stabilization: Review and Policy Proposals*. Coffee Discussion Paper No. 5. Goroka: Coffee Industry Board.

Overfield, D., Smith, D., Kufinale, K., and Kuimbakul, T., 1993. 'Employment levels in the Papua New Guinea coffee industry and the non-potential of downstream processing', in J. Millett, ed., *Seminar on Employment, Agriculture and Industrialisation*. Port Moresby: INA/NRI, pp. 33–46.

Phillips, A., 1989. *The Enigma of Colonialism: British Policy in West Africa*. London: James Currey.

Rural Development Bank of Papua New Guinea, 1994. *1994 Annual Report and Financial Statements*. Waigani: Rural Development Bank of PNG.

Shaw, B., 1985. *Agriculture in the Papua New Guinea Economy*. Discussion Paper No. 20. Port Moresby: Institute of National Affairs.

Simmons, R., 1993. 'Competitiveness in the agriculture sector', in J. Millett, ed., *Seminar on Employment, Agriculture and Industrialisation 14–15 July 1993*. Port Moresby: Institute of National Affairs/National Research Institute, pp. 85–109.

Thompson, H. M., 1986. 'Subsistence agriculture in Papua New Guinea', *Journal of Rural Studies*, 2(3):233–243.

Thompson, H. M., 1991. 'Economic theory and economic development in Papua New Guinea', *Journal of Contemporary Asia*, 21(1):54–67.

Thompson, H. M., and MacWilliam, S., 1992. *The Political Economy of Papua New Guinea*. Manila: JCA Publishers.

Turner, M., 1990. *Papua New Guinea: The Challenge of Independence*. Ringwood, Victoria: Penguin.

United Nations Development Program, 1994. *Papers and Proceedings of the National Employment Summit*. Port Moresby: UNDP.

Fred L. Olson and Tim T. Kan

THE FISHERY RESOURCES OF PAPUA NEW GUINEA

𝒫APUA NEW GUINEA (PNG) has a wide variety of fishery resources. They range from native freshwater and coastal species to pelagic species within its 200-mile Declared Fisheries Zone (DFZ), from introduced species to those in productive waters that can support aquacultural enterprises. (See Perry 1985 for the location of some of these resources.) Some resources are fully exploited, while others remain only a possibility for development.

In addition to its substantial freshwater habitats, including the Fly River, Lake Murray, the Sepik River, and its many lakes, PNG has two million square kilometers within its DFZ. These waters have various resources that are essential for the people to sustain life and become valuable to the economy of PNG when used for domestic and/or export markets.

Natural stocks must be managed when they become overexploited. Stocks not yet fully exploited but with a potential domestic or export market must be developed to contribute to the PNG economy. In some cases, there are opportunities for aquaculture production.

Fish and fishing have been important to the people of PNG for a long time, as indicated by some of the legends that have been passed down (for example, see Anonymous 1986a, 1987; Asong 1986.) It is surprising that many legends from *taim bipo* (time before) have fish or fishing as their subject. As is common with other PNG legends, the fish usually have human qualities and often give advice to the hero or heroine of the legend. However, as pointed out by Pernetta and Hill (1983), fishing activities are undertaken for the dietary necessity much more than simply for pleasure as suggested by some anthropological points of view.

That fish have become an important part of the diet is shown by the large quantity of fish imported annually into PNG (see table 1). In 1986, total fishery imports amounted to about K20 million compared with fishery exports of K10 million. Consumption of canned fish is promoted by food advertisements in Port Moresby newspapers, which usually list special prices on canned fish, particularly mackerel. Papua

Table 1

Papua New Guinea imports and exports of fish and fishery products; quantity and value, 1976–1986.

Year	Value			Quantity		
	Imports		Exports	Imports		Exports
	Total	Canned Mackerels	Total	Total	Canned Mackerels	Total
	US $ thousand dollars			Metric tons		
1976	10,755	9,523	11,484	22,548	21,592	20,092
1977	11,700	11,700	25,494	12,000	12,000	24,976
1978	15,910	15,910	33,268	17,000	17,000	46,698
1979	19,300	19,300	29,800	27,908	27,908	28,485
1980	27,206	24,470	45,288	29,140	26,740	31,444
1981	34,238	32,675	41,428	33,262	31,855	31,207
1982	28,795	26,303	10,714	27,151	24,822	3,811
1983	22,620	22,620	10,882	23,320	23,320	1,712
1984	21,539	19,994	8,639	24,859	22,814	2,844
1985	23,940	21,070	13,875	27,052	23,466	9,882
1986	21,350	17,740	10,784	NA	18,876	NA

Source: FAO, 1986. Yearbook. Fishery Statistics, Commodities, 63: Tables A-6 and J-20.

New Guinea was the world's largest importer of canned mackerel, with 28 percent of the quantity (18,876 metric tons) and 16 percent of the value (US$17,740,000) of the world exports, and 10 percent of world production in 1986 (see table 1). In 1990, the imports of canned mackerel had jumped to about 35,000 metric tons (Agroder 1991). This level may amount to 10 kg of canned mackerel per person in PNG per year. Massive influx of this single import item is creating a *tinpis*[1] phenomenon in PNG (Kan, *et al.* 1995); it appears to have already been a major socioeconomic constraint to the planning and development of fisheries and aquaculture (Kan 1996) in PNG as in several other developing countries in the southeastern Asia region (Lawson 1978).

Before European contact, fishing activity in PNG was mostly for subsistence. This is still an important fishing activity for those living along the coasts or on the lakes and rivers, but commercial fishing activity is gaining (see table 2). Now fishers living in or near coastal villages and cities provide fish for producer markets shopped by homemakers, such as Koki Market in Port Moresby (Lock 1986).

RESOURCES

In the Gulf of Papua, three shellfish resources appear to be fully utilized: spiny lobster, *Panulirus ornatus*; banana prawn, *Penaeus merguiensis*; and giant tiger prawn, *P. monodon*. Spiny lobsters, from a domestic diving fishery, are largely exported to the southeastern Asia countries and the United States. The prawns, from an industrial trawl fishery, are chiefly exported to Japan. Barramundi (giant sea perch), *Lates calcarifer*, a 'good eating' catadromous fish that spawns in the estuaries of the Gulf and matures in fresh water, may by fully utilized by commercial and sports fishers. While natural stocks might be fully exploited, barramundi production could be increased by new aquacultural techniques recently developed in Australia and Thailand (see Copland and Grey 1987). As an example of promotion of a superior product, Air Niugini serves barramundi on its international flights. Other important Papuan Gulf resources are certain shells, sharks, mackerels, and turtles (see Haines *et al.* 1986).

---

[1] *Tinpis* is the PNG Pidgin English word for any processed and merchandised fish, especially canned mackerel.

Table 2
Nominal catches of fish, crustaceans, molluscs, etc., in Papua New Guinea, by
selected species, 1970–1986.

Year	Total	Tuna	Prawns	Barra-mundi	Other
			Metric tons		
1970	15,700	NA	NA	NA	NA
1971	30,700	NA	NA	NA	NA
1972	27,200	NA	NA	NA	NA
1973	45,400	NA	NA	NA	NA
1974	49,963	41,664	508	379	7,412
1975	34,938	17,380	329	201	17,028
1976	50,640	32,941	556	222	16,921
1977	26,648	23,168	538	210	2,732
1978	52,199	48,871	675	170	2,483
1979	29,789	26,857	720	207	2,005
1980	37,468	33,997	756	221	2,494
1981	26,975	24,029	594	308	2,044
1982	1,469	0	507	347	615
1983	1,395	0	732	219	444
1984	6,047	2,755	602	169	2,521
1985	6,100	2,750	610	170	2,570
1986	6,250	2,800	650	200	2,600

Source: FAO, 1986. Yearbook. Fishery Statistics, Catches and Landings, 62: Tables A-2 and E-6.

In contrast, the mangrove crab *(Scylla serrata),* yabbies *(Cherax* spp.), and the giant freshwater prawn *(Macrobranchium rosenbergii)* are widespread through all coastal areas of the Gulf of Papua and as yet do not appear to be fully exploited.

The giant clam resource *(Tridacna derasa* and probably *T. gigas)* found on the coral reef is also fully exploited. Its production can be increased only through aquacultural techniques, some of which are being developed by the University of Papua New Guinea, the International Center for Living Aquatic Resource Management in the Solomon Islands, and the Micronesian Mariculture Demonstration Center in Palau.

About half of the six or more species of bêche-de-mer (dried sea cucumber, *Holothuria* spp.), native to PNG, have an excellent export market among the Chinese populations of Singapore, Taiwan, and Hong Kong. Bêche-de-mer is harvested on the seabed either by diving, or from the surface by dropping a weighted spear. Local stocks of the more valuable species are in urgent need of management because these animals are very sedentary (Shelley 1986). Fortunately, the government has recently taken severe measures of moratorium in harvesting in order to avoid overexploitation of these stocks.

Many schools of skipjack *(Katsuwonus pelamis)* and yellowfin tuna *(Thunnus albacores)* migrate throughout the surface waters of PNG's 200-mile fisheries zone. Certain quantities of bigeye tuna *(Thunnus obesus)* and albacore *(Thunnus alalunga)* may also be passing through. A large export market exists in Japan, southeast Asia, and North America for these tuna resources, which are barely utilized by PNG fishers. Canned tuna is expensive in PNG, compared to mackerel, and makes up only a small part of the shelf space devoted to fish in supermarkets. Tuna resources have been utilized, under agreements or treaties, by the distant-water fleets of the United States, Taiwan, South Korea, Philippines, and other countries (Doulman 1987). These agreements and treaties require the fleets to pay fees and exchange data, and in most cases may also provide for onboard inspection, employment, landings, and provisioning from PNG. Currently, as many as 250 foreign fishing and supporting vessels are licensed to operate in the PNG waters by paying total access fees of about US$20 million a year. Although all of these distant-water fleets are harvesting tuna at a rate of up to 350,000 metric tons per year in PNG waters, nonetheless, these stocks do not appear to have reached their maximum sustainable yield level yet.

Other fishery resources include cyprinids, catfish *(Aridae)*, tarpons *(Elopidae)*, mullets *(Mugilidae)*, gudgeons *(Eleotridae)*, eels *(Anguillidae)*, jacks *(Carangidae)*, drums *(Sciaenidae)*, snappers *(Lutjanus* spp.), groupers *(Epinephelus* spp.) parrotfish *(Scaridae)*, emperors *(Lethrinidae)*, wrasses *(Labridae)*, unique aquarium species, and sharks *(Pristidae, Carcharhinidae,* and *Lamnidae)*. Export markets vary greatly between size and species: for sharks, mainly Great Britain but some in Europe; aquarium species, drums, snappers, and groupers, mainly southeast Asia and America; and for elvers, mainly Japan and Taiwan, where they are used for eel culture. As early as 1924 the pinctada and the trochus shells were also commercial fishery enterprises (see Gash and Whittaker 1975).

There appears to be only a limited variety of commercially useful freshwater fishery stocks in PNG. As a result, tilapia, an algae-feeding cichlid *(Oreochromis mossambicus)* first introduced in the Sepik River in 1954, has spread rapidly. Other introduced species that are used for aquaculture and have dispersed include rainbow trout *(Salmo oairdneri)* and carp *(Cyprinus carpio)* (Kan 1987; West and Glucksman 1976).

MANAGEMENT

Valuable natural, or common property, fishery resources quickly become overfished and therefore require management. Since PNG has established its 200-mile DFZ, it now has the potential for complete management control of its fishery resources, except for those migratory species, such as tuna, and those stocks it shares with neighboring countries. In the case of the spiny lobster and prawns in the Gulf of Papua, PNG has a treaty with Australia providing for the management of these and other shared resources. Similar treaties must be negotiated with Indonesia and the Solomon Islands to cover fishery resources shared with them.

At some point in the future, yellowfin and bigeye tunas, migrating through PNG waters, may be overfished and need to be managed. Establishing that management will now be easy. A regional tuna management authority must be created to have management jurisdiction over the entire migratory range of these transboundary tunas (Munro 1987). This range includes the 200-mile zones of several countries and an area outside of the 200-mile zone of any one country. Since PNG would benefit from a strong regional tuna management authority, it needs to take leadership in establishing that authority. What may be even more difficult is that all countries involved, PNG and the others, must transfer their sovereignty over tuna management to the new tuna management authority.

A good start in the direction of a regional tuna management authority has been made by the South Pacific Forum Fisheries Agency (FFA) which is headquartered in Honiara, the Solomon Islands. This agency is collecting data and conducting research on the tuna economics of the region in order to monitor development of tuna fishing and need for management. It has also been coordinating to deal with a number of issues involving both intra- and extraregional fishing nations, with a recent success, among others (Wright 1993), of two management agreements: Palau Arrangement 1993 and Federated States of Micronesia (FSM) Arrangement 1994. At the moment it does not appear that skipjack tuna and albacore will be requiring management in the near future. But the FFA lacks management authority at this time because its member countries have not given it that authority.

Political and industry leaders must come to a consensus on the purposes, i.e., deciding who benefits and by how much, if any, from schemes to manage domestic resources, or regional transboundary tunas. Once the purposes have been identified, then the fisheries management institutions can be created to carry out the established fisheries management policy.

Regardless of the management scheme selected, domestic PNG or regional, some of the essential elements of any regime would be:

1.   The capability to police and monitor the entire management area;
2.   The collection and analysis of data and information to monitor the resources, and to determine how the management objectives and purposes are being achieved; and
3.   A cash flow or source of financing to accomplish these essentials.

DEVELOPMENT

Development is possible whenever potential markets exist for products that would produce a profit from existing resources with unused but existing technology. By this definition, there are several PNG fishery resources that could be used to support development. But before organized or planned development takes place, PNG needs to define its general development goals:

1.   Can there be development at the expense of subsistence fishers? (Must developers support subsistence fishers who are affected?)
2.   Who should benefit from development? (Can increased employment and value added in a region or port be gained at the expense of decreased or ceased national revenues from export taxes?)

Only when PNG has clarified its development goals can fisheries development take place within that framework (see Wright 1983).

In another dimension, PNG needs to determine how much infrastructure is necessary to provide support for fisheries development, including roads, water and sewage, electricity, training, education, extension activities, exploratory fishing to define available stocks and the like.

Tuna is a resource that appears to have the potential for one of the largest increases in the fishery sector in PNG employment, export earnings, and value added (Doulman 1987). At the present time, export earnings and value added in the tuna fishery in PNG are largely limited to fees paid by foreign fleets. Papua New Guinea tuna development could include at least three separate phases: harvesting, processing, and enhancing production in harvesting by building or licensing more fishing fleets. Issues involved in developing the tuna industry include:

1. The economies of scale in harvesting and processing, to help determine how large vessels and processing facilities should be, and in turn how many and where such facilities should be located;
2. Should the export tax on fishery products be refunded or, as an alternative, exempted? and
3. Should an import tax and/or excise tax on items necessary in the production of exported fishery products be refunded if necessary to initiated PNG tuna development?

Other natural stocks that seem to have a potential for development include crabs, bêche-de-mer, snappers, groupers, and unique aquarium fish. An interesting development issue presents itself with unique aquarium fish. A high-priced market exists for these fish because they are rare. Once these unique fish become available outside PNG, they could be bred and reproduced in large quantities which would then bring down their prices. If PNG is to benefit from exporting unique aquarium fish, it must be prepared to export large quantities during the first three years. Only by doing so can the country benefit from the high initial prices and retain the profits rather than enrich a foreign producer.

In the aquaculture area, development potential exists with trout, carp, tilapia, barramundi, prawns, and the giant clam. Because of its rich fauna and generally unspoiled environment, PNG is promising to become a supply center of the seed and the brood stock for overseas aquafarms, for instance in Hong Kong and Taiwan (Kan 1986).

Papua New Guinea is rich in fishery resources. Through the wise use of management and development strategies (see Anonymous 1986b), its fishery resources can contribute to the increase of employment, export earnings, and value added for the entire economy. Unfortunately, development and allocation of these resources have been hampered by the unduly political interference and corruption as well as a lack of policy, coordination, judgment, and management skills, especially in economics and marketing (Omeri 1996). Papua New Guinea has a fishery sector which, in terms of contribution to the nation's employment, revenue, and exports value, has been disappointing and barely significant in comparison to the mining and forestry industries and cash agriculture (see table 3). For the eleven-year period from 1976, one year after PNG's independence, annual fishery export value fluctuated between about US$9 million (1984) and US$50 million (1980) with an average of only US$22 million. From 1981 to 1986, annual total fisheries export valued at an average of only US$16 million while, ironically, that of the canned mackerel import valued at US$23.4 million.

ADMINISTRATION

Management and development of the fishery resources in PNG are administered in a shared manner by national and provincial governments. However, national government's interest comes first in case there is a conflict between the two levels of government. Major legislation in resource use are the Fisheries Act, the Continental Shelf (Living Natural Resources) (National Seas) Act, and the Tuna Resources Management Act. Major recent international treaties or agreements here include the multilateral one on tunas with the United States, and the bilateral ones with Australia for Torres Strait resources and with Korea, Philippines, and Taiwan, respectively, again on tunas. Coastal, including subsistence, fisheries development activities are centered around two related national government programs: the Coastal Fisheries Development Plan and the International Fund for Aquacultural Development (IFAD)–assisted Artisanal Fisheries Development Project.

Until 1986, national day-to-day and long-term responsibilities for fisheries management and development were undertaken by the Fisheries Division within the Department of Primary Industry. In late 1986,

Table 3
Value of exports from Papua New Guinea 1980–1984.

Item	1980	1981	1982	1983	1984
	US$ million				
Minerals	500.0	441.9	404.8	425.3	347.9
Coffee	183.8	75.7	104.3	108.0	117.3
Cocoa	72.1	50.1	42.6	47.2	71.0
Forestry products	71.0	64.5	82.7	62.4	86.7
Copra products	38.0	28.2	17.3	27.4	52.0
Palm oil	25.7	18.4	16.2	22.8	41.8
Fisheries products	52.5	41.5	11.3	10.9	9.3
Other exports	129.2	111.6	85.0	79.6	138.2
TOTAL	1, 072.3	831.9	764.3	783.6	864.2

Source: Doulman and Kuk (1986) based on data from Papua New Guinea Bureau of Statistics, Port Moresby.

the government upgraded the Fisheries Division to a higher level: Department of Fisheries and Marine Resources (DFMR). In 1995, the DFMR was replaced by the National Fisheries Authority (NFA), which consists of three Divisions: Fisheries Management and Industry support, Licensing, Surveillance and Enforcement, and Planning and Corporate Services. An important mission of NFA is giving support to the fishing industry to achieve the policy of domestication of the tuna fishing industry announced by the PNG government in 1994.

In terms of trophic ecology, the PNG seas are highly productive. This fact, when properly recognised and translated, should derive the needed capital and technology domestically and externally for resource use without difficulty. The single most serious constraint to fisheries management and allocation, therefore, is a general lack of skillful manpower at various levels. Only a few PNG decision makers seem to really understand the fishery's potential contribution to national nutrition and to the economy.

THE FUTURE

In terms of fishery management and development, the only condition which is comfortably possessed by PNG is the huge size of the resources. On the other hand, constraints to a domestically based fishing industry are omnipresent, and range from capital to technology, manpower, and policy (Omeri 1996). However, there are positive signs that the government is now determined to wisely manage and develop the fisheries sector. These include:

1. Replacing the 20-year-old Fisheries Act of 1974 with the Fisheries Act of 1994 and the Fisheries Regulation of 1995 to address the rapid and profound legal, environmental, technological, and socioeconomic changes in regional and global fisheries in recent years;
2. Replacing the bureaucratic DFMR with the task-oriented NFA in 1995 to manage the nation's resources as well as to develop the country-based fishing and aquacultural industries;
3. Vigorously implementing through NFA the policy, proclaimed in 1994, of domesticating the tuna fishing industry; and
4. Offering tax concessions, including in particular the abolishing of export tax on fishery products from 1997 in order to stimulate growth of the fisheries sector.

Therefore, it seems that the stage for a bright future for the growth of PNG fisheries has been set for the dedicated and competent players to perform towards the role 'to ensure that PNG's fisheries and living aquatic resources are used within the limits of sustainable yields and managed in a manner that maximizes the long-term social, economic and environmental benefits to PNG and its people.'[2]

In 1986, PNG determined to develop its tuna fisheries and other marine living resources (Kan and Hill 1988) that are extremely rich in size and variety and readily retrievable as well as marketable worldwide (Philipson 1989). Ironically, this tuna-rich country remains to be, if not the largest importer, one of the largest importers of canned mackerel! Last but not least, it will indeed be beneficial for the country to embark on a simple and delightful initiative in its fishery development in pro-

---

[2] An excerpt from the mission statement of the National Fisheries Authority, based on the PNG National Executive Council Decision No. 157/20 of 22 August 1990.

moting nationwide the canned tuna rather than mackerel consumption and encouraging fresh rather than canned fish and shellfish consumption via intensive programs of fisheries extension such as the distribution of seafood recipes and the demonstration of seafood cooking skills.

REFERENCES

Agrodev (Preparer). 1991. *Fisheries and Coastal Resources Management and Development Project—Papua New Guinea: Midterm Report Prepared for the Government of Papua New Guinea, Port Moresby, and the Asian Development Bank, Manila.* Agrodev Can., Inc.

Anonymous, 1986a. 'The fish at Riwo—a legend from Madang Province', in *Paradise Tales*, Robert Brown & Associates Pty. Ltd. in association with Air Niugini, p. 25.

——, 1986b. *Strategy for Fisheries Management and Development.* Food and Agriculture Organization of the United Nations.

——, 1987. 'Eating fish for the first time in Ambunti'. *New Nation,* July.

Asong, J., 1986. 'How tuna fish came to be—a legend from Siassi Islands, Morobe Province', in *Paradise Tales*, Robert Brown & Associates Pty. Ltd. in association with Air Niugini, p.70.

Copland, J. W., and D. L. Grey, eds., 1987. *Management of Wild and Cultured Sea Bass/Barramundi* (Lates calcarifer), Australian Centre for International Agricultural Research Proceedings No. 20.

Doulman, D. J., 1987. 'Licensing distant-water tuna fleets in Papua New Guinea'. *Marine Policy,* January:16–28.

——, and R. Kuk, 1986. *Papua New Guinea: Fisheries and Their Administration*, East-West Centre PIDP Report.

Gash, N., and J. Whittaker, 1975. *A Pictorial History of New Guinea.* Sydney: The Jacaranda Press.

Haines, A. K., G. C. Williams, and D. Coats, eds., 1986. *Torres Strait Fisheries Seminar.* Canberra: Australian Government Publishing Service.

Kan, T. T., 1986. 'The state of aquaculture in Papua New Guinea', in *Development and Management of Tropical Living Aquatic Resources*, Penerbit University Pertanian Malaysia, pp. 121–125.

——, 1987. 'P.N.G. inland fisheries', in *Fisheries and Marine Resources in the South Pacific*, Occasional Papers No. 13 of Kagoshima University Research Center for the South Pacific, pp. 12–19.

——, J. B. Aitsi, J. E. Kasu, T. Matsuoka, and H. L. Nagaleta, 1995. 'Temporal changes in a tropical nekton assemblage and performance of a prawn selective gear', *Marine Fisheries Review*, 57(3–4):21–34.

——, and L. Hill, 1988. 'Tertiary education in fisheries and marine bioresources in the South Pacific island region', in S. Chang, K. Chan, and N. Y. S. Woo, eds., *Recent Advances in Biotechnology and Applied Biology.* Hong Kong: The Chinese University of Hong Kong Press, pp. 103–114.

Lawson, R. M., 1978. 'Incompatibilities and conflicts in fisheries planning in Southeast Asia', *Southeastern Asia J. Soc. Sci.*, 6:115–130.

Munro, G. R., 1987. 'The management of shared fishery resources under extended jurisdiction', *Marine Resource Economics*, 3(4):271–296.

Omeri, N., 1996. 'Constraints to domestic fishing industry', *P.N.G. National Fisheries Authority Newsletter*, 2(1):17–18.

Pernetta, J., and L. Hill, 1983. 'A review of marine resource use in coastal Papua', *J. de la Société des Océanistes*, 37:175–191.

Perry, K. R., 1985. 'Fishing', in *Papua New Guinea—A Nation in Transition.* Sydney: Robert Brown & Associates Pty. Ltd. in conjunction with the University of Papua New Guinea, pp. 58–59.

Philipson, P. W., 1989. *The Marketing of Marine Products from the South Pacific.* [Suva, Fiji]: Institute of Pacific Studies of the University of the South Pacific.

Shelly, C. C., 1986. 'The potential for re-introduction of a beche-de-mer fishery in Torres Strait', in A. K. Haines, G. C. Williams, and D. Coates, eds., *Torres Strait Fisheries Seminar*, Australian Government Publishing Service, pp. 140–150.

West, G. J., and J. Glucksman, 1976. 'Introduction and distribution of exotic fish in Papua New Guinea', *P.N.G. Agri. J.*, 27(1&2):19–48.

Wright, A., 1983. 'Marine resource use in Papua New Guinea: Can traditional concepts and contemporary development be integrated?' in UNESCO, ed., *The Traditional Knowledge and Management of Coastal Systems in Asia and the Pacific.* Jakarta: United Nations Educational Scientific and Cultural Organization Regional Office for Southeast Asia Proceedings, pp. 81–99.

Wright, A., 1993. 'Trends in the development of western Pacific tuna fisheries', in H. de Soram and N. Krishnasamy, eds., *Tuna '93—Bangkok.* Kuala Lumpur: INFOFISH, pp. 67–74.

Colin Filer

THE MELANESIAN WAY OF MENACING THE MINING INDUSTRY

$\mathcal{J}$N JUNE 1996 Broken Hill Proprietary Ltd., operators of the Ok Tedi mine in Papua New Guinea, finally reached an out-of-court settlement with Slater and Gordon, the Melbourne law firm which represented the claims of various landowning communities living downstream of the mine whose subsistence resources had been extensively damaged by the discharge of waste material into their river system for more than a decade. Under the terms of the settlement, the mining company agreed to fund a substantial compensation package, to pay the legal costs of their opponents, and to find new ways of mitigating the physical impact of the waste material. The settlement has been widely regarded as a victory for what one commentator described as 'a global alliance of landowners, ecological activists, anthropologists and lawyers [who had] mounted a worldwide campaign to stop the mine from polluting the Ok Tedi and Fly Rivers' (Kirsch 1996:14).

This was only the second episode in the recent history of the local mining industry to receive substantial publicity outside of Papua New Guinea, the first being the closure of the Bougainville copper mine by militant landowners and local secessionists in 1989. The amount of publicity which it received was largely due to the fact that it could be readily portrayed and digested as a classic David-and-Goliath struggle between downtrodden indigenous peoples and monstrous multinational companies. Indeed, this was one of the reasons why Slater and Gordon chose to present their case in an Australian court and one of the reasons why one of the company's senior executives was forced to make the public admission, some time before the settlement was reached, that 'BHP had failed in the management of its public position over the Ok Tedi issue and that the company could only blame itself for its failure' (*Post-Courier* 29 September 1995). But one of the reasons why the company had misjudged its public posture, and thus become an easy target for the global green alliance ranged against it, was because it had been locked into a national policy process, inside Papua New Guinea, where the waters are normally as muddy as those of the Ok Tedi River.

The most determined opposition to the green alliance did not come from the company's Australian executives, but from members of Papua New Guinea's own national elite or 'ruling class' who resented the threat to their own conception of national sovereignty and economic priorities. In August 1992, when the German Greens were already persuading the German shareholders to sell their own stake in the Ok Tedi project, the Minerals and Energy Secretary maintained that:

> The State's approach has been to put its cards on the table and formally agree to a certain amount of environmental damage as being acceptable. The government is in control of the situation and I very much resent the attempted interference by outsiders who do not have the knowledge or background information to understand. If these environmental fanatics were able to have a free hand in PNG, they could stir up the mining area and river villages into believing all manner of supposed grievances, recruit the odd politician who might see some short term selfish gain, and destabilise the whole situation. (*Post-Courier* 10 August 1992)

In May 1994, when Slater and Gordon explained their decision to sue BHP in the Victorian Supreme Court by claiming that the company had 'made all the relevant decisions, in particular the environment decisions, about the mine at all times', and therefore expected the action to receive the support of the PNG government, the leader of PNG's parliamentary opposition described it as the work of 'foreign spies, crooks and carpetbaggers' (*Post-Courier* 4–5 May 1994). And in September 1995, when an Australian philosopher accused BHP of making 'fundamental ethical errors', the company's most senior Papua New Guinean manager was said to have replied as follows:

> So people who have never seen my country say they believe that we do not have the right to progress. Australians still feel they can tell us

what to do. They want us to live in a museum, to make countries like ours a zoo for them to visit the past. What people on the river want is to get rid of the mosquitoes from the marshes, to have houses that don't need rebuilding every three months, they want to live longer. These are things that come with progress. (Thomas 1995)

The policy process surrounding the Ok Tedi project was thus seen to exemplify, in an especially acute form, the recurrent argument between representatives of developed and developing countries on all manner of 'environmental' issues. But the intensity of this particular dispute owed as much or more to the 'moral economy' of the mining industry in the colonial and postcolonial relationship between Australia and Papua New Guinea as it did to the actual physical impact of this particular mine. While Australia and Papua New Guinea both have mineral-dependent economies, and Papua New Guinea is still dependent on Australian economic support, the national elite of Papua New Guinea might be forgiven for wondering why they should also be expected to buy into the worldview which one journalist ascribed to the 'chattering classes' of Australia—'that mining is, basically, a filthy rotten business' (Callick 1995).

Now what we seem to have discovered here is not the Melanesian way of menacing the mining industry, but a form of national resistance to the Western way of doing so. BHP's Australian executives made the mistake of thinking that they could profit from, or hide behind, this form of national resistance, while their Western opponents were able to paint the Papua New Guinean national elite as pawns and clients of the mining company, thus permitting the rest of the national population to be portrayed as the natural allies and beneficiaries of the struggle to clean up the company's act.

I do not propose in this chapter to discuss the actual history and relative merits of the various ways of dealing with the physical impact of large-scale mining operations on the natural environment, for the simple reason that I am not qualified to assess either the economic or biological costs and benefits of such measures. My concern is with the structure of the policy process which embraces such issues, and especially with what I take to be a disjunction between the local, national, and international dimensions of this structure. The central question at stake in this multiple process of debate concerns the relationship between 'compensation', 'development', and 'governance' within the nation state of Papua New Guinea and—to some extent—the wider Melanesian 'culture area' with which its people commonly identify themselves. In Papua New Guinea's case, this relationship is constructed around a single problematic fact—that 'customary landowners' own nearly all the land on which 'resource development' takes place, and yet the state claims ownership of nearly all the mineral resources which that land contains in order to maintain its right to set the terms of that development.

If I might be allowed to play the devil's advocate, my argument would be that the Melanesian way of menacing the mining industry has not so far borne much resemblance to the grand struggle of indigenous peoples which takes place in the 'collective conscience' of coffee shop politicians in Melbourne, London, or New York. Of course, Melanesian stakeholders can and do sometimes make appeal to this collective conscience or form alliances with First World activists in order to pursue their own claims against the multinational mining companies. But the indigenous people of Papua New Guinea make life unusually difficult for multinational mining companies, not because they share philosophical assumptions or oppositional strategies which merit the special sympathy or applause of Western environmentalists, but because of the characteristic diversity and instability of political relationships between Melanesian persons, institutions, and communities which constitute their national policy process.

THE RECENT HISTORY OF MINERAL RESOURCE DEVELOPMENT

Although the history of the mining industry in Papua New Guinea reaches back to the beginnings of the colonial period, a new beginning was made with the discovery of the Panguna copper deposit on the island of Bougainville in 1964. In the year preceding the formal declaration of national independence in September 1975, the first Somare government successfully concluded its renegotiation of the 1967 Bougainville Copper Agreement and then caused Kennecott to abandon the Ok Tedi prospect by insisting that it be developed on the basis of the same 'new deal'. In 1981, six years after independence, when the Chan government delivered a new version of the new deal with the official birth of Ok Tedi Mining Limited, it simultaneously failed or refused to undertake the seven-year review which was anticipated in the Bougainville Agreement of 1974, despite the loud noise of protest emanating from North Solomons Province. From the Bougainvillean (or North Solomons) point of view, one can certainly say that what began in 1964 was only redirected or diverted by the deals of 1974 and

1981, and was more obviously, physically terminated by the outbreak of the Bougainville rebellion in November 1988 and the shutdown of Bougainville Copper Limited's mining operations in May the following year. But even in the wider national perspective, it can be said that these calamitous events inaugurated another new phase in the economic and political history of mineral resource development.

In 1988, PNG's mineral exports (gold, silver, and copper) were valued at K861.5 million (equivalent to US$1,042.4 million), which represented 70.5 percent of domestic exports and 27.2 percent of Gross Domestic Product. The bulk of this output came from the two major mines at Panguna and Ok Tedi. In 1988 the national government's Mineral Resources Stabilisation Fund collected K91.8 million from the mining industry, nearly all of which came from BCL in the shape of corporate income tax, dividend withholding tax, and the dividends paid on the government's own equity stake in that company. These receipts alone represented 13.9 percent of the government's nongrant revenues, but a variety of other taxes levied on BCL and OTML would probably have raised at least another K40 million, thus making the mining industry responsible for something between one fifth and one quarter of all nongrant revenues.[1]

Despite the twelve-year gap between the start of mining operations at Panguna (1972) and Ok Tedi (1984), both these mineral deposits were initially discovered by a single burst of exploration in the 1960s, which in turn was prompted and encouraged by the colonial administration, aided and abetted by the World Bank, as one of several ways to dig the economic foundations of an independent nation state. The next main burst of mineral prospecting did not occur until the mid-1980s, and it was this new wave of exploration which did so much damage to the building which had been erected on those earlier foundations, for the institutional capacities of the state have been no match for the proliferating struggle between all sorts of stakeholders over the distribution of real and imaginary mineral revenues. In other words, if it is true to say that the PNG mining industry has entered a new phase of development (or underdevelopment) since 1988, then it is not because there has been any major transformation in the technical, economic, and occupational

---

[1] These figures are all taken from the Bank of Papua New Guinea's Quarterly Economic Bulletin. Confusion sometimes arises because the mining companies record their payments to government as being made in the year before the government records its receipt of them. Government records show that BCL contributed substantially more to nongrant revenues in 1989—the year in which it ceased operations—than it did in 1988.

structure of the industry itself, but because there have been more dramatic changes in its political surroundings. And these are all the more remarkable because so much attention had previously been paid to the formation and maintenance of 'national mineral policy' as one of the truly distinctive achievements of the postcolonial state (see Mikesell 1975; Jackson 1982; O'Faircheallaigh 1984; Pintz 1984).

From this point of view, the flurry of talks and thoughts which bore fruit in the Mining (Bougainville Copper Agreement) Act of 1974 and the Mining (Ok Tedi) Act of 1976 was the climax of a process of economic decolonisation which had already started when Bougainvilleans first took issue with the mining plans of CRA and the Australian administration. While the Bougainville question loomed large in the process of political decolonisation which passed through the deliberations of the Constitutional Planning Committee and the design of the Organic Law on Provincial Government, and while the Bougainville question was also a question of national economic policy, questions of national economic policy could not be settled by new constitutional arrangements. Nor were they. The architects of the new mineral policy were more interested in learning from the mistakes made by governments in other mineral-export economies, from Zambia to Australia, than from those made by the local colonial administration in dealing with the vagaries of Bougainvillean secessionism.

From their point of view, the 1967 Bougainville Copper Agreement was not the detestable tombstone of colonial mineral policy, but an imperfect solution to the problem of achieving the best of all possible deals between a developing national economy and an industry dominated by large foreign companies. But their own solution, like the one which it displaced, was based on the assumption that the nation's interests would have to be defined and guaranteed by certain central bureaucratic institutions of the state engaged in a continuous relationship of regulation and negotiation with their foreign capitalist counterparts (see Garnaut and Clunies-Ross 1983). And this assumption was the cornerstone of a 'technocratic consensus' which, until fairly recently, allowed or enabled a central bureaucratic elite to secure general acceptance of its right to manage the development of the mining industry for the long-term benefit of the new nation.

The Bougainville rebellion was by no means the first sign of a decline in the force of this technocratic policy regime. In light of the recent episode which I described at the beginning of this chapter, we could date the beginning of this process to the night of 6 January 1984, when a catastrophic landslide permanently halted construction work on the Ok Ma tailings dam, thus ensuring that the Ok Tedi mining project would only proceed in defiance of the safeguards announced in its original environmental plan (see Jackson 1993). This was the first big scandal to afflict the local mining industry since independence, and its scale was magnified by rumours that the landslide was deliberately engineered to cut the construction costs of the project. Since that time the popular fear of physical pollution, especially water pollution, has continually combined with the idea that mining companies are by nature bound to operate in bad faith to create an undercurrent of public suspicion, and occasional whirlpools of public outrage, in which 'the wicked multinationals' have been construed, in customary terms, as king-size sorcerers consuming the vitality of hapless Melanesian villagers.

However, during the four years from 1982 to 1986, while the ups and downs of the Ok Tedi project produced occasional headlines or features in the local press, the local technocrats were quietly warming their hands on the 'exploration boom' which, in their own minds, symbolised the continuity and consistency of their efforts to attract foreign investment to the industry. The broader symbolic possibilities of this process only began to be revealed when, in October 1986, it produced a scandal of its own in the shape of the Placer Pacific share issue. Several 'leaders of the nation', most notably the Minister for Finance Sir Julius Chan, were accused of taking windfall profits from a 'share float' which the mining company had organised precisely (or ironically) with a view to giving Papua New Guineans a bigger stake, and thus attracting their political support, in the development of its gold prospects at Misima and Porgera. The Placer Pacific share issue was front-page news for more than two months—long enough to generate a news momentum which had a significant effect on the conduct of the 1987 national election campaign and induced a sort of 'mental mineral boom' in which the production and distribution of mineral resource rent became the subject of continual public debate.

The exploration boom has already produced a succession of new developments which arrived just in time to save the state from serious financial trouble following the closure of BCL's Panguna mine, but which have also provided fresh fuel for public debate over the distribution of the benefits. Placer Pacific secured a Special Mining Lease and Mining Development Contract for development of the Misima mine in Milne Bay Province in December 1987, and Misima Mines began production of gold and silver in June 1989. Placer also became the operating partner in the Porgera Joint Venture (PJV) whose gold mine in Enga Province was granted the necessary approvals in May 1989 and started production in August 1990. The Kutubu Joint Venture received its Petroleum Development Licence in December 1990, with Chevron as its operating partner, and this project started exporting oil in June 1992. The national government has taken a minority equity stake in all these ventures, just as it did in BCL and OTML.

In 1995, PNG's mineral exports were valued at K2,435.4 million (equivalent to US$1,837.5 million), which represented 71.6 percent of domestic exports. Crude oil exports from the Kutubu project accounted for roughly one third, gold for another third, and copper and silver together for the remaining third of this total export value. Exports from the Ok Tedi, Porgera, and Misima mines were worth about K916 million, K431 million, and K172 million respectively. In 1995 the Mineral Resources Stabilisation Fund collected K281.7 million from the mining and petroleum sector, most of it (91 percent) in the form of corporate income tax. These receipts represented 18.9 percent of the government's nongrant revenues, which suggests that the government's overall dependence on revenues from this sector had increased quite considerably since 1988, to the point where they must now account for something between one quarter and one third of all nongrant revenues.

Given the current extent of known mineral reserves, the Kutubu, Ok Tedi, Porgera, and Misima projects are all destined to cease operation before the year 2010. On the other hand, a number of new mining and petroleum projects were still in the pipeline at the end of 1995. Two 'medium-scale' gold mines (Tolukuma and Wapolu) both started production in December of that year, and two or three more are in various stages of development. Of far greater significance, in both its scale and its duration, is the development of the Lihir gold mine in New Ireland Province, where production began in May 1997, and the value of output is expected to average about K287 million a year for the first fifteen years of a 30- to 40-year mine life. The Gobe petroleum project, a virtual extension of the existing Kutubu project, received its development licence in 1996 and thus extended PNG's role as an oil exporter for another few years. There has even been talk of developing a liquid natural gas (LNG) project whose capital cost would be greater than the combined cost of all existing mining and petroleum operations.

Despite these signs of buoyancy, there is also some evidence to suggest that the current pattern of mineral resource development may not be 'sustainable', even if our definition of sustainability is one which allows for the continual discovery of new mineral reserves. For example, the PNG Department of Mining and Petroleum's own figures reveal that hard-rock exploration expenditures have declined from almost K69 million in 1988 to just over K36 million in 1995, which means, in real terms (and in US dollars), a fall of more than 60 percent over that period. In other words, the 'exploration boom' seems to have come and gone. And public statements by industry representatives have been increasingly preoccupied with those features of the local political environment which I have chosen to describe by the title of this chapter.

THE ORIGINS AND IMPLICATIONS OF THE BOUGAINVILLE REBELLION

The outbreak of the Bougainville rebellion and subsequent closure of the Panguna copper mine generated a substantial literature over the period from 1990 to 1992, much of which was concerned with the ways in which the rebellion could be seen as a response to the social, political, and economic impact of the mining operation, and the extent to which these linkages could be seen as characteristic features of the relationship between mining companies, local communities, and the state of Papua New Guinea. All commentators recognised that the initial core of the rebel movement was a group of 'militant landowners', led by Francis Ona, who had for some time been demanding an enormous amount of money from the mining company as compensation for the environmental damage caused by its operations. The question was why the demand had arisen at this particular time, what the militants really wanted, whether and how they might have reached a settlement of their claims, and where they stood or what they represented in the regional or national society of which they were a part.

My own answer to these questions (Filer 1990, 1992) was to say that the rebellion had been nourished by a process of 'local social disintegration' which had been magnified to explosive proportions by the accumulated economic impact of the mining project, especially by the inability of the local community to distribute the economic benefits of mining in an equitable manner. Although it was necessary to recognise a wide variety of contingent factors which were bound to affect the form and extent of this problem in other parts of the country, it could still be said that mineral resource development had a general tendency to exaggerate the political fragmentation of local landowning communities and the larger national society. The rebels therefore represented one section of a community (and a society) whose divisions had driven them to formulate a compensation demand which almost meant the opposite of what it said, because their real aim was to abolish the social conditions of their economic dependency rather than to make a new deal with the mining company which had been damaging their natural environment.

Some commentators (notably Griffin 1990) agreed that the rebels had an ulterior motive, but regarded the claims made against the mining company as an excuse for the resurrection of earlier demands for Bougainvillean independence from Papua New Guinea. No one would deny that Bougainville's political status was added to the rebel agenda at a fairly early stage in the proceedings, and once the mine had been closed it became the main bone of contention in the continuation of civil strife in different parts of the province. But this line of argument can only explain the original social and economic concerns of the militant landowners as a cunning concealment of the truth, even though substantial doses of truth were quite obviously present in their own formulation of these concerns. According to Larmour (1992), the rebellion was fuelled by some potent mixture of ethnic identity and class consciousness, but the timing of this chemical reaction remains something of a mystery. One of the few academic analysts with firsthand knowledge of recent developments on the 'strife-torn island' has suggested that Francis Ona and his original followers traded their own 'compensation' agenda with the 'secession' agenda of other Bougainvillean groups to form a coalition whose social support was then enlarged by the ham-fisted actions of the national 'security forces' initially sent in to quell the rebellion.[2]

Other commentators took the compensation agenda at face value, as a direct and justified response to the fact of massive environmental damage, and therefore took issue with the point in my own argument at which I had suggested that 'the degree of strife within a "landowning community"...is proportional to the size of the "packages" which have been delivered to the community by a mining company and the various agencies of government' (1990:104). From case studies of compensation agreements in Australia and other parts of the world,

---

[2] Tony Regan, personal communication, 1995.

O'Faircheallaigh has argued that damage to the physical environment is itself a major cause of social conflict within landowning communities, and that it

> goes to the heart of the politics of resource development, because it raises starkly the question of power: power over land use, project design and environmental regulation, and over the distribution of benefits from mining which can offer, at least on a material level, compensation for destruction of land and wildlife. (1992:262)

We shall never know what might have happened if the Panguna landowners had obtained a larger amount of this power before they finally blew their tops. But we may still wonder whether Papua New Guinea has the kind of political environment in which their search for economic justice could have reached a satisfactory conclusion, largely because the state resembles the landowning community in its apparent lack of institutional capacity to set the standards for this search.

Amongst the other arguments which have been used to explain the relationship between the mine and the rebellion, most tend either to adopt a voluntaristic perspective, in which BCL's surplus product figured as the prize in a typical Melanesian 'power game' which somehow got out of control (see Quodling 1991; Wolfers 1992), or to 'theorise' the relationship by locating it in a local, national, or global context portrayed with traditional Marxist concepts like 'class struggle' (Thompson 1992), 'mode of production' (Wesley-Smith and Ogan 1992), or 'capital logic' (Gerritsen and Macintyre 1992), none of which appears to throw much additional light on the matter. All these authors recognised the rebellion as a concrete illustration or extreme example of a more general phenomenon, and in this sense they shared the views of those mining company executives, government officials, and members of the general public who all agreed, in the early stages of the rebellion, that it taught some kind of lesson about the politics of mineral resource development in Papua New Guinea. On the other hand, the long duration of the fruitless search for peace on Bougainville seems to have induced a revival in the popularity of Griffin's argument that it really was a 'special case', either because BCL's corporate image has lost its symbolic value in national political debate, or else because people in positions of power and authority believe that they have already done what they can to avoid a recurrence of such violent conflict in other parts of the country.

Does the continuing history of conflict between mining companies
and local communities provide new evidence to support, disprove, or
modify my own inference from the timing of the Bougainville rebellion, that 'mines in almost any part of PNG will generate the same volatile mixture of grievances and frustrations within the landowning
community, and, all other things being equal, blowouts will occur with
steadily increasing frequency and intensity until there is a major deto-
nation of the time-bomb after mining operations have continued for
approximately fifteen years' (Filer 1990:76)? If there is one piece of evidence which should relate to the validity of this hypothesis, it might
appear to be the recent compensation dispute between BHP and the
people living along the Ok Tedi and Fly rivers. But consideration of the
Ok Tedi case also serves to reveal the variety of local contingencies
which are bound to affect the operation of any general 'laws' or 'tendencies' in a country like Papua New Guinea.

The occurrence of the Bougainville rebellion certainly inspired
some of the people harbouring a grievance against Ok Tedi Mining
Limited to express their feelings in terms remarkably similar to those
which had previously been used by Francis Ona and his supporters.
One letter written to a national newspaper shortly after the Panguna
mine had been shut down included the following sentiments:

> We, the people who live along the Fly River, will make sure our river
> system is brought back to normal...rinsed clean by the blood of the
> greedy foxes upstream. We will make sure they drink the waste them-
> selves, and their blood will be poured into the Fly to bring it back to
> normal if the National Government continues to ignore us. It was
> ignorance of the same kind that the Government is displaying over Ok
> Tedi that has led to the Bougainville crisis. The government never lis-
> tened to the landowners' calls, but treated them like rubbish. And now
> what has happened? Francis Ona's mob is on the move and the gov-
> ernment is shivering like a sick monkey, hiding at the back of the
> empty safe for which it sacrificed its country. So—a job well done,
> Francis Ona: Keep it up and get rid of those greedy whites and the
> mentally affected government. You've got silent supporters from
> Western Province. (*Post-Courier* 9 October 1989)

At the same time, OTML and its partners in government had drawn
their own conclusions from the rebellion and agreed that the company
should establish a new funding mechanism (the Lower Ok Tedi Fly
River Development Trust) to compensate the people living downstream
of the mine. This may have moderated the form and extent of local
hostility, but it obviously failed to prevent the litigation which eventu-

ally forced the company to make a far more generous settlement. If the local landowners resorted to court action rather than armed struggle, this choice might be explained by the fact that the mine had been operating for less than ten years when the action began, so their grievances had not yet reached the pitch of intensity which existed on Bougainville, but it might also have been due to the moderating influence of the various foreign stakeholders responsible for internationalising the dispute. There was certainly no history of secessionist sentiment in Western Province which could have served to aggravate local feelings of environmental injustice, but there were substantial numbers of West Papuan refugees living in the area most seriously damaged by the discharge of mine waste, and their presence undoubtedly compounded the pressure on subsistence resources (see Kirsch 1989, 1993).

The one feature of the Ok Tedi dispute which is least consistent with my own model of local social disintegration is the absence from this dispute of those communities which have so far been the main recipients of those mine-related benefits which are dedicated to 'local landowners'. These are the people, roughly 1,500 in number, who hold customary title over the Special Mining Lease, the Tabubil town lease, and a tailings lease which is restricted to the area around the ill-fated Ok Ma dam site. These people have no reason to complain about the discharge of waste material into the river system because they are living upstream of the damage, but even in 1989, five years after the government had allowed OTML to begin mining operations without the tailings dam which has previously been required, these were still the only people receiving any form of compensation from the company. Furthermore, the relatively small size of this landowning group meant that each of its individual members had been getting a larger share of the whole range of benefits reserved for local landowners than their Bougainvillean counterparts. If the intensity of feeling behind the Bougainville rebellion was partly due to the inability of the local community to distribute the economic benefits of mining in an equitable manner, then we might expect to find a higher level of resentment amongst these 'upstream landowners' than amongst the downstream people who had a very much smaller share in the economic benefits of the Ok Tedi mine.

It is certainly true that the 'upstream people' have launched the occasional 'strike' against the mining company—most notably in March 1988, when their action incidentally provoked Francis Ona and his followers on Bougainville to a new level of aggression in pursuit of

their own claims. However, in the first five years of the mine's operation, their protests were primarily directed against the presence and
behaviour of the outsiders hired by the mining company, not against
the fact or value of the damage done to their physical environment. It
was only after the outbreak of the Bougainville rebellion, in June 1989,
that the 'Ok Tedi landowners' began to demand a substantial increase
in their compensation and rental payments from the company, and
even then, the demands were not motivated by any obvious desire to
emulate the Bougainvillean example, but rather by the national government's own stated desire to renegotiate the whole spectrum of
'landowner benefits' in all its mining and petroleum projects. In this
case also, the company learnt its own lesson from the Bougainvillean
example, and began to distribute the cash benefits to individual landowners rather than to clan agents or community leaders who might
later be accused of misappropriation. Although the mine has not yet
reached its fifteenth year of operation, there is very little evidence to
indicate a recent intensification of social conflict within the upstream
community, nor much sign that they shared or supported the justified
resentment of the people who bore the brunt of the downstream
damage and proved most resolute in their pursuit of a new compensation deal.

The Ok Tedi case lends rather more support to O'Faircheallaigh's
claim that social conflict within landowning communities is a direct
outcome of damage to their natural environment and can be mitigated
by the success of their own struggle for reasonable compensation. However, the validity of this point depends in part upon the definition of
the groups involved, since traditional political communities in Melanesia are much smaller than the 'landowning groups' whose identities
are forged by the process of mineral resource development. The series
of 'deals' done between the government and OTML were framed in
terms of an abstract exchange of economic benefits for environmental
losses which signally failed, for many years, to take account of the spatial distribution of these gains and losses amongst the local populations
most directly affected by the operation of the mine. The Ok Tedi case
reveals a complex and enduring pattern of political and economic fragmentation within the general category of 'project impact area people'
which may create a greater menace to the mining industry than any
process of social stratification within their 'natural' political communities. This process of spatial polarisation, extending across the boundaries of those areas which the 'landowners' and the government have

agreed to set aside for mining and related purposes, may also help to explain the spread of support for the militant cause on Bougainville in ways which previous analysis has overlooked.

MOUNT KARE: THE MINE THAT GOT AWAY

Mount Kare, located obstinately on the border between the former colonial territories of Papua and New Guinea, is an excessively remote and miserable place which became famous overnight when a passing 'landowner' discovered large nuggets of gold along the banks of a nearby creek in January 1988. During the course of the next two years it was the scene of a remarkable 'grassroots gold rush' in which a small army of 10,000 Papua New Guinean prospectors and camp followers removed gold worth an estimated K150 million with simple tools and bare hands (see Ryan 1991). While some people saw this as a splendid demonstration of self-reliance, others were more concerned by the inability of the government to either regulate the lucky strike or divert a portion of its output into the long-term development of the adjoining districts and provinces.

All this activity took place within the boundaries of Prospecting Authority (PA) 591, which the government had granted to CRA's local subsidiary, CRA Minerals (PNG), back in 1985. Indeed, it is most unlikely that the discovery would have been made if CRA had not already established its exploration camp in the area. On one interpretation of the Mining Act, the company also had a legitimate claim to some of the gold which was being removed so brazenly from beneath its nose. Given the numbers of people involved in the removal exercise, the pursuit of this claim with a distant and visibly impotent government would not have made much sense. CRA's executives therefore decided that their best option was to form a joint venture with the 'true landowners' of the gold rush site in order to mine those quantities of alluvial and colluvial gold which had not already been taken by these landowners and their 'guests'. In this way they also hoped to reduce the extent of outside interference with their exploration work in the much larger territory covered by PA 591, where it was now reasonable to assume the existence of a substantial hard-rock deposit associated with the newfound wealth of surface material.

Since the gold rush site was located in wild alpine grassland which formed a substantial (though not impassable) barrier between the settlements of the Paiela people in Enga Province and the Huli people in

Southern Highlands Province, the number of people who could (and did) claim some share of its ownership was much larger than it might have been if the fact of ownership had previously had any significant economic value. Nevertheless, the company's consultants were able to establish the existence of sixty-one 'landowning sub-clans' from both sides of the border, and on this basis to construct and register an elaborate hierarchy of business groups and landowner companies whose peak body, the Kare-Puga Development Corporation (KDC), was duly incorporated in May 1989 and entered into the necessary joint venture agreement with its own architects in April 1990. The new joint venture company, Mount Kare Alluvial Mining (MKAM), was a cost- and profit-sharing arrangement in which CRA's own subsidiary, Mount Kare Holdings (the holder of PA 591), held a 51 percent controlling interest. In September 1990 the State granted a Special Mining Lease (SML) to Mount Kare Holdings and entered into a Mining Development Contract with MKAM.[3]

By this time, the easy pickings of the gold rush had been largely picked. But these had only served to whet the appetites of several local businessmen whose own coffers had been swelled by their participation in a range of ancillary activities. This group of local capitalists had excellent political connections: most of them were either past, present, or potential members of the National Parliament or the Enga Provincial Assembly. They saw no reason why their participation in the further development of the Mount Kare prospect should be jeopardised by CRA's determination to erect a metaphorical fence around the 'true landowners' of the area and a real fence around their own mining camp. In sundry combinations and alliances, they did all they could to wrest the fabled golden prize from the wicked multinational monster in its mountain hideout.

They first sought to dissuade the government from granting the SML by claiming that CRA had 'caused' the Bougainville rebellion— hardly a novel idea but one which was guaranteed to raise additional support in the national political arena. They also took a leaf out of Francis Ona's book by complaining that CRA had manipulated the definition and organisation of 'landowners' to exclude its own opponents— an argument which persuaded the Justice Minister to suggest that 'all CRA applications should be stopped and careful landowner studies made' before another mining lease was issued to the company (*Post-*

---

[3] CRA had already submitted its own development proposal and environmental plan to the relevant government authorities at the end of 1988.

Courier 20 August 1990). Meanwhile, in July 1990, an Engan politician persuaded Parliament to amend the Mining Act by granting 'landowners' an automatic right of ownership over all minerals which lay within a certain distance of the surface of the ground. Some MPs may have supported this amendment because they thought it merely gave legal sanction to what had already taken place at Mount Kare, but the KDC directors published a full-page advertisement in the national daily newspaper in which they claimed that it was part of a 'conspiracy' by certain politicians 'to break up the KDC-CRA negotiations and tempt landowners with promises of a better deal with companies with which they have business dealings' (*Post-Courier* 16 August 1990).

Perhaps the advertisers already knew what was about to happen when the SML was actually issued. In the following week, the KDC chairman jumped the metaphorical fence and initiated legal action to challenge the validity of the lease. This was done at the instigation of two other dissident landowners who rapidly added their own names to the proceedings and threw in an extra constitutional challenge to Section 7 of the Mining Act, which declared that all mineral resources were the property of the State. While this case was bouncing back and forth between the National and Supreme courts, the dissidents persisted in their efforts to win over individual members of the KDC board while making loud complaints about CRA's 'divide-and-rule tactics'. To reinforce their point, in March 1991, they organised an armed raid on the MKAM mining camp and forced the manager to sign a written undertaking that CRA would build a road from Paiela to Porgera. And in August 1991 the minister for minerals and energy told Parliament that he had asked Cabinet to deal with CRA's application for a renewal of its prospecting authority (PA 591) because he and his departmental secretary had both been subject to death threats and he felt that 'certain elements of Mt. Kare landowners were threatening another situation similar to Bougainville' (*Post-Courier* 29 August 1991; *Times of PNG* 12 September 1991).

The dissident landowners had lodged their own application for the same glittering prize through a company called Amadio, which had entered into an agreement with two small Western Australian prospecting companies, Ramsgate Resources and Menzies Gold, to share the costs and benefits of removing CRA from Mount Kare. In effect, Ramsgate and Menzies had agreed to foot the bill for the various court battles in which Amadio's directors were engaged, and had promised their 'landowning' partners a 50 percent share in any mining operation which they managed to establish in the wake of CRA's departure. When Cabinet decided to renew CRA's hold on PA 591 for a further two years, the validity of the decision was naturally added to the list of issues in the litigation which Amadio's new benefactors had agreed to fund.

Impatient perhaps with the slow progress of their legal action, the dissident landowners organised another, bigger raid on the MKAM mining camp one night in January 1992. This time they forced the workers at gunpoint to set fire to the installations and equipment, stole all the gold and cash they could find in the company safe, and left behind a note telling CRA to get out of the area. Prime Minister Rabbie Namaliu asked for 'the reaction of those Opposition leaders who have sought to be involved in the question of mine ownership' (*Post-Courier* 13 January 1992), but the only reaction he got was a series of verbal attacks on his own government's failure to address the demands of the 'true landowners' or prevent CRA from using its customary 'divide-and-rule tactics'. As in the case of the earlier raid, some of the truly divided landowners were duly arrested and charged on a number of counts, but most of the charges were eventually dropped or mislaid. One of the individuals charged in connection with the second attack was also one of the plaintiffs engaged in the legal battle over the mining lease and the prospecting authority, and the publicity generated by his various encounters with the law may well have helped to secure his entry to Parliament in the national election of June 1992.

By this time the dissidents were also claiming control of Kare-Puga Development Corporation—a somewhat hollow victory (even if it was real) because the company was almost immediately placed in receivership by its main creditor, the PNG Banking Corporation, on account of 'grave concerns held by the bank over the much publicised litigation which has contributed to delays in re-opening the mine site' (*Post-Courier* 29 June 1992). Yet this was only a minor setback when compared with the political complexion of the new coalition government formed in the wake of the national election. Not only had the new prime minister, Paias Wingti, been the opposition leader who refused to condemn the January raid, but his Engan minister for mining and petroleum, Masket Iangalio, appointed as his personal adviser the very man who had brokered Amadio's deal with Ramsgate and Menzies. The minister made noises about his sincere desire 'to help the landowners settle their differences', but CRA's executives could see the writing on the wall. They offered to transfer the whole of CRA's stake in MKAM to the 'properly identified landowners through their originally established ownership structure' on condition that Amadio and its Australian 'financiers' were persuaded to desist from their legal challenge to CRA's hold on PA 591 and excluded from any beneficial interest in the alluvial mining operation which had recently been recommissioned in an effort to clear KDC's debt to the bank.

The minister at first seemed sympathetic, for he could see that 'CRA was a bit fearful that the West Australian crowd might get in there and manage this on behalf of the people' and therefore gave his 'undertaking that this will not be the case' (*Post-Courier* 12 November 92). But two weeks later he made a statement in Parliament accusing CRA of bribery, corruption, manipulation, and misrepresentation, and would clearly have nothing more to do with them. In February 1993 the company announced that it would suspend the alluvial mining operation 'as an act of goodwill in accordance with the wishes of the Minister' (*Post-Courier* 25 February 1993). By the end of March they had grown so weary of the whole business that they declared *force majeure* and literally walked (or rather flew) away from both the mining lease and the prospecting authority. With a nice touch of irony, the minister described this as a 'provocative act' and an 'ill-conceived move' (*Post-Courier* 29 March 1993).

Within a few days of CRA's evacuation, Ramsgate's managing director announced the conclusion of a new 'management contract' under which the Australian partners would help KDC to pay its debts as soon as the hard-rock rights were in the bag, and apparently had some reason to think that 'it would be futile for anyone else to apply for the exploration licence' (*Post-Courier* 14 April 1993). But he was wrong. Come October there were three different 'landowner groups' in competition for the licence, each with its own joint venture partners, and the mining registrar therefore conducted a ballot under Section 100 of the new (1992) Mining Act to determine which of the applications would be dealt with first. The company which won the ballot, Matu Mining, was the local subsidiary of another Australian company, Carpenters Pacific Resources, which had picked up the support of a landowner faction which had previously been on CRA's side of the fence. Not to be outdone, Amadio's supporters in government produced an amendment to the Mining (Transitional Provisions) Regulation which would have the effect of invalidating the issue of the licence to anyone except the holder of the Special Mining Lease which KDC had inherited from CRA. And so began another round of lucrative employment for the lawyers of Port Moresby. While the matter has remained before the courts, there has been no further exploration or development of Mount Kare's mineral resources except for what little remains to be captured with buckets and spades.

There are two morals which I should like to extract from this tortuous saga. The first is the cumulative absence of any distinctive moral value or any sign of 'indigenous heroism' from the mutually frustrating and denigrating endeavours of the various stakeholders. And the second is the sheer variety of 'strategies and tactics' by which the actors brought about the stalemate none of them had wanted. The Melanesian way of menacing the mining industry is thus revealed as one which has a multitude of menaces but very little in the way of moral messages or purposes.

IN YOUR FACE OR BEHIND YOUR BACK

After the second armed assault on the Mount Kare mining camp in January 1992, the national government decided to create a special police mobile squad, to be known as the Rapid Deployment Unit, to provide 'round-the-clock' security for the country's mining and petroleum projects. The first members of the new squad graduated from their three-week training course at the beginning of June and were promptly deployed to Porgera, whose proximity to Mount Kare was assumed to create a special need for their services. This caused a good deal of confusion in the local community because Porgera already boasted a regular police force and a police mobile squad, as well as the company's own security force. The mining company agreed to accommodate the new squad (with an appropriate deduction from its tax bill) in the absence of any spare government housing. But the management had cause to regret their act of hospitality in October 1992 when an RDU member allegedly shot and killed a 'local landowner', thus provoking an armed assault on the company's residential compound which cost about K1 million in repairs and improvements to security installations, and which also frightened a number of staff and workers into tendering their resignations.

Whether or not the victim of this random yet typical act of police violence was a 'landowner' in the strict sense of the word, many of those who joined in the attack were recruited from the large number of 'squatters' or 'outsiders' attracted to Porgera by its wealth of economic opportunities and social services, and who now greatly outnumber the original inhabitants of the area. In this overcrowded and volatile social formation:

> There are plenty of Porgerans with grievances against the mine and vast numbers of idle outsiders ready to fuel these grievances or join in demonstrations.... Many come for the excitement and form the bulk of the ever ready rent-a-crowd that join in the fights and riotous behaviour which have become a standard feature of pay day. (Bonnell 1994:90–91)

The author of this comment spent three years working in PJV's Community Affairs Division, and most people familiar with the work of that outfit will attest to the accuracy of her analysis. The 'rampage' of October 1992 is only an extreme example of the episodic violence which is a hallmark of 'political' relationships between all sections of the local community, and over which it is the function of the company's community liaison staff to pour large quantities of metaphorical cold water.

Many commentators, inside and outside of the industry, would say that the 'siege mentality' which has been typical of the corporate posture at Porgera and Mount Kare is simply a response to the regional political culture of the central highlands of PNG, where the constant threat and occasional use of violence is the normal form of 'negotiation' or 'dispute settlement'. In the period since independence, central highlanders seem to have developed a form of 'law and order' which features a combination of excessive compensation claims, criminal acts of extortion, riotous mob behaviour, punitive police raids on local villages, and the conduct of 'traditional' tribal feuds with hand grenades and M16s. Although this may sound like a recipe for anarchy, it is a situation in which mining companies can and do continue to operate by bargaining their way through successive confrontations as if they were unusually wealthy tribes or clans whose wealth contributes in equal amounts to the creation and resolution of additional public order problems.

There is certainly much less evidence of outright confrontation between company and community representatives in other parts of PNG. For example, the anthropologist who was engaged to assess the social impact of the Wapolu gold mine in Milne Bay Province wrote that the local villagers had a 'colonial history of neglect and quiet disillusionment' and a 'cultural disposition to be mild and unassertive', which was liable to disguise and prolong the growth of their resentment at the damage caused by the mining operation:

The outburst, if and when it comes, might seem distorted, disproportionate, and not necessarily directed at a solution to the problem.
Their anger is unproductive and inclined to be self-destructive. Being
hurt, they will hurt themselves further to try and hurt the cause of
their resentment. How this could manifest if there was a deep groundswell of resentment against the Company I can only speculate. But it
would not generate (as in the Highlands) a decorated threatening
mob. More likely one would see a campaign of resentful obstruction:
the withdrawal of labour and services, studied avoidance of the camp,
and quietly sabotaged roads. (Young 1987:4)

The superficial or initial absence of hostility need not imply a different
level, but only a different form, of resentment and resistance. Some of
the company and government personnel who negotiated the development of the Porgera mine would say that it is easier to strike meaningful
agreements with the leaders of a 'decorated threatening mob' than
with people whose reticence borders on passive resistance. And the
eruption of the Bougainville rebellion suggests that a 'deep groundswell of resentment' may ultimately prove much harder to manage.

Although Papua New Guineans themselves contribute to the maintenance of such stereotypical contrasts between highland and lowland
(or island) cultures, the volume and form of violent action against
mining and petroleum companies is not simply a function of this
regional diversity. Firstly, the movement of people and ideas between
different parts of the country provides a constant source of novelty or
unpredictability in the approaches which local community leaders can
take to the negotiation of mineral resource development. And secondly, the mining industry, like other sectors of the modern capitalist
economy, is constrained by forms of violence which owe more to the
current formation of national institutional relationships than to the
vagaries of regional custom. It was not only the pent-up anger of militant landowners but also the institutionalised violence of the 'security
forces' which put an end to the mining industry on Bougainville, just as
it provoked the armed assault on PJV's residential compound in 1992.
Wildcat 'strikes' by mineworkers also tend to involve a measure of personal intimidation and physical destruction which would be regarded
as a serious threat to public order in many other national settings, but
which Papua New Guineans seem to accept as part of the definition of a
'strike', even if their leaders still deplore the 'strikes' of workers and
landowners alike as part of a lamentable decline in people's 'respect for
leadership and authority'. In this respect the mining industry is men-

aced by a general breakdown in 'law and order' which both reflects and reinforces a national crisis of governance.

THE RESOURCE DEPENDENCY SYNDROME

It is not difficult to construct a definition of 'dependency' which allows us to describe Papua New Guinea as the owner of a 'mineral-dependent economy'. Such descriptions have often been related to a version of 'dependency theory' which seeks to explain the backwardness or underdevelopment of certain Third World countries in terms of their subjection to specific forms of multinational capital—in this case mining capital (e.g. Girvan 1976; Cobbe 1979; Tanzer 1980). The substantial presence of mining capital in Papua New Guinea clearly does have some negative effects on other sectors of the national economy, mainly because of the way that it affects the domestic market in various factors of production, but if we can therefore say that the mining industry constitutes an 'economic menace' in its own right, it is not this economic form of 'resource dependency' which threatens the industry itself.

The Melanesian way of menacing the mining industry includes a psychological or cultural form of 'resource dependency' which partly reflects the simple economic fact that an ever-increasing proportion of PNG's national income has been collected in the form of mineral resource rent, but which *also* draws part of its inspiration from the 'cargo cult mentality' which postcolonial anthropologists are no longer allowed to talk about, and which, for the sake of political correctness, we might choose to describe as a 'millenarian desperation for development'. Stürzenhofecker has provided a graphic illustration of this state of mind in her portrait of a Duna community whose male members

> blend received notions regarding powerful spirits with rumours regarding the finding of oil resources, in such a way as to move from the picture of a sacred landscape, whose fertility must be preserved for the future, to a picture of an exploitable landscape available for manipulation by a company.... Their peripheral location, coupled with rumours of the centralizing potential of company development, have given them an almost apocalyptic vision of what such a form of development could bring to them, regardless of the likely ecological consequences. (1994:27)

Although there may still only be a minority of the rural population which actually does receive some form of resource rent, the vast majority now seem to subscribe to the belief that their land does contain some valuable resource—whether gold, oil, diamonds, or the truly visible logs—and that their only chance of 'development' lies in their share of the rent to be collected from the extraction of these resources by some 'multinational' company. If and when the company comes, the expectation of deliverance within its field of operations is far too great to be satisfied by the actual conduct of its business, however many special deals or preferences are bestowed upon the local population, since the business it is doing (unlike 'business' in the Melanesian sense) is bound to be directed to the 'bottom line' and not to the consumption or destruction of excessive wealth in the creation of new personal relationships. But while people may not like the experience of 'development' which they actually get from the mining companies (or the logging companies), and can readily be drawn to express their feelings of disappointment, anger, and frustration, they are not cured of their addiction to the drug, they do not choose the path of 'self-reliance' or 'alternative technology'; they simply want the 'company' to give them more, or else to have another 'company' to keep them company.

Bougainville probably was a special case in this respect, because CRA's arrival was not seen as a sign of impending deliverance by any significant fraction of the local population. In the sunset of Australian colonial rule, 'independence' was the natural focus of their aspiration for 'development', just as it was in many other parts of PNG, with or without the addition of millenarian overtones. In those parts of the country where the experience of colonial rule had been more limited and less oppressive, as it had been in the vicinity of the Ok Tedi project, people had other ideas (or no idea) of the relationship between self-government and large-scale mining when they first encountered these two distant concepts. And by the time a foreign mining company made its appearance on Lihir Island in the early 1980s, many people there were seriously disillusioned with the institutions of 'their' nation-state and saw the company's arrival as the outcome of their own communal 'cargo cult'. To understand why mining companies have taken (or been given) more and more of the responsibility for meeting local expectations of 'development' which have been less and less amenable to corporate manipulation, one needs to recognise the existence of a vicious circle connecting the resource dependency syndrome to the apocalyptic elements of Melanesian Christian culture and the secular decline in the legitimacy of the postcolonial regime.

AN UNSTABLE POLICY ENVIRONMENT

One of the more perspicacious remarks made in the wake of the Mount Kare raid in January 1992 came from the national police minister, who said it confirmed police predictions that 'terrorist activities on mines and petroleum installations were going to happen about this time before and after national elections' (*Post-Courier* 16 January 1992). The national election of June 1992 did take place almost exactly midway between this raid and the rampage through PJV's residential compound in October that year. National elections in Papua New Guinea have been held at five-year intervals since 1972. The political cycle which has developed over this period is one in which all matters of public policy have increasingly become the hostages or victims of an unstable succession of coalitions between national politicians whose own electoral survival commonly depends on their ability to reward a very small local constituency with the maximum possible share of government resources. Each successive election has witnessed an increase in the total number of candidates, a corresponding reduction in the proportion of votes required to win a seat, an increase in the number of sitting members who have lost their seats, an increase in the number of winning candidates who have claimed to be independent of the growing number of political parties, and an increase in the intensity of the 'horse-trading' by which a new coalition government has been formed after the declaration of results (see Saffu 1996). And in each of the quinquennial political cycles since 1977, the ruling coalition established after the election has been defeated by a parliamentary vote of no-confidence when one or more of its component factions have crossed the floor and joined the previous Opposition.

In this form of parliamentary democracy, the fluctuating personal interests of individual ministers and their own political patrons and clients have come to undermine the capacity of public servants to maintain the coherence of existing sectorial development policies. In the year preceding an election, all Members of Parliament, whether in government or opposition, try to outbid their prospective opponents by repudiating all existing policies for which they have no personal responsibility in order to recapture some of the permanently disenchanted voters in their own electorates. And in the formation of new coalition governments, the main economic portfolios are often allocated to individuals who have already built their political reputations around a commitment to radical innovations in departmental policies. Successive ministers of minerals and energy (or mining and petroleum) have alternately supported or opposed one or more of the major multinationals which dominate the industry in Papua New Guinea, while candidates standing for election in the growing number of electorates which actually host some form of mineral resource development will almost invariably seek to make some political capital out of the distinctive nature of their own relationship to the developer. Although this form of political competition gives mining companies good cause to perceive the country's policy regime as a cross between a revolving-door and a roller-coaster ride, in which they can expect to be described as 'wild pigs', 'golden rats', or 'economic terrorists' at certain points in the national political cycle, it has also had the effect of destabilising or decomposing the technocratic policy regime which was designed to maximise the share of mineral resource rent being invested for what the National Constitution describes as 'the benefit of future generations'.

Back in 1989, as part of its own effort to avoid a repetition of the Bougainville rebellion and secure a greater degree of local support for the development of new mining and petroleum projects, the national government established a tripartite process of negotiation between national, provincial, and local stakeholders which soon came to be known as the 'Development Forum' (see West 1992). The price which has since been paid for this new level of 'popular participation' has been the development of a zero-sum, short-term, adversarial pattern of relationships between government agencies and local communities as they continually struggle over the distribution of material benefits which can be debited to project revenues.

> Each new forum has increased the share of these benefits which accrue from a specific project to its own 'landowning community', and has correspondingly reduced the share which is retained by the national government. This means that each new mining and petroleum project is liable to be developed under terms and conditions which immediately threaten the deals already done to facilitate the development of all existing projects. In this context, the government is unable to exercise its legitimate role as an agency of effective development planning in project impact areas, but normally stands condemned for its own failure to keep whatever promises it has made in some previous round of negotiations. This kind of failure provokes a corresponding resent-

ment on the part of local communities, whose leaders are thus encouraged to make additional demands on the developers who have increasingly become the surrogate for government itself. And so the wealth, power and authority of the State appears to be trapped in a permanent crisis of governance. (Filer 1996:23)

Other policy measures, most notably the provisions of the new Organic Law on Provincial Government and Local-level Governments (1995), have taken further steps to redistribute mineral revenues from the national government to a small elite of 'lucky-strike' communities and the various 'unofficial stakeholders' who function as their advocates or parasites. Industry spokesmen now complain at regular intervals about the consequent growth of economic inequalities and political conflicts between 'landowners' and other 'project impact area people', even while they chafe under the government's expectation that the companies themselves should carry more of the financial burden of maintaining social order in their fields of operation. This is not something which the companies really want to do, nor something for which they are well prepared, but it happens either at the insistence, or due to the neglect, of the other stakeholders in the policy process, even while these same stakeholders reserve the right to criticise, sue, or assault the mining company's executives at the same time—activities in which they receive a good deal of encouragement from the climate of public opinion in Australia and the other countries where these companies are domiciled.

CONCLUSION

Speaking at a seminar in Germany convened by radical church groups and nongovernmental organisations to reflect upon the problem of environmental degradation in PNG, especially the damage caused by the Ok Tedi mine, the chairperson of the PNG Council of Churches described the problem of governance in her country as one in which local loyalties and traditions inhibit the capacity of politicians and public servants to follow the maxims of distributive justice at a national level.

Thus they may opt for the personal morality of service to kin and friends first rather than the impersonal morality of service to the nation—which in fact means service to non-wantoks. In this sense corruption can be seen as a moral act, or at least not simply an immoral act, in that corrupt politicians are often opting for one set of moral duties rather than another. (Muingnepe 1994:104)

And that presumably is why

Papua New Guinea's politics is so fragmented, parochial and insular and produces political behaviour and attitudes at the national level which in most cases appear incomprehensible and contradictory to national interests. (*ibid.*:105)

She might have added—though this would certainly have put the cat amongst the pigeons—that those Papua New Guineans who have proved themselves best able to pursue the maxims of distributive justice are more likely to be found in the management of 'foreign' mining companies than in the ranks of government at any level. In other words, the corporate sector—including even the mining sector—has ethical standards which may not be as lofty as those of the PNG Council of Churches, but seem to be somewhat higher than those practiced by the various agencies of 'government'.

Once we consider the mining industry to be one of the last bastions of bureaucratic rationality in the State of Papua New Guinea, then we should perhaps be less inclined to represent the multinational companies as unscrupulous and dirty beasts, and think of them instead as tame elephants performing in a circus without a ringmaster or wild elephants consuming the resources of a national park whose gamekeepers are all ivory hunters in disguise. It is fairly easy to conclude from such analogies that 'Melanesian society' has an in-built tendency to resist any form of bureaucratic or corporate regulation, whether by the state or multinational capital, but it is rather more difficult to conjure up a sustainable alternative. Although we may detect a superficial resemblance between the way that Melanesian villagers and Western environmentalists perceive the 'pollution' of the mining industry, we need to bear in mind that the Melanesian perception (and the actions which stem from it) owes much less to the desire for a 'clean natural environment' than it owes to the search for a new social and economic order.

Is there another form of 'development' whereby the people of Papua New Guinea can (if they wish) escape the clutches of the resource dependency syndrome? In theory (and in the discourse of the coffee shop), there may be something beautiful and small and user-friendly which will do the trick. But in practice it is not so clear. In the discourse of the coffee shop, 'indigenous peoples' living in harmony with nature should not really need 'development' of any kind, since 'we all know' that 'development' is an unfashionable social construct ripe for deconstruction (Escobar 1995). If the people of PNG are crying out for 'development', shall we then declare that they are suffering from some form of false consciousness, that they do not know their own true needs, and what they do need is a serious dose of such new-fangled medicines as 'participatory rural appraisal' to open their eyes to the wonders which they have inherited from their stone age ancestors?

The technocrats in the mining industry and the environmentalists in the coffee shop are both liable to beg the question posed in the aftermath of the Bougainville rebellion—whether mining projects in PNG have a uniform and predictable impact on their local social environment, or whether the vagaries of local and national history dictate that there can only be a series of unique relationships between projects and communities, or between a set of 'stakeholders' whose own identity is constantly at stake. Any attempt to construe the 'real' needs and desires of the national population will normally be based on the assumption that these relationships do have regular and general features from which deductions can be made about the merits of specific policies, but when we actually document the 'multitude of menaces' to the corporate strategies of mining capital at national, provincial, and local levels, it is much harder to figure out the general direction in which this history of 'resistance' is leading the various stakeholders.

My own conclusion would be that the struggle of these 'indigenous peoples' is not a conscious or deliberate battle against the demons of mineral imperialism, but an internal struggle which threatens the fabric of their state and has the accidental or unintended effect of creating an increasingly problematic investment climate for the mining companies. The problem here is not the contemporary fact of capitalist exploitation, but the very limited scale of cooperation which has always been characteristic of Melanesian society, and which Papua New Guineans nowadays refer to with the one word 'politics'. Despite the best (or worst) efforts of Western colonialism, the political fragmentation of Melanesian society has continued to defy the binding powers of fear, trust, shame, or guilt. The Melanesian way of menacing the mining industry is not just a failure to cooperate with the industry itself, which many people might applaud as a heroic act of resistance, but a lack of mutual cooperation in the pursuit, and even the definition, of that 'development' which everyone agrees they want.

REFERENCES

Bonnell, S., 1994. *Dilemmas of Development: Social Change in Porgera, 1989-1993.* Thornlands (Qld.): Subada Consulting P/L for Porgera Joint Venture (Porgera Social Monitoring Programme Report 2).

Callick, R., 1995. 'Think about the future: think about stability', *The Independent,* 2 September.

Cobbe, J. H. 1979. *Governments and Mining Companies in Developing Countries.* Boulder, Colorado: Westview Press.

Escobar, A., 1995. *Encountering Development: The Making and Unmaking of the Third World.* Princeton: Princeton University Press.

Filer, C., 1990. 'The Bougainville Rebellion, the mining industry and the process of social disintegration in Papua New Guinea', *Canberra Anthropology,* 13(1):1-39. Reprinted (1990) in R. J. May and M. Spriggs, eds., *The Bougainville Crisis.* Bathurst: Crawford House Press, pp. 73-112.

———, 1992. 'The escalation of disintegration and the reinvention of authority', in M. Spriggs and D. Denoon, eds., *The Bougainville Crisis: 1991 Update.* Canberra: Australian National University, Department of Political and Social Change Monograph 16, pp. 112-140.

———, 1996. 'Resource rents: distribution and sustainability.' Paper presented to the conference on 'Papua New Guinea's Economic Performance: A 20/20 Vision', Port Moresby, August.

Garnaut, R., and A. Clunies-Ross, 1983. *Taxation of Mineral Rents.* Oxford: Clarendon Press.

Gerritsen, R., and M. Macintyre, 1991. 'Dilemmas of distribution: the Misima Gold Mine, Papua New Guinea', in J. Connell and R. Howitt, eds., *Mining and Indigenous Peoples in Australasia.* Sydney: Sydney University Press, pp. 35-54.

Girvan, N., 1976. *Corporate Imperialism: Conflict and Expropriation.* New York: Monthly Review Press.

Griffin, J., 1990. 'Bougainville is a special case', in R. J. May and M. Spriggs, eds., *The Bougainville Crisis.* Bathurst: Crawford House Press, pp. 1-15.

Jackson, R. T., 1982. *Ok Tedi: The Pot of Gold.* Waigani: University of Papua New Guinea Press.

———, 1993. *Cracked Pot or Copper Bottomed Investment? The Development of the Ok Tedi Project 1982-1991, a Personal View.* Townsville: James Cook University (Melanesian Studies Centre).

Kirsch, S., 1989. 'The Yonggom, the refugee camps along the border, and the impact of the Ok Tedi mine', *Research in Melanesia,* 13:30-61.

———, 1993. *The Yonggom People of the Ok Tedi and Moian Census Divisions: An Area Study.* Waigani: Unisearch PNG P/L for Ok Tedi Mining Ltd. (Ok-Fly Social Monitoring Programme Report No. 5).

———, 1996. 'Anthropologists and global alliances', *Anthropology Today,* 12(4):14-16.

Larmour, P., 1992. 'The politics of race and ethnicity: theoretical perspectives on Papua New Guinea', *Pacific Studies,* 15(2):87-108.

Mikesell, R. F., 1975. *Foreign Investment in Copper Mining: Case Studies of Mines in Peru and Papua New Guinea.* Baltimore: Johns Hopkins University Press.

Muingnepe, R., 1994. 'What kind of ethical standards do we need in Papua New Guinea?' in H-M. Schoell, ed., *Development and Environment in Papua New Guinea: An Overview.* Goroka: Melanesian Institute (Point No. 18), pp. 99-108.

O'Faircheallaigh, C., 1984. *Mining and Development: Foreign-Financed Mines in Australia, Ireland, Papua New Guinea and Zambia.* London: Croom Helm.

———, 1992. 'The local politics of resource development in the South Pacific: Towards a General Framework of Analysis', in S. Henningham and R. J. May, eds., *Resources,*

Development and Politics in the Pacific Islands. Bathurst: Crawford House Press, pp. 258–289.

Pintz, W. S., 1984. *Ok Tedi: Evolution of a Third World Mining Project*. London: Mining Journal Books.

Quodling, P., 1991. *Bougainville: The Mine and the People*. St. Leonards (NSW): Centre for Independent Studies (Pacific Papers 3).

Ryan, P., 1991. *Black Bonanza: A Landslide of Gold*. South Yarra, Victoria: Hyland House.

Saffu, Y., ed., 1996. *The 1992 Papua New Guinea Election: Change and Continuity in Electoral Politics*. Canberra: Australian National University, Department of Political and Social Change Monograph 23.

Stürzenhofecker, G., 1994. 'Visions of a landscape: Duna premeditations on ecological change', *Canberra Anthropology*, 17(2):27–47.

Tanzer, M., 1980. *The Race for Resources: Continuing Struggles over Minerals and Fuels*. London: Heinemann.

Thomas, M., 1995. 'BHP finds itself in the firing line', *Post-Courier*, 4 October.

Thompson, H., 1992. 'The Bougainville Rebellion: costs, causes and consequences', in H. Thompson and S. MacWilliam, *The Political Economy of Papua New Guinea*. Manila: *Journal of Contemporary Asia*, pp. 14–49.

Wesley-Smith, T., and E. Ogan, 1992. 'Copper, class, and crisis: changing relations of production in Bougainville', *Contemporary Pacific*, 4:245–267.

West, G., 1992. 'Development forum and benefit package: a Papua New Guinea initiative'. Port Moresby: Institute of National Affairs (Working Paper 16).

Wolfers, E. P., 1992. 'Politics, development and resources: reflections on constructs, conflict and consultants', in S. Henningham and R. J. May, eds., *Resources, Development and Politics in the Pacific Islands*. Bathurst: Crawford House Press, pp. 238–257.

Young, M. W., 1987. *Wapolu Gold Mining Project: A Socio-Economic Impact Study*. Canberra: Anutech P/L (for Department of Minerals and Energy and City Resources P/L).

Part Three

THE NEW SOCIETY

𝒥N TRADITIONAL PAPUA NEW GUINEAN societies, old and young, male and female had their special roles to play (cf. Brown and Buchbinder 1976; Glasse and Meggitt 1965; Strathern, M. 1972). While some anthropologists have demonstrated that there was more inequality in traditional Papua New Guinean societies than commonly believed (see the articles by Morauta and Reay in May 1984), with few exceptions, social stratification of the kind familiar in the West seems to have been absent, and the attributes that most differentiated individuals were their age, sex, and clan affiliation, but most especially personal characteristics such as ambition or sloth, assertiveness or timidity. In today's more complex and unequal society, personal networks include foreigners, co-workers, and unrelated neighbors as well as *wantoks* and close kin. And an individual's identity may include, for example, a sense of belonging to Papua New Guinea's 'grassroots' and of being a 'Highlander' in addition to being a person from a particular Chimbu village in Simbu Province. The experience of change and multiple and sometimes conflicting identities has been captured in a spate of autobiographies (e.g., Mell 1993 and Strathern, A. 1993). Likewise, the often very personal and often difficult relationships between Papua New Guineans and outsiders is depicted in Dame Josephine Abaijah's semifictional autobiography (1991) and the accounts of expatriate women and anthropologists (e.g., Bourke *et al.* 1993 and Read 1986). As the following chapters show, modern PNG society is far from set and there is much experimentation and contest, especially between men and women over the content and shape of development and their relation-ships (there is also debate amongst older and younger generations of women as illustrated in articles in Dickerson-Putman, ed., 1996). A decade after independence, Papua New Guinean women leaders criti-cized their government for failing to live up to its promises of equality for women (King *et al.* 1985). Women's calls for change continue, focus-ing primarily on economic and political issues (Stratigos and Hughes 1987; Zimmer-Tamakoshi 1993) but also calling for more supportive per-sonal relationships with men (Rosi and Zimmer-Tamakoshi 1993; Zimmer-Tamakoshi 1993). Rich sources of deeply felt concerns about development and men and women's desires for new relationships, can be found in contemporary music and literary productions (Powell 1987; Webb 1993; Zimmer-Tamakoshi 1995). Also interesting is to contem-plate just what it is 'rascals' are saying about modern PNG society, espe-cially when many are educated and economically solvent when they choose a life of crime. In a recent paper, anthropologist Michael God-dard has suggested 'they are big-men in a crime-fed gift economy that involves social relations typical of precapitalist Melanesian societies in general' (1995:64). If so, PNG society is evolving in a very specific man-ner, making easy generalizations about the process impossible.

SUGGESTED READINGS

Abaijah, J., 1991. *A Thousand Coloured Dreams: The Story of a Young Girl Growing Up in Papua*. Mount Waverley, Victoria: Dellasta Pacific.

Bourke, M. J., Holzknecht, S., Kituai, K., and Roach, L., eds., 1993. *Our Time but Not Our Place*. Melbourne University Press.

Brown, P., and Buchbinder, G., eds., 1976. *Man and Woman in the New Guinea Highlands*. Washington, D.C.: American Anthropological Association.

Dickerson-Putman, J., ed., 1996. *Women, Age, and Power: The Politics of Age Difference among Women in Papua New Guinea and Australia*, Special Issue, *Pacific Studies* 19(4).

Glasse, R. M., and Meggitt, M. J., eds., 1965. *Pigs, Pearlshells and Women*. Englewood Cliffs: Prentice-Hall.

Goddard, M., 1995. 'The rascal road: crime, prestige, and development in Papua New Guinea', *The Contemporary Pacific* 7(1): 55-80.

King, P., Lee, W., and Warakai, V., eds., 1985. *From Rhetoric to Reality? Papua New Guinea's Eight Point Plan and National Goals after a Decade*. Waigani: University of Papua New Guinea Press.

May, R. J., ed., 1984. 'Social stratification in Papua New Guinea.' Canberra: Australian National University, Department of Political and Social Change, Research School of Pacific Studies Working Paper No. 5.

Mell, M. Y., 1993. *The Call of the Land*. Boroko, Papua New Guinea: The National Research Institute.

Morauta, L., 1984. 'Social stratification in lowland Papua New Guinea: issues and questions', in R. May, ed., 1984, *ibid.*, pp. 3-28.

Powell, G., ed., 1987. *Through Melanesian Eyes: An Anthology of Papua New Guinean Writing*. South Melbourne: The Macmillan Company of Australia Pty. Ltd.

Read, K., 1986. *Return to the High Valley: Coming Full Circle*. Berkeley: University of California Press.

Reay, M., 1984. 'Pre-colonial status and prestige in the Papua New Guinea highlands', in R. May, ed., 1984, *ibid.*, pp. 29-52.

Rosi, P., and Zimmer-Tamakoshi, L., 1993. 'Love and marriage among the educated elite in Port Moresby', in R. Marksbury, ed., *The Business of Marriage: Transformations in Oceanic Matrimony*. Pittsburgh: University of Pittsburgh Press, pp. 175-204.

Strathern, A., trans., 1993. *Ru: Biography of a Western Highlander*. Boroko, Papua New Guinea: The National Research Institute.

Strathern, M., 1972. *Women in Between*. London: Seminar Press.

Stratigos, S., and Hughes, P. J., eds., 1987. *The Ethics of Development: Women as Unequal Partners in Development*. Port Moresby: University of Papua New Guinea Press.

Webb, M., 1993. *Lokal Musik: Lingua Franca Song and Identity in Papua New Guinea*. Boroko, Papua New Guinea: The National Research Institute.

Zimmer-Tamakoshi, L., 1993. 'Nationalism and sexuality in Papua New Guinea', *Pacific Studies* 16(4): 61-97.

———, 1995. 'Passion, poetry and cultural politics in the South Pacific', in R. Feinberg and L. Zimmer-Tamakoshi, guest editors, *The Politics of Culture in the Pacific*, a special issue of *Ethnology*, Spring and Summer, pp. 113-127.

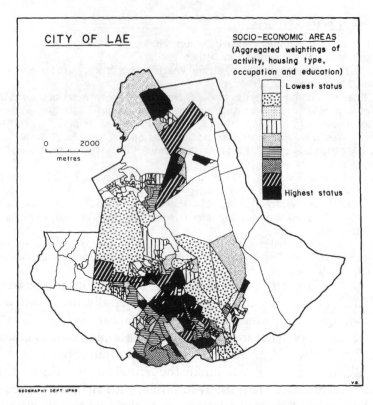

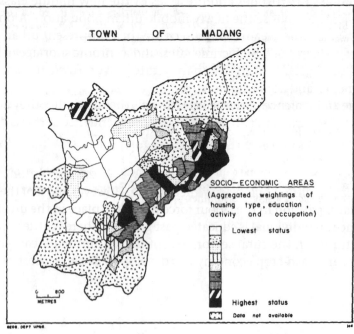

David King

ELITES, SUBURBAN COMMUTERS, AND SQUATTERS
The Emerging Urban Morphology of Papua New Guinea

*T*HE IMAGE OF MODERN Papua New Guinea is an urban image. Despite the fact that the rural sector is also changing rapidly, the growth of the big towns and cities offers all that is new and exciting as well as that which is dangerous, negative, and squalid. Shopping centres multiply, offering a dazzling array of goods and luxury items. High-rise office buildings are beginning to dominate the central business districts, prestigious elite areas are increasingly localised, with all of the consequential changes in attitudes and lifestyles of the new middle class, and traffic jams symbolise the newly mobile urban population. Alongside television, football teams, and discos are the ever-present urban problems of unacceptably high crime rates, and a chronic shortage of housing that results in high occupancy rates, overcrowding, squatter settlements, and domestic violence.

The ambivalence of the people towards the towns that they occupy is as strong more than two decades after independence as it was during the late colonial period, when the Levines (1980) reviewed the attitudes, adaptations, and general dissatisfaction of 'ambivalent townsmen'. The towns have become bigger, and less obviously colonial, but they remain difficult places in which to live. However, most of the post-colonial expansion in the labour force has taken place in the urban sector. Once an individual is educated past grade six there is little apparent opportunity in the rural sector, except for the limited areas where a strong rural cash-crop economy has developed. Besides, most of these successful rural enclaves are close to, or well served by, nearby large towns. Thus the wage jobs are to be found in the towns, whether or not people are attracted to urban living. Despite high rates of urban unemployment, the trend is towards stagnant or declining rural wage-earning opportunities, and a slow but steady increase in urban employment as the country shifts its development priority to extractive industry and the services and support industries that are located in the largest towns. The growth in new jobs, however, remains far below the expanding demand from new migrants and urban-born youth. Options and opportunities are severely limited.

URBAN-RURAL CONTRAST

The strongest urban-rural contrast is urban diversity and rural homogeneity. Within villages and rural communities, housing styles and materials are relatively uniform, even where modern materials, such as tin roofs and sawn timber walls, have been introduced. Added to the contrast is the juxtaposition of villages beside the urban areas themselves. But the contrast of urban forms and housing styles themselves is even greater. Homogeneity and uniformity are rejected in the Papua New Guinean city. Alongside prestigious elite houses are small shabby squatter settlements, squeezed into dry valleys and on steep slopes. Large housing estates and suburbs achieve a kind of drab uniformity, but sizes of houses vary considerably, and there is a further subdivision into high cost, medium cost and low cost. Clearly Papua New Guinean urban society is neither homogeneous nor equal.

This chapter examines some of the aspects of the urban contrast as they are represented in urban morphology and socioeconomic differentiation. Why are the towns socially differentiated, how did stratification develop, and to what extent are the urban populations socially stratified?

COLONIAL ORIGINS

Towns were established in Papua New Guinea as colonial control and administrative centres. There was a proliferation of small centres in remote and isolated parts of the country. There were no towns at the time of the colonial invasion, although there were a number of large villages with populations much greater than those of the centres that were established alongside them. The first colonial centres were mainly ports, built on offshore islands or easily defensible peninsulas, but as the purpose of these places was control rather than serious trade, the inconvenience of some of the sites was unimportant until the last thirty years when rapid urban expansion began to take place.

From the coast new administrative centres were founded inland, but usually on rivers or estuaries. It was not until the opening up of the Highlands in the 1930s that significant inland centres were founded. However, the pattern was still one of many tiny centres, often built around an airstrip and having poor links with other neighbouring centres. Christian missions very often established separate centres. The result was a proliferation of tiny administrative centres, missions, and patrol posts. Although they provided some services to the surrounding rural populations, few of them could be called towns. They offered few sources of employment and were dominantly Australian colonial outstations.

The colonial administrators did not plan to found great cities. Because trade and industry were not part of colonial policy, the land that was alienated for administration was the minimum necessary for the limited numbers of buildings and structures. In some cases the airstrip occupied up to half of the area of the station land. While this made negotiations easy for the administration, the effect was to create a chronic land shortage in most of Papua New Guinea's embryonic urban centres. The existence of extensive areas of customary land contiguous to towns has subsequently enabled uncontrolled incursions of both local people and squatters.

Where larger centres developed, zoning was enforced to separate both populations and urban functions. Jackson (1978) argued that zoning and urban regulations were designed specifically to exclude Papua New Guineans and their settlement patterns from towns. As increasing numbers of Papua New Guineans began to work for the administration and were housed in towns, residential areas were zoned into High, Medium, and Low Covenant areas in order to separate the races. Thus began the practice of employers' providing housing for their employees and stratifying them according to the social status and skill level of their jobs. This has added to the housing shortage and created an unreal housing market.

The towns initially borrowed nothing from indigenous forms. Using mostly imported materials they were typical of the form and housing style of north Queensland towns; suburban dwellings standing in plots of nonproductive gardens. Existing villages and the later introduction of squatter settlements have given towns their Papua New Guinean features. However, zoning and the haphazard siting of government land have caused some towns to be extremely dispersed with the inconvenience to residents of long commuter journeys and traffic jams.

Thus the basic urban morphology in Papua New Guinea is Australian residential segregation with the addition of remnant villages and self-help settlements, of which some, but by no means all are squatter settlements. An urban form that was left by the colonial power has thus shaped the modern Papua New Guinean towns and bequeathed to society an introduced idea of social stratification that is expressed in the different levels of urban housing. This absorption of western social values in the urban sector has been aided by the disinterest shown by successive governments towards the nation's towns.

URBAN POLICY

Postindependence policies have played a part in controlling urbanisation. In 1975 most towns were still small and cash crop prices were high so that the eight aims of development, stressing rural development and decentralisation, boosted the hierarchy of small towns and outstations. District and provincial headquarters acted as service centres to their rural hinterlands. However, the small towns were very small in relation to their hinterlands and they did not act as growth poles. Rural development was successful in the 1970s more because of high cash crop prices than because of government policy. Consequently the recession of the early 1980s was a severe blow to rural development. The drop in commodity prices caused severe retrenchment in the plantation sector. In the face of declining earnings, smallholders and subsistence farmers looked increasingly to the towns for other income-earning opportunities (Goodman *et al.* 1985).

Small towns, with little or no employment base, merely provided the route for outmigration. Although jobs in the large towns were being cut back as private enterprise felt the recession and the government retrenched the public service, it was still easier for unemployed urban migrants to wait for an opportunity by staying with urban relatives or in the squatter settlements, than to wait in the rural sector. Todaro (1983) has described this as a general Third World unemployment problem. Consequently the recession encouraged urbanisation, although some real jobs were created in new mining towns and exploration camps.

Despite the fact that economic policy has remained the highest priority, a shift in emphasis has inadvertently benefited urban employment. The expensive process of decentralisation stopped at the provincial government headquarters, leaving the district office towns to stagnate. The abolition of provincial governments in the mid-1990s introduced a new boost to decentralisation by relocating many more services to the district centres. This was accompanied by a reorganization of districts themselves and should have created greater efficiencies in service provision. However, funding cutbacks at the same time left provincial administrations unable to do much to achieve real decentralisation. The reality is that new positions have been created at district level, but the public servants remain in the provincial headquarters town, unwilling or unable to relocate to the district that they serve. Thus no real economic boost has yet percolated to the small centres. At the same time national governments which have included Julius Chan, have consistently emphasised growth areas and expansion in production. To encourage greater economic self-sufficiency and to pay for the costs of development, the government encouraged mineral exploitation. Despite the problems of dealing with large mines and multinational companies, many new jobs have been created both at mine sites and in the urban-based mining service industries. Inevitably this has provided a boost to the largest towns, especially Port Moresby, Lae, and Mount Hagen.

RURAL-URBAN MIGRATION

During the 1980s Port Moresby (N.C.D.) increased its population at a rate of 4.6 percent a year, while Lae at 2.7 percent a year, and the other large towns, have grown much more slowly (NSO 1991). Although much of this increase has been due to higher birth rates and natural increase in the urban areas than in the rural sector (Bakker 1986), it still means that the largest city, Port Moresby, has been receiving an annual mean of more than 3,500 new migrants during the 1980s. Although there is a strong positive relationship between the number of jobs in a place and the number of migrants to that place (Walsh 1985), this increase in migrants is not related to the absolute number of jobs that have been added. For one new job there have usually been three or four new migrants, as well as a steady increase of urban-born adolescents entering the work force. The result has been a steady increase both in unemployment and crime rates in Papua New Guinea's towns.

Table 1
Urban Growth 1966 to 1990

	1966 census	1971 census	1980 including NSP	1980 excluding NSP	1990[a] excluding NSP
National Population	2,150,300	2,435,400	3,010,727	2,881,933	3,529,583
Total Urban Population	103,600	285,016	395,713	370,223	536,860
Percent Urban	4.8	11.7	13.1	12.8	15.2

Source: National Statistical Office.

[a] Note: The rebellion in Bougainville, North Solomons Province, prevented the proper conduct of the 1990 census.

The rate of urbanisation in Papua New Guinea has been steady but is not dramatic. The fact that relatively small numbers of migrants have moved to the towns is as much an indicator of continuing ambivalence as it is a potential for much greater rural-urban migration. Already half the towns of the Pacific island nations are located in Papua New Guinea alone, while the urban population of well over half a million Papua New Guineans exceeds the total population of every Pacific island state except Fiji. Yet, as a low 15 percent of the population remains urban, the potential for further growth is enormous. Against a background of existing inequality, lack of job opportunities, and high crime, such a migration can only increase urban social problems.

THE NEW MIDDLE CLASS, ZONING, AND SOCIAL STRATIFICATION

Urban zoning during the colonial era assumed a structure to society that did not at that time exist amongst Papua New Guineans (MacPherson 1982; MacPherson and Midgley 1987). The provision of housing according to occupational status began to separate people according to newly emerging social and economic differences. Thus towns have stratified society in a way that did not occur in precolonial society. It may be expected that a rigid residential segregation will continue to exist in modern towns. The mapping of socioeconomic census characteristics from the 1980 census, in Port Moresby, Lae, Goroka, Mount Hagen, Wewak, and Madang showed spatial patterns and variations (see table 2). There were clear visual patterns of distribution, and some characteristics appeared to be strongly related. These were tested for correlation by giving them rank values and calculating coefficients for

Table 2
Socioeconomic Characteristics in PNG Towns

Characteristic	Rank No.	Characteristic	Rank No.
Housing Type		**Occupations**	
High Cost	1	Professionals	1
Flat	1	Admin./Managerial	1
Duplex	4	Clerical Workers	2
Domestic Quarters	2	Sales Workers	3
Nonprivate dwelling	3	Service Workers	4
Self-help high cost	1	Agricultural Workers	6
Low Cost	4	Production Workers	5
Makeshift	5		
Traditional	6	**Activity**	
Self-help low cost	5	Wage job	1
		On leave	1
		Business	2
Education		Farming & fishing	6
No grade or nil	6	Subsistence farming	6
Grades 1 to 6	4	Student	3
Grades 7 to 12 (including tertiary)	2	Housework	4
		Too old or young	4
		Job hunting	5
		Other—not job hunting	5

Source: 1980 Census.

the large towns. Four groups of characteristics showed strong positive relationships: housing type, educational level, occupations (employed population only), and activity (all population over ten years).

These thirty social and economic population characteristics are mutually exclusive within each of the four main groups. Number 1 represents the highest status and number 6 represents the lowest. Domestic quarters were classified along with the high cost houses to which they are contiguous, as they often (these days) house friends, relatives, and wantoks. Traditional houses are accorded the lowest status rank as these buildings show the least urban adaptation and require the least income for construction, maintenance, or rent.

Education only had three useful categories. More could have been created, but an equal weighting for each group was preferable, although the choice of rank numbers 2, 4, and 6 instead of 1, 3, and 5 was arbitrary. The full census list of occupations was used to determine their ranking. Service work contains a great variety of levels of occupations, but is dominated by the lower status occupations. The same is true for production workers, in which labourers and unskilled people form a high proportion. Agricultural workers also includes some higher paid plantation and commercial farm workers, but these are generally not in the town, while this category is otherwise dominated by smallholders and subsistence farmers. Peri-urban areas, squatter settlements, and traditional urban villages contain significant numbers of such farmers.

While occupations relate only to adults in the work force, activity supplies information on all people over the age of ten years. A wage job is accorded the highest status, as the level of job is qualified by the occupation category. It is further assumed that the more dependants there are in a census unit, the lower will be the standard of living, although farming, while counteracting some of this dependency, is again allocated the lowest rank as it is the least urban, and is less likely to contribute to an urban lifestyle. The category of students includes any student above ten years of age, so that many people defined as students are community school pupils. Housework, and too old or young increase the dependency rate, so that these are ranked low, while rank 5, other activities, includes the unemployed and idle.

A criticism of any ranking system is that when used numerically it creates equal spaces between characteristics that do not possess such equal distinctions. Consequently the ranking will tend towards smoothly separated categories. However, the continuum of census units that emerged was greater than the ranking system would have suggested. Clear zoning differences were expected but the data show a smooth continuum with no natural breaks between high cost, low cost, village, or settlement, although of course on this continuum, high cost and squatter settlement or village are at opposite, separated ends of the scale.

The aggregated scores shown in table 3 were obtained by multiplying the percentage in each category by the rank number and adding for each census unit. The four scores for each category were then added to obtain a total for each census unit. Scores varied between 900 and 1,900 (the absolute limits were 600 and 2,400). For the maps an arbitrary scale of nine categories was adopted with breaks at every 100.

The maps (see p. 182) illustrate the gradation of socioeconomic areas in selected towns. However, the scores for all of the census units form a smooth continuum without any natural breaks and the difference between the highest and lowest status areas only represents the gulf between areas in Papua New Guinean towns. There is no external measure involved and no indication of income. Compared to other Third World cities in Africa, Asia, or South America, Papua New Guinean towns are remarkably homogeneous, with no strong extremes of rich and poor.

Table 3 lists the mean score for each of the towns in rank order of mean status level. Smaller towns have less reliable means, and the position of the town boundary is very important in including or excluding semi-rural peri-urban areas. However, on a scale of just over 900, a difference of 300 is quite significant, between Arawa/Kieta/Panguna etc., the highest-status town, and Goroka, the lowest-status town. Such differences may have a powerful effect upon the ability of an urban council to raise revenues to pay for its basic services. (It should be noted that by 1991, Arawa, Loloho, and Panguna had ceased to exist as urban centres following the Bougainville uprising.)

If the aggregated scores for all census units are ranked, they demonstrate a smooth continuum from one extreme to the other. It is not possible to predict where an urban zoning boundary occurs. The mean high cost is of a higher status level than the mean low cost or the mean informal settlement, but between each type of residential area there is a massive overlap. This is probably because people of all socioeconomic groups accommodate numbers of relatives and wantoks, while the urban housing shortage causes significant numbers of well-educated, well-employed individuals to stay with relatives in low-cost settlement or village areas.

Table 3
Mean Status Levels of Papua New Guinean Towns

Rank	Town	Education	Activity	Occupation	Housing	Total
1	Kieta/Arawa/Panguna/Loloho	392	240	370	320	1322
2	Rabaul	423	273	360	301	1357
3	Port Moresby	429	278	333	327	1367
4	Mendi	444	305	303	353	1405
5	Alotau	418	297	360	353	1428
6	Kimbe	430	295	334	379	1438
7	Popondetta	415	316	342	390	1463
8	Mount Hagen	443	275	434	357	1499
9	Lae	459	298	381	367	1505
10	Kundiawa	475	306	354	373	1508
11	Madang	458	325	367	395	1545
12	Vanimo	468	280	381	428	1557
13	Wewak	456	327	376	438	1597
14	Daru	470	336	358	451	1615
15	Goroka	476	349	388	413	1626

Source: 1980 Census.

A sample survey of family type residences in high-cost, low-cost, and informal areas of Port Moresby[1] in 1987 showed a significant homogeneity between these apparently very different areas. Household size, dependency, and unemployment rates varied within a limited range,

[1] A stratified random sample of 160 family households was selected from high-cost, low-cost, and informal residential areas of Port Moresby. Single persons' dwellings and expatriates were excluded from the survey which was carried out by students of the University of Papua New Guinea during 1987.

although high-cost areas predictably fared better on most characteristics while informal areas fared least well. Occupational levels and levels of education also varied little between these residential zones, although levels of income were significantly higher in high-cost areas.

CONCLUSION

Social stratification is certainly occurring in urban areas of Papua New Guinea, but census and survey data suggest that the differences between social groups and residential areas are not yet great. However, despite an apparent socioeconomic homogeneity, it will probably be the income differentials that will separate the urban populations during the next two decades and result in wider social differences as the emerging middle class entrenches its presently fragile advantages. Higher incomes will encourage a lifestyle that concentrates on the urban environment, slipping steadily away from the village origins and the redistribution mechanisms of rural society, while ensuring a future place in the elite for middle class children by investment in expensive private education. Children growing up in the settlements and urban villages, on the other hand, are likely to be faced with chronic unemployment and a continuing lack of good housing and the opportunity to participate in the urban economy. We can then expect to see an entrenchment of social classes and a widening of the gap both between classes and residential areas.

Against these processes of social separation it is inevitable that urbanisation will increase and that the urban growth will be concentrated in a small number of larger towns, especially Port Moresby. As job opportunities are likely to continue growing at a much slower rate than the urban work force, it also is inevitable the social separation between the classes of those that have regular employment and those that have not, will increase. The frustration and inequality that this will fuel can only exacerbate the crime rate, urban political volatility, and domestic violence. Papua New Guinea's urban future will not be peaceful, although good social planning may ease some of the tensions.

References

Bakker, M., 1986. *Fertility Situation in Papua New Guinea.* Research Monograph No. 6. Port Moresby: NSO.

Goodman, R., Lepani, C., Morawecz, D., 1985. *The Papua New Guinea Economy: An Independent Review.* Canberra: ANU.

Jackson, R., 1978. 'Housing trends and policy implications in Papua New Guinea: flaunting the flag of abstracted empiricism', in Rimmer, P., ed., *Food, Shelter and Transport in South East Asia and the Pacific.* Canberra: ANU.

Levine, H., and Levine M. 1979. *Urbanization in Papua New Guinea: A Study of Ambivalent Townsmen.* Cambridge: Cambridge University Press.

MacPherson, S., 1982. *Social Policy in the Third World: The Social Dilemma of Underdevelopment.* Brighton: Harvester.

MacPherson, S., and Midgley, J., 1987. *Comparative Social Policy and the Third World.* Sussex: Wheatsheaf Books; New York: St. Martins Press.

National Statistical Office, 1991. *Preliminary Figure: 1990 Population Census.* Port Moresby: NSO.

Strathern, A., ed., 1982. *Inequality in New Guinea Highlands Societies.* Cambridge: Cambridge University Press.

Todaro, M., 1985. *Economic Development in the Third World.* 3d edition. New York: Longman.

Trotman, P., and Ravusiro, R., 1985. *Medium Term Development Strategy: Employment and Growth Prospects in Selected Urban Areas.* Working Paper No. 3. Port Moresby: Department of Physical Planning and Environment.

Walsh, A. C. 1985. *Migration and Urbanization in Papua New Guinea: The 1980 Census.* Research Monograph No. 5. Port Moresby: NSO.

Laura Zimmer-Tamakoshi

WOMEN IN TOWN
Housewives, Homemakers and Household Managers

$\mathcal{A}$CCOUNTS OF THE LIVES OF Papua New Guinean women in town are sparse.[1] Early on there was Oeser's work on the urban adaptation of women in Hohola—Papua New Guinea's first low-cost housing estate (1969)—and Whiteman's work on Chimbu family relations in Port Moresby (1973). More recently there are Rosi and Zimmer-Tamakoshi's paper on elite marriage (1993), Zimmer-Tamakoshi's short biography of a former Air Niugini air hostess (1996a), and Josephine Abaijah's semi-fictional portrayal of her rise to political prominence in colonial Papua New Guinea (1991). Other works on urban women focus on specific problems such as violence against women and women's involvement in crime (Borrey 1994; Dinnen 1993; Toft 1985, 1986; Zimmer 1990; Zimmer-Tamakoshi 1997c), and women's unequal participation in education (Weeks 1977; Wormald and Crossley 1988) and development (King *et al.* 1985; Stratigos and Hughes 1987).

Although not well documented, the lives and domestic relations of urban women vary significantly according to the contributions they are able to make to household affairs and men's perceptions of the rela-

---

[1] This paper is based on fieldwork carried out between 1982 and 1995, including fifteen months in Gende villages in Madang Province, several months in towns others than Port Moresby and Goroka, a total of three months in the Goroka settlement described in this paper, three and a half years teaching at the University of Papua New Guinea and doing research in Port Moresby, and more recent visits focusing on agricultural and mining developments involving Gende and other Madang Province peoples.

tive value of women's contributions. In Papua New Guinea, men who
pay large brideprices for their wives often expect a substantial return on
their investments (Carrier 1993; Filer 1985; Zimmer-Tamakoshi 1993). In
some cases, young husbands may see their unemployed wives as not-so-
glorified servants or, if the men's social and political ambitions exceed
their incomes, obstacles in the way of their success. In marriages where
both the husband and wife work, husbands often expect their wives to
spend their salaries on household expenses while they themselves use
some or all of their own income on social activities and drinking.
Although husbands may feel justified in their behavior, their wives
may disagree, sometimes to the point of open resentment and conflict
(Rosi and Zimmer-Tamakoshi 1993).

Not all wives are treated this way, however. In the following
description of the lives of Gende townswomen, my main focus is on the
women of a small migrant settlement on the outskirts of Goroka, the
capital of Eastern Highlands Province and the home of several hundred
Gende. The women of the Okiufa settlement are representative of a category of urban wives and mothers I characterize as 'homemakers' as
opposed to unemployed 'housewives' and employed 'household managers'. Although unemployed outside the home, the women at Okiufa
have earned the respect of their husbands—all of whom are low-
income wage earners—for the stable and relatively safe home environment they have created at Okiufa and their successful presentation of
themselves as overseers of the family purse and the 'tamers of men'
(Zimmer-Tamakoshi 1997b). I also look at the lifestyles of Gende housewives and household managers, although because wealthier households are more spread out in the urban community my focus here is on
individual women's situations rather than a community of women
such as those living at Okiufa.

This account of Okiufa women is theoretically important as, with
few exceptions, feminist anthropology has been slow in recognizing
the value of women's domestic contributions to their households in
both developed and developing countries (Lamphere 1997; Murcott
1983, reprinted 1997). Renewed interest in women's gender rituals (Lutkehaus and Roscoe 1995) and age stratification systems (Dickerson-
Putman 1996) has, however, revealed the richness of women's involvement in and shaping of their societies both in the past and in today's
rapidly changing and complex world (Zimmer-Tamakoshi 1996b). And
developments in the study of 'life histories' and other autobiographical
representations have alerted anthropologists to the powerful meanings

and symbolism in women's songs and stories (Abu-Lughod 1993; Behar 1993; Okely and Callaway, eds., 1992), sometimes subversive of men's interests (Zimmer-Tamakoshi in press), but often constructively realized as in Okiufa women's collective 'biography' of their economic and social importance to their husbands and families.

OKIUFA

For fifty years Okiufa has been home to a small number of Gende families and a home away from home for visitors and newly arrived migrants from the Gende's traditional homeland in southern Madang Province. Located on a narrow, tree-lined ridge amidst other hills and with a view of more distant mountains, Okiufa engenders the feeling of being back in the village instead of within easy walking distance of the second largest town in the Papua New Guinea highlands. Two rows of small, mostly bush-material houses enhance this impression, while most Okiufa homes consist of two or three rooms with earthen floors and central firepits around which family members gather to cook food and warm themselves on cold nights. Further down the slope are latrines, a pig pen, and a large communal vegetable garden.

Okiufa is not, however, a remote mountain village. It is an urban settlement whose residents are dependent on the town for their livelihood. Two or more times a day—on their way to and from work, school, church, or market—residents pass through a gate in the fence which separates Okiufa from the playing fields behind Goroka Teachers College. If, on their return, they are delayed beyond the time when the gate is locked for the night, they must return home along a dark road which winds up the slope from the other direction past a factory, a lonely stretch of woods and tangled undergrowth, and finally, the homes and commercial pub belonging to the Gende's landlord and his sons. On occasion, latecomers are harassed by drunken troublemakers hanging outside the social club or by rascals lying in wait to rob them of their fortnightly pay packets.

In spite of the nuisance of living next to a popular drinking and dance club, the Gende maintain cordial relations with their neighbors. Once a year each of the eight or so households living at Okiufa pay K50 in rent to the landlord. They also purchase small amounts of food and other items from the landlord's tradestore, visit his pub just often enough to demonstrate their goodwill, and when passing their neighbors on the road, share cigarettes or betel nut with them. In return, the neighbors' sons sometimes give Okiufa residents a lift home from town in the back of their truck or, on the rare nights one or more Gende men visit the club, buy them drinks.

THE FOUNDING AND SOCIAL ORGANIZATION OF OKIUFA

In 1987, when I began my study of Okiufa, there were eight families living there. As indicated in table 1, all of the Okiufa households at that time had some connection to two particular Gende villages—Orobo-morai and Boganogoi—a connection that remains true among newer residents as I learned during subsequent field trips to Okiufa in 1988, 1989, and 1994. Many of these ties were through women. Of the eight male heads of household, four (in households 1, 2, 3, 4) had a connection to Orobomorai village through their mother or wife's mother or father, while another (7) had a direct link through his own father. Two of the remaining male household heads had links to Boganogoi village through their mother (6) or wife (5), while another (8) had a link through his father. Since there have been many marriages between members of Orobomorai and Boganogoi villages, it is not surprising that four male heads of household (in households 1, 2, 4, 7) had links to both villages. What is surprising about the Okiufa households is that although postmarital residence back in the villages is strongly patrilo-cal, at Okiufa it is more matrilocal, with women and their male and female relatives forming the core of the settlement.

That women have played a prominent role in the settlement of Okiufa becomes clear when we look at its history. Four generations of Gende migrants have lived at Okiufa. The first came during and after the Second World War, as carriers for Allied troops and later as police under the lead of then Assistant District Commissioner of Eastern Highlands District, James Taylor. Later on, Gende men built Goroka's present airstrip. The original airstrip was where Goroka Teachers College is now located, adjacent to Okiufa. At first, the local landowners at Okiufa allowed the Gende to settle rent-free at Okiufa. When the Gende became better educated and better paid, the local people claimed that the Gende were 'stealing' their ground and, in the early 1970s, began charging each household a yearly rental fee of K50. The first generation of settlers at Okiufa are all dead. The second includes the adult members of households 3, 5, and 8—all of whom have lived at Okiufa for thirty years—and more recent arrivals in households 1, 2, and 7. The third generation includes the young adults in households 4

Table 1
Okiufa Households in 1987

House-hold	Household Members[a, b]	Length of Residence at Okiufa in Years
1	A widower (Orobomorai, mother's place) whose wife (Boganogoi) died at Okiufa in 1986.	6.5
	His widowed sister (Orobomorai, mother's place) and five of her six children (Bogai).	0.5
2	A widow (Orobomorai), her four children (HAGEN).	3.0
	Her second husband (Karasokara) and his two children (Karasokara).	2.0
3	A husband (Tigina) and his wife (Orobomorai) and three of their five children (GOROKA).	20.0 plus years for both
4	A husband (Yandera) and his wife (Orobomorai, mother's place) and his nephew (Yandera).	4.5
5	A husband (Bogai) and his wife (Boganogoi) and four of their five children (GOROKA).	20.0 plus years for both
6	A young husband (Karasokara) who was raised by his mother's brother (Boganogoi) in Goroka.	15.0
	His wife (KAINANTU) and their child (GOROKA).	2.0
7	A husband (Orobomorai) and his wife (Kindakebi) and their four children (Orobomorai).	4.5 years for all
8	A divorced man (Boganogoi) and two of his four children (GOROKA).	20.0 plus years

[a] The birthplaces of Okiufa residents are given in parentheses. Where the birthplace is the birthplace of the individual's mother, this is pointed out. All of the names are Gende villages except for towns in the Highlands that are given in all capitals.

[b] Some households have grown children who are living elsewhere and are not included in this table.

and 6 and the children of the second-generation households. The fourth includes the children of households 4 and 6.

One woman who has been particularly influential in the current composition of Okiufa is Julie, the wife in household 3. Julie and her husband came to Goroka when they were first married. Their five children were all born in Goroka. Although they first lived in a rented house with running water and electricity located near the hospital where Julie's husband worked as a cook until recently, Julie soon decided it would be less expensive to live at Okiufa. She was particularly keen on moving to Okiufa because there she could raise pigs and plant a small garden, and there were also relatives from her mother's natal village of Boganogoi living at Okiufa (in households 5 and 8). In succeeding years, Julie provided a link for relatives from her own village of Orobomorai to move into Okiufa for short or long periods of time. Four of the households currently residing at Okiufa are there as a result of Julie's instigation. These households are numbers 1, 2, 4, and 7. The widower in household 1 is from the same Orobomorai clan as Julie. He and his deceased wife settled in Okiufa in 1981 when he came to Goroka to work as an actor for the highly acclaimed, nationalist Raun Raun Theater. His only son is now a doctor in charge of health services in another Highlands town. The wife in household 2 is Julie's half-sister (same father) who came to Okiufa from Hagen (at Julie's urging) when her first husband died leaving her with four young children. Once her half-sister was at Okiufa, Julie convinced her to marry a widower with two children, whose mother comes from Boganogoi. The wife in household 4—whose mother's brother is the head of household 1 and whose father came from Boganogoi but raised his children in his wife's village of Orobomorai—is married to a man from Yandera village. In 1983, when her husband found work in Goroka, she joined him there, at first living in company housing but later moving to Okiufa at Julie's invitation. Household 7 also came to Okiufa around the same time. Their reasons for coming were to find work and put their younger children into school. Again it was Julie who urged them to come and who offered them assistance in getting their household set up at Okiufa and in finding work.

THE ROLE OF HOMEMAKER AND DEFENDERS OF HEARTH AND HOME

At Okiufa, women have created a stable home environment for themselves and their families. Contrasting their way of life with that of other townswomen—including other Gende women in town—the Okiufa women attribute their success to the circumstances which have allowed them to create a pocket-sized, closely related community, insulated from the interethnic and interclan strife that mars the peace of larger urban settlements, and to their self-consciously and collectively constructed role as defenders of hearth and home, something different from most middle-class Americans' views of a homemaker's role.

What that role consists of can in part be illustrated by describing the women's daily routine. A typical day at Okiufa begins with a woman cooking breakfast for her family and then escorting her children to school or sending them off under the watchful eyes of several other women, whose turn it is to see that the children arrive safely and are actually in their classrooms at the start and finish of the school day. On one memorable occasion I witnessed, when all the women were engaged for the day in helping a local landowner pick coffee, several of the younger schoolboys took advantage of the opportunity to leave school early and went swimming with some of their non-Gende schoolmates in a river several miles outside of town. Arriving home well after dark, the boys were severely scolded and in one instance thrashed for their truancy and for unnecessarily scaring their parents. Throughout the evening, the little boys' sobs could be heard intermingled with the grumblings of several of the older men who berated the younger generation of mothers for not looking after their children properly. Their criticism was unfair, for all the adults of Okiufa are conscious of the fact that, however long they have lived in Goroka, they remain 'outsiders' in the eyes of many local residents and as such are susceptible to aggressive acts against themselves and their children.

While the older children are in school, women attend to the daily chores of washing dishes, doing laundry, and sweeping. Although there is a communal water tap, women often do their laundry in a nearby wooded stream where they can also bathe and collect firewood for the evening meal. When the tap goes dry, which it often does, women make numerous trips to the stream to keep water buckets filled for cooking and washing purposes. In the afternoons, two or three women may go into town together to do their marketing while other women stay behind to tend small children or work in the garden. Although the lack of refrigeration necessitates frequent shopping forays, trips to the market and downtown stores are also an opportunity to meet other Gende and to exchange news of happenings in town or back in the village. On their way home, women will pick up children from school. In the late afternoon, women begin preparation of the evening meal or engage in friendly games of cards with other women. Although few of the women at Okiufa have enough education to be of much help with their children's homework, most encourage their children to do at-home assignments during the remaining hours of daylight. One reason parents give for staying in town is the opportunity for children to acquire a better education than they would receive if they stayed on in the village. Indeed, many of the children of the older generation of Okiufa residents are either in the process of completing their high school educations or have gone on to promising careers or further education.

Women's comportment away from Okiufa is in marked contrast to their more relaxed behavior at home. Walking into town with them, I was regaled with stories of rascal attacks on naive and suspecting persons and kept in a state of nervous surveillance. My companions, some as fearful as I, adopted the stance of a crack combat team, striding with presumed confidence into town and marketplace, emoting a willingness to fight, if need be, but all the while engaging in friendly banter and exchanging small gifts with other Gende or with other Goroka residents with whom they had established tentative friendships. Once back in Okiufa, where it was safe to be expansive, the women told stories of how they had tricked other men and women in card games and foiled rascal attacks with their strong presence and reputations for lethal sorcery. Such bravura aside, many likened their behavior to that of Gende women of the past, who survived the dangers of tribal warfare and had to marry into enemy clans by using their wits and creating well-oiled networks of friendship and reciprocity with other women and men. Among the Gende, women are as involved in exchange as men are, encouraged to increase their productivity and cooperate with others in female initiation rituals and by the social and political rewards associated with women's formal repayment of their brideprices and women's ascension to full adult status and eventual ancestral glory (Zimmer-Tamakoshi 1993 and 1997a).

WOMEN, FINANCE, AND MEN

As important as their homemaking and childcare efforts are, Okiufa women's self-proclaimed roles as the tamers of men and guardians and investors of their husbands' incomes enable Okiufa residents to lead comfortable lives and to rest secure in the knowledge that having maintained rural links with exchanges and hospitality—largely through women's thrift and hard work—they can return home to the village whenever they wish. Women achieve these things in part because their husbands cooperate with them and recognize that without their wives they would be 'lost men' (*lusman*), unable because of low salaries to raise a brideprice for a new wife and subject to the urban excesses that befall lonely men and bachelors. Women play on their husbands' fears of losing them by keeping fit and threatening to return to the village whenever their husbands become abusive or indifferent to family welfare. The underlying threat is that the women can find other husbands as women remain valued producers of pigs and sweet potato gardens. Women also contrast their own successes in money and personal management with ample cases of men's lack of judgment and foresight, putting themselves and other, mythical and near-mythical, examples of female hardheadedness forth as almost impossible exemplars for men to follow (Zimmer-Tamakoshi 1996a and 1997a; see also Sexton 1982 and 1995).

Women's role as guardians of their husbands' paychecks becomes apparent every fortnight. On payday, wives meet husbands at the bank where their paychecks are cashed or at their workplace. Men give most of their wages to their wives for safekeeping, sometimes banking a portion of their pay as a means of making it difficult to spend. Paydays are hazardous intervals in a family's efforts to budget their income since impecunious *wantoks* (members of the same language group) or persons who have loaned them money will descend on a couple, knowing they haven't had a chance to spend (or hide) their money. Other drains on family income are unexpected or prolonged visits from village relatives and the occasional drinking sprees that husbands get drawn into when entertaining visitors or when egged on by less dutiful acquaintances. For the most part, however, wives can be counted on to lessen the cost of drinking sessions by refusing to give their husbands more money or to deflect the advances of borrowers and lenders by lying about their finances. If need be, wives will stage fits of outrage that send offenders scurrying away. Husbands, who are in collusion with their wives, are able to maintain a front of manly dignity in the face of their wives' dominance by claiming they are afraid of their wives' anger and their alleged powers of sorcery.

In addition to buying everyday necessities, paying rent and school fees, and being able to afford an occasional movie or new clothes, every household at Okiufa is enmeshed in a network of exchanges which binds them to one another and to other Gende in town and in the village. Important exchange payments facing every Gende household are brideprice, *tupoi* (a repayment of the brideprice which gives a couple rights over their own labor and income), and death payments. The latter are important since making major contributions to the mortuary and death payment ceremonies of deceased kin is essential to securing rights to land once used by the deceased man or woman. Because they are generous to village kin, several long-term Okiufa residents have extensive landholdings in Orobomorai village, which they rent out to less fortunate villagers. The rent usually consists of a pig every few years and is charged more as a way of publicizing the absent landowner's continuing ownership of the land than as a business venture. Because of their close family ties, Okiufa residents sometimes act as a unit, as they did, for example, in 1987 when they were planning a mortuary ceremony back in Orobomorai in honor of the dead father of two Okiufa women. Several months before the ceremony, one of the older men at Okiufa returned to Orobomorai to build a house for those Okiufa residents who would attend the ceremony. The pigs being reared at Okiufa and fed on rice and leftovers were earmarked for this important exchange event as were the carefully guarded savings of most of the Okiufa households.

HOUSEWIVES AND HOUSEHOLD MANAGERS, AND THE WIDER SOCIAL ENVIRONMENT

Not all urban Gende women live in makeshift settlements or possess the ability or need to guard and spend their husbands' income so carefully. Some, like the Gende women described here, are members of Papua New Guinea's small middle and elite classes. Nonetheless, although the living conditions of women married to more prosperous husbands are usually better than those of the Okiufa women, certain aspects of their lifestyles and domestic relations are less enviable. While the women may live in large houses equipped with microwave ovens and electric washing machines, they may also be forced to share their homes with numerous live-in in-laws who criticize the women for not contributing any income to the household budget or expect to be waited on as if the women were servants and not 'the lady of the house'. Such was the case with Cecelia (not her real name), a young housewife married to a government employee. However much she tried to please her husband's family, both they and her husband made Cecelia the butt of frequent insults and jokes about her housekeeping skills and 'greedy relatives'. On the rare occasions when members of her own family came to visit Cecelia, her in-laws and husband were rude to them, often refusing to allow Cecelia to cook a meal for them or to loan them money.

Not well acquainted with the other women in the high-income neighborhood she and her husband lived in, Cecelia sought the company of other Gende women by going every day to the market. On the advice of other Gende women, Cecelia eventually left her husband and returned to her parents' home in Yandera village. With no children and no lack of female admirers, Cecelia's husband made no effort to stop her. Although her parents loathed their son-in-law, they were unhappy about having to return most of the large brideprice he had given for Cecelia, and at first tried to convince her to return to her husband. Cecelia steadfastly refused, however, settling back into village life, helping in her mother's gardens, and rather quickly attracting the interest and marriage proposal of an ex-migrant who was himself disillusioned with town life.

Married women who are employed outside the home are usually spared the indignity of being treated like servants and, unlike working wives and mothers in Western societies, they are able to avoid the pressures of the double workday by mobilizing live-in relatives and in-laws to do some or all of the childminding and household chores. While there are notable exceptions, they may, however, be less successful in achieving balanced relations with their husbands or in having any control over their husbands' (or even their own) incomes (Rosi and Zimmer-Tamakoshi 1993). A case in point is that of one Gende 'household manager' whose husband regularly spends most of his income on drinking with *wantoks* or carousing with friends at expensive nightclubs. Although she has often expressed her unhappiness over this behavior, her husband's response is that since he paid most of her brideprice he is entitled to spend his and her incomes as he pleases. This husband's attitude reflects a negative side of today's high brideprices, especially when it is the husband who contributes the major portion of his wife's brideprice.

Traditionally, much or all of a brideprice was paid by a young man's family and it was expected that a young couple would work together to pay it back. Today, however, some young Gende men are able to pay for their own wives and many feel that their wives are indebted to them and that their wives' incomes should, at the very least, be spent on everyday household expenses while their own incomes are spent on advancing their social connections. However logical such attitudes are in the context of Gende exchange patterns, the women's loss of a sense of partnership with their husbands and their suspicions over the value of some of their husbands' 'social connections' are a source of bitter conflict and quarrels.

From the perspective of the women at Okiufa, these women's biggest problems are their social and economic distance from other women. More than their inability to convince their husbands of their importance to family well-being, these women's dependence on their husbands' incomes—in the case of 'housewives'—or their greater economic independence in the case of working women, leaves them pretty much out of or in opposition to the main concerns and biographical hegemony being fashioned by the women of Okiufa and by women in the villages who are coping with difficult development situations (Zimmer-Tamakoshi 1996b). Left to their own resources, these women are more on their own in their relations with men, more vulnerable to domestic violence and male domination (see Toft 1985; Ranck and Toft 1986; Zimmer-Tamakoshi 1997c); in the case of more economically (and often ideologically) independent women, more likely to be seen as troublemakers by women in more straightened circumstances, these women must also deal with the effects of brideprice inflation, and growing misogyny and violence against women (Dinnen 1993; Borrey 1994).

CONCLUSIONS

In the foregoing pages I have described certain variations in the lifestyles and domestic relations of Gende townswomen and have, in part, linked these variations to differences in the women's contributions to household and kin-related affairs and to their husbands' judgments regarding the relative value of the women's contributions when compared with their own. In those cases where a man has paid much of his wife's brideprice himself, a salient feature of domestic relations is the husband's expectation that he has a right to control or direct the use of his wife's labor and income as he sees fit. This expectation was objectionable to many of the women I interviewed, including women in both high- and low-income households. Nonetheless, it received indirect support from the behavior of the Okiufa women who, because their husbands were not wealthy and had not been major contributors to their brideprices, exhibited and expected a much higher degree of equality in their relations with their husbands.

Given the small size of the Okiufa settlement, the fact that I have not carried out a full survey of all Gende townswomen, and the absence of comparable studies on other urban women in Papua New Guinea, it is not possible to assert that my findings are representative of the lives of most Gende women, much less others. My study is suggestive, however, of some of the dynamics in urban marriages, and similar research should be carried out by other researchers. That such research will be fruitful in terms of a better understanding of the nature of urban women's existence and changes in their relationships with men can be illustrated by applying what I have learned in my research on Gende townswomen to the findings of the Law Reform Commission on domestic violence in Papua New Guinea.

In their analysis of the data from three surveys covering both rural and urban sections of Papua New Guinea society, Stephen Ranck and Susan Toft (1986:21) explain the fact that rural violence is more common even than among urban groups by referring to urban men's changing attitudes towards the use of violence in domestic altercations. That the incidence of violence among higher income households in town is much greater than among lower income urban households is explained as being caused by the greater social and professional pressures being experienced by high income urban males. My data suggest additional forces at work such as the men's attitudes towards their wives' contributions to household finances and family exchange obligations as well as the women's own attitudes, which are also changing and not always in the same directions as men's.

If men in other low income groups are as dependent on their wives' help as the men at Okiufa, it is not surprising that they would think twice about the use of violence in their domestic relationships. At the same time, in cases where men feel they are carrying more of the economic burden or that the payment of high brideprices gives them more right to dictate the conditions of their wives' lives, a difference of opinion on the part of the wives would result in higher levels of domestic tension than even added social and job pressures would explain.

In other research on Papua New Guinea's educated elite, both Pamela Rosi and I found significant differences in men and women's attitudes towards their roles in urban marriages (Rosi and Zimmer-Tamakoshi 1993). On the whole, women wanted more supportive, egalitarian, and Westernized relationships while men expected more submissiveness out of their educated wives than was usually the case. This dissonance is matched by an increasing number of educated Papua New Guinean women who choose to marry non–Papua New Guinean husbands (Zimmer-Tamakoshi 1996a; Rosi and Zimmer-Tamakoshi

1993) or to engage in de facto relationships that do not bind the woman into a desperate marital situation (Abaijah 1991). That such strategies for self-fulfilment do not always work out as planned (see Deklin 1987 and Zimmer-Tamakoshi 1996a) should not blind us to the fact that Papua New Guinean women are actively involved in creating valuable and secure places for themselves in Papua New Guinea's urban society. This paper has presented one such positive case.

Okiufa women's power to construe history to their own advantage and to take precedence in the construction of urban society is the result of a number of factors. Papua New Guinean men's situations generally are not good in the cash economy (see Dickerson-Putman's paper, this volume) and as a result they are often not able to live up to either traditional or modern standards of politically and financially solvent manhood and their relations with women suffer as a result (Zimmer-Tamakoshi 1993 and in press). Women as a group have more secure, albeit generally less exciting or new, opportunities for making productive contributions to society. The women at Okiufa, for example, have the option of returning to the village to raise pigs should their efforts to make the most of marriage to low-income migrants fall through, while the same is not true for men, increasing numbers of whom, at least among the Gende, remain bachelors or are left by their wives because they cannot keep up with today's circumstances and exchange imperatives. Okiufa women also have the advantage over their husbands of time together and cultural models to construct powerful historic selves and, because they can always do something useful, to attain the moral high ground over their low-income husbands. Far from being 'shadow biographies' as in Behar's *Translated Woman* (1993), Okiufa women's stories are accepted by men, at least some of them, even used to strengthen men's position vis-à-vis other migrants. Okiufa women's constructions help women make sense of and control changes going on in their lives, portraying themselves as powerful survivors and instigators of changing gender roles, in short as primary 'defenders of hearth and home'. Okiufa women have made a space for themselves in the male-dominated urban social scene—that of low-income urban homemaker—a role in which Okiufa women can, for the near future at least, achieve both old and new social goals.

REFERENCES

Abaijah, J., 1991. *A Thousand Coloured Dreams: The Story of a Young Girl Growing Up in Papua*. Mount Waverly, Victoria: Dellasta Pacifica.

Abu-Lughod, L., 1993. *Writing Women's Worlds: Bedouin Stories*. Berkeley and Los Angeles: University of California Press.

Behar, R., 1993. *Translated Woman: Crossing the Border with Esperanza's Story*. Boston: Beacon Press.

Borrey, A., 1994. 'Youth, unemployment, and crime'. Paper presented at the National Employment Summit, 11–12 May, Port Moresby.

Carrier, A., 1993. 'The effects of economic change on marriage and exchange on Ponam Island, 1920–1985', in R. Marksbury, ed., *The Business of Marriage: Transformations in Oceanic Matrimony*. University of Pittsburgh Press, pp. 27–55.

Deklin, F., 1987. 'Women in development: some reflections on the experience of Papua New Guinea women in Australian society', in S. Stratigos and P. J. Hughes, eds., *The Ethics of Development: Women as Unequal Partners in Development*. Port Moresby: University of Papua New Guinea Press, pp. 100–107.

Dickerson-Putman, J., 1996, guest editor. *Women, Age, and Power: The Politics of Age Difference among Women in Papua New Guinea and Australia*. Special Issue of *Pacific Studies* 19(4).

Dinnen, S., 1993. 'Big men, small men and invisible women', *Australian and New Zealand Journal of Criminology*, (March) 26: 19–34.

Filer, C., 1985. 'What is this thing called "Brideprice"?' *Mankind*, 15(2): 163–183.

King, P., Lee, W., and Warakai, V., eds., 1985. *From Rhetoric to Reality? Papua New Guinea's Eight Point Plan and National Goals after a Decade*. Port Moresby: University of Papua New Guinea Press.

Lamphere, L., 1997. 'The domestic sphere of women and the public world of men: the strengths and limitations of an anthropological dichotomy', in C. B. Brettell and C. F. Sargent, eds., *Gender in Cross-Cultural Perspective*, 2d edition. New Jersey: Prentice Hall, pp. 82–91.

Lutkehaus, N. C., and Roscoe, P. B., eds., 1995. *Gender Rituals: Female Initiation in Melanesia*. New York and London: Routledge.

Murcott, A., 1983 (orig.), 1997. '"It's a Pleasure to Cook for Him": food, mealtimes and gender in some South Wales households', reprinted in C. B. Brettell and C. F. Sargent, eds., *Gender in Cross-Cultural Perspective*, 2d edition. New Jersey: Prentice Hall, pp. 92–101.

Oeser, L., 1969. *Hohola: the Significance of Social Networks in the Urban Adaptation of Women in Papua New Guinea's First Low-Cost Housing Estate*. New Guinea Research Unit Bulletin No. 29. Canberra: Australian National University.

Okely, J., and Callaway, H., eds., 1992. *Anthropology and Autobiography*. New York: Routledge, ASA Monograph 29.

Ranck, S., and Toft, S., 1986. 'Domestic violence in an urban context with rural comparisons', in S. Toft, ed., *Domestic Violence in Urban Papua New Guinea*. Law Reform Commission of Papua New Guinea, Occasional Paper No. 19, pp. 3–51.

Rosi, P., and Zimmer-Tamakoshi, L., 1993. 'Love and marriage among the educated elite in Port Moresby', in R. Marksbury, ed., *op. cit.* pp. 175–204.

Sexton, L., 1982. 'Wok Meri: a woman's savings and exchange system in highland Papua New Guinea', *Oceania*, 52:167–198.

———, 1995. 'Marriage as the model for a new initiation ritual', in N. Lutkehaus and P. Roscoe, eds., *Gender Rituals: Female Initiation in Melanesia*. New York and London: Routledge, pp. 205–216.

Stratigos, S., and Hughes, P. J., eds., 1987. *The Ethics of Development: Women as Unequal Partners in Development*. Port Moresby: University of Papua New Guinea Press.

Toft, S., ed., 1985. *Domestic Violence in Urban Papua New Guinea*. Law Reform Commission of Papua New Guinea, Monograph No. 3.

——, 1986. *Domestic Violence in Urban Papua New Guinea*. Law Reform Commission of Papua New Guinea, Occasional Paper No. 19.

Weeks, S. G., 1977. *The Social Background of Tertiary Students in Papua New Guinea: A Survey of Students in Fifteen Institutions*. Educational Research Unit Report, No. 22, University of Papua New Guinea.

Whiteman, J., 1973. *Chimbu Family Relationships in Port Moresby*. New Guinea Research Bulletin No. 52. Canberra: Australian National University.

Wormald, E., and Crossley, A., eds.,1988. *Women and Education in Papua New Guinea and the South Pacific*. Port Moresby: University of Papua New Guinea Press.

Zimmer, L., 1990. 'Sexual exploitation and male dominance in Papua New Guinea', *Point*, Series No. 14, Human Sexuality in Melanesian Cultures, Mel. Institute, pp. 250–267.

Zimmer-Tamakoshi, L., 1993. 'Bachelors, spinsters, and *Pamuk Meris*', in R. Marksbury, ed., *op.cit*. pp. 83–104.

——, in press. 'The Last Big Man', *Oceania*.

——, 1996a. 'Role models for contemporary Gende women', in H. Levine and A. Ploeg, eds., *Work in Progress: Essays in New Guinea Highlands Ethnography in Honour of Paula Brown Glick*. Frankfurt au Main, Germany: Peter Lang, pp. 317–341.

——, 1996b. 'The women at Kobum Spice Company: tensions in a local age stratification system and the undermining of development', in J. Dickerson-Putman, guest editor, *Women, Age, and Power, ibid.*, pp. 71–98.

——, 1997a. 'Empowered women', in W. Donner and J. Flanagan, eds., *Social Organization and Cultural Aesthetics: Essays in Honor of William H. Davenport*. Philadelphia: University of Pennsylvania Press, pp. 45–60.

——, 1997b. 'The taming of men on the outskirts of Goroka: historic selves and biographical hegemony'. Paper presented at working session on History, Biography, and Person, ASAO Meetings, San Diego, 19–22 February.

——, 1997c. '"Wild Pigs and Dog Men": rape and domestic violence as "Women's Issues" in Papua New Guinea', in C. B. Brettell and C. F. Sargent, eds., *Gender in Cross-Cultural Perspective*, 2d edition. New Jersey: Prentice Hall, pp. 538–553.

Martha Macintyre

THE PERSISTENCE OF INEQUALITY
Women in Papua New Guinea since
Independence

NINETEEN SEVENTY-FIVE WAS United Nations International Women's
Year as well as the year of independence for Papua New Guinea. The
rhetoric of women's rights and improvement in women's status and
economic position resounded in Papua New Guinea as it did throughout the world. The seventh of the Eight Aims drawn up by Somare in
1972 had called for:

> A rapid increase in the equal and active participation of women in all
> forms of economic and social activity.

Given the very high level of involvement of women in economic
activity in rural areas, this call must be viewed as a policy for incorpo-
rating women in economic activities that are deemed to be 'modern',
'developmental', or part of the cash economy. These ideals were later
enshrined in the national Goals and Directive Principles relating to the
Constitution. The principles and goals invoke Western liberal ideals of
individual autonomy and personal freedom of action whereby 'each
man or woman will have the opportunity to develop as a whole person
in relation with others' (No. 1). This capacity of individual development is basic to the further aim:

> Equal participation by women citizens in all political, economic,
> social and religious activities. (No. 5).

This statement is radical indeed in a state where so many different traditions of male-female social relations existed. Most Papua New Guinean societies had sexually segregated religious activities and in very few could women participate in political decision-making processes as the equals of their menfolk.

Unlike their counterparts in Western societies, Papua New Guinean women did not have to struggle for suffrage. Their Constitution immediately conferred equality of status and allegedly protected them from discrimination on grounds of '...race, tribe, place of origin, political opinion, colour, creed, religion or sex'. Decolonisation and government policies for economic and social advancement necessarily assume an identity of interest across the nation at the same time as they confront problems of cultural variation and inter-regional inequities that are the legacy of colonial developmental policies. The contradictions and paradoxes that are generated by the political necessity of assuming national unity are especially poignant in the case of Papua New Guinean women.

Government attitudes towards women have often been overtly nonsexist. There are many policy statements and research projects that acknowledge women as an economically and socially disadvantaged group. Papua New Guinea women took up the legacy of white women's struggles when they were granted jural adult status and the right to vote for political representatives, without having to fight for these rights on a united front. I suspect that this piece of neocolonial liberality is in fact one of the main reasons why highly educated Papua New Guinean women eschew so-called Western feminism—it has no historical roots in their modern state. So the inequalities and inequities are often obscured or veneered over as men and women in positions of authority appeal to letters of the law and the achievements of a small group of educated women. But the majority of Papua New Guinean women are uneducated or undereducated and they live in rural areas, far away from the centres of government. They have few ways of earning cash and are marginally involved in development projects. Their distance, physically and metaphorically, from their sisters in urban employment means that they can be simultaneously idealised and neglected or ignored with impunity.

The rhetoric of decolonisation, of economic development, and modernisation all draw on very powerful images of nationalism. The forms and expressions of that nationalism as a populist ideology owe much to the colonial past and little to indigenous cultural or political realities. For example, the displays of costumes, dancing, and music that are part of public celebrations of state visits or national events follow a mode of ethnic representation rooted in a British imperial tradition. Cultural practices are rendered folkloric and divorced from their social context. Pageants, displays, flag-waving, and processions diminish and tame cultural presentations so that regional variation becomes a mere matter of 'local colour'—manageable, superficial, and apolitical. Pig fat, poster paint, and decorative headpieces provide a glossy medium for obscuring the conflicts between different groups in the Highlands or between coastal and highland immigrants to urban centres such as Lae or Moresby. In Papua New Guinea the link between nationalist ideology and representation of cultural diversity in terms of dress and decoration is very strong and is now featured in television advertisements as well as tourist publications. In form, and the contexts in which the displays of cultural differences through dress are encouraged, the emphatic uses of 'tradition' as visual entertainment continue rather than challenge colonial representations of Papua New Guinea. In contrast to their use in postcolonial contexts of resistance, such as the assumption of Maori dress in New Zealand or Polynesians in Hawaii, in Papua New Guinea, where the colonisers made it illegal to dress like whites, dressing 'traditionally' carries quite different meanings.

Anthropologists and other researchers have stressed the environmental, linguistic, and cultural diversity of Papua New Guinea. The rhetoric of independence included much about national unity and cultural variation. Appeals to a 'Melanesian Way' assume an ethnic or regional identity that draws heavily on a colonial model of an homogeneous society. While the cultural divisions that existed before independence did not become the bases for major political divisions in the first fifteen years of independence, the Bougainville crisis has fractured unity. Bougainvilleans and people from the Fly River area affected by Ok Tedi mining have opposed the State's authority and constructed it as alien and against its own people's interests. Regional and cultural variations have become increasingly relevant in discussions of 'modernisation' and 'development', particularly since the 1980s, when the government's decision to industrialise through resource extractive industries (mining and logging) ensured that projects are highly localised and not sustainable in terms of long-term economic development. All major development projects use advanced technology and employ a predominantly male work force. The women of Papua New Guinea remain marginalised in the development process.

'Papua New Guinean woman' is a necessary fabrication in an independent state. But as we move from mountain to coast or island to island, the variations obscure our attention and we find that the differences in the cultural meanings of 'femaleness' seem to militate against formulations about a national female identity. The same could be said of the differences in cultural constructions of masculinity—yet this problem is rarely addressed when policies of development are discussed. To talk incorporation or exclusion of women in policy, assumes that the citizen/subject is invariably male. This assumption now permeates economic decision making, where mining lease agreements are regularly made with 'clans' and 'landowners' and women are ignored, both in terms of traditions of land rights and participation as citizens.

Similarly, the rhetoric of equality between the sexes and the publicity given to the few women in high status government jobs disguises informal but systematic discrimination against women in education and employment. The problems of assessing or discussing women in Papua New Guinea are many, but I shall attempt a cursory examination of the contemporary status and condition of women by looking at public proclamations and, insofar as I can, pragmatics and practices.

Political independence generated a series of changes in the lives of Papua New Guinean women. For the few highly educated women it meant that they were rocketed to stardom in government bureaucracies. For the many rural or village women it meant that they were willy-nilly and in varying degrees expected to join in the process of 'development', specifically, economic development, that would draw them into the cash economy. From the beginning, government agencies concerned with development have recognised the gap between words and actions. The White Paper 'National Development Strategy' of 1976 noted that the beneficiaries of the government aid aimed at generating income-earning projects were not those envisaged in initial guidelines. These inequalities, acknowledged one year after independence, have not vanished. Indeed many rural people are of the opinion that the gulf between those who can earn money and those who subsist in rural villages is widening. My own field research in Milne Bay Province suggested that people in small communities, remote from the new centre of administration in Alotau, believed that they were doomed to economic marginality. They saw their main hope in the education of their children to take up salaried positions in the bureaucracy. Problems of transport and fluctuations in prices for cash crops made people wary of commitment to community projects. Josephides, in a study focusing on the socioeconomic condition of women in fishing villages, observed similar responses to economic development in Sepik and on Daugo Island. She concluded that people did not see that their material conditions had altered in seven years of independent government. Furthermore, she found that in all fishing villages:

> The invariable opinion was that if their children did well in school they could expect to land good town jobs but if they failed they must come and shift for themselves in the village. (1982:62)

The period of rapid localisation that followed independence saw many educated Papua New Guineans step into well-paid positions. All over the country, the phenomenon influenced expectations about education that could not be fulfilled after the first few years (see for example M. Reay, 1981:38). More to the point, the existence of a highly paid educated elite, fiercely protecting its jobs and urban living standards, perpetuates the divisions between haves, have-nots, and hopefuls. But one thing is definitely established—the villagers in areas remote from towns and the services or facilities linked to them see themselves as having failed in crucial ways. This has profound implications for rural women who define economic and social progress as gaining access to these urban privileges. Moreover, in cases of the Sepik villagers interviewed by Josephides, and the villagers in Milne Bay with whom I worked, 'development' was viewed as imposed improvements.

> The overall feeling was that they, being uneducated villagers, by definition could not suggest how their situation could be improved. It was the job of the educated town dwellers to do it for them. (Josephides. *ibid.*)

Since independence the government of Papua New Guinea has pursued economic policies that favour the development of extractive industries—mining, logging, and fishing—where the capital investment comes from large transnational companies. While these are justified in terms of their capacity to raise capital that can be directed towards local development projects, there is little evidence that this is achieved (Jackson 1991:19). The Bougainville crisis that led to the shutdown of the copper mine is an illustration of the level of local discontent over the inequities in distribution and the gap between national rhetoric and practice.

If we look more closely at the problems of social and economic impact on local people where such projects exist, we find that women are particularly disadvantaged. Mining, fishing, and logging are internationally male-dominated industries. Insofar as local people are employed in them, they are almost all unskilled men. Women constitute a small minority and their work is invariably defined as serving males—as typists, clerical assistants, cleaners, and the like. This perpetuates a view of modernisation and development being 'men's business' as it introduces the dual labour market of industrial societies that so discriminates against women.

Furthermore, as men move out of the village into wage labour on mining or other similar projects women are forced to continue the work of subsistence production without the assistance of men. House maintenance and construction, garden clearing and fencing—work normally performed by men—is left to the women, along with their usual tasks. In some areas this means that the quality of life in the village declines as men rarely send back money, houses fall into disrepair, and garden land is degraded through overplanting (Rogers 1985:174). While the role of women as food producers is often invoked as the source of their value, they are excluded from programs that train them in aspects of agricultural development or marketing (Cox and Aitsi 1991:24–30). At present, very few women benefit from the enhanced wage labour opportunities that extractive industries bring, and for some it introduces new problems such as an absentee husband, increased alcohol consumption by men as wages are spent on beer, and a greater subsistence workload. In some areas, especially those where coffee plantations and markets were already established, women have set up small businesses which they manage co-operatively (see Sexton, L. 1982; Zimmer-Tamakoshi, L. this volume) and throughout the 1990s betelnut selling in towns has provided women with opportunities to earn and organise income-generating activities on their own terms.

The International Labour Office (ILO) is one of several organisations involved in promoting development projects for women in Papua New Guinea. In an ILO report on rural employment policies in developing countries, Martha Loutfi characterised rural women as 'the most silent participants in the economic life of developing countries' (1980:1). She argued that the fundamental issues are: the incorporation of women in directing and effecting projects and their equitable participation in reaping the benefits. If we look at these fundamentals in the Papua New Guinean case there needs to be a resolution of the definitional questions: Is there a 'woman problem' in development policy? and do women constitute a separate group, requiring distinct policies and positive discrimination?

Nationalist ideals entail a vision of social unity and assumed shared goals. A dominant theme in nationalist rhetoric is that the endeavour and benefits of development involve all citizens equally. Papua New Guinean women have the vote; they have equality before the law; they face no institutionally ratified discrimination in pursuing education, employment, or election. Yet, they do not share government with men—at present, in 1997, there are no women in parliament. Males outnumber females in every sphere of the modern state—there are more of them being educated at every level; there are more of them in employment; there are more of them at every level of politics. Within the modern state women are underrepresented and their interests are viewed either as identical to those of their menfolk, or as the specifically problematic diversions of a minority group. In short, the state apparatus of modern, independent Papua New Guinea is male dominated. Furthermore, as bureaucratic powers are centralised and in urban environments the future for rural women looks bleak.

It is very difficult to index or even evaluate the lives of women in underdeveloped countries. Improvements in living standards and the elimination of gross inequities in health, education, material wealth are hard to assess. Jenny Cory, in her Report to the Department of Community and Family Services, observes that if we look simply at the provision of health, legal, and education services to rural women, we find that almost half the population has easy access to an aid post. A mere 3.6 percent of people are more that four hours away from medical assistance. Legal advice and services are generally accessible to rural women and a wide range of educational facilities are available in the formal system and Non-Formal Education Service.

If we look at the provision of services, the government's record is good but in decline. If we then scrutinise the use of services, a different picture emerges. Cory's survey suggested several reasons for the under-utilisation of social services by rural women. Ignorance, relative inaccessibility, and lack of time emerged as three significant factors in women's failure to avail themselves of facilities. Established inequalities that are historically grounded in colonial or traditional practices tend to be perpetuated, to the extent that customary law is invoked as a proper reason for discrimination against women. For example, in many societies women did not have the same legal rights as their menfolk;

they were jural minors whose interests were subsumed in those of father and brothers or husband. Such views were often endorsed by colonial laws and by the attitudes of colonial administrators—who, after all, came from a society with an equally long tradition of the legal subjugation of women. The legal service is seen by many rural women as an institution devoted primarily to law enforcement and punishment. The administration of the law in Papua New Guinea is almost exclusively the business of men. Women are often unaware of their rights, and because of their lack of rights according to customary law, they rarely initiate legal action or avail themselves of the services of the law.

Papua New Guinean men on the other hand have become enthusiastic litigants and there is ample evidence of their desire to legitimate the subjugation of women by extending customary law into other areas. I shall give some illustrations of the process. In 1975 a survey of village courts in the Mendi subdistrict reported several instances where women were clearly discriminated against in ways that contravened the national law demanding that men and women be treated equally. A woman had been fined K40 for smoking in a Mendi street on the grounds that this was forbidden by customary law. A village court magistrate explained this harsh penalty by appealing to the rising rate of adultery and divorce that coincided with the introduced habit of smoking (Martin 1975:6). In another case a magistrate in Tulum Village Court believed that the court should enforce customary restrictions on women by punishing those who did not go into menstrual seclusion. Both of these examples reveal that reactionary and discriminatory ideologies can be (and are) legally maintained in the face of overarching legislation for equality. Sexual discrimination against illiterate rural women is largely unacknowledged by people in urban centres. First because the women affected have no public voice; second, because such activities do not fit the highly selective and romantic view of 'the village woman' that figures prominently in nationalist rhetoric. Once we enter the town, however, there is more publicity and debate on the issues of equality and sexual discrimination. During September 1979 there were between twenty-two and seventeen young women imprisoned in Popondetta jail on charges of adultery. Not one man was jailed and, according to reports, the local magistrate Mr. Haembo did not call all parties involved before deciding on the sentence (*Post-Courier* 26 September 1979:4). Before the introduction of codified law, in many societies, adultery was treated as a female crime. Customary punishments included pack rape and mutilation (see Berndt 1962:147–178 and Meggitt 1989:137). In other societies the matter was sorted out by compensatory payments and/or a 'good belting' to one or both of the adulterers. The Popondetta cases revealed the problems inherent in attempts to accommodate customary laws relating to sexual offences in a uniform national code. Clearly, Mr. Haembo believed that his judgements followed principles of customary law. Equally clearly, public opinion was divided on the issues of apportioning guilt and imposing suitable punishment. Blanket legislation for equality between the sexes looks good on the books and buttresses Papua New Guinea's international reputation as a progressive state. But it is precisely the gap between the national legal policies and regional or village legal practices that is the locus of sexual discrimination within the modern legal system. Not that there is an exemplary record in this judicial realm— the Papua New Guinea government refused to ratify the United Nations Convention on the Elimination of All Forms of Discrimination Against Women and has consistently rejected criticism of breaches of women's human rights in its penal system and the defence force's treatment of Bougainvillean women. Solutions to these problems cannot be imposed from above—the resolution of contradictions can only come from those whom they affect. The starting point for female participation in the institutions of the modern state is an education that communicates possibilities and rights, elucidates policies, and prepares women for rapid social change.

The call for an appropriate education policy directed towards the specific needs of Papua New Guinean women has long been a litany by female anthropological observers (see Wedgwood 1957:294–502; Reay 1965:166–184). While it is in some ways satisfying for me to set myself in a line of Western feminist commentators, it is depressing to note that the terms of debate have not altered with independence and that Papua New Guinean women have now made the call their own (see for example Daro 1975:9 and Kekedo 1978).

Opposition to the education of women is widespread and vocal. The Northern provincial secretary spoke for many of his countrymen in 1979 when he said:

> There should be no special provisions to assist girls and women to further their education. It is true that fewer women are in all stages of education—but that is what people want. I believe that educated women lead to a breakdown of our society. They become big-headed,

leave their husbands and run off with other men. (cited by Johnson from Grieve 1979:58)

And in 1980, a report from the Ministry of Education confirmed that after five years of independence, 'Education is readily available to those who can pay a small fee, and to those who are geographically close to a school, and those who are male' (Minister of Education 1980, cited in Johnson 1983:138).

The Papua New Guinea Department of Education has produced detailed statistical analyses of education for many years (see Annual Reports of the Planning Branch, Department of Education 1975:83). While these show an impressive expansion in the provision of primary education, the data on female education reveal that there have been few significant advances since independence. The proportion of girls enrolled in all primary schools increased by 6 percent from 36 percent in 1976 to 42 percent in 1983. Over the past decade it remained fairly constant, declining in several major rural regions. Secondary school enrolment patterns are even more telling, for although the number of students has increased from 26,356 to 41,702 the proportion of women has remained static at around 31 percent for over fifteen years. National High Schools between 1974 and 1979 saw a decrease of 4 percent in female enrolment, from 27 percent to 23 percent. At the University of Papua New Guinea, female students constitute a mere 12 percent of undergraduates—in 1974 there were 175 Papua New Guinean women enrolled, in 1980 there were 162. There has, however, been a substantial increase in the numbers and proportion of women enrolling in teacher education institutions. Ten years after independence the figures for women's education remained deplorable: 'About 30 percent of all high school students, 15 percent of all university students and 25 percent of all vocational trainees were females' (Cox and Aitsi 1988: 28). As employment in both public and private sectors requires educational qualifications, women are beset by dual inequalities, access to education and opportunities to work—both consistently reinforced by persistent informal patterns of discrimination. The pattern is emerging whereby trained women are clustered in a few service occupations such as nursing, community school teaching, and lower level clerical positions. During the 1990s, the Chan government cut funding to these departments and many female employees in health, education, and welfare have lost jobs or been forced to work with ever-decreasing budgets. These postindependence developments indicate that Australian colonial policies are alive and well in Papua New Guinea. Camilla

Wedgwood had commented on the pervasive attitudes of expatriate administrators in 1957:

> Many Europeans see dangers in any forms of education which might encourage indigenous girls to look for a satisfying life outside marriage and the home, or which might make them dissatisfied with the seeming inevitability of their role of wife and mother. (1957: 499)

These expatriates and the Papua New Guinea provincial secretary concur on the dire effects of female education. In some respects their predictions are correct. Education does enable women to make choices that may result in divorce from an oppressive husband, or even to remain unmarried and financially independent of any men. Increasing divorce rates should not be seen as a pathological social development; rather they reflect the choices available to women when they can earn their own living. Education is integral to policies of development and rural Papua New Guineans have responded to educational opportunities with enthusiasm. But unless there is some change in the proportion of women who are educated, the participation of women in the modern economy is likely to decrease. Hogan has demonstrated the ways in which male hostility towards educated and employed women is manifest in urban environments (1982:97–99). Young educated men who were at high school during the period of localisation leave with expectations of white-collar employment. When these are not fulfilled, their disappointment and frustration is often directed towards women, and particularly married women. This response is not exclusive to Papua New Guinean men—in Australia there are many people who condemn married women for working while young men are unemployed. The form of the argument is also similar, being an appeal to an imaginary past when women were allegedly entirely economically dependent on husbands. But in the case of Papua New Guinean men, the attacks on employed women often invoke ideologies of female inferiority and subordination.

Antagonism towards female education and paid employment is inconsistent and variable. In an article on Hagen gender ideology, Marilyn Strathern recorded the postindependence remarks of a man whose view of women in the late 1960s was 'They are little rubbish things that stay at home simply, don't you see!' (1981:166). By 1976 he had accommodated economic change to the extent that he valued those women who earned money—and gave it to their husbands. Indeed, most Papua New Guineans, regardless of their views on women, acknowledge that rural women work very hard. Women's work as gardeners, as producers of children, and as swineherds was differentially valued and the regional variations persist. Indeed, there is evidence of a polarisation of views on women since independence.

When Frideswide Lovell spoke at a graduation ceremony in 1972, she called upon Papua New Guinean men to treat women as equals. This provoked an angry response from at least one educated Papua New Guinean man who argued that as a woman, Mrs Lovell was inferior and that her 'status in Papua New Guinea society is, and always will be, less important' (*Post-Courier* 6 September 1972:14). In her reply, Lovell maintained that traditionally there was no subordination of women in spite of the fact that she was 'prepared to admit that the traditional division of labour in most societies in Papua New Guinea made the position of women similar to the position of water buffalo in Southeast Asia'. The appeal to tradition by those who want to circumscribe the role of women in the modern state comes more often from men than women, but the shifts in ground are illuminating. For example, in a Mendi court case, a woman claimed that her husband's failure to support her by giving her money he earned constituted grounds for divorce. The magistrate replied: 'You're are talking about being maintained with money, but you must remember we never had anything to do with money in the past. I don't think that we should bring such a grievance about money as grounds for divorce' (Martin 1975:5). By the same token, the appropriation of women's savings by clansmen or husbands is often justified as a functional extension of traditional arrangements (see Zimmer-Tamakoshi, this volume).

This brings me back to the question I posed about the existence of a 'woman problem' in Papua New Guinea. Let me first draw the lines as they are expressed by Papua New Guineans.

Firstly, there are those who maintain that the 'problem' is simply that of development and there is no gender distinction between its subjects. What will benefit one will benefit all. This is the view taken by many educated Papua New Guinean women and expressed most vehemently in the writings of Bernard Narokobi. He argues that Western commentators have misinterpreted the position of Melanesian women (see for example his article in the *Post-Courier* 29 July 1977 and 1980:45). As an elaboration upon this theme, Melanesian nationalists have attributed contemporary discrimination to colonialism (Mandie 1982). This representation of the Melanesian way of distinguishing on the grounds of sex takes a number of forms but can be briefly summarised as follows:

> Women were traditionally equal/complementary/occupied incomparable social domains, but the balance was upset by colonial intrusion so that inequities now exist. These inequities are particularly noticeable in those aspects of life that are concerned with a modern or postcolonial Papua New Guinea.

The alternative version is different but with a tendency to converge with the first view and therefore to focus on aspects of urban or postcolonial life as the cause of problems associated with women and the relations between the sexes. Violence against women in Port Moresby is a constant subject of debate. Women are frightened to walk alone at night, and whether or not the incidence of assault is higher in Moresby than elsewhere, the atmosphere is one of chronic, low-level terror. The debates on violence against women reveal a deep conservatism among men from those societies where women are defined as subordinate and where female sexuality is traditionally under the control of her clan and then her husband. Freedom of movement or independence of mind that is expressed in dress, appearance, or idiosyncratic behaviour is interpreted as rebellion against rightful (male) authority. In particular, if a woman is known to act (or suspected of acting) autonomously in her choice of sexual partner, then this is seen as renunciation of authority and protection, so that the woman is perceived as being sexually uncontrolled and therefore promiscuous. The cluster of 'modern' attributes—European-style appearance, independence from family, and sexual promiscuity are so linked that the one is viewed as evidence of the other. For example, in a letter to the *Post-Courier,* responding to an editorial, several male university students argued that: 'Some rape cases have been the result of females walking by themselves. This provides somebody with the appropriate situation. You have only to prevent the right situation. This includes "extreme" make-up too' (*Post-Courier* 22 April 1977).

Since the 1980s the government has been forced to recognise the extent of violence against women in both rural and urban settings. While some writers attest to traditions of male violence against women that prevailed in precolonial times (Meggitt 1989:141; Chowning 1980:72) many stress the pressures of social change as the source of current high rates. In Port Moresby it was estimated that in 1985 the rate of reported rapes was twice that of any American city (Cox and Aitsi

1988:35). Examination of homicide statistics reveals that during the
1980s, almost all female murder victims were killed in the context of
'domestic' conflict—by husbands, sons, co-wives, or brothers (Kivung,
Doiwai, and Cox 1985:79). In all countries, rape and domestic violence
statistics under-represent the actual situation. In Papua New Guinea
the publicity that has attended such violence may have given more
women the courage to report to the police, but there is little evidence
that the situation is improving. A Solomon Island woman, the poet
Jully Sipolo, observed of Papua New Guinean women, 'They talk a lot
and fight but their men still beat them' (McCoy 1992:36). It is an ironic
and disturbing insight for it conveys the confidence and assertiveness
that observers and Papua New Guinean women appeal to when coun-
tering stereotypes of female passivity and mute inferiority, as it highlights the pervasiveness of male dominance in national culture.

Over the years, invitation to rape has included wearing miniskirts,
long jeans and shirts, high-heeled shoes, and not being appropriately
deferential. Solutions to the problems of sexual assault vary from suggestions that offenders be castrated or hanged to the more usual ones
involving strict limitations on women's freedom of movement, style of
dress, and normal social behaviour. Since 1979 there have been several
demonstrations calling for government action on the issue of sexual
assault, and some women demanded a curfew for unaccompanied
men. Such militancy is rare in Papua New Guinea, but it does indicate
that female passivity cannot be depended upon. Indeed, research into
other aspects of women's lives, in towns and villages, suggests that
there is resentment of discrimination in all forms, and that women
organise independently of men in order to protect or further their own
interests.

The co-operative organisations of women in some coffee-growing
areas of Simbu Province, called alternatively Kafaina or Wok Meri,
reveal in their aims and achievements that some rural women do see
their interests as different from those of their menfolk. Sexton argues
that the formation of the women's co-operative savings societies
reflects women's resentment of their powerlessness and lack of autonomy compared with men. Wok Meri is a critical response to men
'squandering their money on beer and gambling' (Sexton 1982:13).
These women's organisations at present do not retain very much control over the money they save; most of it eventually goes on things that
men decide on and use (see Sexton 1982:31 and Warry 1983, passim).
These spontaneous or institutional movements such as the demonstra-

tions in Moresby or the Wok Meri groups in Simbu suggest that Papua New Guinean women have not completely internalised the male social evaluation that defines them as social inferiors. Zimmer-Tamakoshi (this volume) observes that marital arguments about gender roles in urban families arise because women resist the restraints imposed by men in terms of 'tradition'. However, in Papua New Guinea none of these manifestations of resistance have developed beyond particular issues in village locations, nor have they extended their influence to the provincial or national spheres. Even the National Council of Women, the only national body that has any political policy on women's issues, has no force within government, nor any voice in either of the main political parties.

I worked on a tiny island in Milne Bay Province—a region which, statistically and impressionistically, produces exceptional women. In 1981 I participated in a farewell feast for a group of six girls who had been selected to go to secondary school. That six girls from a total population of less than 200 were chosen is remarkable in itself—1981 was one of the few years when no boys at all reached the quota from the small community school on Tubetube. Parents felt pride and anxiety as their daughters sailed away and a few old people voiced their regret that the community was probably losing its greatest asset, the cream of its youth. In the years since independence many young girls from the island have gone off to secondary school. A journalist, a nurse, a dentist, and several highly trained clerical workers are among the women who have benefited from the expansion in education and employment for women. But for all the pride derived from these achievements, they must be examined in terms of their relationship to the local and national position of women. These women go off and the distinction between the urban 'haves' and the village 'have-nots' in some respects denigrates their less scholarly sisters. At the national level, the outstanding performances of girls from Milne Bay Province (or for that matter New Ireland or Manus) must be set in the context of interregional variations. While Tubetube girls sail off, leaving families who work extremely hard making copra to pay fees, there are parents in the Southern Highlands Province who are flatly refusing to send their daughters to primary school. R. J. Clarke of the Planning Department in Education attributed the low enrolment number of girls in Southern Highlands Province schools to several factors including parental reluctance to lose their daughters' labour and the fear of loss of brideprice. He also discovered that girls at high schools were 'sometimes the target for unwarranted ridicule and improper attention by male teachers'. Boys often reinforce feelings of inadequacy because, according to Clarke, they 'consider girls to be inferior in both intellectual and practical skills and tend to belittle all their efforts' (Clarke 1980:159–60). At tertiary level women's participation is slowly increasing, but employment opportunities are few.

In a recent fascinating study of five eminent Papua New Guinean women, Ann Turner observed that their public prominence, the fact that they were outstandingly successful leaders in their fields, distinguished them from the majority of women in Papua New Guinea (Turner, A. 1993:1). They were all educated outside Papua New Guinea before independence and they all testified to a strong Christian ethic of self-motivation, autonomy, and internalised personal values. None had ever been 'representative' of the village society of their origins. The daughters of missionaries, patrol officers, and men who identified strongly with ideals of development and progress, these women became the beneficiaries of the first flush of an egalitarian ethos which existed for a short period after independence. It enabled them to gain recognition for their qualifications and their achievements. In the intervening period the masculinisation of government administration, business development, and the professions has proceeded apace. The hypermasculinity of the Melanesian elite has been criticised by numerous Melanesian women (See Zimmer-Tamakoshi 1995) who locate its roots in the traditions that subjugated women and excluded them from the realms of politics and decision making. Ironically it is those Melanesian men in power who are prone to sentimentalise and romanticise women's roles in traditional society, in ways reminiscent of some functionalist anthropological defendants of a traditional status quo. They appeal to a past where women's 'informal' powers allegedly complemented those of men, in harmonious homeostasis. Radical Melanesian women are beginning to question the colonial origins of all forms of inequality and to trace current male violence and oppression of women to customs which constituted women as inferior to men.

The romanticism in the rhetoric of decolonisation that sets up a vision of a Melanesian woman living in perfect and harmonious equality does women a disservice. It obscures fundamental differences, it fails to provide the basis for national policies that can confront and transform the subordination and relative disadvantage of women in many areas of Papua New Guinea. In 1976 it was clear that some form of positive discrimination was going to be necessary to increase the proportion of women to men in tertiary education. Weeks pointed out:

> There is an inherent contradiction in the development of women's education that most planners have not been made aware of: the expansion of opportunities for further education for females is at the price of their coming from a more limited and elitist segment of the population. Female tertiary students are more likely to come from non-rural areas, to have gone to an urban primary school and to have fathers who are more educated and higher up on the educational hierarchy, than male students' fathers. Female tertiary students come from fewer Districts than male tertiary students and a few Districts lead in the production of female students. This holds particularly true for the islands and for Milne Bay. (1976:89)

Research into the areas of access to and involvement in education and development projects has repeatedly revealed that prevailing male attitudes affect the levels of participation by women (see, for example, Weeks 1976; Johnson 1984; Nakikus 1985). Their findings do suggest that if Papua New Guinea has any problems with equality of the sexes then they come from male-focused ideologies, not female ones.

In 1995, the Papua New Guinea delegation to the NGO Forum on Women in Beijing presented accounts of the ways in which women have been held back from representing their views as citizens of a modern independent state. The Eight Aims acknowledged that following independence there was a need to develop female participation specifically so their voices could be heard. Twenty years later, the political participation of women has declined at every level. Women's education, health, and welfare have not improved. Women have sustained the subsistence sector during the mining boom, but very few have received any direct economic benefits from the wealth it has generated. In Papua New Guinea societies women are beginning to give voice to their concerns in new ways. The Beijing Forum produced a collection of poetry that included poems signalling the fact that the analyses by outsiders are being superseded by those of literate Papua New Guinean women. Their words are stronger and more telling than any that an observer can offer:

> We must be incorporated into the emerging social forms
> if our society is to survive.
> Let the women and men of PNG,
> The government and churches listen.
> Stop the violence and abuse of women in PNG

Stop the beatings, the rape and killings,
Educate women to read and write their own lives,
Recognise and value women's roles
and contributions, in every culture,
in the childrearing and daily tasks,
Share political, economic and social benefits with us,
as equal partners in development....

('Hear us, The women of PNG', Linda Passingen, Rabaul, 1995)

REFERENCES

Berndt, R. M., 1962. *Excess and Restraint: Social Control among a New Guinea Mountain People*. Chicago: University of Chicago Press.

Chowning, A., 1980. 'Kove women and violence: the context of wife beating in a West New Britain society', in S. Toft, ed., *Domestic Violence in Papua New Guinea*. Papua New Guinea Law Reform Commission Monograph No. 3, pp. 72–91.

Clarke, R. J., 1980. 'A chance of girls to take their place: education of girls in Southern Highlands Province', *Education Gazette*, pp. 158–163.

Cory, J., 1981. 'Rural women's access to legal, health and education services in Papua New Guinea'. Port Moresby: Department of Community and Family Services.

Cox, E., and Aitsi, L., 1988. 'Papua New Guinea', in Taiamoni Tongamoa, ed., *Pacific Women: Roles and Status of Women in Pacific Societies*. Suva: Institute of Pacific Studies of the University of the South Pacific, pp. 23–39.

Daro, B. B., 1975. 'The Papua New Guinea women in education: today and tomorrow', in J. Brammall and R. J. May, eds., *Education in Melanesia*. Canberra: Australian National University Press.

Hogan, E., 1982. 'Two liberations or one? Gender ideologies in Papua New Guinea, 1971 to 1980'. B.A. Honours Thesis, Australian National University, Canberra.

Jackson, R., 1991. 'Not without influence: villages, mining companies and government in Papua New Guinea', in J Connell and R. Howitt, eds., *Mining and Indigenous Peoples in Australasia*. Sydney: Sydney University Press.

Johnson, D. D., 1984. '"The government women": gender and structural contradiction in Papua New Guinea', unpublished doctoral dissertation, University of Sydney.

Josephides, L., 1982. 'The socio-economic condition of women in some fisherfolk communities', report on ESCAP/FAO Survey, June.

Kivung, P., Doiwai, M. And Cox, S., 1985. 'Women and crime: women and violence', in P. King, W. Lee, and V. Warakai, eds., *From Rhetoric to Reality? Papua New Guinea's Eight Point Plan and National Goals after a Decade*. Port Moresby: University of Papua New Guinea Press, pp. 74–80.

Loutfi, F. F., 1980. 'Rural women, unequal partners in development'. Geneva: ILO.

Mandie, A., 1982. 'Institutional and ideological control of gender in transitional society'. Waigani Seminar Paper, University of Papua New Guinea.

Martin, J., 1975. 'Some notes on the village courts based on a visit to the Mendi sub-district, 5–10 July, unpublished report.

Meggitt, M., 1989. 'Women in contemporary central Enga society, Papua New Guinea', in M. Jolly and M. Macintyre, eds., *Family and Gender in the Pacific*. Cambridge: Cambridge University Press, pp. 135–155.

Nakikus, M., 1985. 'Planning for women's advancement in Papua New Guinea', in P. King, W. Lee, and V. Warakai, eds., *From Rhetoric to Reality? Papua New Guinea's Eight Point Plan and National Goals after a Decade*. Port Moresby: University of Papua New Guinea Press, pp. 39–50.

Narokobi, B., 1980. *The Melanesian Way*. Port Moresby: Institute of Papua New Guinea Studies.

Passingen, L., 1995. 'Hear Us, The Women of PNG', in *Beneath Paradise: A collection of poems from the Women in the Pacific NGOs Documentation Project*. IWDA, Melbourne.

Rogers, B., 1985. 'Women's perspective on development', in P. King, W. Lee, and V. Warakai, eds., *From Rhetoric to Reality? Papua New Guinea's Eight Point Plan and National Goals after a Decade*. Port Moresby: University of Papua New Guinea Press, pp. 172–177.

Sexton, L. D., 1982. *Customary and Corporate Models for Women's Development Organisations*. IASER Discussion Paper No. 42.

Strathern, M., 1981. 'Self-interest and the social good: some implications of Hagen gender imagery', in S. Ortner and H. Whitehead, eds., *Sexual Meanings: The Cultural Construction of Gender and Sexuality*. Cambridge: Cambridge University Press, pp. 166–191.

Sunderland, J., 1977. 'Sin begins with a woman: an account of some aspects of sexism at the University of Papua New Guinea', Hecate 3(2):62–76.

Turner, A., 1993. *Views from Interviews*. Melbourne: Oxford University Press.

Warry, W., 1983. 'Chuave politics', unpublished doctoral dissertation, Australian National University.

Wedgewood, C. H., 1957. 'Some educational problems of women and girls in the Pacific', *South Pacific*, 9(9):294–502.

Weeks, S., 1976. *The Social Background of Tertiary Students in Papua New Guinea*. University of Papua New Guinea Educational Research Unit Report No. 22, Port Moresby.

Zimmer-Tamakoshi, L., 1995. 'Passion, poetry and cultural politics in the South Pacific', in R. Feinberg and L. Zimmer-Tamakoshi, eds., *The Politics of Culture in the Pacific*. Special issue of *Ethnology*, 34(2):113–127.

Acknowledgments

This article could not have been written without major assistance from Diane Johnson whose research provided much of the material on which my argument is based. I thank also Evelyn Hogan for making her thesis available to me. Ms. M. Daroa of the library of Papua New Guinea was most helpful in providing me with articles unavailable in Australia and I am grateful for her prompt attention to my requests.

Jeanette Dickerson-Putman

MEN AND THE DEVELOPMENT EXPERIENCE IN AN EASTERN HIGHLANDS COMMUNITY

SINCE THE MID-1970S much scholarly research has been focused on the ways in which gender influenced an individual's experience of development in both Melanesia and worldwide (Boserup 1990; P. Brown 1988; Cox and Aitsi 1988; Gardner 1976; Hughes 1985; Preston and Wormald 1987; Sexton 1986; A. Strathern 1982b; Stratigos and Hughes 1987). In many of these works, women's negative experience with development was opposed to men's positive and beneficial experience with development. This paper will compare and contrast the life course, and associated gender models and roles, of Bena Bena men in the community of Ganaga in the Eastern Highlands Province of Papua New Guinea in both the past and in contemporary times. The comparison of the male life course provides a structure for understanding men's experiences and the relationships among men. A particular emphasis will be on how the development process was experienced differently by men of various ages and how this heterogeneity of experience and values has also affected community life and social control in the contemporary Eastern Highlands village of Ganaga.

THE MALE EXPERIENCE IN PRE-CONTACT GANAGA

My understanding and partial reconstruction of life in Ganaga prior to Australian contact was acquired through both interviews with informants of both genders and from comparative insights drawn from other anthropological research on the Bena (Keil 1974; Keil and Johannes 1974; Langness 1963, 1964a, 1964b, 1967, 1969, 1971, 1974; Young 1974).

The perspectives of various Melanesian ethnographers who have explored the nature of gender relationships in Highland societies have informed my understanding and interpretation of the past in Ganaga (Brown and Buchbinder 1976; Faithorn 1976; Hays and Hays 1982; Herdt 1981, 1982a; M. Strathern 1972). A few ethnographers have also considered how age and age stratification affect the lives of men and women (Gelber 1896; Godelier 1982; Modjeska). According to Foner (1984a:xi), age stratification exists in any society when 'individuals in a society, on the basis of their location in a particular age stratum, have unequal access to valued social roles and rewards'. More recently, Dickerson-Putman (1986, 1992, 1993, 1994a, 1994b) has explored the ways in which hierarchical age patterns structure relations among Highland men and women.

Bena Bena refer to the time period prior to Australian contact as 'the fighting time'. During this period, the Bena Bena participated in sweet potato horticulture, pig and cassowary husbandry, regional partner-to-partner fixed equivalence trade, and life course exchanges. Endemic warfare based on the bow and arrow and organized through Bigman leadership was another key feature of the past. The most important patrilineal kinship groups were the clan (*moneconare*) and lineage (*naneyarapanatna*) (Langness 1964a). Clan members resided in a fortified village ideally located in an easily defensible position during the 'fighting time'.

During the 'fighting time' systems of both age and gender affected the lives of men and women. The impact of these systems on the lives of women and the nature of age stratification among women prior to Australian contact and in contemporary contexts has been explored elsewhere. A complex web of gender ideologies appears to have structured pre-contact relations between men and women. A male-dominant ideology characterized such extradomestic activities as male cults, warfare, exchange, and leadership as culturally superior because it was these activities that provided a 'road' (*rot* Pidgin English) through which men could acquire prestige and renown and thus be referred to as someone 'who had a name'. Another ideology emphasized the complementary roles of men and women. When a couple married, they were expected to form a cooperative and interdependent economic unit. Men relied on the economic cooperation of their wives because the resources women produced (pigs, cassowaries, and surplus produce) were crucial to men's achievement of adulthood and their acquisition of a name.

THE MALE LIFE COURSE IN THE PAST

A person's functional age (involving a complex interplay of physiological changes, personal achievements, and role performance) affected the kinds of roles and activities that were considered culturally appropriate for him or her at different points along the life course. The Bena Bena believed that men's lives could be divided into four stages called: *Panae* (Child), *Kokolobo* (Youth), *Aloopabo* (Adult), and *Ayafa* (Old Man).

The most important life experiences for men occurred in the first three life course categories. While male children or *Panae* would accompany and help their fathers with various tasks, they spent most of their time playing with peers and practicing with bows and arrows. Between the ages of six and ten, they experienced the first two stages of *nama* cult initiation. It was after completion of the last two stages of initiation that male children became known as *Kokolobo* or Male Youths.

In the past, the initiation process, carried out by members of the secret, male *nama* cult, performed an important educational role in Bena Bena culture (Langness 1974; Read 1952). During this four-stage ritual education young men were trained as warriors, they learned appropriate gender roles and the purificatory rituals used by men to maintain personal strength, and they came to understand the importance of respect for one's elders and cooperation and identification with age-mates. Continued participation in male cults and communal residence provided structure to men's lives, was crucial to men's gender identity, and created a unified and strong fighting force (Herdt 1982b; M. Strathern 1995).

These rituals of initiation also introduced young men into a system of male age stratification in which older men would exert much control over the life events of younger men. It was assumed that younger men would extend the feelings of respect and obligation they had for their fathers to all senior men. The transfer of knowledge controlled by older men was crucial to the successful performance of men's roles throughout the life course and older men in general were expected to act as role models for younger men. In pre-contact Ganaga, an ideal gender stereotype provided a model for what an adult man could be. The ideal adult Bena Bena man cooperated with his wife in the production of resources and children, gave up courting, built a house for his wife, performed cult rituals, upheld male concerns, started to pay back his brideprice, and proved himself in war.

Although all senior men tried to emulate the behavior of the ideal man, it was the behavior of *gipina* or Bigmen that most closely conformed to this ideal model. A *gipina* among the Bena Bena ruled by influence and personality in a consensus-based society. To be a *gipina* was to have a name and thus have renown and influence beyond one's local group. Most clans (*moneconare*) had more than one *gipina*. A *gipina* acquired prestige and was able to draw and keep followers not because of entrepreneurial or oratorical skill but primarily because he took a 'road' that developed his skill as a battle strategist. In warfare (*luva*) (Langness 1971), a *gipina* had unlimited authority and this could be diffused to other situations such as dispute settlement between the clans and decisions concerning the timing of certain rituals.

The continued transfer of knowledge between older and younger men also created the general consensus of values (Dahrendorf 1957) that was necessary for the maintenance of social control. Older men and Bigmen could only pressure young men to conform to the role model for their gender if younger and older men agreed on the value of the model in the first place. A general consensus of values was also critical to the control of inappropriate or deviant behavior in Ganaga. It was the respected old men (*man bilong tok*) and retired *gipina* in a clan that most often oversaw and managed its daily activities. If the deviant behavior of younger men could not be controlled by these informal leaders, then a *gipina* would be called in to resolve the situation. Most young men eventually conformed because they valued their cultural traditions and feared and respected older men who were in a position to control and punish them.

During the course of their initiation, young men also learned the importance of their relationships with their age-mates (*faloo*). The bonds of endurance, mutual loyalty, obligation, cooperation, and closeness that men had with their biological brothers should also characterize their relationships with age-mates. And like biological brothers, the ties between age-mates remained salient until death. Until they achieved the status of adults, age-mates were perceived as a group and experienced major life course events as a group (Langness 1964a:101).

After completing the final stage of initiation male youths in Ganaga spent part of their time as warriors and part of their time participating in formal courting parties (Langness 1969). Courting, however, had little direct bearing on marriage. In Ganaga, Bigmen and older men controlled the choice of a marital partner for a young man because their wide personal networks could be utilized to find a bride for each member of an age-set (since the age-set married as a group) and because they were in the best position to amass and control the vast amount of resources necessary for the two types of brideprice. The skillful allocation of resources in these payments was a 'road' that helped older men to both acquire and maintain their renown and in the process indebt younger men to them.

For various reasons the early stages of marriage were very difficult for a young couple (Dickerson-Putman 1986, 1995). Older members of the community pressured the young couple to settle down and begin working as a responsible team and this pressure often resulted in wife beating. When the behavior of a married man demonstrated his responsibility and commitment to marriage, he entered the life stage of *Aloopabo* or adult.

Being a socially recognized adult was also the first prerequisite for acquiring a name. Having a name meant that one had achieved prestige and renown in the eyes of community members. Although all men eventually became adults not all men acquired a name. There were two 'roads' that men could take to acquire prestige. First, a man could acquire a name as a brave warrior who killed many men. Another 'road' for acquiring a name was to strategically contribute to brideprices, life course exchanges, and alliance payments within one's group to build up one's network and reputation. Men who combined these skills with expertise in battle competed for Bigman (*gipina*) leadership. We will now consider how men's lives and the nature of community life during the 'fighting time' were transformed by the development process.

EASTERN HIGHLANDERS AND THE DEVELOPMENT PROCESS

In a period of sixty years the Bena Bena have been transformed into coffee-producing peasants. I follow the lead of various Pacific scholars who consider that the introduction of cash crops (such as coffee) into agricultural communities is a key element in the transformation of these societies into peasantries. This is because the introduction of cash crops links a local economy to that of global economy over which local residents have little control (Healey 1989; Howlett 1962, 1973; Meggitt 1971; A. Strathern 1982b). An explicit goal of the Australian Administration was to transform Highlanders into peasants through the cash cropping of coffee. As we shall see, Australian development policies were particularly concerned to change men's roles. The cash cropping of coffee, conversion to Western religions, and new forms of leadership were explicitly introduced to Bena Bena men to replace the roles they lost in warfare, Bigman leadership and ritual.

The Australian Colonial Administration, believing that colonies should pay for themselves, focused its efforts on extracting resources from core areas in Papua New Guinea. Various authors have documented how the activities of both explorer-miners and missionaries led to the exploration of the Eastern Highlands and the beginning of the development process (Brookfield 1972; Connolly and Anderson 1987; Dexter 1961; Dickerson-Putman 1986; Downs 1980; Munster 1979).

Evangelical responsibility for the Goroka area fell to the German Lutheran or Neuendettelsau Lutheran missionaries based in Finschafen (Munster 1982). The Upper Bena Bena people had their first contact with these missionaries in 1932. In 1934, the German Lutherans established their first Mission Station in the Bena Bena area. These missionaries, however, appear to have had little long-term impact on the lives of Ganaga residents. In 1937, Seventh Day Adventists (SDA) entered the Goroka Valley and established a mission in the Bena Bena area.

The rumblings of the Second World War interrupted the activities of both missionary camps. When the SDAs returned to the Bena Bena area after the war (1946–1947) one of the first things they did was establish a primary school for the natives and two schools (at Sigoiya and Megabo) to train missionaries. One of the first men to return to Ganaga as an SDA missionary was a former resident who had received SDA training. Sometime in the early 1950s the missionaries came to the village and asked some of the converts to break their sacred flutes as a sign of their faith.

After this event most men abandoned the communal men's house and either resided full-time with their wives or spent much of their time in an individual men's house of their own construction. The conversion of some residents to Seventh Day Adventism introduced a new 'road' into communities like Ganaga—the church road or church-based activities. Men who travelled this 'road' believed that their involvement in church-based activities could help them acquire access to both prestige and cash. These men also provided a new and important role model for local men.

Encouraging rumors of gold deposits brought Australian explorers into the Eastern Highlands. In 1932, Bena Bena labor helped in the construction of an airstrip for the prospecting party of Mike Dwyer and the Leahy Brothers. The explorers pulled out of the Bena Bena area in 1933 when their search for significant mineral deposits was abandoned. In 1934 Jim Taylor established a patrol post near the abandoned airstrip. Between 1935 and 1936 *kiaps* used this post as a base from which to patrol their territories and begin both the pacification of the natives and the introduction of a decentralized form of government that would be administered through the positions of the *luluai* and *tutul*. It was probably during these patrols that the village of Ganaga was first contacted. It took six years to pacify the Bena Bena and they were not considered fully under administrative control until 1941. The threat of the Second World War led to the establishment of military control in the Highlands by the Australian New Guinea Administrative Unit (ANGAU) from 1942 to 1945 (Dexter 1961).

After the end of the war, *kiaps*, based in the Administrative Headquarters at Goroka, reintroduced decentralized government in the Eastern Highlands. Although some Ganaga men took advantage of the opportunities offered them through the Highlands Labor Scheme in 1950, the process of change and development did not really resume in the Eastern Highlands until after the reconstruction period (1946–1950). In summary, during the early years of Australian development in the Eastern Highlands, male cults were broken up, pacification was established, new forms of leadership were introduced, and conversion to Western forms of religion was begun.

It was after the Second World War that Australian development policies transformed the Highlands. The Eastern Highlands was officially opened to European settlers in 1953. Shortly thereafter, Bena Bena and other local men began to work on coffee plantations. Later in 1953 and 1954, smallholder coffee production was introduced to men. Policy makers believed that cash cropping and other forms of income-earning activities should be introduced to men to replace men's precolonial activities and roles eliminated in earlier stages of the development process. As noted earlier, Bena Bena horticulturists became peasants because the cash cropping of coffee linked local economies into the world economic system.

When the settlers entered the Goroka Valley in 1953, the local population was eagerly awaiting their arrival. For one thing, Eastern Highlanders were anxious to earn the newly introduced money from the sale of their land, their labor, and their food crops. From the local perspective any income-earning activity was called 'business' (*bisnis* Pidgin English). Equally important was the feeling that if settlers lived nearby, one would be certain to learn of the source of their wealth and power.

Ben Finney (1973, 1993) has suggested that Eastern Highlanders so quickly and enthusiastically responded to the introduction of coffee production and other forms of *bisnis* because their culture preadapted them to do so. He traces the evolution of several Gorokan business leaders (some of whom were Bena Bena) who were regarded as 'big men of business' because of their great skill and leadership in the new economy. During this phase of development in the Eastern Highlands, then, this first generation of business leaders forged a new 'road' to achieve a name and in the process provided a new role model for indigenous men.

New and more 'modern' forms of leadership and government, introduced during this period, provided men with another path or 'road' for the achievement of prestige. On a local level people would learn about representative government through locally elected government councils. In 1968, all other local councils in the Eastern Highlands were merged into the Goroka Local Government Council (Langness 1963). By the early 1970s the Administration decided that local government councils should be limited to administrative functions such as road building and that law and order, at the local level, should be implemented through a system of local courts and native magistrates (Downs 1980:150). Since 1980 one of the magistrates on the Sigerehe Village Court has been a man from Ganaga.

The introduction and expansion of educational facilities at the community, provincial, and national level also took place at this time. In the Eastern Highlands this meant that most 'villages' had greater access to community schools. In fact, many parents believed that educating their children (primarily boys) was a strategy that would improve their chances of sharing in the wealth of development.

At independence in 1975 the Papua New Guinean government hoped to diversify its economy and take control of its own development (Amarshi, Good, and Mortimer 1979; Good 1986). To date, the government has unfortunately experienced difficulty realizing this aim. As a result, some scholars believe that a distinctive style of peasantry persists in Eastern Highlands communities such as Ganaga. Diana Howlett (1973, 1980), for example, has characterized the peasantry of the Eastern Highlands as a terminal stage of development because of the lack of agricultural diversification and the general failure of investment activities in the region. More recently, Lawrence Grossman (1984) examined peasant commodity production in the Eastern Highlands community of Kapanara to understand why peasantry persists. He concluded that it was the ability of community residents to vary their participation in commodity production that largely accounted for the persistence of this stage of economic growth.

Some commentators have described some of the characteristics of contemporary Eastern Highlands peasantry. Donaldson and Good (1981) found that stratification of opportunity and economic differentiation have emerged as definitive characteristics of the peasantry of this province. This growing pattern of differentiation in opportunity has also exacerbated intergenerational differences among men. Researchers differ on whether younger or older men in the Highlands have benefited most from development (Boyd 1985; Donaldson and Good 1980; Howlett 1973; Meggitt and Gordon 1985).

These inequalities and biases have undoubtedly contributed to the growing level of frustration manifested in the Eastern Highlands in both the increase in the types and use of sorcery (Amarshi, Good, and Mortimer 1979; Keil and Johannes 1974; Westermark 1981) and in the resumption of tribal warfare (P. Brown 1982; Koch 1983; Meggitt 1977; Podelefsky 1984; A. Strathern 1984). Recently a growing number of researchers have postulated a relationship between the frustrating nature of the development experience and the increased incidence of both village and urban rascal crime (Bray 1985; Clifford *et al.* 1984; Hart Nibbrig 1992; Iamo 1993; Kolma 1993; Kulick 1992; Morauta 1986; Schiltz 1985; Toft 1985).

Some researchers, who have explored the activities of rascals in both rural and urban areas, suggest that 'rascalism', rather than being labeled as an identity or behavior related to organized crime, might better be viewed as the activities of acephalous and situationally responsive groups. Rascal groups are led by leaders whose behavior is not only often held up as a role model for members, but also strongly parallels that of Bigmen and entrepreneurs (Borrey 1993; Kulick 1993; Sykes 1994). Goddard (1995) feels that rascal behavior is best understood as a 'road' used by individuals to get money and prestige. We will now explore how the development processes outlined above have affected both the men of Ganaga and the community in which they live.

MEN IN THE PEASANT COMMUNITY OF GANAGA

Change and development have created a new world for Ganaga residents. The contemporary community of Ganaga consists of eighty-seven households (347 people) dispersed over seventeen named territories/hamlets. A vacant Seventh Day Adventist (SDA) church serves as a meeting house for the 18 percent (sixteen households) of the population that have converted to this religion. Contemporary Ganaga also includes a Health Post, Community School, and a formal market area.

As peasants, Ganaga residents must achieve a delicate balance between subsistence and income-earning activities (Meggitt 1971; A. Strathern 1982). Like MacWilliam (this volume) I view production in rural agricultural smallholdings in the Highlands as being sensitive and responsive to both the subsistence needs and capacities of household members and to the operation of an international economic system. Residents combine sweet potato horticulture and the animal husbandry of pigs, goats, and cassowaries with the cash cropping of coffee and various investment-based activities. Income-earning activities (such as coffee production and investment-based activities including tradestore operation) are considered 'business' and are afforded high cultural value and renown by both men and women.

Ganaga residents appear to view the introduction of cash-generating activities as the most important impact that development has brought to their rural community. So for Ganaga residents, the road to development is the path that leads to the acquisition of cash. As we shall see, although most Ganaga residents of Ganaga tend to emphasize the 'business' participation as a way to acquire this modern form of wealth, some people also recognize that development and cash can also be acquired through church-based fund-raising activities and through the activities of rascal gangs.

Breakup of the male cult, cessation of male and female group initiation, and pacification mean that some of the ideological boundaries between the sexes have blurred with development. Although Ganaga has been transformed into a peasant community, residents agree that a marital relationship, characterized by cooperation, complementarity, and mutual support, is still a crucial requirement for the achievement of adulthood for both men and women. Many aspects of the male life course, however, have been altered by the development process. The ramifications of these changes mean that men of contemporary Ganaga are confronted by a crisis of masculinity as they attempt to redefine both the appropriate roles for men and the meaning of the achievement of manhood and adulthood in a modern world.

The structure and nature of the development process as it unfolded in the Eastern Highlands has meant that Ganaga men of different ages have been offered differing opportunity structures (S. Barnes 1990) and different pathways to adulthood and prestige. Observation of and discussion with contemporary residents of Ganaga suggested that there were at least three 'roads' that men could take to acquire cash and achieve adulthood, recognition, and community prestige. The presence and allure of these differing paths has eroded the value consensus, intergenerational ties, and age stratification system (favoring older men) that were crucial to both community leadership and social control in the past. The diversity of experiences available to Ganaga men of different ages also means that men can't agree on how to define contemporary adulthood. In the following discussion I divide contemporary Ganaga men into three groups to highlight the diversity noted above.

OLD MEN

The group I refer to as old men subsumes the life course categories of *aloopabo* and *ayafa*. Men who were adults or who were on the road to adulthood prior to Australian contact are the older (forty or older) men of contemporary Ganaga. All of these men have participated to some degree in the group-based *nama* cults but none of them acquired a Western-style education. In short, these older men were educated into a system of values, gender roles, and ideology that prepared them for participation in male cults, warfare, and competition for Bigman leadership and renown.

It was the combined impact of the cessation of warfare and the abolition of group *nama* cults that most profoundly affected the older men of Ganaga and their response to subsequent forces of development. These events mean that older men have lost some of the most important means for maintaining their strength and identity as adults and their differentiation from women.

Pacification and the cessation of warfare have also eliminated the most important extradomestic role for men. This void has prevented men from achieving the adult status, has removed the main criterion for the definition of leadership and acquisition of a name (prestige), and has eliminated one of the most important means for creating and maintaining male gender identity.

Unlike the pattern of age stratification among women in the past (Dickerson-Putman 1992, 1993, 1994a), the pattern of age stratification among Ganaga men has been transformed by the development process. The abolition of male cults and the full-scale initiation system undermined one element of older men's control of younger men. The control that older men exerted in the marriage process has also diminished because they no longer have a monopoly of the resources used in brideprice. And finally older men do not participate to the same extent in new forms of leadership and in 'business' because they often lack the education and requisite skills required for these activities. In contemporary Ganaga then, the scale of age stratification has been tipped in favor of younger men because they now have greater access to valued social roles and rewards.

The current older men of Ganaga were eager to become involved in the cash cropping of coffee because they thought it would enable them to quickly achieve the wealth and success of the Australian expatriates. Although all of these older men actively participate in the opportunities available to Ganaga peasants, many are disillusioned and disappointed that the new 'road' of development has not brought them the wealth, meaning, success, or prestige that they had hoped for. They also have little faith in the introduced leadership roles of village magistrate and councilor because these positions have no legitimate power. And even if they acknowledged the legitimacy of these roles, older men do not have the requisite skills to participate in them. Conversion to Seventh Day Adventism has also not replaced the meaning and structure provided by pre-contact ritual and ideology. The disillusionment of older men is reflected in their lack of confidence in 'business' and education and their failure to support new leadership roles. Despite the great transformations that these older men have experienced, most still believe that the road to adulthood of the past has the most meaning, validity, and legitimacy.

YOUNG MEN

Unlike older men, the young men of Ganaga did not have to adjust to a radical change in their cultural environment. The group that I refer to as young men subsumes the life course category of *aloopabo* and includes Ganaga men who are roughly between the ages of twenty-five and forty. Most of these men have undergone the individual *nama* cult initiation and some have received an SDA education.

These young men of contemporary Ganaga have grown up in a peasant community that offers individuals the opportunity to participate in various income-generating and investment-based activities. While these young men demonstrate respect for the values of older men, they also have great confidence that participation in 'business' can lead to individual success.

Most contemporary young men in Ganaga have shared in the common experience of the voluntary, individual *nama* cult initiation. This 'modern' style of initiation evolved in the early 1950s when the fifteen-year group-based cult education was abolished. This contemporary form of initiation includes only the monthlong rituals of the Stage Three *nama* rites. Though some may have been coerced by their fathers, most young men say that they willingly took part in the initiation because, in the eyes of their community, it was the first step toward becoming a man. Many young men were also anxious to learn love magic so that they could attract women. Even though young men experience initiation on an individual basis, those men who have undergone the rituals consider themselves to be age-mates.

Unlike the system of rituals of the past in which young men learned the roles and pathways to manhood, the modern form of initiation functions as more of a public ceremony than as a system of education. It appears that during this initiation ritual, contemporary young men gain a knowledge and perhaps respect for their culture and for older men but these lessons do not necessarily form the basis for a system of age stratification or for a value system that would orient their subsequent behavior. This is of course because the peasant community in which these young men live is very different from life during the 'fighting time'.

Some of these contemporary young men in Ganaga also received a formal education at the SDA school that was introduced into the region in the late 1940s and 1950s. A community school education only became available in the Ganaga area in the early 1970s. The SDA educational system includes instruction in agricultural and business management. In fact, many of the leading businessmen in the Eastern Highlands have received an SDA education. Many young men who received an SDA education did not go beyond high school because they were anxious to become involved in coffee production. Though many of these young men did not receive secondary educational training in agriculture and business, the value of these activities may well have been communicated during the course of their primary education. The SDA education some of these men received, then, may have facilitated their adaptation to peasant life.

A few of the young men from Ganaga who obtained a primary education at he SDA schools went on to high school and/or received other forms of training. These young men may also have been influenced by the activities of second and third generation businessmen in the Goroka area who had ventured into both individual and group-based entrepreneurial activities such as the operation of coffee plantations and development corporations (Finney 1993:110). Two SDA-educated age-mates and active church members have used 'business' activity as a way to finance their efforts to acquire newly introduced leadership positions. The activities of these men and their combination of 'business' and church participation provide important role models for other young men and for male youths in contemporary Ganaga.

Carles was born in Ganaga and attended the SDA school through grade four. During my residence in Ganaga, Carles was elected as the new village magistrate. He believes that his election to this position was related to his reputation as a rising young businessman in Ganaga. Carles combines coffee production/processing and tradestore operation with coffee buying and the running of a family business corporation. Unfortunately, the older men in Ganaga do not recognize or support his position as magistrate and this fact often undermines Carles' efforts. Despite these difficulties, he provides an important example and model of a young man who has combined 'business' activity, political participation, church participation, and full-time residence in a rural peasant community.

John is a young man who is striving for a political position in national politics. Though he does not now reside full-time in Ganaga his behavior and his inclusion of male youths in his campaigns means that he provides another important role model for contemporary men. John received a primary education at the SDA school at Megabo and went on to complete grade ten at Goroka High School. For about ten years, John has been involved in politics, first at the regional and provincial level and most recently as a candidate for a seat in the National Parliament. In 1982, John became involved in coffee buying as a way to finance his campaign. Like Carles, he bought a modern coffee pulper and established it in one of the hamlets in Ganaga.

Although he lost as the Pangu Party candidate in the Bena-Unggai elections in 1982 and the by-election in 1983, John was proud of the way he conducted his campaign. His campaign visits also provided a stark contrast to those of other candidates which were characterized by the consumption of beer and physical fights. John's campaign visits to villages were quiet affairs and, because of his strong SDA beliefs, did not include the consumption of beer.

Through the years, John has gained a reputation as a fair man and a *man bilong tok*. When tribal fighting resumed in the Upper Bena Bena area in the late 1970s and various times in the 1980s, John negotiated a peace agreement between the principal communities.

Although Carles, John, and other young men in Ganaga appear to respect the values and achievements of older men, a formal, Western-style education is the context in which they develop their values, identities, and expectations. This education stressed the value and importance of 'business' and all other village-based activities and newly introduced leadership positions. In fact, younger men in this age group not only evaluate each other on the basis of individual achievement in 'business' but view success in 'business' as a springboard to national and local-level politics. So for the young men of contemporary Ganaga, Western-style education, 'business' activity, and for some church participation, are the crucial components of their path to adulthood and acquisition of a name (prestige).

MALE YOUTHS

Male youths, as an age group, are between the ages of eleven and twenty-five. In the past these youths would have been called *kakolobo*. Some of these youths have undergone individual *nama* cult initiation. While some male youths currently attend the community school in Ganaga or high school, most leave school. Although some male youths have experienced the modern form of initiation, they do not demonstrate very much respect for their elders or their past culture and they also do not appear to see the value of a peasant way of life.

Unlike the SDA-educated young men of Ganaga, most male youths attended the local community school. Ganaga residents told me that community schools stress that education is the key to finding a job, earning money, and becoming a success in the modern world. During their time in school, many Ganaga youths seem to have developed a set of expectations and values that led them to believe that they could break their ties with Ganaga and obtain a lucrative job in the city. These jobs would then allow them to purchase all the attractive Western-style goods that they saw in Goroka.

Although the male youths left school for various reasons, many shared the experience of having to return to life in Ganaga. Understandably, some experienced anger, frustration, and embarrassment at their failure to meet their own and their parents' expectations.

The community school experience appears to have alienated many male youths from village life. Though parents encourage their sons to help in the gardens and pick coffee, male youths don't have much desire to participate in these activities. This lack of interest is not a function of the life course but appears to reflect their attitude that horticulture and cash cropping are low status activities. And though some fathers and older men make overtures, male youths do not care to listen to the advice and guidance given to them by their elders. This is probably because male youths feel that their parents and elders do not have the appropriate knowledge to help them. The only interests many of these youths seem to have are in card playing, beer drinking, and contemporary forms of courting.

Both older men and young men alike told me that it is education that has spoiled male youths and many contemporary parents do not encourage or support their children's desire to attend school. This accounts for the low level of school attendance by Ganaga children. Regrettably, this further highlights the failure of school leavers and creates frustration in those who desire a Western education. The alienation that some male youths experience is often exacerbated by the reactions of parents and other men (see also Yauwi and Sipian 1978) who may show little understanding for the difficult transition their sons may be experiencing.

Some older men, who can't understand the failure and disinterest of male youths, react by publicly berating and nagging them. This behavior was expected and successful in the past when older men controlled various aspects of younger men's lives. But in contemporary Ganaga older men have little success in this role. This is largely because older men and male youths do not value the same roles, experiences, or social reality. As a result male elders feel that they have lost the support and respect and the ability to control and coerce male youths into action. The young men of contemporary Ganaga also appear unable to control the behavior of male youths. Again this is largely because young men and male youths do not value the same experiences and activities. Male youths show little respect for the 'business' and political participation that are so highly valued by the young men of Ganaga. The lack of strong intergenerational bonds and value consensus among men in Ganaga means that older men and young men are often unable to enforce social control. This failure has affected the community's ability to deal with the rascal problem.

During the course of my stay in Ganaga various community residents were the victims of rascal crime. Many parents in Ganaga feel that there is a strong relationship between education and 'rascalism', and this has apparently led them to withdraw their support from education.

I also became the target of rascals when I was away on a short field break. It was this incident that sensitized me to the fact that there was a vacuum of leadership and absence of social control in the community of Ganaga. My efforts to deal with this crime within the village court system are detailed elsewhere (Dickerson-Putman 1986). Eventually the two rascals who were responsible for that crime and most of the other crimes in Ganaga were identified. They turned out to be two male youths from Ganaga. These two youths both left school and spent part of their time living in Ganaga, processing coffee for John (the political candidate discussed above), and part of their time living in Goroka, helping John with his campaign. It appeared, then, that these two youths alternated their time between 'rascalling' and working as campaign workers.

Though community residents appeared to deplore the behavior of the rascals, the threats and pressures exerted on the youths by their older male relatives and the local village magistrate did not seem to affect the behavior of the village criminals. I would also argue that the lack of an even partially shared social reality and set of values among men has affected the ability of community members (especially older men) in Ganaga to control the disruptive and sometimes criminal behavior of male youths. These youths do not heed the criticism and pressure exerted by older men and young men because many feel that the values and 'roads' these groups have taken to acquire prestige have no relevance or meaning for them.

Although it did not occur to me at the time it is also possible that in some ways the residents of Ganaga supported the behavior of the rascals. In fact, both villagers and fellow rascals may view rascals as heroes and role models (Kulick 1993; A. Strathern 1993). Male youths, who don't see much value in the ways of the past, or in the 'business', church, and political participation valued by young men, may view 'rascalism' as a socially legitimate way to acquire both cash and prestige (Goddard 1995).

CONCLUSION

This article has attempted to compare and contrast the life course, role models, value system, educational experience, and activities of Bena Bena men of different ages in the Eastern Highlands community of Ganaga. The world of Bena Bena men prior to Australian contact has been radically transformed by colonial and postcolonial policies for development and culture change. During the 'fighting time', the male life course offered men roles and activities in male cults, warfare, exchange, and leadership. Successful performance in these arenas throughout the life course provided men with 'roads' to adulthood and prestige. A prolonged period of group initiation and ritual education combined with shared life experiences led to the development of a fairly homogeneous set of values, strong intragenerational ties and stratified intergenerational ties among men. All of these elements provided a strong base for community stability and social control.

Over sixty years of change have brought great heterogeneity to the lives of Ganaga men. Ritual education and group initiation no longer lead to the development of shared role models, stratified relations between generations, or form the basis for the development of a general consensus of values. In contemporary Ganaga Western-style education, 'business' activity, church activity, and rascal activity are the 'roads' to prestige valued by young men and male youths. The culturally appropriate roles and role models through which older men developed their gender identity, achieved adulthood, and acquired extradomestic prestige have been largely eliminated by change and development. Today the older men of Ganaga not only suffer role discontinuity but have also lost confidence in the hope that 'business' and Western forms of religion and education could replace the meaning they now find only in their past.

The heterogeneity of development experiences, values, role models, and perceived 'roads' to prestige associated with men of different ages has also affected community life and social control in Ganaga. This diversity suggests that it is imperative for contemporary Ganaga men to begin the process of redefining culturally appropriate roles, values, and intragender relationships for men. They must also reach for some level of consensus concerning a contemporary male life course and associated pathways to prestige. Until this process is under way the differential life experiences and aspirations of men will prevent residents from regaining social control and community stability and from defining a place for the community of Ganaga in the modern, developing world.

REFERENCES

Amarshi, A., Good, K., and Mortimer, R., 1979. *Development and Dependency: The Political Economy of Papua New Guinea*. Melbourne: Oxford University Press.

Barnes, S., 1990. 'Women, property and power', in P. Sanday and R. Goodenough, eds., *Beyond the Second Sex*. Philadelphia: University of Pennsylvania Press, pp. 253–280.

Borrey, A., 1993. *Talking about Revolution: The Law and Order Situation along the Highlands Highway Simbu Province of Papua New Guinea*. Fieldwork report, Papua New Guinea National Research Unit.

Boserup, E., 1990. 'Economic change and the roles of women', in I. Tinker, ed., *Persistent Inequalities: Women and World Development*. New York: Oxford University Press, pp. 14–24.

Boyd, D., 1985. 'Intergenerational discord and the politics of personal resource management in Papua New Guinea'. Paper presented at the annual meeting of the American Anthropological Association, Washington, D.C.

Bray, M., 1985. *Education and Social Stratification in Papua New Guinea*. Melbourne: Longman Cheshire.

Brookfield, H., 1972. *Colonialism, Development and Independence*. Cambridge: Cambridge University Press.

Brown, P., 1982. 'Chimbu disorder: tribal fighting in newly independent Papua New Guinea', *Pacific Viewpoint*, 22:1–21.

——, 1988. 'Gender and social change: new forms of independence for Simbu women', *Oceania*, 59:123–142.

Brown, P., and Buchbinder, G., 1976. 'Introduction', in P. Brown and G. Buchbinder, eds., *Man and Woman in the New Guinea Highlands*. American Anthropological Association: Washington, D.C., pp. 1–15.

Clifford, W., Morauta, L., and Stuart, B., 1984. *Law and Order in Papua New Guinea*. Volumes 1 and 2. Port Moresby: Institute of National Affairs.

Connolly, R., and Anderson, R., 1987. *First Contact*. New York: Viking.

Cox, E., and Aitsi, L., 1988. 'Papua New Guinea', in T. Tongomoa, ed., *Pacific Women: Roles and Status of Women in Pacific Societies*. Suva (Fiji): Institute of Pacific Studies of the University of the South Pacific, pp. 23–39.

Dahrendorf, R., 1957. *Class and Class Conflict in Industrial Society*. Stanford: Stanford University Press.

Dexter, D., 1961. *The New Guinea Offensives*. Canberra: War Memorial.

Dickerson-Putman, J., 1986. *Finding a Road in the Modern World: The Differential Effects of Culture Change and Development on the Men and Women of an Eastern Highlands Community*, unpublished doctoral dissertation, Bryn Mawr College.

——, 1988. 'Women's contribution to the domestic and national economy of Papua New Guinea', *Research in Economic Anthropology*, 10: 201–222.

——, 1990. 'Development or disillusionment: the rise and fall of a women's development organization in the Eastern Highlands Province of Papua New Guinea'. Paper prepared for the annual meetings of the American Anthropological Association.

———, 1992. 'Age and gender stratification in the highlands of Papua New Guinea: implications for participation in economic development', *Human Organization,* 51(2):
109-122.

———, 1994a. 'Old women at the top: an exploration of age stratification among Bena
Bena women', in J. Dickerson-Putman and J. K. Brown, eds., Special Issue entitled
Women's Age Hierarchies, *Journal of Cross-Cultural Gerontology,* 9(2): 193-206.

———, 1994b. 'Women, development and stratification in the Eastern Highlands Province of Papua New Guinea', in J. Dickerson-Putman and L. Zimmer-Tamakoshi, eds.,
Special Issue entitled Women and Development in the Pacific. *Urban Anthropology
and Studies of Cultural Systems and World Economic Development,* 23 (1): 13-38.

———, 1996. 'From pollution to empowerment: women, age and power among the Bena
Bena of the eastern highlands', in J. Dickerson-Putman, ed., Special Issue entitled
'Women, Age and Power in Papua New Guinea and Australia'. *Pacific Studies,* 19(4).

Donaldson, M., and Good, K., 1980. *Development of Rural Capitalism in Papua New Guinea:
Coffee Production in the Eastern Highlands.* Institute of Papua New Guinea Studies
Occasional Paper No. 1. Boroko, Papua New Guinea.

Donaldson, M., and Good, K., 1981. 'The Eastern Highlands: coffee and cash', in
D. Denoon and C. Snowden, eds., *A Time to Plant, A Time to Uproot.* Boroko (PNG):
Institute for Papua New Guinea Studies, pp. 143-170.

Downs, I., 1980. *The Australian Trusteeship: Papua New Guinea 1945-1975.* Canberra: Australian Government Press Service.

Faithorn, E., 1976. 'Women as persons', in P. Brown and G. Buchbinder, eds., *Man and
Woman in the New Guinea Highlands.* Washington, D.C.: American Anthropological
Association, pp. 86-95.

Finney, B., 1973. *Bigmen and Business.* Canberra: Australian National University Press.

———, 1993. 'From the Stone Age to the Age of Corporate Takeovers', in V. Lockwood, T.
Harding, and B. Wallace, eds., *Contemporary Pacific Societies.* Englewood Cliffs: Prentice Hall, pp. 102-116.

Foner, N., 1984. *Ages in Conflict.* New York: Columbia University Press.

Gardner, S., 1976. 'Sir Paul and the Sleeping Beauty', *Research in Melanesia,* 2(3&4): 22-31.

Gelber, M., 1986. *Gender and Society in the New Guinea Highlands.* Boulder: Westview Press.

Goddard, M., 1995. 'The rascal road: crime, prestige and development in Papua New
Guinea', *The Contemporary Pacific,* 7(1): 55-80.

Godelier, M., 1982. 'Social hierarchies among the Baruya', in A. Strathern, ed., *Inequalities
in the New Guinea Highlands,* Cambridge: Cambridge University Press, pp. 3-34.

Good, K., 1986. *Papua New Guinea: A False Economy.* London: Anti-Slavery Society.

Grossman, L., 1984. *Peasants, Subsistence Ecology and Development in the Highlands.* Princeton: Princeton University Press.

Hart Nibbrig, N. E., 1992. 'Rascals in paradise: urban gangs in Papua New Guinea', *Pacific
Studies,* 15(3): 115-134.

Hays, T. E., and Hays, P. T., 1982 'Opposition and complementarity of the sexes in
Ndumbu initiation', in G. H. Herdt, ed., *Rituals of Manhood.* Berkeley: University of
California Press, pp. 201-238.

Healey, C., 1989. 'The anthropology of development', *Canberra Anthropology,* 12: 1-18.

Herdt, G. H., 1981. *Guardians of the Flutes: Idioms of Masculinity.* New York: McGraw Hill.

Herdt, G. H., ed., 1982a. *Rituals of Manhood: Initiation in Papua New Guinea.* Berkeley: University of California Press.

Herdt, G. H., and Poole, F. J. P., 1982b. 'Sexual antagonism: the intellectual history of a
concept in New Guinea anthropology', in F. J. P. Poole and G. H. Herdt, eds., *Gender
and Social Change in Papua New Guinea.* Social Analysis 12: 1-25.

Howlett, D., 1962. *A decade of change in the Goroka Valley,* unpublished doctoral dissertation. Australian National University.

————, 1973. 'Terminal development: from tribalism to peasantry', in H. Brookfield, ed., *The Pacific in Transition*. Canberra: Australian National University Press, pp. 249–273.

————, 1980. 'When is a peasant not a peasant? Rural proletarianism in Papua New Guinea', in J. N. Jennings and G. L. R. Linge, eds., *Of Time and Place: Essays in Honor of OHK Spate*. Canberra: Australian National University Press, pp. 193–210.

Hughes, H., 1985. 'Introduction', in H. Hughes, ed., *Women and Development in the Pacific*. Canberra: Australian National University, pp. 3–10.

Iamo, W., 1992. 'Misunderstood and misrepresented: the plight of today's youth', *Current Issues*, 1 (1).

Keil, D. K., 1974. 'The inter-group economy of the Nekematigi, Eastern Highlands District, New Guinea', unpublished doctoral dissertation, Northwestern University.

————, and Johannes, A., 1974. 'Fighting with illness'. Paper presented at the annual meeting of the American Anthropological Association, Mexico City.

Koch, K. F., 1983. 'Pacification: perspectives from conflict theory', in M. Rodman and M. Cooper, eds., *The Pacification of Melanesia*. New York: Lanham, pp. 199–208.

Kolma, C., 1993. 'Youth leader suggests ways to tackle crime'. *Papua New Guinea Post-Courier*, Tuesday, 27 July, 23.

Kulick, D., 1992. *Language Shift and Cultural Reproduction: Socialization, Self and Syncretism in a Papua New Guinea Village*. New York: Cambridge University Press.

————, 1993. 'Heroes from Hell: representations of rascals in a Papua New Guinean village', *Anthropology Today*, 9(3): 9–14.

Langness, L. L., 1963. 'Notes on the Bena Bena Council, Eastern Highlands', *Oceania*, 33: 151–170.

————, 1964a. 'Bena Bena Social Structure', unpublished doctoral dissertation.

————, 1964b. 'Some problems in the conceptualization of highlands social structure', *American Anthropologist*, 64(4): 162–182.

————, 1967. 'Sexual antagonism in the New Guinea highlands: a Bena Bena example', *Oceania*, 27: 61–77.

————, 1969. 'Marriage in the Bena Bena', in R. Glass and M. Meggitt, eds., *Pigs, Pearlshells and Women*. Englewood Cliffs: Prentice Hall, pp. 38–55.

————, 1971. 'Bena Bena political organization', in B. Berndt and P. Lawrence, eds., *Politics in New Guinea*. Perth: University of Western Australia Press, pp. 298–316.

————, 1974. 'Ritual, power and male dominance in the New Guinea highlands', *Ethos*, 2: 189–212.

Leahy, M. J., 1991. *Exploration into Highland New Guinea*. Tuscaloosa: University of Alabama Press.

Meggitt, M., 1971. 'From tribesmen to peasants', in L. R. Hiatt and C. J. Awardena, eds., *Anthropology in Oceania*. Sydney: Angus and Robertson, pp. 191–209.

————, 1977. *Blood is their Argument*. Palo Alto (CA): Mayfield Publishing Co.

Meggitt, M., and Gordon, R. J., 1985. *Law and Order in the New Guinea Highlands*. Hanover (NH): University Press of New England.

Modjeska, N., 1982. 'Production and inequality: perspectives from central New Guinea', in A. Strathern, ed., *Inequality in the New Guinea Highlands*. Cambridge: Cambridge University Press, pp. 50–108.

Morauta, L., ed., 1986. *Law and Order in a Changing Society*. Canberra: Australian National University Press.

Munster, P., 1979. 'Makarai: A History of Early Contact in the Goroka Valley, New Guinea Central Highlands', unpublished doctoral dissertation, University of Papua New Guinea.

————, 1982). 'My rifle is above', *Catalyst*, 12(3): 226–243.

Podelefsky, A., 1984. 'Contemporary warfare in the New Guinea highlands', *Ethnology*, 23(2):73–88.

Preston, R., and Wormald, E., 1987). 'Culture, ideology and the subordination of women in transitional societies', in S. Stratigos and P. Hughes, eds., *Ethics of Development: Women as Unequal Partners in Development*. Port Moresby: University of Papua New Guinea, pp. 50–58.

Read, K., 1952. 'The Nama Cult of the central highlands', *South Pacific,* 23:1–25.

Salisbury, R., 1962. *From Stone to Steel*. Melbourne: Melbourne University Press.

Schiltz, M., 1985. 'Rascalism, tradition and the state in Papua New Guinea', in S. Toft, ed., *Domestic Violence in Papua New Guinea*. Port Moresby: PNG Law Reform Commission.

Sexton, L., 1986. *Mothers of Money, Daughters of Coffee: The Wok Meri Movement*. Ann Arbor: University of Michigan Press.

Strathern, A., 1982. 'Tribesmen or peasants?' in A. Strathern, ed., *Inequality in New Guinea Highland Societies*. Cambridge: Cambridge University Press, pp. 137-157.

——, 1984. *A Line of Power*. London: Tavistock.

——, 1993. 'Crime and compensation: disputed themes in Papua New Guinea's recent history', *Polar,* 55–65.

Strathern, M., 1972. *Women in Between*. New York: Seminar Press.

——, 1995. 'Gender and identity in the New Guinea highlands', in J. D. Faubion, ed., *Rethinking the Subject*. Boulder: Westview Press, pp. 46–59.

Stratigos, S., and Hughes, P. J., eds., 1987. *The Ethics of Development: Women as Unequal Partners in Development*. Port Moresby (PNG): University of Papua New Guinea Press.

Sykes, K., 1994. 'What do rascals want? a critique of education as national development in Papua New Guinea'. Paper presented at the American Anthropological Association Meeting, Atlanta, Ga.

Toft, S., ed., 1985. *Domestic Violence in Papua New Guinea*. Port Moresby: Papua New Guinea Law Reform Commission.

Westermark, G., 1981. 'Sorcery and economic change in Agarabi', *Social Analysis,* 8:89–100.

Yauwi, J. P., and Sipian, S. J., 1978. 'The role of school leavers in rural development in the Goroka District'. Seminar paper on Rural Development in the Eastern Highlands Province. Administrative College.

Young, R., 1974. 'The social hierarchy of the Bena Bena', in R. D. Shaw, ed., *Kinship Studies*. Summer Institute of Linguistics, pp. 137–168.

Acknowledgements

I acknowledge with thanks the organizations that made possible the research on which this paper is based. Specifically, funding was provided by the National Science Foundation, the Wenner Gren Foundation for Anthropological Research, the Bryn Mawr College Max Richter Travelling Scholarship and the Sigma Xi Scientific Society. Special thanks to the residents of Ganaga who shared their lives and experiences with me.

Part Four

THE PEOPLE'S WELFARE

$\mathcal{P}$APUA NEW GUINEANS' INVOLVEMENT with the outside world has resulted in problems and opportunities that challenge both old and new cultural imaginations and the small political scale of most Melanesian societies (Smith 1994; Kirsch 1997). From communal safety nets to urban crime and rural poverty, from medical systems focused on restoring social relations to one requiring mass inoculations and the monitoring of such new diseases as AIDS and diabetes, and from small-scale farming to large-scale developments and environmental destruction, Papua New Guineans must make decisions about a future that is contested and only partly under their control. How to harmonize, for example, the people's desire and need to secure the land for future generations with their own and the government's commoditization of the environment and the selling off of Papua New Guinea's natural resources? Or how to understand and satisfy the conflicting interests of men and women when they live in a world in which, on the one hand, a western-educated Papua New Guinean man might yet feel himself a victim of his wife's treachery and sorcery when she suffers a miscarriage and, on the other, a young village girl, having been exposed to western ideas through her experiences at a mission school, might dream of having a new kind of relationship with her future husband. In the following chapters, education is highlighted as a primary means for Papua New Guineans to handle the challenges they face. One compelling challenge is improving the distribution and quality of health care to more equitably care for the needs of persons living in rural areas of

Papua New Guinea as well as the special needs of women and children (Gillett 1990; Stratigos and Hughes 1987; Townsend 1985). Other important challenges include educating the public in ways to prevent the further spread of AIDS and other sexually transmitted diseases throughout Papua New Guinea (The National Sex and Reproduction Research Team and Jenkins 1994), solving Papua New Guinea's 'Law and Order Problem' (Morauta 1986), and eradicating domestic violence and the sexual abuse of women (Counts 1990; Toft 1986), and protecting Papua New Guinea's environment from rapacious capitalism and greed (Hyndman 1994; May and Spriggs 1990; Oliver 1991; Polomka 1990; Quodling 1991). It is worth keeping in mind, however, that education itself has introduced problems into Papua New Guinea society by promoting increased social stratification and economic inequality (Bray and Smith 1985). While there is a concerted effort to educate females as well as males, Papua New Guinea's education system is still riddled with the results of sexism (Wormald and Crossley 1988). And, as both Crossley and Monsell-Davis point out in this volume, the expectations education raises among both students and their parents are not likely to be met in most instances, resulting in increasing dissatisfaction with the system and more law and order problems.

SUGGESTED READINGS

Bray, M., and Smith, P., eds., 1985. *Education and Social Stratification in Papua New Guinea*. Melbourne, Australia: Longman Cheshire.

Counts, D. A., ed., 1990. *Domestic Violence in Oceania*. Special Issue, *Pacific Studies*, 13(3).

Gillett, J. E., 1990. *The Health of Women in Papua New Guinea*. Goroka: Papua New Guinea Institute of Medical Research Monograph No. 9.

Hyndman, D. C., 1994. *Ancestral Rain Forests and the Mountain of Gold: Indigenous Peoples and Mining in the New Guinea Highlands*. Boulder: Westview Press.

Kirsch, S., 1997. 'Regional dynamics and conservation in Papua New Guinea: the Lakekamu River Basin Project', in K. Barlow and S. Winduo, eds., *Logging the Southwestern Pacific: Perspectives from Papua New Guinea, Solomon Islands, and Vanuatu*. Special Issue, *The Contemporary Pacific*, 9(1): 97-120.

May, R. J., and Spriggs, M., eds., 1990. *The Bougainville Crisis*. Bathurst, NSW: Crawford House Press.

Morauta, L., ed., 1986. *Law and Order in a Changing Society*. Canberra: Department of Political and Social Change, Australian National University.

National Sex and Reproduction Research Team and Jenkins, C., 1994. *National Study of Sexual and Reproductive Knowledge and Behaviour in Papua New Guinea*. Goroka: Papua New Guinea Institute of Medical Research Monograph No. 10.

Oliver, D., 1991. *Black Islanders: A Personal Perspective of Bougainville, 1937-1991*. South Yarra, Victoria: Hyland House.

Polomka, P., ed., 1990. *Bougainville: Perspectives on a Crisis*. Canberra: Strategic and Defence Studies Centre, Research School of Pacific Studies, Australian National University.

Quodling, P., 1991. *Bougainville: The Mine and the People*. Pacific Papers Series No. 3. St. Leonards, NSW & Auckland: Centre for Independent Studies.

Smith, M. F., 1994. *Hard Times on Kairiru Island: Poverty, Development, and Morality in a Papua New Guinea Village*. Honolulu: University of Hawaii Press.

Stratigos, S., and Hughes, P. J., eds., 1987. *The Ethics of Development: Justice and the Distribution of Health Care*. Port Moresby: University of Papua New Guinea Press.

Toft, S., ed., 1986. *Domestic Violence in Papua New Guinea*. Papua New Guinea Law Reform Commission Monograph No. 3.

Townsend, P. K., 1985. *The Situation of Children in Papua New Guinea*. Boroko: Papua New Guinea Institute of Applied Social and Economic Research.

Wormald, E., and Crossley, A., eds., 1988. *Women and Education in Papua New Guinea and the South Pacific*. Port Moresby: University of Papua New Guinea Press.

Lawrence Hammar

AIDS, STDS, AND SEX WORK IN PAPUA NEW GUINEA

$\mathcal{G}$LOBALLY, SOMEWHERE BETWEEN 25 and 30 million people are now infected with Human Immunodeficiency Virus (HIV), the pathogen alleged to cause Acquired Immune Deficiency Syndrome (AIDS) (Altman 1996; Krieger 1996; Purvis 1997). As of 1992, 'only' 6,070 AIDS cases had been reported to the World Health Organization (WHO) for countries in the Western Pacific/Southeast Asia region, but the situation is worsening (United Nations 1996:10). At 1995's end there was an estimated HIV antibody seroprevalence (or presence in blood samples of antibodies to HIV) in the Western Pacific of 43,500 (*STD Nius* 1995:2), a rate increasing so rapidly that some (e.g., Elford and Dwyer 1993:259) predict that by the year 2000 there will be HIV epidemics greater than in North America and Europe combined. The official HIV antibody seroprevalence in Papua New Guinea climbed to 247 and 342 by the ends of 1994 and 1995, respectively, but the real numbers may be decimally greater (cf. van der Meijden and Malau 1991; O'Leary *et al.* 1993; Purvis 1997; *The Health Worker* 1995a:3; *STD Nius* 1995:1; Sarda and Harrison 1995).[1] Papua New Guineans are infecting one another

---

[1]Mounting a national HIV antibody serosurveillance program is incredibly complicated since one has accurately to link data derived from surveys conducted at particular sites (e.g., STD or antenatal clinics, army barracks) to an imputed 'general population' in whose members immune system distress can already be common. One must employ often unreliable, variably interpretable tests and report on findings derived therefrom without inducing public alarm or apathy (cf. van der Meijden and Malau 1991; NSRRT and Jenkins 1994; United Nations 1996; Whitaker and Edwards 1991; Mondia 1990; Mondia and Perea 1990; Gillett 1990:25).

and are linked sexually to Australia and Indonesia, where figures are high and increasing quickly, respectively (Mulhall, Haret, and Harcourt 1995; Ford, Wirawan, and Fajans 1995; Stevenson 1994; Lubis *et al.* 1994). Papua New Guinea's HIV/AIDS ratio is roughly 2:1, the lowest among all countries in the Western Pacific reporting more than two cases. This suggests that Papua New Guineans are developing AIDS more quickly than other Western Pacific islanders, dying from it faster (e.g., Sarda and Harrison 1995), and that gross underreporting of HIV infection is occurring.

Serosurveillance programs (which track pathogen spread via blood testing) may yet be insufficiently monitoring immune systems compromised by HIV, for example, tuberculosis, or *Pneumocystis carinii* pneumonia, that is being activated specifically by HIV infection (or vice versa). Complicating matters further is that HIV relates synergistically (in co-related fashion) with sexually transmitted diseases (STDs), particularly with genital ulcer diseases (GUDs), which can facilitate HIV transmission and hasten the clinical presentation of AIDS (Wasserheit 1991; Bennett 1996). Mann, Tarantola, and Netter (1992:165) write that those 'who have histories of STD are at increased risk of acquiring HIV, while HIV-infected persons are likely to have greater susceptibility to infection with other STDs and, if co-infected, may experience them in an unusually severe and protracted course'. In Papua New Guinea, significant GUDs and their 'causal agents' (see below) include chancroid (*Haemophilus ducreyi*); syphilis (*Treponema pallidum*); Donovanosis (*Calymmatobacterium granulomatis*); a chlamydial infection, Lymphogranuloma venereum; and genital herpes (herpes simplex virus). GUD prevalence (or extent of untreated cases) and incidence (of new cases) may also be taken to be mimicking HIV transmission and to be standing proxy for the extent of 'unprotected sex' in a community.

HIV has been present in Papua New Guinea in a critical mass at least since the early 1980s, perhaps mimicking STD transmission that occurred along the Highlands Highway in the 1960s (*STD Nius* 1995:3). Some suspect that Papua New Guinea has the 'highest per capita prevalence of HIV in the Pacific region' (Purvis 1997:77). '[D]evastatingly low levels of knowledge about the disease' (*STD Nius* 1995:3) and the fact that 44 percent of women in a nationwide survey either knew 'nothing' or only vaguely (in Western terms) about STD dynamics (NSRRT and Jenkins 1994)[2] suggest that several serious social and medical crises are

---

[2] This ingenious publication was unfortunately deemed unfit for nonmedical readership.

afoot. STDs are often related to lowered self-esteem, and can induce sorcery accusations and retribution and spousal abandonment. Non-marriedness can lead women into commercialized sexual relations and the occupational and health hazards thereof. Women's often absent 'sexual citizenship' (Goldstein 1992), or power to consent to and control the timing, meaning, and implications of sexual intercourse, bodes ill particularly for women suffering from AIDS or suspected to be so (United Nations 1996:18).

GOALS OF THIS CHAPTER

In this essay I want to link the current AIDS crisis in Papua New Guinea ultimately to European introduction of STDs, and then explore two historical questions related to colonial and postcolonial developments. One involves processes by which sex industries, or multiple locales and systems of prostitution, now flourish throughout Papua New Guinea, and the other links 'traditional' forms of sexual transaction to such sex industries. I want to make clear at the outset that my analytic lens is explicitly gendered, inspired by feminist critique, and trained upon three intertwined theses. First, I believe that STDs and AIDS, no less so than prostitution, are evidence of acutely gendered relationships *between* people, not just biomedical phenomena operating *in* people or upon them. In Papua New Guinea, therefore, syphilis infection is a problem of the Social Body, the Body Politic, too, not just Body Individual. Consider the following, literally: (1) *sexually transmitted* disease/ sexually transmitted *dis-ease;* (2) *acquired* immune deficiency syndrome; (3) prostitution equals the exchange of sex for money and/or goods. Convention tells us that syphilis is a disease whose cause is the spirochete and whose cure is now penicillin. But perhaps syphilis (and GUDs generally) is not the real *dis-ease* so much as that women lack sexual citizenship, that men are having unprotected intercourse, that extreme sexism's manifestation is syphilis, and that the cure is not so much penicillin as concrete measures taken to improve women's status, to redress gendered legal inequities, and to increase sexual citizenship. My second thesis is that prostitution is the *solution* to extreme sexism, not the cause. Women have to exchange sex for money and goods casually and institutionally because they do not have access to the means of production equal to men's. My third thesis, more optimistically, is that if AIDS evinces *dis-ease* in the Body Social, it can be healed, socially, *in* the community, not just *at* the clinic, biomedically. If prostitution is caused by men's biologically greater sex drive, then not much can be done about it, but if prostitution is a contradiction social in origin and perpetuation, then it can be unraveled and made unnecessary. If *disease* is sexually transmitted, then AIDS, STDs, and sex work can be healed.

THE INTRODUCTION OF STDs TO THE PACIFIC

With the sole exception perhaps of a genetically close 'cousin' of syphilis (yaws), each of the STDs above was introduced to (Papua) New Guinea by Europeans beginning a century ago, where they have ravaged (Papua) New Guineans ever since.[3] Being new, introduced diseases, local peoples lacked both immunity to them and the cultural and medicinal repertoire requisite to recognizing, treating, and preventing them. This 'gift' of civilization (e.g., Bushnell 1993) Europeans wrote about in shades that swung between ignorance, neglect, blame, and concerned paternalism. When they recognized themselves as having *introduced* STDs, they blamed alleged Melanesian sexual laxity and medical ignorance for their *further spread*, on, for example, 'marathon dancing...accompanied by sexual license' (Gunther 1972:754). When Europeans expressed culpability for the devastating bodily effects that STDs had upon Melanesians, they argued for the latter's racial inferiority (Lambert 1928:363). When European knowledge of and treatments for STDs began to improve, Europeans began not only to treat afflicted Melanesians but to surveil upon them accordingly—STDs became for Europeans subject and object of discourse and administration. They used the information gained thereby (say, on high village STD infection rates) to justify colonial rule, to inspire Christian discipline, and to introduce sweeping behavioural changes. 'Moral' educational policies were designed so as to induce Marind-anim, for instance, 'to monog-

[3] I have to use some terms somewhat confusingly, since 'Papua', 'New Guinea', 'Papua New Guinea', and '(Papua) New Guinea' or 'Papua-New Guinea' each mean different things throughout the colonial period. Unless otherwise noted, 'New Guinea' refers to the entire mainland of this, the world's third largest island, plus neighboring, offshore islands. 'Papua New Guinea' refers to the independent nation-state thereof, 'Papua New Guineans' to its citizens, and '(Papua) New Guinea' and '(Papua) New Guineans' to the same geographic locale and peoples prior to independence. 'Papuans' refers to those living along the southern coast of the mainland of New Guinea, stretching from what is now the Milne Bay Province in the east through the Papuan Gulf westward to the border between Papua New Guinea and Indonesia. 'New Guineans' includes 'Papuans' but extends beyond it. 'Melanesia' includes island and archipelagic New Guinea plus the Solomon Islands, Buka, Bougainville, and so on.

amy, by building houses according to a given model and by combating superstition and sexual excesses' (Thierfelder 1928:406).

STD epidemics occurred almost upon contact and often with devastating effect. In 1874, there was no STD reported in Papua, but by 1908 there was an STD prevalence of 5 percent in the Trobriand islands (Lombange 1984:145) and of 5 percent in Rabaul, having spread 'enormously' in the six years from 1920 (Lambert 1928:368). Donovanosis introduced first to Australian aborigines then Torres Strait islanders then south coastal New Guineans eventually infected upwards of 12 to 35 percent of Marind-anim in some villages.[4] Syphilis outbreaks occurred in the Torres Strait and at Cairns in 1900–1901, due partly to the brothels established there in the 1870s in which were kept prostituted Japanese women (Sissons 1977:488, n. 69). Others in the Torres Strait/South Fly river area had by then already made evident to the pearl-sheller, Edward Beardmore (1890), their familiarity with genital afflictions. Gonorrhea and Donovanosis epidemics occurred in the (Papua) New Guinea highlands region in context of the Second World War and gold-mining exploration (Zigas 1971). A syphilis epidemic occurred in the highlands only nine years after its introduction during construction of the Highlands Highway (Garner, Hornabrook, and Backhouse 1972; Hornabrook 1972), and epidemics of all three have ensued at other times in and around Port Moresby (Maddocks 1967; Maddocks, Enders, and Dennis 1976).

STDs IN BIOMEDICAL PERSPECTIVE

Most historical references to the introduction of STDs to the Pacific are tantalizingly sketchy (e.g., Fischer 1963; Salmond 1991; Wright 1959; Watt 1979; Moorehead 1966; Furnas 1947), so those either greatly or specifically about STDs (e.g., Lambert 1928; Richens 1985; Vogel, with Richens 1989; Willcox 1980a-c; Hughes 1991; Hughes and Dyke 1993) or about social aspects thereof (e.g., Ree 1982; Pataki-Schweizer and Tabua 1980; Hart 1974; Clark 1993; Clark and Hughes 1995) are therefore precious. Most references either glance at the controversy surrounding the introduction of STDs either by English crew of Captains Wallis, Cook,

[4] Donovanosis had been introduced to Australian aborigines and Torres Strait islanders to the south beginning in the 1880s (e.g., Jackson 1911). In Australia it now plagues almost exclusively Australian aborigines, particularly in remote Central Australian communities (Mitchell, Roberts, and Schneider 1986) and in more urbanized Northern Queensland settings (Watsford and Alderman 1953; Ashdown and Kilvert 1979).

and Bligh, or French crew of Captain Bougainville and others of STDs to Tahitians, Tongans, and Hawaiians, or mention them but only so as to blame 'the indiscriminate sexual intercourse of the inhabitants' (Naval Intelligence Division 1945:223) or to charge that 'unmarried [New Guinean] women are practically all prostitutes' (Calov and Weir 1925:722). Rare is a primary source such as the following, a journal entry written by one of Captain Cook's lieutenants on 1 March 1779, which noted that one Hawaiian man

> told us that we had left a disorder amongst their women [probably both gonorrhea and syphilis], which had killed several of them, as well as men. He himself was infected with the Venereal disease, & described in feeling terms the havock it had made, & its pains, &tc—I was never more thoroughly satisfied...that we were the authors of the disease in this place. (quoted in Bushnell 1993:36–37)

Non-GUDs in Papua New Guinea
Chancroid, Donovanosis, and syphilis, because they quickly and obviously manifest themselves on the 'outside' of the body, often obscure the seriousness of the less easily visible and identifiable gonorrhea, chlamydia, trichomonas, and non-gonococcal urethritis (NGU). Gonorrhea is the most frequently *reported* STD in Papua New Guinea, indeed, the third most frequently reported communicable disease in the Pacific, with Papua New Guinea contributing 86.8 percent of those cases as of 1973 (Willcox 1980c:207). The infertility which, when left untreated, it induces factored in the depopulation of New Ireland between 1930 and 1951 and a high infant mortality there (Gunther 1972). Hart found in 1974 in Port Moresby that 62 percent of all Army STD Clinic patients at sergeant's rank or below were infected with it (and that 38 percent were infected with two or more other STDs). Almost all pre-term babies, stillbirths, and miscarriages show evidence of it (Gillett 1990:91; see also Everett 1987), as did, according to Rooke (1982), 43 percent of all the gynecology admissions to one hospital and 50 percent of all maternity patients to another clinic (Kish, in Gillett 1990:91). Other non-GUDs do damage, too. Wesche (1989) reports high levels of chlamydia which, when left untreated, can also induce infertility (Jenkins 1993). Between 1978 and 1988, incidence of PID, tubo-ovarian abscess, and extra-uterine pregnancy rose from 67, 5, and 6, respectively, to 270, 19, and 26 (Gillett 1990:92). Madang Hospital admissions between 1976 and 1984 for PID-related illness increased tenfold (NSRRT and Jenkins 1994:6; see also Mola 1989), and it accounted

for 15 percent of all Port Moresby General Hospital gynecological admissions by the early 1980s (Rooke 1982). Between 1974 and 1983, the crude incidence of gonorrhea plus syphilis equaled the crude birth rate (Lombange 1984:151).

Donovanosis

Donovanosis (see also Hammar 1997a) was introduced first to coastal New Guinean villages and then spread up, down, and between waterways due to both colonial policies and indigenous sexual practices. The Marind-anim, for instance, practiced ritualized hetero- and homosexual serial intercourse (vaginal, anal, and masturbatory) so as to encourage plant, human, and animal fertility, to mark important events, and to acquire mixtures of semen and vaginal fluids for use in medicinal and ritual contexts (see especially Van Baal 1966). These practices had disastrous effects once Donovanosis was introduced. However, the Dutch also forcibly installed model nuclear-family-type dwellings, which pushed men and women together sexually more frequently. They prohibited head-hunting and encouraged labour migration and intertribal trade, which opened up former 'no-man's lands' to disease transfer. Generally, they contributed to imbalanced sex ratios and facilitated sexual liaisons between male soldiers, police, and carriers and local females. Lambert's study (1928:368) showed 'the results of breaking the ancient quarantine of intertribal enmity', and Zigas (1971) found similar processes at work in the Goilala region of Papua and resultant high prevalence of Donovanosis. It has been a particular problem in Papua at least since 1917 (Kettle 1979:17; Maddocks 1967), and is now extremely common in the National Capital District (NCD), and in Morobe and Highlands provinces (Ree 1982:33). Given that it has an incubation period of 8–80 days and produces beefy-red ulcers and grooved nodules which can erupt into expansive lesions, Donovanosis, when left untreated, can have long-term, constitutional (Richens 1985, 1991), and social effects by its propensity to disfigure genitalia, induce infertility, and smell peculiarly and particularly bad.

Syphilis

(Papua) New Guineans once enjoyed natural immunity to syphilis due to exposure to another disfiguring treponemal disease, yaws ('serologically indistinguishable from syphilis' [Gershman *et al.* 1992:599]), until its near eradication by the WHO campaign launched in 1957 (see Garner, Hornabrook, and Backhouse 1972:141).[5] Syphilis was first reported in the highlands in the 1960s, but by 1969 a full-scale epidemic was on (Lombange 1984:145). It produces initial 'hard' sores (in contrast to chancroid, or 'soft' chancre) on and in genital, oral, and anal membranes. These sores typically heal by themselves but then erupt later and shed infectious material rich in spirochetes. These later multiply rapidly, circulate throughout the body, and insinuate themselves into tissue, blood, and organs, leading often to blindness, insanity, arthritis, heart disease, liver and kidney dysfunction, cartilage damage, and sometimes congenital infection, from mother to fetus through the placenta or during normal, vaginal births.

Syphilis prevalence has steadily increased throughout the past three decades, doubling between 1973 and 1977 (Willcox 1980a:280), tripling between 1973 and 1980 (Willcox 1980c:207), and continuing to increase thereafter (Elias 1989:87; see also Jenkins 1993). Clark and Hughes (1995:335) similarly note a tripling of STD cases in the Tari Hospital STD Clinic between 1984 and 1989. Increased human traffic, increased efforts to track, treat, and prevent infection, and generally the breakdown of some sexual mores and facilitation of others have each contributed to what Pataki-Schweizer and Tabua dub national STD incidence 'out of proportion to other social indices such as demographic and urbanization rates' (1980:17). One health official said in 1986 that STDs were 'out of control.... I don't need figures to prove it—the whole thing is beyond our control' (Kaime, quoted in *Post-Courier* 7 January 1986). Determining STD prevalence clinically or serologically is difficult in view of inconsistent census data collection and reporting strategies, an unevenly developed health care infrastructure, and incomplete diagnoses (see Gillett 1990:93; van der Meijden and Malau 1991).

HIV and AIDS

The 'official' story of AIDS in Papua New Guinea began in 1987 with a *Post-Courier* article about a policeman from the Morehead area in Western Province who died of AIDS in his own village after being diagnosed in Port Moresby and staying briefly in the hospital on Daru, the small island capital of Western Province. His apparently HIV-infected wife and infant daughter both died soon thereafter, as did at least seven other Papua New Guineans by the following year. Increasing numbers of apparent HIV infections and AIDS diagnoses raise the question as to

[5] Gershman *et al.* (1992) and Lambert (1928) discuss anti-yaws campaigns.

how best to provide treatment and prevent transmission in a country that has nineteen provinces, many hundred different languages and local traditions, often inadequate case-finding and follow-up, lack of transport, fuel, and personnel (van der Meijden and Malau 1991:62). Institutional inertia around politically sensitive issues and insufficient programs for counseling prior to and following HIV antibody testing are other problems. A letter writer from Daru (2-28-95) noted that during 1993–1994, there were '6-7 hundred cases of gonorrhea, syphilis, and Donovanosis and others except HIV.... Since you left we had two more HIV positives [but] they are not here in Daru, must have gone back home. We have not followed them up due to no transport'. These problems are multiplied by contention over what Health Department policies really are in terms of reportage, confidentiality, and anonymity with respect to antibody testing, and multiplied again when applied to the interpretation of data derived from serosurveillance. By 1992, 103 Papua New Guineans had tested antibody positive (*Post-Courier* 20 February 92, p. 13), 161 by December of 1993 (NSRRT and Jenkins 1994:6), and since 1993, seropositivity has seemingly risen along a trajectory from 'slow burn' to 'explosive growth' (United Nations 1996), 308 by June of 1995, and 342 by the end of the year. The vast majority of antibody seropositivity has been detected in the NCD, regardless of where infections occurred. The transmission source(s) and dynamics were still 'unknown' in two-thirds to three-fourths of those first 342 cases (cf. Sarda and Harrison 1995:9; *The Health Worker* 1995b:3; *STD Nius* 1995:1).

STDs in Social Perspective

Transmission dynamics, therefore, are open to interpretation. STDs seem to be afflicting ever younger persons, are often going untreated, and are widespread in both urban and rural environs. During interview many men narrated STD infections they acquired when young from even younger girls, so STDs are 'spreading among children in some communities' (NSRRT and Jenkins 1994:125).[6] Many STDs are going untreated despite full knowledge of both partners. One married woman told NSRRT and Jenkins (1994:128) that

> my body pained and I didn't know it was gonorrhea. [A] health worker...told me it was gonorrhea and that I should go tell my hus-

[6]Zigas (1971) and Vogel, with Richens (1989) also provide evidence of young victims.

band and come for a test. My husband gave me gonorrhea but didn't
want to go to the hospital. So I have had gonorrhea for about 6 years
now. Still I have sex with my husband every day.

They found that 22 percent of male informants had been infected at
least once, and 8 percent more than once. 'Despite smelly discharges
and pain', they noted, '71% of these men described continuing to have
sex' (NSRRT and Jenkins 1994:125). Too many STD sufferers are delay-
ing treatment, too. In one study 59 percent of women who had anogenital lesions requiring hospitalization had delayed seeking treatment
for at least four weeks (Vacca and MacMillan 1980). In another study, 73
percent of those afflicted with Donovanosis delayed for two months or
more (Lal and Nicholas 1970). A survey of pregnant women found that
4.5 percent tested positive for syphilis and that 10–20 percent of
women attending antenatal clinics tested positive for gonorrhea
(Mugrditchian and Jenkins, cited in United Nations 1996:17; cf. Gershman *et al.* 1992; Hotchin *et al.* 1995).

Many factors are implicated here. Some people know that they are
afflicted with something, but suspect sorcery or something else, not a
specific microorganism *sexually* transmitted. As a man from Houston,
Texas, explained to Fritz *et al.* (1976:1464), his almost completely muti-
lated-by-Donovanosis penis meant that 'somebody played a mean trick
on me'. Edward Beardmore visited the South Fly river area of Papua in
1890 and found that 'venereal diseases are traced back to one man who
was chafed on the penis with a rope whilst harpooning dugong. The
wound grew into a sore and the disease spread' (Beardmore 1890:461).
One of my Daruan informants, a century later, aged fifty, explained his
lingering genital ulcer by saying, 'well, I was climbin' da, what, tree at
da kona, droppin' da coconuts, and den dat, what, sore, it came up.
Monin', scretch'.[7] Other informants active in sea cucumber work and
crayfish diving attributed genital ailments to the effects of sitting too
long in the hot sun in wet shorts in aluminum boats. Other Daruans
talked about how easily, in an extremely hot and humid environment,
fingernail scratches can turn into sores (something I can personally
vouch) whether or not in the genital area, and forcible, painful intercourse can have the same effect.

In my opinion, these informants (Beardmore's in 1890 and mine in
1990) are telling the truth such as to suggest that we expand our per-

---

[7] I have in places quoted directly from informants speaking in English, and wish to indicate further that Daruans, like most Papua New Guineans, are incredible polymaths, all.

spective on the social sides of STDs accordingly. On Daru, *mido dubu* (sorcery men) are alleged to cause sores to 'come up' on genitalia by 'poisoning' victims via the laundered clothing they leave too long to dry on the clothesline. This makes abundantly clear to all, including the eventual sufferer, that spurning such men's sexual advances has consequences. Other *mido dubu* can 'spoil' genitalia by 'throwing' 'magic' onto or into drying pants, panties, and trousers or by applying irritative substances which have the same effect. Social analysis, therefore, reveals that sexually transmitted *dis-ease*, whether manifested in genital ailments or not, is also constituted *in* social relationships.

High STD prevalence may also be attributed to short supply of condoms and distribution problems thereof, to great expense involved in their purchase, to lack of cultural acceptance, and to individual awkwardness at their usage (see also Hotchin *et al.* 1995). One study conducted in Tari found that the suggestion that condoms be made available for purchase via tradestores was met with near universal disgust (Hughes and Dyke 1993).[8] Men and women thought oppositely about proposed condom availability despite knowing that condom use could prevent STDs, women fearing that men would 'go wild', and vice versa. The United Nations concluded that

> If a woman [in the Pacific] was to ask her husband to use a condom…it would be an accusation of his infidelity, and he would probably become angry, defensive, and even violent. The double standard has it that sex is 'a man's game'. An unmarried woman often has little access to condoms in any case, for in some Pacific island countries they are not sold commercially outside of the main urban centres and some health clinic nurses refuse to supply them except to married people. Using a condom to protect herself from HIV is therefore not a choice that many Pacific women have. (1996:39)

Condom usage threatens men apparently by calling attention to the sexual double standard, that no one and nothing should impinge upon a man's sexual prerogative. For both obvious and complicated reasons, too, condoms can decrease male (and female) sexual pleasure, irritate

---

[8]Condoms were introduced en masse throughout the Pacific by servicemen during and following the Second World War specifically for STD preventive not contraceptive purposes, and in many Pacific island communities condoms still have a terrible ring to them. In Tonga and Samoa, *of* women regularly using contraceptives, only 12 percent use condoms, and the rate is 0.5 percent in women of childbearing age in the Solomon Islands (see United Nations 1996:37).

genitalia and come off during intercourse, and induce individual and relational genitophobia.

Sexually transmitted *dis-ease*, therefore, can be viewed both under the microscope and in context of knowledge and experience people have in local sex/gender systems (Rubin 1975) or gender/class systems (Hammar 1989). Women's lack of sexual citizenship can disempower both men and women, therefore, though differently, from their ability and propensity to avoid pathogens,[9] even in the presence of the most aesthetically obvious and bodily painful genital ailments; the highlands woman quoted above *and* her husband are good examples.

Three components of this problem deserve special mention here. First, *contemporary* men still exercise *customary* sexual prerogatives to hurt women via their genitalia (e.g., Fortune 1931:98; Berndt 1962; Meggitt 1965:143; Glasse, in Clark and Hughes 1995:318), to enact husbandly 'payback' for real and imagined infidelities (e.g., United Nations 1996:35), or to keep female war captives for use sexually themselves or to take them on what Mead called 'money-making tours' (cf. Fortune 1931:95; Mead 1953). Onlookers to women's public abuse by a husband, 'frequent cause of female clinic attendance' in Tari (Clark and Hughes 1995:319; see especially Counts 1990), often look the other way (or blame the woman for her abuse) if he be a wage-earner. This seems to take two patterns. An abusive husband's consanguines (blood relatives) either explain away his behaviour ('he was drunk', not 'normal sense') or blame the wife for her own abuse ('she was playing cards', 'she did not stay home', 'she was refusing him [sexually]'). An abusive husband's affines (wife's blood relatives) now tend to look the other way ('that's their business') for fear that he will take off and take his pay packet with him. For the Telefolmin, marriage is fast becoming a purely 'family' affair in an entirely new way: where one family's daughter goes in marriage is now nobody else's business, 'a matter of concern solely to the immediate families of bride and groom' (1988:263). One Anga informant told NSRRT and Jenkins (1994:104) that '[i]f she refuses [me sexually] I will beat her or do bad things to her. She has to follow my likes.... Now young men round and if the woman doesn't want sex,

----

[9] In 1995, the United Nations announced a set of 'Shared Rights, Shared Responsibilities', two among them being that '*Everyone* has the right to sexual self-determination, including the right to refuse unsafe sex and to take the steps of his or her choice to avoid infection', and that '*Everyone* has the right to freedom from sexual violence and sexual coercion. This includes rape in and outside marriage, trafficking, forced prostitution, and harmful traditional customs. All of these practices increase the risk of infection' (1996:112).

they beat them badly. Sometimes they kill them for refusing sex' (1994:104). Nowadays many women do not have even the nominal protection of brothers and other male relatives.

These trends are implicated in STD transmission such that *being* married can be considered an added risk factor; 85 percent of women who were hospitalized for anogenital lesions in one study were married (Vacca and MacMillan 1980; see also Sittitrai *et al.* 1992:46, for a Thailand example). Sexual violence heightens women's risk in at least three ways. First, men seem to be fetishizing it (cf. Sanday 1990; NSRRT and Jenkins 1994:101–107) such that STDs can both literally *mark* such violence and facilitate its future occurrence. A female informant on Daru who had suffered for two years from several persistent genital sores without treatment beyond washing them with Omo (a soap powder) and water, and application of Detol (see below), attributed them to a pack rape perpetrated on her by '*kona* boys', young men living in adjacent settlements. Her female cousin said that 'with boys, if they rape you, not only one or two, they can make mark on you and sore will start up. Men and boys, they will rape you.... They will hurt her [a woman, her cousin, in this case] when they are doing sex and sore will come up' (field note, Daru, 18 October 1991). Women who spoke of their own or of others' sexual assaults confirmed the 'marked'ness of such assaults, bodily, in terms of sores 'coming up', and also socially, their now being rendered 'fair game' (see also NSRRT and Jenkins 1994:105–107).

Second, 'traditional' sexuality-, marriage-, and reproduction-related double standards (Johnson 1979; Counts 1990; Zimmer-Tamakoshi 1993b; NSRRT and Jenkins 1994) are now being fueled by Western-derived film, music and music video, and other media that glorify sexual violence even as they normalize, possibly even democratize, sexual desire and activity.

Third, I want to speculate about knowledge and beliefs held by women and particularly men about female genitalia, beliefs that seem to swing between 'the wet' and 'the dry'. I believe that some women imagine 'dry' vaginas to evince both genital 'cleanliness' (that is, not STD-infected) and genital 'safety', that is, lack of sexual desire, nonpromiscuity. Like women the world over, some Daruan women insert substances into or apply them onto genitalia for aesthetic, cleansing, possibly contraceptive or spermicidal reasons, such as Detol, a household cleanser, stronger than Lysol in effect, clearly not meant for human tissue. One woman informant said that on the advice of her friend she sometimes daubed into a rag and applied vaginally a clear liquid that '*sikrapim sikin bilong mi nogut tru*' (that irritated her genitalia; field note, 23 October 1991, Daru). To another woman informant it was suggested by a female health lecturer in Australia to apply warm, diluted Detol to her genitals prior to sexual intercourse (field note, 11 November 1991, Daru), and I suspect that more than a few Daruan women engage in similar practices. Such behaviours are common cross-culturally, witness U.S. practices of douching and use of tampons and other 'feminine hygiene products'; pubic shaving, waxing, and pubic hair trimming; and adding the extra, 'husband stitch' following (often unnecessary) episiotomies. These practices accord with stated male desires for 'dry and tight' sex; for 'sweet-smelling', tightened, narrowed genitalia; for 'young' genitalia, sometimes even immature; and for *apparently* absent female sexual desire.[10] These practices can facilitate HIV transmission to and from women for inducing breaks in skin and irritation of genitalia.[11]

On the other side, while Daruan men may not actually fetishize dry vaginas, neither do they appear always to distinguish between vaginas rendered 'wet' due to desire, to immediately prior insemination (in case of serial intercourse), to vaginal discharge due to yeast infections, NGU, gonorrhea, trichomonas, or chlamydia, or perhaps to use of certain artificial lubricants to facilitate sex, but which can both irritate genitalia and compromise the integrity of condoms if used. Two Daruan informants had between them already twenty-five *different* STD episodes of five different STDs in the past decade. The young wife of one

---

[10]See also Brown, Ayowa, and Brown (1993); Brown, Brown, and Ayowa (1992); Runganga, Pitts, and McMaster (1992); and Tanzanian Red Cross Society (1994). During the 1996 United Nations Women's Conference held in Beijing a large Chinese pharmaceutical company made the following special offer for (male? female? both?) 'VIP' delegates: purchase of 'Women's Spring', a traditional herbal medical product designed to narrow vaginal walls, a 'marvel of medical world in 20th century' (*Newsweek*, September 18, 1995, p. 6). The *double entendre* of the aqueous referent here (Woman's *Spring*) should not be missed. Some Kiribati women engage in 'the risky practice of vaginal cauterization designed to inhibit vaginal mucous production and female sexual secretion' or the use of vaginal inserts to 'promote dry and sweet-smelling genitalia, considered by women to be sexually pleasing to men' (Brewis 1992:204, 209). *All* married women on the Kiribati atoll of Butaritari, Brewis notes, 'manually evacuate the vagina of all mucus daily', as well as following all intercourse (1992:209).

[11]Studies done in the Rakai District of Uganda have shown that all manner of GUDs and genital discharges, particularly in women, are considered more normal than abnormal. As the director of one international program launched to decrease prevalence and incidence of untreated STDs put it, 'you go through your entire life thinking that discharges are normal. Your mother has one, your aunt has one—you think it's part of being a woman' (Wawer, cited in Bennett 1996:A2). These studies have enormous relevance for contemporary Papua New Guinea.

suffered gonorrhea thrice during her first married year and two miscarriages, though it was she, not he, who was marked linguistically—*ai nibo* (smelly vagina) or *gonoria ai* (gonorrhea [infected] vagina). He told me, however, that at least *'samting bilong en igat gris istap long en'* (that thus her vagina was lubricated). To that point, her sexual desire had been precluded by her young age, his violence, their lack of privacy, and strained family relations. Some informants explained that even visibly diseased female genitalia were 'just better', 'really good food', that they only cared about 'pumping it' (field note, Daru, 14 April 1991). Other younger informants recounted to me their experiences of 'going in line' (serial intercourse), of going 'on-top' (right behind) a male drinking buddy sharing a sexual partner (see also NSRRT and Jenkins 1994; Van Baal 1966).

STDs are thus not just isolated, isolable biological phenomena, but are eminently social relations in dynamic tension between social structure and individual agency. They express the contours of and give shape to normative behaviour at the same time as they evince 'deviance' from them and justify stigmatization thereby. My fear is that 'traditional' male fears of females, female bodies, and female body parts, known in Melanesianist studies under the rubric of 'sexual antagonism', will be given, in a sense, new life under perhaps increasing statistical support for contentions that *'kain kain ol sik nogut'* (all these STDs) *'bai kamap olsem samting bilong ol meri tasol'* (will be interpreted increasingly as having their source *in* women, not men, or in women and men equally). STDs may manifest on and in human bodies, but as signs—in the form of lesions, infertility, discharges, odor, and pain—in a larger Social Body they also signal and mediate relations *between* bodies—in terms of stigmatization, symbolic violence, and marital dissolution. STD research priorities should thus extend from virology and pathology, from clinical methods and nomenclature, to all manner of genital hygienic practices and their consequences, to sexual behaviours and systems of sexual networking (Caldwell, Caldwell, and Quiggin 1989), to barriers to full sexual citizenship, and to STD-related stigmas.

TALKING AIDS IN PNG

Many of these issues are similarly implicated in public AIDS discourse, if articles about and letters to the editor of the *Post-Courier* regarding transmission knowledge and dynamics, sexuality, and preventive measures are any clue.[12] Like Americans, many Papua New Guineans theorize STDs and AIDS more in terms of lax bodily hygiene and sexual immorality than in terms of HIV and transmission dynamics. One young (eighteen-year-old) Daruan informant attributed the lingering GUD of a girlfriend of hers thusly: '[s]he got da, what, sore, because she was doing dat no good one [oral sex, in this case]...and she nevah wash, dat one'.[13] Papua New Guineans have rich and dynamic, constantly-in-flux models for understanding HIV transmission and prevention that extend well beyond the often too narrow tenets of Western-style germ theorizing (Patton 1994; Farmer 1992). They make use of both 'common-sense' understandings and 'scientific' ones (Maticka-Tyndale 1992). They reenact and author existing AIDS knowledge (Balshem *et al.* 1992:147) regarding skin cleanliness, morality, germs, and perceived risk (see also Waddell 1996), as well as enact themselves new knowledge based on changed circumstances and new information, as two disease narratives rendered partially below indicate.

> She ['P', a 31-year-old married woman] thinks that there are essentially two ways of getting [STDs and AIDS]. One is poison, the other [is] 'going around with the boys...'. [As to the former...] 'If clothings is hanging on the line, the poison fellow will come and he will see clothings on the line and he will put the word on them and then you will put the clothings on. In the morning you will wake and say 'hey, what is this eetch?' You will scretch scretch and sore will come up. [Later,] sore will 'come up' [that is, become, turn into] AIDS (field note 1 March 1992, Daru).

> K: [a 32-year-old married man, when asked to recount possible HIV transmission routes, said] 'Umm, (pause) umm, and what's that, plastic that we are using for the water. To water and wash with it, on the bucket. When the bucket is underneath, her two legs, while she is washing that, the one who is having this, *auwo temeteme* [Kiwai=pain, sickness, e.g., AIDS], while this, that bucket is underneath, and that plastic, already, it's over there, and when you are not using this, but, you are using your own bucket, but you using your own plastic to wash. And you get the water from the well, and fetch the bucket. You fill the bucket take it where, where, the washing place or where the bathroom. And you using that same plastic to wash. And easily, because we have holes on our skins.... That water is going inside through the holes' (field note 3-3-92, Daru).

---

[12] See also *Pacific Health Dialog* 2(2), 1995, which details grassroots-level responses.

[13] See also Hyams' proclamation: 'Maybe venereal disease [incidence in India under the Raj] was loosely defined, and some of the "syphilis" cases might have been no more than festering abrasions caused by "impure coition" (that is, fellatio) in a hot climate' (Hyams 1990:126).

These Daruans have authoritatively blended both 'traditional' and 'modern' models of sickness based upon knowledge of sorcery, contagion, germ theory, and sexual transmission. Knowledge of 'magic fellows', 'poison fellows', 'black magic', and so forth, is certainly alive and well, and is woven interestingly into several different kinds of disease narratives (see Hammar 1996c:chapter 9). Sorcery *is* not only a causal explanation, but also a metaphor for other social relations, including one's own culpability and/or others':

> Learning why agents cause illness leads to a deeper grasp of relations between a people's medical ideas, other aspects of their cultural philosophy, and their social system. In some societies, illness is thought to be primarily the fault of the victim, and the diagnostic question is: What have you done, or who have you offended, that you are now suffering retaliation? (Glick 1972:756)

Most of my fifteen to twenty informant interviews specifically about STDs mentioned clothing left too long to dry on the line but also *zelasi* (jealousy) of those spurned in love, e.g., the following:

> She says that she washed a bunch of clothing, her own panties, her *nakimi*'s [in-law's] trousers, some baby's trousers, and her *bubus'* [grandparents'] things, too, and then hung them up on the line. Her big sister was doing the cooking, she said. Her mother then went to play cards and then she followed her to the cards place, and played cards, forgetting all about the panties on the line. She said that she hung them up on the line, and that someone came along and put magic in them. She...put the dry and clean panties on, went to sleep, woke up, and then in the morning when she went to pee found that she had a sore in her vulva. She and [another informant] claimed that there is some other *mido dubu* in the corner [about sixteen] 'doing magic to other girls, too'.

As in the U.S., beliefs in HIV transmission via everyday, casual contact are also alive and well, though in Papua New Guinea they focus more intently on shared utensils, clothing, beer bottles, and cigarettes. A nineteen-year-old Ok informant told NSRRT and Jenkins (1994:130) that he 'got to know about AIDS from a book. AIDS can be spread by talking, eating, washing, etc. This education was taken from a book'. Indeed, printed matter is a second major source of information and disease narrative construction in Papua New Guinea, some indication of which is rendered below in table 1, which is comprised from a manual search of back issues of the *Post-Courier* for AIDS-related discourse. Early

AIDS narratives in Papua New Guinea featured themes (e.g., promiscuity, alcohol, migration, immorality) that blamed the already stigmatized, such as women who were dubbed *pamukus* or *disko meris* and thereby constructed as harbors and reservoirs of infection. Men, their wives, and children were constructed as their hapless, largely unwitting victims despite highly imbalanced male/female ratios of infection. The origins of AIDS were *dis*placed overseas and into the bodies of non–Papua New Guineans, but domestically located on and in the bodies and activities of already marginalized people, such as 'nontraditional', primarily single women, promiscuous, and so forth. Partly because prostitution was seen throughout the 1960s, 1970s, and 1980s as the institutional framework within which STDs were being transmitted, the country spoiled, and patterns of sexuality thereby changed, it became a convenient trope for mostly blame-happy discourse (e.g., Patton 1994).

Table 1
Post-Courier Stories about AIDS, 1985–1992

Year	No.	Representative Article Titles
1985	1	'Test kits here for AIDS'
1986	4	'Fight to halt sex disease'
1987	18	'Another AIDS carrier' 'Premier fears AIDS in Isle of Love'
1988	47	'AIDS trio vow to leave disco scene' 'Sex habits the key to prevention' 'AIDS tests for single expats' 'More heat on Suckling's Discos' '2000 AIDS carriers' 'Group tackles condom image'
1989	14	'Baby is among PNG's AIDS cases' 'Condoms aren't the answer to AIDS: Minister'
1990	19	'Contraception available now without spouse's consent' '18 die of AIDS, among them 3 children'
1991	8	'Break the custom on sex: Kwarara'
1992	11	'The young more prone as HIV positive carriers'

PROSTITUTION IN PAPUA NEW GUINEA

Like exchange, kinship, and production, prostitution is also a 'total social phenomenon' (Mauss 1967). Historically and cross-culturally, prostitution is protean, ubiquitous *and* often highly patterned, and supported tacitly or explicitly by capital, church, the state, patriarchy, medicine, and law (e.g., Walkowitz 1980; Rosen 1982; Waddell 1996). It is a social contradiction that flourishes in context of others, such as when the frankness of discussion about sexuality does not match its occurrence empirically or metaphorically.[14] Sexual networking transmits ideas, money and goods, offspring, favours and obligations, love and affection, and, to be sure, pathogens. Changing forms and intensities of sexual networking both reflect and produce myriad historical, economic, and social changes, to which I shall now turn.

Issues of History

Since prostitution is 'total social fact' and because bias often gets in the way, one cannot state the precise 'arrival' of it to the Pacific (see also Hammar 1996c:chapter 8). Caroline Ralston (1988:77) notes that for Polynesian history 'the use of terms such as "prostitution", "promiscuity", and "debauchery" to describe the behaviour of Polynesian women' reveals more about (male) European subjects than (female) Polynesian objects. Even when Hawaiian women began to exchange sexual services for 'a range of highly desired goods of western manufacture', she argues, it neither constituted prostitution categorically nor was stigmatized locally (1988:77), despite voluminous European commentary to the contrary. The Reverend J. H. Holmes, for instance, attributed 'concubinage' to Papuan Gulf peoples (1924) and was repulsed thereby, though he may actually have been seeing polygyny and observing sexual relationships and activities between men and second and subsequent wives. Ralston has raised a key issue but hardly solved it, since she also implies that prostitution did not exist in the Pacific prior to European contact, that female sexuality was never deployed by husbands or male relatives without their consent, that

---

[14]The Papua New Guinea Office of Censorship in September of 1992 also requested that all pharmacies 'remove every instruction leaflet contained in the packets of the Protector Condom before selling them' since those instructions contained a line drawing of an erect penis that was deemed pornographic. This was also precisely what the American Red Cross decided to do when it was determined by board members and its then president, Elizabeth Dole, that drawings of penises be rendered more clinically, and that material contained in brochures, handouts, videos, and so forth, was too 'highly explicit' (Berke 1995:A9).

sexual aspects of polygyny were never nonexploitive in a material sense, and that 'prostitution' was necessarily evidence of female agency (cf. Nash 1981). Imputing prostitution where it does not exist can be racist and ethnocentric, but putting it necessarily beyond the pale of Pacific islanders is not necessarily any less so.

We non-Pacific islander explorers, missionaries, and anthropologists, therefore, are thus left to distinguish as responsibly as we can between concubinage and polygyny, to disentangle gifts from commodities, and to tell the difference between payments and ties of reciprocity. Prostitution was never a *thing* the origin of which in Melanesia can be empirically discovered, but rather, an ongoing, eminently social *process* that twists, turns, and unfolds along the way. As such, both exogenous and endogenous factors were involved, including social structure, individual agency, collective action, historical accident, and the collision of conceptual systems. The transition from, say, gift-relations *in* sex to payments *for* it obviously had an impact upon social structures and relations, and disease was often an unforeseen consequence of social and cosmological precepts that enjoined sexual transactions. Key throughout were cultural meanings tied to and produced in sexuality, as were the place and function of sexuality in the political economy (see Kelly 1991; Bushnell 1993; Hori 1981; Bailey and Farber 1992; and Fletcher 1996, for Polynesian examples; see especially Knauft 1993 for several Papuan case studies).

Like Ralston, I, too, am raising more questions than I can definitively answer. 'Sexuality and Empire' literature (e.g., Hyams 1990; White 1991; Kelly 1991) is still poorly developed for colonial (Papua) New Guinea. A history of sexual 'contacts, collisions, and relationships' during the colonial encounter, to use Bitterli's schema (1989), would necessarily include sexual contacts between village women, on the one hand, and native carriers and police/military forces, on the other, during initial contact and exploration, and later, routine patrols or punitive expeditions (e.g., Kituai 1988:160, n. 14; Bjerre 1964:148). Racist discourse was fueled, too, by ubiquitous sexual unions between European males and (Papua) New Guinean females (Connolly and Anderson 1987). Almost wholly imagined sexual unions between European females and (Papua) New Guinean males, however, were made a capital offense, induced by the enactment in 1926 of the White Women's Protection Ordinance (Inglis 1975).

Prostitution of/or Tradition?

In his 1972 contribution to the *Encyclopaedia of Papua and New Guinea*, Burton-Bradley states that commercial promiscuity and the associated 'emotional indifference characteristic in European society' was not traditional in (Papua) New Guinea. He did note 'dissociated components' of it in which women were provisioned sexually to provide 'hospitality', incur obligations, or cancel debts (1972:977–978). This imputes partial but not total European culpability for the introduction of prostitution to (Papua) New Guinea, since prostitution could not logically have been introduced without there being already something onto which to 'latch', some social contradiction, some already existing deployment of female sexuality. For instance, it was reported in the *Post Courier* that new tax rules were introduced in one local setting that provided that a man's 'pigs or wife [would] be put on the market' should he be in tax arrears (cited in Johnson 1979:19). The writer of a letter to the *Post-Courier* (26 March 1975, n.p.) asked whether someone 'may care to relate the way village elders looked on prostitution in pre-contact days', and a response a week later (8 April 1975, p. 2) noted that '[i]n some Solomon societies, a big man usually brought a widow with him on trading voyages. She would be used by a person from those the big man was visiting or trading with, if they wished. But the goods received for that act would all go to the big man' (1975:2). The following must be consulted if one wishes to engage this debate (Armstrong 1922; Beben 1990; Codrington 1972; Cotlow 1966; Davenport 1971; Fortune 1934; Hogbin 1946–47; Maher 1961; Malinowski 1929, 1961; Mead 1953; Oliver 1967, 1973; Ouellette 1971; Roheim 1940, 1946; Serpenti 1977; Thomas 1941).

Contemporary Tradition?

Given the 'traditional' backdrop of female sexuality deployment raised in such publications as the above and the rapidity of colonial social change, it is not surprising that in urban settings women were increasingly pressured by husbands, male relatives, and financial exigency to begin selling sexual services (e.g., Anonymous 1973) or later that they began to deploy their own sexually. Of Port Moresby Joan Johnstone notes that

> To-day [what were in the 1970s called *bisnis-meris*] are called Two-kina meris and they are found in many urban centres in P.N.G. I just happened to be on the spot when they first developed amongs[t] the Guminis in Port Moresby as a consequence of contact with Goilalas

and Goaribaris, who were already practicing this form of prostitution.
(1996:1)

In this snippet are raised three key historical questions. First, if Gumini
'got' their prostitution from Goilalas and Goaribaris, can prostitution,
therefore, be said to be necessarily European-induced? Second, were
such Goilala and Goaribari practices thereby 'modern, European-style'
prostitution, or did they reflect nonprostitutive 'traditional' deploy-
ments of female sexuality? Third, even if prostitution *is* modern, why
are Goilala, Goaribari, and Gumini involved, and not, say, Gende,
Gogodala, and Gimi? By the early 1970s the *Post-Courier* was already full
of articles about and letters to the editor complaining of prostitution
that was becoming too visible in important business and administrative centers and that it was apparently following too closely certain
ethnic/tribal designations. Most commentators attributed it to rising
cash needs, to rural-to-urban migration, to breakdown of social mores,
European inducement and seduction, and to 'traditional' male sexual
prerogatives exercised in new settings. Malinowski, for instance, noted
Trobriand chiefs who prostituted their wives to whites, who married
particularly young women for that purpose, and who encouraged such
behaviours in sons (1929:323; see also Fletcher's fascinating Maori/
European case study, 1996). By 1930, prostitution flourished in the bus-
tling port/town/aerodrome of Lae when local women were deployed by
husbands to service sexually New Guinean, Chinese, and European
pilots, clerks, sailors, and labourers (Willis 1974:107–108).

Economic Factors at (Sex) Work

Other factors that mediated the general pattern of declining local sovereignty included what Jorgensen calls 'the commercialisation of life'
(1988:256). Rural-to-urban migration, already marked by gender imbal-
ances, combined with bridewealth inflation and the adoption of European ideas, goods, and behaviours, simultaneously set forth new
possibilities *of* sexual networking (e.g., different partners, locales, fre-
quencies, and meanings) and new uses *for* it (e.g., to pay school fees,
obtain food and alcohol, buy transportation, attend social functions).
At independence and thereafter these factors were only heightened by
a *Constitution*-guaranteed right of free movement and increasing consumption of alcohol (Ryan 1993; Marshall 1988). Already gender-imbal-
anced and increasing human traffic stripped villages of valuable male
labour but redoubled women's productive workload thereby in gardening, animal tending, and child care (e.g., Filer and Jackson 1988:165).

Insufficient male remittances, however, encouraged females to sell casual sexual labour, both domestically and in migration.

Colonial policies, too, even inadvertently, facilitated commercialized sexual networking. Perhaps because same-sex relations while on patrol were considered the greater sin, Australian patrol officers and their largely Papuan carriers were encouraged to engage village women sexually (Willis 1974:75). Missionaries also prohibited polygyny, but in so doing brought divorce into being and precluded subsequent marriage. This left these 'released women', as missionaries euphemistically called them, stigmatized, without support, and unmarriageable, thus leading women ironically further into the very commercialized sexual unions and forms of 'village prostitution' that so troubled them (cf. Willis 1974:57; Nilles 1953:24; Thomas 1941; Maher 1961; Roheim 1940, 1946). Prohibitions of polygyny had 'unintended' consequences for women since (Tari) men still 'prefer, as they become older, to take younger and more attractive wives. This often leads to serial monogamy and the casual abandonment of the first wife, who then has to fend for her family by herself' (Clark and Hughes 1995:321). Women, not men, can be jailed for having 'unsufficient means of support' (e.g., *Post-Courier* 15 May 1975, p. 13).

Labour Forms of Prostitution

These historical, economic, and social processes ramified unevenly on women, on gender relations, and on sexual networking, but as they did they eventually crystallized or hardened into empirically observable, spatially discrete forms such as I studied on Daru. Luise White (1991) has staked out theoretically the notion of 'labour forms' of prostitution that encoded these different spatial, economic, and behavioural parameters during colonial Nairobi, Kenya. These forms included *watembezi*, or streetwalking, the solicitation of men in public places, the 'only form available to homeless women and ... runaways' (1991:13). *Malaya* women, by contrast, waited in their own rooms for male customers for whom they also performed a host of domestic services, such as the cooking of food, drawing of bathwater, making of tea and conversation, and doing of laundry, for each of which they charged set prices (1991:15). The third form involved *wazi-wazi* women who waited for customers to appear outside their homes, who maximized the number and minimized the duration of primarily sexual encounters (1991:19).

In (Papua) New Guinea, too, there was not and is not now one Prostitution but many prostitutions. They can be found at administrative centers such as Goroka, Hagen, Port Moresby, Rabaul, Lae, and Wewak. On Daru, for instance, there exists a 'family' form of prostitution[15] in which husbands, fathers, and other male relatives solicit paying sexual partners 'for' their wives, daughters, and other female relatives (see also Reaves 1993) at tradestore and *kai ba* (or fast food) fronts, at public drinking environments, and at the wharf when ships visit, in exchange for money, beer, food, tobacco, and/or promises thereof. There is also a 'freelance' form in which women solicit paying sexual partners at the hotel and at various clubs and barracks, private houses and com-pounds, bush areas behind and between settlements, or simply out on the road at dusk and later. They may employ all manner of 'messengers' to convey availability, intent, desire, locale, and timing. A third form involves 'sex brokers' who find women for potential customers (and sometimes vice versa) while roaming to and between the public market and wharf, businesses, drinking establishments, provincial govern-mental offices, tradestores, barracks and compounds, and private houses. They can end up with 25 percent of the earnings derived there-from, and may also receive free alcohol, tobacco, food, or possibly a vid-eocassette watching and a shower in case of having arranged a hotel-room sexual encounter (see Hammar 1996c). A fourth form, *sagapari*, or *tu kina bus* ($2 bush prostitution), involves only married Bamu women who sell brief, cheap sexual services to, by definition, non-Bamu cus-tomers in a bush area, a form existing on Daru for at least three decades (Hammar 1996a).

These different labour forms are found throughout Western Prov-ince and the South Fly/Torres Strait region generally. Coupled with the rural-to-urban migration and imbalanced sex ratios in towns men-tioned above, the easy availability of alcohol, difficult economic condi-tions for women, and male sexual prerogative, both traditional and contemporary as, once, facilitators and now also purchasers of sexual services, it is not surprising that such often highly patterned labour forms as *tu kina bus* emerged and now flourish throughout Papua New Guinea. 'Liberal Minded', for instance (*Post-Courier* 7 October 1977, p. 2), noted that 'everybody knows where the K2.00 bush is in Port Moresby, and also in places like Lae, Rabaul, Goroka, Madang, Wewak, and others'. *Masawa* is the name by which another such *tu kina bus* is known at the Wawoi-Guavi timber camp in Western Province, and

---

[15] Not to be confused with mere family arrangements of marriage in which money or brideprice became increasingly a feature. One Telefolmin man put it to Jorgensen (1988:272) that his daughter was his 'tradestore'.

Balimo, Kerema, Kiunga, and Tabubil have been similarly reported now to have *tu kina bus* not unlike Daru's *sagapari*, Port Moresby's Paga Hill, and Goroka's *sikrap maunten*.[16] One University of Papua New Guinea student reported from Kamusi(e) timber camp that

> most of the prostitutes [at Kamusie and such other sites] are married women whose husbands have been unable to secure employment with the company. About 50% of the prostitutes are single mothers employed by the company. Low wages have been the major driving factor that have encouraged them into this activity. (Goinau 1995:27)

Other labour forms and prostitutive monikers can be found throughout the Pacific in hotels and dance and social clubs, at wharves, mines, and sawmills, and at public taverns and lounge bars, as the monikers 'loose girls', 'ship girls', and so forth (United Nations 1996) indicate. Sadly, in Papua New Guinea *tu kina bus meri* is one of the monikers by which women are coming to be known to international audiences. '*Hotel meris*' and '*disko meris*' (both essentially 'freelance' forms) and '*meri wokabaut*' and '*rot meris*' (streetwalkers) indicate another form, as does '*pasindia meris*' (passenger women), who began to be prostituted out of public motor vehicles on roadways first in context of large road-building projects. The existence of brothels in (Papua) New Guinea was presumably noted by those who drafted the Child Welfare Act (of 1961), in which it was decided to label children, by definition, 'neglected' if they lived in a house occupied by more than two women presumptively dubbed prostitutes (Johnson 1979). By the early mid-1970s these forms of prostitution and their visibility were such as to arouse the ire of townsfolk, church leaders, politicians, and business-people for reflecting ill on this fledgling nation. A fourth-year law student at the University of Papua New Guinea noted that prostitutes operating in bush areas or openly soliciting in night clubs annoyed 'decent members' of the community and were 'injurious to the business communities' (Kombagle 1986:6), a sentiment echoed by many letters written to and articles written for the *Post-Courier*. Table 2 indicates some of the range and content of these sentiments.

Who knows how many other labour forms are coming into being or are going into decline, changing their contours to meet changes in the

---

[16] An Eastern Highlands Province informant, however, recently told me that houses have now replaced *sikrap maunten*. He confirmed my speculations about the logistics of Port Moresby's sex industry in the main, too, having served for a time as facilitator thereof.

Table 2
Post-Courier Articles about Prostitution, 1972–1986

Year	No.	Representative Article Titles
1972	1	'Low pay forces girls into prostitution'
1973	10	'Two brothels in Papua New Guinea'
1974	6	'Independence Day upstaged by prostitution worries'
1975	6	'Drift to town and prostitution'
1976	3	'Women's meeting against prostitution'
1977	45	'Selling bodies: 'what is brideprice'?' 'Prostitution—product of modern society' 'Pamuks must stay illegal'
1978	9	'Schools used as brothels at night'
1979	5	'Two Kina ladies'
1980	12	'K2 bush business is a disgrace' 'Stop selling women on Paga Hill'
1981	10	'Capitalist evil' 'Red light for West New Britain brothel'
1982	8	'Can the rapes stop by opening brothels?'
1983	3	'Brothels could work'
1984	15	'Modern problem'
1985	2	'Filipino women used as bribes on officials: MP'
1986	17	'Three arrests at city brothel' 'Don't legalise prostitution, says church' 'Prostitutes not at my hotel: manager'

political economy and in popular culture? Clark and Hughes note, for instance, that a new kind of sexual networking has arisen in Tari centered around the *'pasindia meri'*, a 'deviant woman from the outside, who figures as the ultimate source of pollution illness [now STDs]. Women say that they are identifiable at the market by their painted cheeks and scant clothing, and that they ply their trade at the courting parties where their sexual services are offered' (1995:336). The task is not an easy one: to operationalize the *exchange* (payment, favour, gift, fee, present, equal or unequal, prior to sex, during, later, how much later, etc.?) *of sex* (penile/vaginal penetration, digital/vaginal or oral/

vaginal or oral/penile contact, kissing, nonpenetrative foreplay, pornography viewing, nudity, with and without condoms, how many times, in what positions, for what duration, etc.?) *for* (directly, indirectly, now, delayed, equivalent, equal, nonequal, once, twice, thrice, etc.?) *money* (how much, how frequently, currency versus the promise of it, in kind, for school fees, clothing, etc.?) *or goods* (food and household items, beer, t-shirts, audio cassettes, tobacco, sweets, betel nut, etc.).

Good luck. Ethnographic research conducted by Clark and Hughes in the Tari region in context of widespread social and sexual networking changes revealed that whereas Huli men may have given presents to their betrothed and to second wives they met at courting parties, now single men are giving such presents even to single women with whom they are friendly, and married men are now giving tobacco, food, and beer. Women receiving such gifts in such contexts are thus dubbed *pamuku* or *pasindia meri* not because it is inherently prostitutive to do so, but because it is assumed immediately to precede sex, not marriage (1995:339–340, n. 6). This (changing) dynamic was the subject of my ethnographic fieldwork, conducted mostly on Daru. The question of the transition from gift to payment, from marriage to sex, is not easily resolved. Near the end of fieldwork, in the context of free condom distribution, and once we figured out how (not) to do so, one of my research assistants and I carried out fifty-four brief (twenty- to twenty-five-minute) but formal (scheduled interview), on-the-spot (around town, on the road) interviews with small groups (three to six persons, in all-male, all-female, and mixed groups) of recipients (267 in all, 19.68 years old on average, 13 male and female virgins) of free condoms. We inquired of recipients' age, gender, birthplace, and residence; history (if any) and recency (if any) of condom usage; location and circumstances of the last sexual contacts they had; locations of material exchanges that occurred prior to or following most recent sexual activity, rendered in table 3. Table 4 tabulates the frequency with which 'the exchange of sex for money or goods' occurred.

Serious caution is warranted with respect to how best such data may be interpreted. It should be noted here that (a) not every male 'customer' at *sagapari* is paying for sexual intercourse, at least not at the time, which may indicate some degree of material support by 'boyfriends' in between sexual encounters; (b) many more places than one's own or one's partner's house are being employed for sexual encounters, which may have significant public health implications in terms of likelihood

Table 3
Location of Last Sexual Intercourse

Location	Female	Male	Totals	Proportion of Total
House	37	51	88	0.35
Party Place	28	30	58	0.23
Bush	7	27	34	0.13
Sagapari	5	12	17	0.07
Video	8	9	17	0.07
Motel	1	8	9	0.04
Village	0	5	5	0.02
School	0	1	1	0.00
Other	0	5	5	0.02
No Sex Yet	3	10	13	0.05
Totals	99	168	267	1.05

Table 4
Exchange Relations by Location

Location	No. of Acts	Instances of Material Exchange	Percentage of Exchange per Act
Sagapari	17	15	88.2
Hotel	9	6	66.6
Video Place	17	11	64.7
Bush	34	17	50.0
Road	20	10	50.0
Party Place	58	23	39.6
House	88	27	30.6
Village	5	0	0.0

of genital inspection for disease and genital hygiene following intercourse, likely availability of condoms, and so on; (c) almost 44 percent
of all respondents, including not a few married and otherwise part-
nered persons, were engaged in exchange relations of some sort or
another during and following sexual encounters.

Although these 44 percent do not represent the entire nation,
these findings return me to the starting point of this essay and to my
three theses. Such findings stretch to the breaking point the definition
of prostitution as being 'the exchange of sex for money and/or goods',
unless one is willing to dub 44 percent of all Daruans as involved in
prostitution, which I am not. However, fairly predictable patterns of
the material transactions themselves (for details, see Hammar 1996c)
sharply underscore the likelihood that *the* fundament of AIDS, STDs,
and sex work in Papua New Guinea is that women exchange sex for
money and goods because they have to, while men exchange money
and goods for sex because they can. There are, of course, 'traditional'
and 'contemporary' explanations for facets of this sexual double standard that do not involve male prerogative *per se*—e.g., female agency,
adherence to sound postpartum sex taboos—and (Papua) New Guinean men did not 'choose' the kinds of changes that Europeans induced
by ruling colonially. I still think, however, that the *real* problem is
women's absent sexual citizenship.

DIRECTIONS FOR THE FUTURE: THE NEED FOR HYPER-
GENDERED ANALYSIS

Though I am not alone in believing that HIV is not perhaps even a,
much less *the* cause of AIDS (see, e.g., Root-Bernstein 1993), AIDS would
appear to be causing and signaling profound distresses in Papua New
Guinean communities, however much they may differ across time and
between body. AIDS will continue to manifest itself in protean fashion
in the decades to come, too, indicating ongoing distress between
bodies *in* the Body Politic. HIV is constantly changing, too, and its
transmission dynamics are far more complicated than what you may
already have read or heard. AIDS will continue to have both empirically
'real' and constructed aspects to it, since it is simultaneously built upon
sociopolitical relations and seemingly able itself to inscribe them. STDs
and sex work, too, have traveled along the 'fault lines' of Papua New
Guinean communities in fairly predictable ways (e.g. Lindenbaum
1979; Bateson and Goldsby 1988). There is, as Adams reminds us, a
'political economy of AIDS' (1992:9), no less so in Port Moresby than in
Port-au-Prince, Haiti (see also Farmer 1992; Hunt 1988).

Peter Piot has noted that even despite the happy discovery of pro-
tease inhibitors and so-called 'drug cocktails', 'the AIDS gap only
becomes wider' (quoted in Purvis 1997:76). The 'AIDS gap' to which he
refers is not just between 'First World' and 'Third', rich and poor, but
also man and woman, husband and wife. This does not have to happen.
As concerned citizens of a planetary village increasingly connected by
human traffic, commodity flows, and pathogens, we must grasp this
fundamental, though admittedly complicated point, that STDs are
afflictions simultaneously of and between bodies. We need, therefore,
not just a few million more condoms, a cure for AIDS or vaccine against
HIV, and a better HIV antibody test kit, but also to begin thorough-
going healing of social relations. Papua New Guinea women's status is
second-class in ways that clash not only with the country's Constitution, with all manner of publicly spouted pledges and homilies, but
with universally valued determinations regarding human rights for all
(cf. Counts 1990; Zimmer-Tamakoshi 1993b; Gillett 1990; NSRRT and
Jenkins 1994; Johnson 1979; United Nations 1996). Women face obstacles that men do not, are held to behaviour standards in ways men are
not, have bodies that are stigmatized in ways that men's are not, bear
the brunt of fists, bush knives, and beer bottles thrown at them in fre-
quencies and with consequences that are patently unfair, and are
blamed for myriad ills not very much of their own making. Women do
not currently have the social power to negotiate their own sexuality,
which should be their own birthright. Men are losing out thereby, too,
though surely in different ways.

For these reasons and many more, our prescriptions for social
change, whether from academic, popular, or 'high' sources, need to be
far more gender-saturated than they are. Let me conclude with three
brief examples. As an example of the latter, in laying out the 'role of the
churches' with respect to AIDS education, the United Nations
(1996:110) proclaimed that 'abstinence and monogamy needed to be
stressed as the safest ways of protection'. The naivete and wronghead-
edness of such a proclamation are stunning, since throughout Papua
New Guinea neither sexual abstinence nor monogamy is much in
women's control (as the United Nations' own data and conclusions
make clear; see below). Such thoughtless exhortation to 'monogamy'
per se can foster further sexual violence and can stigmatize women who
wish to leave abusive relationships. It overlooks the possibility that one
or another spouse is *already* infected, and neglects to consider what
'monogamy' might mean in regions in which polygyny in various

forms might still be normative (please note that I am not at all against polygyny *per se*). Multiple-partner sexual unions, despite the frequent hazards and dislocations thereof, are often for women the only way to survive. Being monogamous, remaining sexually 'full of faith', can for wives increase their risks of infection if and when their husbands have other wives to whom they might *also* be faithful, still more if they have other sexual partners. Exhortations to monogamy are too simple in the face of often incredibly complicated STD/HIV transmission dynamics. Schopper, Doussantousse, and Orav (1993:407) found that 19.4 percent of couples in 'polygynous' marriages in one African study disagreed as to the number of wives the husband had! For women on Daru in various forms of marriage/prostitution I found this also to be true, that the line dividing 'single' from 'married', gifts *in* sex from payments *for* it was not a fixed quality so much as a marker of ongoing material support and social practice.

More popular literature, too, often naively construes 'risk' to be gender-blind and tilts confusingly between plugging reliance on technology and exhorting 'common sense'. In the latter case, comic booklets, church pamphlets, and public health posters all exhort people to 'Follow God's Way', 'know your partner', 'avoid contact with *pamukus*', and 'be faithful'. Unfortunately, *extra* violence is often meted out to women thereby. As well, neither 'God's Way', 'knowing', nor 'partner' is easily operationalizable. People are at risk when in contact with bodily fluids and tissues, medical technologies and techniques, not moral precepts and abstract philosophies. The flip side seems equally true, that too often new pieces of technology such as condoms or antibody test kits are seen as the solution to STD and HIV transmission. Condoms are potentially rarely bad *per se* (when used, that is, 'properly'), but non-Oxynol 9–laden condoms have *now* been dubbed the added risk factors they *always were* for some people. Condoms are feared to become entangled with fetuses if they come off during or following intercourse, or are feared to be the agents of *infection*, not prevention, when used twice between different vaginas. Condom usage, therefore, is less about the technical properties of latex or polyurethane than about social relations, genitophobia, and absent sexual citizenship. The United Nations (1996:39) has concluded:

> If a woman was to ask her husband to use a condom as a precaution against disease, it would be an accusation of his infidelity, and he would probably become angry, defensive, and even violent. The double standard has it that sex is 'a man's game'. An unmarried

woman often has little access to condoms in any case, for in some Pacific island countries they are not sold commercially outside of the main urban centres and some health clinic nurses refuse to supply them except to married people. Using a condom to protect herself from HIV is therefore not a choice that many Pacific women have.

Finally, even the very most sterling of our academic discourses could use a shot of gender. Colin Filer's key theoretical piece on the Bougainville Crisis (1990) *is* gendered with rich, but nevertheless telling metaphors, such as that the early stages of the Panguna project were a sort of 'honeymoon' between geologists and landowners (1990:7). In terms of the presumed heterosexual logic by which most of us write, he has thus either feminized either 'geologist' or 'landowner', though no women are mentioned explicitly in context of these developments, or has made this new 'marriage' not just homosocial, but male homosocial, and then backed away from deserved commentary thereabout. He notes that neither absence nor presence of such a 'honeymoon' affects the long-term stability of such a 'marriage', but the homosocial nature of such marriages (between capital and, what, patriarchy?) emerges clearly with the following:

> It could even be argued that those landowners who have experienced a romantic engagement with mining companies during the process of exploration will be even more disappointed by the sordid realities of extraction than those whose marriage has been arranged against their will. (1990:7)

This deflects if not erases fully the specifically gender-saturated nature of development. The 'fact' to which Filer refers in this and other illuminating writings—the sordid realities of extraction—disadvantages all Papua New Guineans vis-à-vis foreign capital, but surely women triply so since (a) they seldom relate straightforwardly *qua* women to land, (b) development pains are often felt more acutely by women (in context of alcohol, prostitution, and disease), and (c) development functions *precisely and according to* existing gendered cleavages. 'Gender-neutrality' is paradigmatically imbricated precisely when hyper-genderedness is called for.

It has fallen to me to discuss several serious sociomedical issues in Papua New Guinea, though I have done so uneasily. Blame and responsibility surely fall mostly upon me and my European ancestors, but they fall also upon Papua New Guinean men and women *na ol tumbuna bilong ol* for the tangled histories of AIDS, STDs, and sex work we have collectively and individually, though not always mutually, woven. As we move away from what has been for most Pacific islanders and Pacific island communities probably the bloodiest and swiftest century ever and toward a brand-new millennium, I believe that we need to awaken or reawaken ourselves and each other to the deleterious effects of double standards with respect to sexual citizenship, since they clearly ramify in so many ways on the issues I have raised above. I have tried to show that STDs, HIV, and AIDS have far more than mere medically felt effects or biological precursors. That so many women and families engage in sex work contravenes the very human rights, Christian precepts, and traditional laws that we hold most dear.

REFERENCES

Adams, B., 1992. 'Sociology and people with AIDS', in J. Hunter and B. Schneider, eds., *The Social Context of AIDS*. Newbury Park, California: Sage, pp. 3–18.

Altman, L., 1996. 'AIDS epidemic spreads around world', *The Oregonian*, 29 November, p. A10.

Anonymous, 1973. 'Double trouble for PNG women in today's changing society', *Post-Courier*, 7 September, p. 33.

Armstrong, W. E., 1922. 'Reports I, Anthropology of South Eastern Division (Excluding Woodlark Island), Engineer Group, Bosilai, East Cape, Normanby Island (South Coast), and of Morima, Fergusson Island', in *Annual Reports for the Territory of Papua*, Native Taxes Ordinance, 1917–1922.

Ashdown, L. R., and Kilvert, G.T., 1979. 'Granuloma Inguinale in Northern Queensland', *Medical Journal of Australia*, [1]:146–148.

Baal, J. Van, 1966. *Dema*. The Hague: Martinus Nijhoff.

Bailey, B., and Farber, D., 1992. 'Hotel street', *Radical History Review*, 52:54–77.

Balshem, M., Oxman, G., van Rooyen, D., and Girod, K., 1992. 'Syphilis, sex and crack cocaine', *Social Science and Medicine*, 35(2):147–160.

Bateson, M. C., and Goldsby, R., 1988. *Thinking AIDS*. Reading, Massachusetts: Addison-Wesley.

Beardmore, E., 1890. 'The natives of Mowat, Daudai, New Guinea', *Journal of the Royal Anthropological Institute of Great Britain and Ireland*, 19:459–468.

Beben, W., 1990. 'An anthropological view of sexuality', in J. Ingebritson, ed., *Human Sexuality in Melanesian Cultures*, Point Series, No. 14. Goroka: The Melanesian Institute.

Bennett, A., 1996. 'A new regime: Africa's AIDS experts turn to antibiotics', *Wall Street Journal*, 27 December, A1.

Berke, R., 1995. 'Red Cross alters AIDS material at Elizabeth Dole's request', *The Oregonian*, September 13, p. A9.

Berndt, R., 1962. *Excess and Restraint*. Chicago: University of Chicago Press.

Bitterli, U., 1989. *Cultures in Conflict*. Stanford: Stanford University Press.

Bjerre, J., 1964. *Savage New Guinea*. New York: Tower.

Brewis, A., 1992. 'Sexually transmitted disease risk in a Micronesian atoll population', *Health Transition Review*, 2(2):195–213.

Brown, J., Ayowa, O. B., and Brown, R., 1993. 'Dry and tight: sexual practices and potential AIDS risk in Zaire', *Social Science and Medicine*, 37(8):989–994.

Brown, R., 1992. 'Letter: vaginal inflammation in Africa', *New England Journal of Medicine*, 327(8):572.

Burton-Bradley, B. G., 1972. 'Prostitution', in P. Ryan, ed., *Encyclopaedia of Papua and New Guinea*. Melbourne: Melbourne University Press, pp. 977–978.

Bushnell, O. A., 1993. *The Gifts of Civilization*. Honolulu: University of Hawaii Press.

Caldwell, J., Caldwell, P., and Quiggin, P., 1989. 'The social context of AIDS in sub-Saharan Africa', *Population and Development Review*, 15:185–234.

Calov, W. L., and Weir, H., 1925. 'Gonorrhoea in natives of New Guinea: a record of twelve months' work in a venereal disease campaign in Rabaul', *Medical Journal of Australia*, [2]:720–724.

Clark, J., 1993. 'Gold, sex, and pollution: male illness and myth at Mt. Kare, Papua New Guinea', *American Ethnologist*, 20(4):742–757.

Clark, J., and Hughes, J., 1995. 'A history of sexuality and gender in Tari', in Aletta Biersack, ed., *Papuan Borderlands*. Michigan: University of Michigan, pp. 315–340.

Codrington, R. H., 1972 [1891]. *The Melanesians*. New York: Dover.

Connolly, B., and Anderson, R., 1987. *First Contact*. New York: Viking.

Cotlow, L., 1966 [1942]. *In Search of the Primitive*. Boston: Little, Brown.

Counts, D., 1990. 'Beaten wife, suicidal woman: domestic violence in Kaliai, West New Britain', *Pacific Studies*, 13(3):151-169.

Davenport, W., 1971 [1962]. 'Red feather money', in L. L. Langness and J. Weschler, eds., *Melanesia: readings on a culture area*. Scranton, Pennsylvania: Chandler, pp. 83-93.

Department of Health, 1986. *Papua New Guinea National Health Plan, 1986-1990*. Hohola: Department of Health.

Elford, J., and Dwyer, J., 1993. 'Editorial: HIV and AIDS in Asia and the Pacific', *AIDS Care*, 5(3):259-260.

Elias, I. F., 1989. 'Epidemiology of sexually transmitted diseases', in *STD/AIDS Training Course*, held in Port Moresby, July 31st to August 4th, Port Moresby: Department of Health.

Everett, V. J., 1987. 'The M of MCH', *Papua New Guinea Medical Journal*, 30:121-125.

Farmer, P., 1992. *AIDS and Accusation*. Berkeley: University of California Press.

Filer, C., 1990. 'The Bougainville Rebellion, the mining industry and the process of social disintegration in Papua New Guinea', *Canberra Anthropology*, 13(1):1-39.

Filer, C., and Jackson, R., 1988. *The Social and Economic Impact of a Gold Mine on Lihir*. Lihir Liaison Committee.

Fischer, A., 1963. 'Reproduction in Truk', *Ethnology*, 2:526-540.

Fletcher, A., 1996. 'Indigenous female bodies and colonialism'. Paper presented during the 1996 meetings of the American Anthropological Association, San Francisco.

Ford, K., Wirawan, D. N., and Fajans, P., 1995. 'AIDS knowledge, risk behaviors, and condom use among four groups of female sex workers in Bali, Indonesia', *Journal of the Acquired Immune Deficiency Syndromes and Human Retrovirology*, 10:569-576.

Fortune, R., 1931. 'Manus Religion', *Oceania*, 2:74-108.

———, 1934. *Manus Religion*. Lincoln, Nebraska: University of Nebraska Press.

Fritz, G., Hubler, W., Dodson, R., and Rudolph, A., 1976. 'Mutilating Granuloma Inguinale', *Archives of Dermatology*, 111:1464-465.

Furnas, J. C., 1947. *Anatomy of Paradise*. New York: William Sloane Associates.

Garner, M. F., Hornabrook, R. W., and Backhouse, J. L., 1972. 'Treponematosis along the Highlands Highway', *Papua and New Guinea Medical Journal*, 15(3):139-141.

Gershman, K., Rolfs, R., Larsen, S., Zaidi, A., and Palafox, N., 1992. 'Seroepidemiological characterization of a syphilis epidemic in the Republic of the Marshall Islands, Formerly a Yaws Endemic Area', *International Journal of Epidemiology*, 21(3):599-606.

Gillett, J., 1990. *The Health of Women in Papua New Guinea*. Papua New Guinea Institute of Medical Research Monograph No. 9. Goroka: Papua New Guinea.

Glick, L., 1972 'Medicine, indigenous', in P. Ryan, ed., *Encyclopaedia of Papua and New Guinea*. Melbourne: Melbourne University Press, pp. 756-757.

Goldstein, D., 1992. 'From condom literacy to women's empowerment: AIDS and women in Brazil', *Proteus*, 9:25-34.

Goinau, W., 1995. 'The impact of Wawoi Guavi logging in the Bamu area of the Western Province'. Department of Anthropology and Sociology, Social Work Programme, University of Papua New Guinea. Unpublished manuscript.

Grant, J., Saito, H., and Zelenietz, M., 1986. 'Where development never comes: business activities in Kilenge, Papua New Guinea', *Journal of the Polynesian Society*, 95(2):195-219.

Gunther, J. T., 1972. 'Medical Services, History', in P. Ryan, ed., *Encyclopaedia of Papua and New Guinea*, Melbourne: Melbourne University Press, pp. 748-756.

Hammar, L., 1989. 'Gender and class on the fringe: a feminist analysis of ethnographic theory and data in Papua New Guinea', Working Paper No. 189 in the Michigan State University Series, *Women in International Development*, Rita Gallin, ed.

———, 1992. 'Sexual transactions in Daru: with some observations on the ethnographic enterprise', *Research in Melanesia*, 16:21-54.

————, 1996a. 'Brothels, Bamu, and *Tu Kina Bus* in South Coast New Guinea: human rights issues and global responsibilities', *Anthropology and Humanism*, 21(2):140–158.

————, 1996b. 'Bad canoes and *Bafalo*: the political economy of sex on Daru Island, Western Province, Papua New Guinea', *Genders*, 23:212–243.

————, 1996c. 'Sex and political economy in the South Fly: Daru Island, Western Province, Papua New Guinea', 2 volumes, unpublished doctoral dissertation, City University of New York, Department of Anthropology.

————, 1997a. 'The dark side to Donovanosis: color and climate, race and racism in American South Venereology', *Journal of Medical Humanities*, 18(1):29–57.

————, 1997b. 'Caught between structure and agency: the parameters and punishments of prostitution in Papua New Guinea', *Transforming Anthropology* (forthcoming).

Hart, G., 1974. 'Social and psychological aspects of venereal disease in Papua New Guinea', *British Journal of Venereal Diseases*, 50:453–458.

Health Worker, The, published by the Department of Health of Papua New Guinea. 1995a 1(1), April.

————, 1995b 1(3), October.

Hogbin, H. I., 1946–1947. 'Puberty to marriage: a study of the sexual life of the natives of Wogeo, New Guinea', *Oceania*, 16:185–209.

Holmes, J. H., 1924. *In Primitive New Guinea*. London: Seeley and Service.

Hori, J., 1981. 'Japanese prostitution in Hawaii during the immigration period', *Hawaiian Journal of History*, 15:113–124.

Hornabrook, R. W., 1972. 'Syphilis', in P. Ryan, ed., *Encyclopaedia of Papua and New Guinea*. Melbourne: Melbourne University Press, pp. 1108–1109.

Hotchin, P., Tapelu, E., Chetty, V., Hakwa, R., and Phillips, D., 1995. 'Knowledge, attitudes and behavior of reinfected patients—Suva STD Clinic, Fiji 1994/95', *Pacific Health Dialog*, 2(2):45–47.

Hughes, J., 1991. 'Impurity and danger: the need for new barriers and bridges in the prevention of sexually-transmitted disease in the Tari Basin, Papua New Guinea', *Health Transition Review*, 1(2):131–141.

Hughes, J., and Dyke, T., 1993. 'Barriers and bridges to the spread of sexually transmitted diseases among the Huli of Southern Highlands Province, Papua New Guinea', in *Population, Family Health and Development*, papers from the 19th Waigani Seminar, Port Moresby: University of Papua New Guinea, pp. 200–204.

Hunt, C., 1988. 'AIDS and capitalist medicine', *Monthly Review*, 39:11–25.

Hyams, R., 1990. *Empire and Sexuality*. Manchester: Manchester University Press.

Inglis, A., 1975. *Not a White Woman Safe*. Sussex: Oxford University Press.

Jackson, E. S., 1911. 'Notes on Ulcerative Granuloma', *Australasian Medical Gazette*, 30:133.

Jenkins, C., 1993. 'Fertility and infertility in Papua New Guinea', *American Journal of Human Biology*, 5:75–83.

Johnson, D., 1979. 'Aspects of the legal status of women in Papua New Guinea: a working paper', *Melanesian Law Journal*, 7(1–2):5–81.

Johnstone, J., n.d. 'The Gumini Bisnis-Meri', unpublished doctoral dissertation, University of Queensland, Department of Anthropology.

————, 1996. Personal Communication, January 14.

Jorgensen, D., 1988. 'From sister-exchange to "daughter-as-tradestore": money and marriage in Telefolmin', *Catalyst*, 18(3):255–280.

Kelly, J., 1991. *A Politics of Virtue*. Chicago: University of Chicago.

Kettle, E., 1979. *That They Might Live*. Sydney: F. P. Leonard.

Kirsch, S., 1989. 'The Yonggom, the refugee camps along the border, and the impact of the Ok Tedi Mine', *Research in Melanesia*, 13:30–61.

Kituai, A., 1988. 'Innovation and intrusion: villagers and policemen in Papua New Guinea', *Journal of Pacific History*, 23(2):156–166.

Knauft, B., 1993. *South Coast New Guinea Cultures.* Cambridge: Cambridge University Press.

Kombagle, D., 1986. 'Prostitution: the great debate (again)', *The Times of Papua New Guinea,* January 11, p. 6.

Krieger, L., 1996. 'AIDS conference marks quiet revolution', *San Francisco Examiner,* 7 July, pp. A1, A8.

Kuberski, T., 1986. 'Granuloma Inguinale (Donovanosis)', *Sexually Transmitted Diseases* 7(1):29–36.

Lal, S., and Nicholas, C., 1970. 'Epidemiological and clinical features in 165 cases of Granuloma Inguinale', *British Journal of Venereal Diseases,* 46:461–464.

Lambert, S.M., 1928. 'Medical conditions in the South Pacific', *Medical Journal of Australia,* [2]:362–378.

Lindenbaum, S., 1979. *Kuru Sorcery.* Palo Alto: Mayfield.

Lombange, C., 1984. 'Trends in sexually transmitted disease incidence in Papua New Guinea', *Papua New Guinea Medical Journal,* 27:145–157.

Lubis, I., Master, J., Bamban, M., Papilaya, A., and Anthony, R., 1994. 'AIDS related attitudes and sexual practices of the Jakarta Waria (Male Transvestites)', *Southeast Asian Journal of Tropical Medicine and Public Health,* 25(1):102–106.

Maddocks, K., 1967. 'Donovanosis in Papua', *Papua and New Guinea Medical Journal,* 10:49–53.

Maddocks, I., Anders, E. M., and Dennis, E., 1976. 'Donovanosis in Papua New Guinea. *British Journal of Venereal Disease,* 52:190–196.

Maher, R., 1961. *New Men of Papua.* Madison: University of Wisconsin Press.

Malinowski, B., 1929. *The Sexual Life of Savages.* New York: Harcourt, Brace.

———, 1961. *Argonauts of the Western Pacific.* New York: Dutton.

Mann, J., Tarantola, D., and Netter, T., eds., 1992. *AIDS in the World: a global report.* Cambridge, Massachusetts: Harvard.

Marshall, M., 1988. 'Alcohol consumption as a public health problem in Papua New Guinea', *International Journal of the Addictions,* 23(6):573–589.

Maticka-Tyndale, E., 1992. 'Social construction of HIV transmission and prevention among heterosexual young adults', *Social Problems,* 39(3):238–252.

Mauss, M., 1967. *The Gift.* New York: Norton.

Mead, M., 1953 [1942]. *Growing Up in New Guinea.* London: Pelican.

Meggitt, M., 1965. *The Lineage System of the Mae Enga.* London: Oliver and Boyd.

Meijden, W. van der and Malau, C., 1991. 'The STD/AIDS control programme in Papua New Guinea. *The Courier,* 126:61–64.

Mola, G., 1989. 'Standard treatment of pelvic inflammatory disease', *Papua New Guinea Medical Journal,* 32:27–31.

Mondia, P., 1990. 'Editorial: The impact of Acquired Immunodeficiency Syndrome (AIDS) on tuberculosis control in Papua New Guinea', *Papua New Guinea Medical Journal,* 33:81–83.

Mondia, P., and Perera, J., 1990. 'A limited serosurveillance of HIV infection among tuberculosis patients attending a tuberculosis clinic: a preliminary report'. Paper presented to the 26th Annual Medical Symposium, Goroka.

Moorehead, A., 1966. *The Fatal Impact.* New York: Harper and Row.

Mulhall, B. P., Hart, G., and Harcourt, C., 1995. 'Sexually transmitted diseases in Australia: a decade of change, epidemiology and surveillance', *Annals of the Academy of Medicine, Singapore,* 24(4):569–578.

Nash, J., 1981. 'Sex, money, and the status of women in aboriginal South Bougainville', *American Anthropologist,* 8(1):107–126.

National Sex and Reproduction Research Team and Jenkins, C., 1994. *National Study of Sexual and Reproductive Knowledge and Behavior in Papua New Guinea.* Papua New

Guinea Institute of Medical Research Monograph No. 10. Goroka: Papua New Guinea Institute of Medical Research.

Naval Intelligence Division, 1945. *Pacific Islands, Vol. 1: general survey*. Geographical Handbook Series, #B.R. 519. Naval Intelligence Division, no place of publication listed.

Nilles, J., 1953. 'The Kuman People: a study of cultural change in a primitive society in the central highlands of New Guinea', *Oceania*, 24(1):1-27, 119-31.

O'Leary, M., Meijden, W. van der, Malau, C., Delaware, O., and Pyakalia, T., 1993. 'HIV serosurveillance in Papua New Guinea', *Papua New Guinea Medical Journal*, 36:187-191.

Oliver, D., 1967 [1955]. *A Solomon Island Society*. Boston: Beacon Press.

———, 1973. *Bougainville: a personal history*. Honolulu: University of Hawaii Press.

Ouellette, S. M. L., 1971. 'The Hahalis Welfare Society and the Baby Garden', *Papua and New Guinea Medical Journal*, 14(1):3-6.

Pataki-Schweizer, K. J., and Tabua, T., 1980. 'Psychosomatics of venereal disease: toward a programme for the 1980s', *Papua New Guinea Medical Journal*, 23:17-21.

Patton, C., 1994. *Last Served?* London: Taylor and Francis.

Purvis, A., 1997. 'The global epidemic', *Time*, January 6, pp. 76-78.

Ralston, C., 1992. 'Dialogue: the study of women in the Pacific', *The Contemporary Pacific*, Spring:162-175.

———, 1988. '"Polyandry," "Pollution," "Prostitution": the problems of eurocentrism and androcentrism in Polynesian studies', in B. Caine, E. A. Grocz, and M. de Lepervanche, eds., *Crossing Boundaries*. Sydney: Allen and Unwin, pp. 71-80.

Reaves, G., 1993. 'Flesh traders turn Thai girls into sex slaves', *The Oregonian*, 6 June, p. A4.

Ree, G. H., 1982. 'Knowledge and attitudes of young people regarding sexually transmitted diseases', *Papua New Guinea Medical Journal*, 25(1):33-36.

Rhodes, F. A., and Anderson, S. E. J., 1970. 'An outbreak of Treponematosis in the Eastern Highlands', *Papua and New Guinea Medical Journal*, 13(2):49-52.

Richens, J., 1985. 'Donovanosis: a review', *Papua New Guinea Medical Journal*, 28:67-74.

———, 1991. 'The diagnosis and treatment of Donovanosis (granuloma inguinale)', *Genitourinary Medicine*, 67:441-452.

Roheim, G., 1940. 'Professional beauties of Normanby Island', *American Anthropologist*, 42:657-661.

———, 1946. 'Ceremonial prostitution in Duau (Normanby Island)', *Journal of Clinical Psychopathology and Psychotherapy*, 7:753-764.

Rooke, P. W., 1982. 'Pelvic inflammatory disease in Port Moresby General Hospital', *Papua New Guinea Medical Journal*, 25:29-32.

Root-Bernstein, R., 1993. *Rethinking AIDS*. New York: The Free Press.

Rosen, R., 1982. *The Lost Sisterhood*. Baltimore: Johns Hopkins Press.

Rubin, G., 1975. 'The traffic in women', in R. Reiter, ed., *Toward an Anthropology of Women*. Boston: Monthly Review Press, pp. 157-210.

Runganga, A., Pitts, M., and McMaster, J., 1992. 'The use of herbal and other agents to enhance sexual experience', *Social Science and Medicine*, 35(8):1037-1042.

Salmond, A., 1991. *Two Worlds*. Honolulu: University of Hawaii.

Sanday, P., 1990. *Fraternity Gang Rape*. New York: New York University Press.

Sarda, R., and Harrison, G., 1995. 'Epidemiology of HIV and AIDS in the Pacific', *Pacific Health Dialog*, 2(2):6-13.

Scheper-Hughes, N., 1994. 'AIDS and the social body', *Social Science and Medicine*, 39(7): 991-1003.

Schopper, D., Doussantousse, S., and Orav, J., 1993. 'Sexual behaviors relevant to HIV transmission in a rural African population', *Social Science and Medicine*, 37(3):401-412.

Serpenti, L., 1977. *Cultivators in the Swamps*. Assen: Van Gorcum.

Sissons, D. C. S., 1977. '*Karayuki-San*: Japanese prostitutes in Australia, 1887–1916, part II', *Historical Studies*, 17(69):474–488.

Sittitrai, W., Phanuphak, P., Barry, J., and Brown, T., 1992. *Thai Sexual Behavior and Risk of HIV Infection*. Bangkok: Chulalongkorn University.

STD Nius, The, 1995. No. 1, December.

Stevenson, M., 1994. 'Acquired Immune Deficiency Syndrome in Indonesia', *Antara Kita*, the Indonesian Studies Committee 39:1–5.

Tabet, P., 1991. '"I'm the meat, I'm the knife": sexual service, migration, and repression in some African societies', *Feminist Issues*, 11(1):3–21.

Tanzanian Red Cross Society, 1994. *Changes in Sexual Behaviour and Effects of Health Education: a community based study*. Red Cross Society of Tanzania.

Thierfelder, M. U., 1928. 'The control of Granuloma Venereum among the Marindinese in Dutch South-New-Guinea', *Mededeelingen van den Dienst der Volksgzondheit in Nederlansch-Indie*, 17:393–423.

Thomas, K. H., 1941., 'Notes on the natives of the Vanimo Coast, New Guinea', *Oceania*, 12:163–186.

United Nations, 1996. *Time To Act*. Suva, Fiji: United Nations.

Vacca, A., and MacMillan, L., 1980. 'Anogenital lesions in women in Papua New Guinea', *Papua New Guinea Medical Journal*, 23:69–73.

Vete, S., 1995. 'Sex and AIDS: myths that kill', *Pacific Health Dialog*, 2(2):132–139.

Vogel, L. C., and Richens, J., 1989. 'Donovanosis in Dutch South New Guinea: history, evolution of the epidemic and control', *Papua New Guinea Medical Journal*, 32:203–218.

Waddell, C., 1996. 'HIV and the social world of female commercial sex workers', *Medical Anthropology Quarterly*, 10(1):75–82.

Walkowitz, J., 1980. *Prostitution in Victorian Society*. Cambridge: Cambridge University Press.

Wasserheit, J., 1991. 'Epidemiological synergy: interrelationships between HIV infection and other STDs', in L. Chen, J. Amor, and S. Segal, eds., *AIDS and Women's Reproductive Health*. New York: Plenum, pp. 47–72.

Watsford, S.D., and Alderman, L.W., 1953. 'Extragenital Granuloma in North Queensland', *Medical Journal of Australia*, [2]:50–52.

Watt, J., 1979. 'Medical Aspects and Consequences of Cook's Voyages', in R. Fisher and H. Johnstone, eds., *Captain Cook and His Times*. Seattle: University of Washington Press, pp. 129–157.

Wesche, D. L., 1989. '*Chlamydia trachomatis* Infections: therapeutic implications', *Papua New Guinea Medical Journal*, 32:65–70.

Whitaker, R., and Edwards, Y., 1991. 'A model-based approach to U.S. policy on HIV-1 infection and immigration', *AIDS and Public Policy Journal*, 6(1):3–14.

White, L., 1991. *The Comforts of Home*. Chicago: University of Chicago Press.

Willcox, R. R., 1980a. 'Venereal diseases in the Pacific Islands', *British Journal of Venereal Diseases*, 56:277–281.

———, 1980b. 'Venereal diseases in the islands of the North Pacific', *British Journal of Venereal Diseases*, 56:173–177.

———, 1980c. 'Venereal diseases in the islands of the South Pacific', *British Journal of Venereal Diseases*, 56:204–209.

Willis, I., 1974. *Lae: village and city*. Melbourne: Melbourne University Press.

Wright, H., 1959. *New Zealand, 1769–1840*. Cambridge: Harvard University Press.

Zegwaard, G. A., 1959. 'Headhunting practices of the Asmat of Netherlands New Guinea', *American Anthropologist*, 61(6):1020–1041.

Zigas, V., 1971. 'A Donovanosis project in Goilala (1951–54)', *Papua and New Guinea Medical Journal*, 14(4):148–149.

Zimmer, L., 1990. 'Sexual exploitation and male dominance in Papua New Guinea', in J. Ingebritson, ed., *Human Sexuality in Melanesian Cultures*, Point Series No. 14. Goroka: The Melanesian Institute, pp. 250–267.

Zimmer-Tamakoshi, L., 1993a. 'Bachelors, spinsters, and *Pamuk Meris*', in R. Marksbury, ed., *The Business of Marriage*. Pittsburgh: University of Pittsburgh Press, pp. 83–104.

———, 1993b. 'Nationalism and sexuality in Papua New Guinea', *Pacific Studies,* 16(4):61–98.

Acknowledgments

I thank all Daruans and Ngao and Doumori villagers in particular for taking care of me so well. Particular thanks also go to health workers on Daru and elsewhere, to the Wenner-Gren Foundation for Anthropological Research (Grant #5250), to Carol Jenkins and Michael Alpers, and to the Institute of Papua New Guinea Studies. Extraordinary library help was given, too, by Johanna Sherrer and Kathy Creely: thank you! Kathy Poole provided a key document, and Leslie Butt, Tanya King, and Laura Zimmer-Tamakoshi improved this essay greatly by sharing with me their keen insights and editorial criticism. Where I have erred the fault is wholly mine.

Michael Crossley

IDEOLOGY, CURRICULUM, AND COMMUNITY
Policy and Practice in Education

*J*N THIS CHAPTER the development of the school curriculum in Papua New Guinea is examined in the light of two ideological perspectives that have shaped the education system since Western schools were first introduced in the late nineteenth century. The first of these ideological perspectives orientates the curriculum towards the 'needs' of the village community and the improvement of rural life. The second perspective focuses more upon education for modern economic development and participation in the cash economy. An understanding of these historical and ideological foundations helps to explain the tensions and controversies that dominate the following analysis of recent curriculum trends and of the policy issues concerning the relevance of schooling in modern Papua New Guinea society. The discussion begins with a brief theoretical consideration of the political and ideological dimensions of curriculum planning and development in the light of recent sociological critiques of the process of curriculum change and of the role played by education in national development.

Curriculum Planning and Development
There is in the field of curriculum planning and development a tendency in much of the literature to portray the task as a rational, technical process in which educational experiences are simply tailored to the emerging skills and intellectual abilities of the learner. This line of

thinking reflects the scientific approach to curriculum 'engineering' that first emerged in the United States of America during the 1920s, when rapid educational change was seen as essential for national development. The work of Bobbitt (1924) and Tyler (1949) has been especially influential in this respect, with Tyler's 'objective model' for curriculum development being widely refined and applied in developed and less-developed countries worldwide.

While the influence of the curriculum engineers continues—especially in the modern social climate dominated by concepts of economic efficiency and accountability—the social and intellectual upheavals of the 1970s challenged the dominance of the rational-technical model by reasserting the importance of the 'political', cultural, and ideological foundations of education and of the school curriculum itself. Leading this challenge, sociologists of education drew attention to the significance of conflicting interests in educational decision making, the processes of the legitimation of educational knowledge, and the role of the school curriculum in social stratification and control. Education was no longer assumed to be a 'good thing' for all—the implications of policy for different clients were increasingly questioned, and curriculum planning and development processes became the focus of renewed scrutiny.

Paralleling initial research on the role of education in metropolitan societies, critical sociologists began to question the impact of education in the international development process. Dependency theorists, for example, presented a fundamental critique of the international influence of Western education. Carnoy's (1974) *Education as Cultural Imperialism* articulates this challenge well:

> Our thesis is that educators, social scientists and historians have misinterpreted the role of Western schooling in the Third World and in industrialized countries themselves. We argue that far from acting as a liberator, Western formal education came to most countries as part of imperialist domination. It was consistent with the goals of imperialism: the economic and political control of the people in one country by the dominant class of another. The imperial powers attempted, through schooling, to train the colonized for roles that suited the colonizer. (1974:3)

With respect to policy analysis and reformulation the intellectual response has included calls for total 'deschooling' (Illich 1970), an emphasis on adult education and 'conscientization' (Freire 1971), and the decolonization of the curriculum in both its formal and hidden dimensions (Graham-Brown 1991; Turner 1993).

This is not to say that the perspectives of the 'new' sociologists and dependency theorists have been, or should be, accepted as such; for the shortcomings and limitations of 'critical theory' and alternative educational models have themselves been acknowledged in more recent years (Watson 1994; Crossley and Vulliamy 1997).

On the other hand, the contemporary study of the curriculum is now a more complex and challenging arena than it used to be. The critical perspectives have challenged so many assumptions relating to, for example, issues of learning and gender, class reproduction, selection, common or diversified curricula, language of instruction and cultural analysis that curriculum studies now hold a central place in educational research worldwide. The dominance of the rational, technically oriented curriculum engineers has also been shaken as the political and ideological dimensions of curriculum planning and development have come to the fore. As Bacchus (1986) argues with reference to the development of the curriculum in the Caribbean over the past hundred years:

> What was actually taught in Caribbean schools over this period was not the outcome of a rational planning process, but instead reflected a struggle for control between different interest groups. The curriculum at any given time reflected the relative amount of effective power which a particular group—whether it was colonial administrators, planters, missionaries, teachers, or parents—was able to exert. (1986)

THE SCHOOL CURRICULUM IN PAPUA NEW GUINEA: HISTORICAL FOUNDATIONS

Intellectual perspectives sensitive to the ideological and political issues raised above help to throw new light upon the study of the curriculum in Papua New Guinea. The importance of embedding educational debate more firmly within the broader sociopolitical context of Papua New Guinean society is also emphasized. Indeed, Bacchus's argument has much relevance in Papua New Guinea, where the colonial economy and associated external influences have had a similarly marked impact upon the nature of schooling and curricula.

Historically the nature of the school curriculum has long been a contentious issue that has generated heated debate between conflicting pressure groups and ideologies. Having said this, few studies of the national curriculum in this context have, as yet, gone far beyond the parameters set by mainstream literature. We can do little but sketch out the major controversies and issues here, but the potential for further research, both theoretical and empirical, is considerable.

Two Divergent Ideologies

At the risk of oversimplifying the issues, two conflicting ideologies have influenced the broad patterns and shifts in curriculum policy since the origins of Western formal education in Papua New Guinea.

The first of these perspectives or educational ideologies stems from mission educational policies that emphasized Christian upbringing and values, combined with an orientation towards 'improved' village life. The first missionaries to establish a permanent school in the country were London Missionary Society pastor-teachers from the Pacific Islands. They settled near Port Moresby in 1873 and were joined by the European W. G. Lawes the following year. While variations in the curricula of missionary schools reflected differing priorities of the Christian denominations, the following extract from a 1916 directive issued by Catholic Bishop de Boismenu vividly portrays the nature and tone of the Christian ideology:

> The religious teaching takes in school the first rank. From your Priests, you will know which religious matters you have to teach. Follow carefully this program.
> The text of the approved catechism has to be taught exactly as it stands without any change whatever. Teach this text, lesson after lesson, question after question, in the order of the book, so that the whole doctrine may be seen in the course of the year. However, this order may be, exceptionally, interrupted by direction of the Father. (cited in Smith 1987a:79)

Beyond this religious core of the curriculum, mission philosophy emphasized the 'three Rs', vernacular literacy, and agricultural and practical skills. These skills and qualities, it was assumed, would be applied by school graduates when they returned to improve material conditions in the village and proselytize within the community.

Following the turn of the century the second major ideological influence emerged as interest in the curriculum was increasingly expressed by colonial administrators. Language policy was an important stimulus in this respect because government objectives favored the spread of the colonial languages. In 1913, for example, the German Imperial Governor Albert Hahl agreed to pay subsidies to mission schools that helped to spread the German language. A similar scheme was established in Papua by Lieutenant Governor Murray in 1920 to promote the English language. Administration schools were eventually established in both Papua and New Guinea and these developed a more secular curriculum much of which was transferred from metropolitan society.

In contrast to the missions, administration curriculum ideology was directed more towards serving the emerging cash economy. Basic literacy and numeracy were emphasized along with the industrious work habits and discipline needed by a low level indigenous work force. It was not until 1960 that official education policy shifted to emphasize the development of an educated indigenous elite.

Both Church and State, however, aimed to change indigenous society and to introduce Western values and lifestyles into Papua and New Guinea. But, to reiterate the basic point, the ideological divergence that has dominated curriculum policy was apparent from the start with the missions focusing upon social cohesion, the subsistence economy and community development (in their terms), and the secular authorities' emphasis of education for modernization and participation in the cash economy. In the words of Smith and Guthrie (1980:7):

> In providing formal education, the missionary societies and the colonial governments saw schools as powerful agents for change. There was never any intention that the schools should serve merely to reproduce the values, beliefs and lifestyles of the societies in which they were placed: in fact their explicit intention was the opposite. Perhaps on the whole the missions were more concerned than the governments to preserve the social cohesion of local communities (but in the process the communities were to be transformed, evil practices eliminated, and replaced with Christian ways). Governments by and large were content to support the missions in their work, for their aims of pacification, civilization and native development were equally served by the mission schools. Where missions and governments differed was in their view of 'development'.

Blending of the Cultures

Before leaving the Church-State curriculum dichotomy it is revealing to examine how from the 1920s efforts were made to bring mission and government curricula closer together in policy and practice. The stimulus for such initiatives throughout many British colonies came from official Colonial Office policy of the times (see, for example, Advisory Committee 1925; Crossley 1984).

In Papua, British Colonial Office influences were best articulated by F. E. Williams, government anthropologist, in his essay 'The Blending of Cultures' (1936). Williams' ideas were later taken up by W. C. Groves, the first director of education for Papua and New Guinea in the late 1940s and 1950s. The Blending of the Cultures policy argued for the development of a Westernized (but Christian) school curriculum, based upon a (selective) foundation of indigenous culture, values, and economic activities. To cite Groves' introduction to the 1951 edition of Williams' monograph:

> Appreciative of the distinctive pattern of Papuan cultures, he [Williams] held fast to the principle that the development of the Papuan, in its early phases at any rate, should be on the sure foundation of Papuan interests. A discriminating student of Papuan art, Papuan music and the communalistic pattern of Papuan social and economic life, these he desired to see interwoven into the texture of new Papuan life, and given expression in Papuan education—the old blending with the new!

In this respect educational policy, for the times, displayed 'enlightened' respect for indigenous ways of life—despite the fact that the selection of what was deemed to be worthwhile for 'blending' was made by colonial and mission authorities.

In practice, however, the story was very different, for Groves proved to be an ineffectual administrator who failed to see his policies implemented. To be fair, he also faced concerted opposition from expatriate pressure groups, such as planters and businessmen, for concerning himself with the educational aspirations, rights, and values of the indigenous population at all (Dickson 1978).

The picture was further complicated by the very significant fact that the children of the colonial elite continued to receive a metropolitan style academic curriculum that did not emphasize the practical skills and agriculture that were also central to the mission/Groves curriculum alliance. This obvious fact was not lost upon the indigenous school clientele, especially following the Second World War when aspirations for personal and political advancement became more acute. Despite the apparent cultural sensitivity of Groves' policy, Papuans and New Guineans clearly recognized the political implications of the dualistic curricula. They rightly saw the practical and village-oriented ('blended') curriculum as inferior in status, and feared it would exclude their children from access to the modern sector of life where jobs, high income, and social and political power were to be obtained. Indigenous parents thus came to demand that their children have the 'best' foreign, academic education because this carried most value and prestige in society (Smith 1975).

By the mid-1950s efforts to orient the school curriculum towards community needs and values were, along with Groves, largely discredited (Smith 1987b). Under the influence of G. T. Roscoe, then the deputy director of education, new centralized academic syllabuses were drawn up for Papua and New Guinea based upon those used in Queensland. The community orientation was virtually abandoned as official policy and government authority began to exert an increased influence upon the curriculum in all schools, whether they were administration or mission controlled.

THE CURRICULUM AND MODERN PAPUA NEW GUINEA SOCIETY

Reproduction and Dependency?

The brief historical sketch presented above is especially interesting in the light of the work undertaken by critical sociologists referred to earlier. It is to such an analysis that we now turn, followed by an exploration of its relevance for an understanding of more contemporary trends and developments in Papua New Guinean schools and society.

Given the indigenous rejection of the Blending of Cultures ideology, it is interesting to reconsider popular criticism of the present school curriculum as a 'colonial imposition'. Clearly this issue is more complex than is usually acknowledged. The academic model of the late 1950s was transferred directly from Australia but, because of the personal rewards that academic success conferred, this was fervently wanted by Papua New Guineans.

On the other hand, the practical and community oriented curriculum favored by Groves was rejected—despite its cultural sensitivity. This model also reflected colonial motives and ideologies by emphasizing a dualistic nature for schooling where the elite (then Europeans) received an academic education suitable for leadership and control, and the general populace received a practical education appropriate for low level service in the administration or for village life.

This can be seen as reproducing the existing colonial social order; and similar dualistic provision was characteristic of metropolitan societies such as Britain itself. There the working classes received a practically oriented curriculum, while children of the educated elite

attended academic grammar or public schools. Western social class
reproduction was thus replicated within the colonies in the Blending
of Cultures ideology as well as through the more commonly discredited
academic model. This has implications for the analysis of contemporary policy as we shall argue later.

In the years leading up to independence members of the indigenous community were responding vociferously to 'adapted' curricula
as a form of social control; but in opting for the academic model they
played a part in legitimizing distinctly Western educational structures,
content, and values. As McKinnon (1976) points out, the academic
model then dominated throughout the 1960s and early 1970s.

Independence and Curriculum Change

With political independence in 1975 came renewed criticism of the
'colonial curriculum'. This emanated from articulate Papua New
Guineans as well as from influential foreign critics. The Eighth Waigani
Seminar on Education in Melanesia held at the University of Papua
New Guinea, for example, provided a forum for many educationalists,
including Ivan Illich (1970) who inspired others within the Pacific with
his radical notions of de-schooling (1973).

Concern was expressed about the dependency of the new nation
upon the structures, influence, and resources (material and human) of
the former colonial power. In education the search was for ways of
decolonizing the school curriculum—with an emphasis upon challenging the academic model.

Since these early days of independence the twin and competing
ideologies of education for village life or the modern economy have
surfaced in the curriculum policy debate time and time again. The
1970s were characterized by the ascendance of the community orientation which was seen to be compatible with the principles of the new
National Constitution and the ideology of the Eight Point Plan and
National Development Strategy (1976). During this period a succession
of National Education Plans was drafted and redrafted (Cleverley 1976),
primary schools were redesignated 'community schools', selection to
high school was influenced by quotas to improve the representation of
rural students, and efforts were made to 'adapt' the content of the curriculum to the needs of rural development. The influence of the Tanzanian Philosophy of Education for Self Reliance was notable, the
attendance of indigenous students at International Schools was discouraged, the Generalist Teaching innovation (Field 1981) was intro-

duced to provincial high schools, the Secondary Schools Community Extension Project (SSCEP) was born (Crossley and Vulliamy 1986); and efforts (largely unsuccessful at the time) were made to introduce *Tok Ples* languages into the school curriculum as a medium of instruction in the early years (Weeks and Guthrie 1984). This was a time when optimism in education led to expectations of major change and reconstruction in society.

Challenges to many of these initiatives soon arose, however, often led by members of the new indigenous elite, whose chances of reproducing their own social advantages for their children were now being threatened. The expatriates (who continued to influence postindependence ideology) now had less to win or lose directly from such change since their own futures lay elsewhere.

Somewhat ironically, while striving to maintain educational advantages for their own children, many of the new elite expressed support for new forms of dualistic curricula that would better prepare the majority for life in the village and the subsistence sector, and their own children for leadership positions in modern society via selective academic institutions or curricula. In this way reflections of colonial educational ideology began to appear in 'alternative' and 'independent' educational policy, despite official rhetoric to the contrary. As modern sector employment opportunities became more difficult for school leavers to obtain during the 1980s, such views became increasingly common.

CONTEMPORARY CURRICULUM ISSUES

Modern Papua New Guinea has thus assumed a complex educational heritage complete with a long-standing range of curriculum controversies and dilemmas. Given the central position of education in the social fabric of the nation, the way such curriculum issues are resolved often has a marked influence upon other dimensions of social policy and upon the course of development itself. Often the wider influence of educational factors upon society may be less than is commonly assumed—but popular perceptions and false assumptions may also have a powerful influence upon public policy. We have only to think, for example, of how frequently so-called 'poor' or 'irrelevant' education is blamed for the contemporary ills of society—for unemployment, rascalism, urbanization—to realize the extent of the pressures and dilemmas facing educational decision makers and practitioners. As other papers in this volume demonstrate, conflicting pressures also abound, for many of the central problems and issues facing modern Papua New Guinea society have implications (or perceived implications) for educational and curriculum policy. Michael Monsell-Davis' paper, for example, calls for a curriculum that serves the needs of both the modern economy and village community.

Cost-Effectiveness

At the broadest level tensions between the twin ideologies of education for community life or the modern economy persist in educational policy and practice. The last decade has seen the influence of the tightening of the world economic situation reflected in renewed support for traditional academic standards, improved cost-effectiveness, and greater efficiency from education in terms remarkably similar to those of the 1920s, when business and industrial principles were first applied to curriculum development. In this international context, enthusiasm for spending upon unproven 'alternative' initiatives has diminished in Papua New Guinea.

Pressures for education that is demonstrably useful for modern sector economic development have, on the other hand, assumed increased importance. The academic standards of schools and formal examinations have reasserted themselves as criteria for measuring efficiency (Kenehe 1981); and the budget to the educational sector as a whole is repeatedly challenged to redirect funds to economic sectors and income generating activities. Concern for improved cost-effectiveness also continues to reinforce curriculum policy that emphasizes preparation and training for the modern economy. Indeed, the launching of a National Training Policy (1989) to stimulate, direct, and coordinate improved training programs throughout the public and private sectors is indicative of the emphasis placed upon such activities beyond the school level. The Resource Management System (RMS), introduced by the Government at the end of the 1980s to better coordinate all public sector spending, also emphasized the need for community-based education initiatives to be increasingly supported by the communities themselves (Tetaga 1989).

Relevance

The relevance of the school curriculum is still strongly debated, with calls for improved academic standards being articulated at the same time as demands are made for increased cultural sensitivity and practical education that will generate entrepreneurial skills and prepare youth for a productive return to village life. In practice, curriculum planning and policy formulation is complex and somewhat confusing, as new decision makers search for ways of reconciling these long-standing and apparently contradictory pressures.

Throughout the 1970s emphasis was placed upon building a unified education system with a common curriculum for all. Efforts were made to meet the needs of students destined for higher education and modern sector employment, through the same program of study as that provided for potential school leavers likely to remain unemployed or return to the village. SSCEP, for example, was developed on these lines to apply academic learning to practical and developmental projects that could be established within village communities. Through SSCEP it was argued that academic standards would be maintained while the relevance of the provincial high school curriculum for rural development could be improved. The achievements and failures of SSCEP are considered elsewhere (Crossley and Vulliamy 1986) but it is interesting to note how, at the broader political and administrative levels, pressures for a movement away from the common curriculum approach that sustained this initiative have increased in recent years.

It is at the secondary school level where the implications of these trends are most significant, because proposals for the restructuring of secondary education and the reintroduction of dualistic secondary curricula are repeatedly articulated (Deutrom 1989). The needs of both the modern economy and village life can better be met, it is argued, if 'able' secondary students are selected to follow an academic curriculum, while the majority undertake a practical, vocational, and community-oriented program relevant for a return to village life. Paramount in such deliberations is recognition that, for example, in 1988 only 33.8 percent of tenth-grade graduates were receiving offers of modern sector employment or further education on leaving school. Concern about the increasing numbers of unemployed secondary school leavers and attendant social problems is certainly a major issue in modern Papua New Guinea society, but what shifts in curriculum policy will come to pass remains to be seen. In view of Papua New Guinea's own educational history, if dualistic models emerge the political and ideological implications will be considerable.

Meanwhile, schools continue to emphasize examination performance in practice, and this is the dominant criterion for measuring their success. The rhetoric of community and cultural relevance remains sig-

nificant but, while subjects such as expressive arts have received attention, secondary education clearly gives priority to the academic needs
of the modern economy.

At lower levels similar dilemmas continue to affect curriculum
planning and development, although community and cultural relevance are given greater prominence in policy, even though this is far
from always the case in practice. To cite the Secretary for Education at
the start of the 1990s:

> Community-based education will play a big role in making basic edu-
> cation more attractive because it makes education relevant and useful
> to everyone. At the same time, as more and more children are spend-
> ing their time in school, schools must spend more time ensuring that
> the traditional knowledge of their community is preserved and built
> upon. These factors make universal basic education a catalyst in the
> development of a much closer relationship between schools and com-
> munities. (Tetaga 1989:3)

Such initiatives are further supported by the Philosophy of Education for Papua New Guinea (the Matane Report) which is considered
below.

National Philosophy

Since its approval in October 1987 the Matane Report has been the official 'Philosophy of Education for Papua New Guinea'. Central to this
report are notions of integral human development, equal access to educational resources and opportunities, and, above all, Papua New
Guinea values. Matane called for a broadening of the basis of the curriculum (for all), emphasizing spiritual and social goals in addition to academic standards. Interestingly, much of the flavor of mission
educational ideology is reflected in the Matane Report, and Matane
himself was a primary school teacher and inspector who tried to implement the Blending of Cultures rural bias (Matane 1972).

The introduction of vernacular education in early grades is supported again to help remove barriers between school and community,
and to improve standards in the English language. Indeed, increased
community involvement in the work of the school features strongly
throughout the Philosophy of Education, recognizing the need for education to be seen as the responsibility of all members of society. Parents
are discouraged from viewing education solely as a means of securing
paid employment, and community and provincial high schools are to
emphasize a more practical curriculum. The eventual reintegration of

school leavers into village life is therefore central to the Matane Report—as is the persistence of concern for the plight of unemployed school leavers and associated problems of social control and stability.

Tensions in Policy and Practice

In view of the trends and proposals outlined above, the continuation of ideological tensions between pressures supporting education for modern economic development and education for community life clearly persist in contemporary curriculum policy and practice. The Philosophy of Education reiterates the importance of education for community life, while contrary policy proposals, the influence of the broader economic climate, and actions of the educated elite demonstrate continued pressures for an education suited for employment in the modern economic sector.

We have already noted proposals for a restructuring of secondary education but also of significance here is explicit support by the Government for the further opening up of fee-paying 'International Schools' (following Western academic curricula) for the children of the wealthy elite. Growth in Papua New Guinean enrolments in international primary schools, for example, saw the proportion of national pupils rise from 6 percent in 1976 to 47 percent in 1987 (see also Smith and Bray 1985). This selective avenue clearly provides an alternative, non-community-based curriculum for those who can afford it. Agreements were also made in late 1988 to spend increasing amounts of tied Australian aid on the provision of high school places in Australia for specially selected Papua New Guineans. Twenty-five such candidates were chosen in 1988, and further increases have characterized recent years. If these trends are indicative of future educational policy the implications for the national system need to be fully considered and there are clear lessons to be learned from past experience. Reflecting the importance of the issue at the end of the 1980s, the *Times* of Papua New Guinea responded rapidly to the tied aid announcement by maintaining that: 'What the PNG education system needs is not better educated minorities but an improved and revitalized system' (1988:7).

Clearly, increased reliance upon Australian schools (and curricula) and International Schools within the country, poses serious questions about cultural values that even the opponents of reproduction and dependency theories must recognize. The 'backwash effect' of this form of dualism has major implications for the national curriculum today, as it did in the past. The tensions between education for the modern economy or for village life, between academic and community-based curriculum policy, are particularly noticeable in this context.

Emerging Trends

One thing is clear from the above discussion and that is the fact that the course of curriculum development is as much a product of broad political decision making as it is of the specialist and technically oriented efforts of educational personnel. As political ideologies change so too do the ideologies that steer the course of the school curriculum. At the present time broader political uncertainties are clearly reflected in curriculum ambivalences and tensions, and in the conflicts between curriculum policy and practice that characterize contemporary education.

It will certainly be interesting to compare the course of educational and curriculum change in the future with the guiding principles established in the Matane Report. This is already quite a revealing exercise if we look again at the evolution of SSCEP, an innovation of the 1970s that influenced Matane and that has endured to become incorporated into the continuing structures of the National Department of Education. As we noted earlier, SSCEP was based upon efforts to meet the educational needs of both the modern economy and the local community. Under SSCEP all provincial high school students were to emphasize local cultural values and the practical applications of academic learning. Today, similar rhetoric prevails in some quarters but broader educational policy has clearly shifted away from this orientation.

Another significant development is that some indigenous perspectives are now becoming more prominent as Papua New Guineans are assuming senior positions in the curriculum field (Martin 1987). Through the influence of the work of such people there is increased potential for indigenous values, practices, and ideologies to renew and reorientate the curriculum of the future. In this way it may be that elements of traditional education and village culture come to be more easily accepted as a distinctive and legitimate component of education in modern Papua New Guinea society. The promotion of vernacular languages in schools with the active support of the National Department of Education (NDOE) Curriculum Unit, for instance, is one central initiative that is gaining widespread support.

Perhaps it is at the local level, through local people, that the emphasis upon indigenous culture, values, and perspectives will be most strongly and more appropriately pursued. Certainly there is much to be gained from initiatives where the relevance of learning applies less to job training and social control, and more to the cultural values and identity that are so essential for personal confidence and intellectual maturity. Could this lead to the foundation of an educated, satisfying, and productive life in both village community and the modern economic society?

CONCLUSIONS

In many respects the curriculum controversies and dilemmas characteristic of modern Papua New Guinea society have their roots firmly embedded in educational history. Times have changed dramatically, but certain key educational issues continue to prevail. Foremost of these issues is concern for the relevance of the school curriculum—a concern that pulls the policy in two apparently opposing directions. On the one hand, the ideology of modernization and economic development is reflected in pressure for improved academic standards and schooling that can be favorably equated with the 'best' international criteria and models. On the other hand, fear of growing numbers of unemployed school leavers and potential social unrest lends support to those who favor a school curriculum designed to prepare youth for a productive return to the village economy and culture. Somewhere between these two positions are proposals for a dual curriculum favoring academic study for a small elite and practical applications for the majority.

This debate is more complex than it is often portrayed for, as our historical and sociological analyses demonstrate, the vested interests of different sectors of society influence both what is proposed as educational policy and what is possible as educational practice. The curriculum issue is not simply a rational, technical matter but it is characterized by ideological influences and questions of political shifts in the balance of power and the nature of social control and stratification.

In modern Papua New Guinea society, just as in the colonial era, different pressure groups compete to influence the nature and orientation of the school curriculum. Informing each group are ideological perspectives relating to the role and aims of education. Today many of the issues and controversies of old continue, while some of the interest groups have changed—and some have stayed the same.

Because education acts as a key mechanism for social stratification, all sectors of society recognize the importance of successful competition at each level of the system. Similarly, all clients of schools value access to the academic type of education that confers such success; and efforts to introduce a more community-oriented curriculum continue to face resistance or criticism—most notably from those who are 'destined' to receive it. It is this basic dilemma that educational decision makers must deal with if the principles of integral human development for all are to be upheld. This, however, depends in turn upon consistent support from other powerful sectors of society—support that in the past has proved hard to find.

Perhaps because this is the heart of the dilemma we should conclude on a realistic note. Curriculum change has been quite dramatic since independence and much of the basic content has been adapted to the Papua New Guinean context. A thriving and active Curriculum Development Division has been created generating an impressive range of home-produced textbooks and materials (NDOE 1987; Peril 1984). Much more can certainly be done, especially to strengthen indigenous values and perspectives, but we should not expect curriculum (or educational) change to solve broader social problems alone. To do this is to expect too much of education and to foster the sort of unproductive and disillusioning debate that attracts unwarranted criticism to the educational sector and the personnel within it. Rather, it is both more realistic and helpful to accept that, while educational change may play an important part in the process of development, this role is constrained by the extent of parallel support forthcoming from other sectors of the society; from economic policies that influence rural incomes; from social policies that determine the distribution of resources between urban and rural dwellers; and from the ideological orientations of politicians themselves.

REFERENCES

Advisory Committee on Native Education in British Tropical African Dependencies, 1925. 'Education Policy in British Tropical Africa'. London: Cmd 2374.

Bacchus, M. K., 1986. *The Myth and Reality of Curriculum Planning: Insights from the Educational Development of the Caribbean*. London: University of London Institute of Education.

Bobbitt, F., 1924. *How to Make a Curriculum*. Boston: Houghton and Mifflin.

Carnoy, M., 1974. *Education as Cultural Imperialism*. New York: Longman.

Cleverley, J., 1976. 'Planning educational change in Papua New Guinea', *Comparative Education*, 12(2):16–25.

Crossley, M., and Vulliamy, G., 1986. *The Policy of SSCEP: Context and Development*. ERU Report No. 54, Waigani: University of Papua New Guinea.

Crossley, M., and Vulliamy, G., eds., 1997. *Qualitative Educational Research in Developing Countries: Current Perspectives*. New York: Garland.

Deutrom, B., 1989. 'Current initiatives and possible future strategies in education'. Paper prepared for the Education Seminar in Kiunga, Western Province, 17–22 April.

Dickson, D. J., 1978. 'W. C. Groves: Educationalist', in J. Griffin, ed., *Papua New Guinea Portraits: The Expatriate Experience*. Canberra: Australian National University Press, pp. 101–135.

Field, S. G., 1981. *Generalist Teaching Policy and Practice*. ERU Report No. 36, Waigani: University of Papua New Guinea.

Freire, P., 1971. *Pedagogy of the Oppressed*. Harmondsworth: Penguin.

Government of Papua New Guinea, 1989. *National Training Policy*. Waigani.

Graham-Brown, S., 1991. *Education in the Developing World*. London: Longman.

Illich, I., 1970. *De-schooling Society*. New York: Harper and Row.

———, 1973. 'A convivial society for Melanesia', in R. J. May, ed., *Priorities in Melanesian Development*. Canberra: Australian National University and University of Papua New Guinea, pp. 210–227.

Kenehe, S. (Chairman), 1981. *In Search of Standards*. Waigani: Papua New Guinea Ministry of Education.

Martin, N., 1988. 'Community participation in schooling', unpublished doctoral dissertation, University of Alberta.

Matane, P., 1972. *My Childhood in New Guinea*. London: Oxford University Press.

———, 1986. *A Philosophy of Education for Papua New Guinea*. Waigani: Papua New Guinea Ministry of Education.

McKinnon, K. R., 1976. 'Curriculum development in primary education: the Papua New Guinea experience', in E. B. Thomas, ed., *Papua New Guinea Education*. Melbourne: Oxford University Press, pp. 49–56.

National Department of Education, 1987. *Curriculum Development Division*. Waigani: Papua New Guinea, NDOE.

Papua New Guinea, Central Planning Office, 1976. *The Post-Independence National Development Strategy*. Port Moresby: Government Printer.

Peril, M. B., 1984. 'Integration of curriculum development, in-service training and the community school inspectorate', *Papua New Guinea Journal of Education*, 20(1): 23–28.

Smith, G., 1975. *Education in Papua New Guinea*. Melbourne: Melbourne University Press.

Smith, P., 1987a. *Education and Colonial Control in Papua New Guinea: A Documentary History*. Melbourne: Longman Cheshire.

———, 1987b. 'A department of native development: W. C. Groves and non-school education 1946–1955', in M. Crossley, J. Sukwianomb, and S. G. Weeks, eds., *Pacific Perspectives on Non-Formal Education*. Suva and Port Moresby: Institute of Pacific Studies and University of Papua New Guinea Press, pp. 177–188.

Smith, P., and Bray, M., 1985. 'Educating an elite: Papua New Guinea enrolment in International Schools', in M. Bray and P. Smith, eds., *Education and Social Stratification in Papua New Guinea*. Melbourne: Longman Cheshire, pp. 115-145.

Smith, P., and Guthrie, G., 1980. 'Children, education and society', in G. Guthrie and P. Smith, eds., *The Education of the Papua New Guinea Child*. Port Moresby: University of Papua New Guinea, pp. 1-15.

Tetaga, J., 1989. 'Minister for Education's closing speech', Community-based Education National Seminar. Port Moresby, 3-7 July.

Times of Papua New Guinea, 1988. Leader article, 17 November, p. 7.

Turner, J. D., ed., 1993. *The Reform of Educational Systems to Meet Local and National Needs*. Manchester: Manchester University Press.

Tyler, R., 1949. *Basic Principles of Curriculum and Instruction*. San Francisco: Fearon.

Watson, J. K., 1994. 'Technical and Vocational Education in Developing Countries: Western Paradigms and Comparative Methodology', *Comparative Education*, 30(2):83-97.

Weeks, S. G., and Guthrie, G., 1984. 'Papua New Guinea', in R. M. Thomas and T. N. Postlethwaite, eds., *Schooling in the Pacific Islands*. Oxford: Pergamon Press, pp. 29-64.

Williams, F. E., 1936. *The Blending of the Cultures: An Essay on the Aims of Native Education*. Port Moresby: Government Printer.

Acknowledgments

Mark Bray and Sheldon Weeks provided useful comments which helped in the refinement of this paper.

Michael Monsell-Davis

EDUCATION AND RURAL DEVELOPMENT
Social Considerations in Expanding High
School Education to All

$\mathcal{J}$N PAPUA NEW GUINEA, as in many Pacific island nations, there has
been a ferment of discussion in recent years concerning such matters as
rural development, village entrepreneurs, the quality of education,
crime and delinquency, and urban squatter settlements. In particular
much debate has centred on the question of growing numbers of
young people with good education, but unable to obtain formal jobs,
and their dissatisfaction as a result. A recent estimate suggested that
52,000 youngsters leave school every year hoping to enter a wage economy that can cater to only 10,000 (Barber 1993). A related issue therefore, has been that of whether or not these youngsters can fit back into
the village and use their new skills there.

Most recently there has been pressure to keep youngsters in school
right through to grade 10, with the Manus Provincial Government stating, in 1988, that their policy is now 'High School Education for all'. As
other provincial governments follow this lead, there is a pressing need
to consider what we expect youngsters to do when they leave school,
thus a need to discuss the wider social context of education, hence my
choice of topic.

One comment is appropriate: my remarks in this chapter are based
in part on my experiences as a teacher and anthropologist for more
than thirty years in various parts of Melanesia and the wider Pacific,
and in part on published writings by other people. Only those immediately concerned can decide how much is relevant to their own provinces,

either directly or indirectly. Officials in some provinces appear to believe that youth problems are of no concern to them.[1] It is, therefore, worth noting in the context of Manus, that one visitor wrote:

> To an outside observer, Manus youth have always been very busy, not only in group projects but in other activities which involve the whole family or community.

But she added that 'older community members' make reference to

> the restless groups of young people who are considered to be an increasing problem.[2] (O'Collins 1984:100)

To introduce the main part of this chapter, I would like to recount two short tales of recent experiences. The first concerns a young man, about nineteen years old, from one of the settlements in Port Moresby. I knew him slightly, but not well. From the accounts of all in his community he was a pretty good sort of youth—a bit rough when he got drunk, but otherwise a youth who normally sat with his parents and family in the evenings and talked with them, rather than run around with a gang.

He was not a rascal, but in June 1988 two older youths who were rascals persuaded him to drink with them, and when he was drunk they took him to the old Boroko RSL Club and together they broke in. They were caught and he was beaten to death by the security guards.

He was unemployed, unoccupied, and poorly qualified. Alcohol and the activities leading from it were a temporary stimulation, a quick release from boredom.

My second tale concerns a village man in his late thirties, educated to grade eight. For three years in the mid-1980s, he was very active as chairman of the local community school—a new school that needed a

---

[1] This is a revised version of a paper first prepared for a seminar/workshop on high school education for all in Manus, 11–13 July 1988, sponsored by the Manus Provincial Government and the Hanns Seidel Foundation. While this paper was written for the Manus seminar, many of the examples cited are from other areas.

Extracts from the original version were published in Community Education: South Pacific News. The Newsletter of the International Community Education Association (Pacific), September 1989.

[2] Some Manus participants in the 1988 seminar argued that the implications of disaffected youth and increasing social problems contained in this work were not relevant to Manus. It is worth noting that in the eighteen months or so following the seminar there were a number of serious incidents in Lorengau, including armed robbery, arson at the high school, and the murder of a local hotelier.

lot of work to get it underway. In 1988 he became seriously ill with malaria, and when he consulted a village diviner, she told him that he was ill because he was too active in the community—his work for the school was making other people jealous. When he returned to the house, he wrote his letter of resignation from the school committee.

These two stories serve as an excuse to divide social context into two broad, closely interrelated aspects:

1. the individual students themselves; and
2. the community.

I shall discuss these in turn, and then try to draw conclusions. Perhaps much of what I say is not especially new, but there is sometimes a need to review the issues.

INDIVIDUAL STUDENTS THEMSELVES

Probably in most societies of the world, the period of youth—broadly between puberty and marriage—has been a time of sharp contrasts, especially for boys. It was often a time of self-indulgent wildness, a time of idleness and lack of responsibility, and yet at the same time it was a learning period when the youth were drawn into the adult world of work and war when necessary.

It was understood that youths should run wild from time to time, but even in their wildness they were expected to be ready to act, when society needed them, as warriors, gardeners, fishermen, dancers, hunters, house builders, and so on. Young unmarried people were commonly on the periphery of society, but everything they did was a kind of on-the-job preparation for adult life and status within the community.

The point here is that in the traditional context, youths had important tasks *in* the community that enabled them, when required, to contribute to, and participate in the community (Monsell-Davis 1986a). Many of these tasks have been removed and replaced by school as a role or status of its own, supposedly to lead to adult-worker status, but as we know, for many it appears to lead to nothing.

Carrier has written that some Manus parents think of their children as their garden, which they spend some years cultivating, and when the child gets a job, they can begin to harvest. The same author also said, 'Parents think of their children's education as the cost of producing a commodity that will generate a cash return' (Carrier 1984:47).

Some parents put enormous pressure on their children to succeed at school: I have often heard Papuan fathers say such things to their children as, 'I'm relying on you. Don't let me down. Why do you think I pay your school fees? You have to pay me back when you are working, and you will help to pay for your younger brothers and sisters. Look at your cousin Raho—I helped with his school fees his first year, now he's finished school and I've got *nothing* from him. Not even K1. When you're working, I'll retire and you'll look after me...', and so on.

It is variable, of course. The chairman of one community school in the Bereina area of Central Province complained to me that parents objected to a fee increase from K5 to K7. Yet the same parents easily and unthinkingly spend K20 on a carton of beer, and hundreds on gambling. The same parent who cannot find the school fees is often the one who puts the greatest pressure on his children to succeed at school.

This kind of pressure can create great anxiety in youngsters, and if they then fail to get the expected job, it can induce strong feelings of guilt and resentment, which in turn may lead to behavioural problems.

In addition, people today have much broader aspirations than in the past: lessons in school, on the radio, through advertising, on films and video, through migration, travellers' tales, letters from relatives, and so on, all combine to inform youngsters that there is a whole different world outside the village—a world of new experiences, new sights, new tastes, new consumer goods.

The Western Samoan government acknowledged in 1982 that

> the consumer goods to which the farmer aspires are not within reach
> without a quantum leap in income, something which [the village
> farmer] rarely sees as possible in agriculture...a major constraint is
> thus that village agriculture as practised now is not [seen as] economi
> cally competitive with the wage sector. (MacPherson and MacPherson
> 1987:318)

There are obvious exceptions, in that those with good coffee or cocoa holdings can raise large sums of money for consumer goods. Most people, however, especially the young, do not have access to these cash crops, and thus do not see agriculture as an avenue to consumer goods.

I do not want to dwell on this, but the point is that from the perspective of the young—especially those who do not go on to jobs—all this can appear to add up to nothing. We put them in school and the whole of their early lives we seem to say to them, 'do well in school and you'll get a good job and earn money to help yourself and your family: this is your way to contribute'. This is the goal we give them, with great promise and pressure—and then they leave school, and for the majority, what happens?

Nothing. We have given them hope and an aim, and then suddenly stripped everything away. They are no longer part of the community with something positive to contribute—and this is reflected by those parents who angrily reject those of their children who do not get jobs or win places in higher education.

For such youngsters the result can be the loss of any sense of purpose, and other frustrations that can lead to behavioural problems such as the high crime rates in Fiji and PNG, or suicide in Micronesia and Samoa—in both those places suicide in the fifteen to thirty age group, particularly for males, is horrifyingly high (see, for example, Hezel 1977; Oliver 1982; MacPherson and MacPherson 1987).

Young people need direction and goals. They need a strong clear point in their lives that provides direction and discipline. A strong anchor point such as this should ideally be in the family and the community and the church; otherwise they may seek it in the gang on the street.

This is the period in their lives that Michael Crossley has called the 'transition from school' (Crossley 1987:51), and Maev O'Collins characterized as

> the transition of young people to adult status in their societies, not only as possible future leaders, but also as members of their families, clans and communities. (O'Collins 1984:131)

This 'transition' that youth has to make is, in fact, a complex series of closely interrelated transitions: there is the transition from school to community and work; the social transition from childhood to adulthood; the sexual transition from the immaturity of childhood, to the active maturity of adulthood; the transition from a selfish awareness of the self, to an awareness of the needs of others; from having most significant decisions made for them, to making decisions themselves; from being occupied by others, to making choices and learning to occupy themselves; and so on.

It is a difficult time in their lives when they are neither children nor adults, hence the need for a strong anchor point and guidance, which, as I just remarked, should lie within the family and community. In this context, it seems opportune to remind ourselves that 'youth cannot be seen in isolation from the rest of society' (O'Collins 1984:131; compare Monsell-Davis 1986b; Preston 1987:35–36), and this leads us into the second of my two main headings.

The Community

When I was first teaching in PNG, in the mid-1960s, I was based in what were then called Junior Technical Schools in Mt. Hagen and Yule Island. In about 1967 these schools were succeeded by Vocational Centres. Both had similar aims: to provide training relevant to self-employment and use of skills in rural areas. Graduates, in other words, were expected to return to the village, with their new skills.

There were differences in curricula in that Junior Technical Schools included general subjects along with the technical skills, while Vocational Centres downgraded the general subjects and made a greater attempt to orient their skills training to local enterprises—fishing, cattle, coffee, or whatever was relevant to the local economy.

It turned out that most youngsters had no intention of returning from the Junior Technical Schools to the local economy, at least not before they had seen a bit of the world. Almost every one of my students at that time went to Moresby and obtained jobs or continued their education: a number transferred to Idubada (Port Moresby Technical College), some continued through to Sogeri Senior High School, and one eventually completed a degree in engineering at the University of Technology. Today, twenty years later, at least half *are* back in their villages, married with children, and using their Junior Technical skills in the context of their village lives.

In 1977 a survey of Vocational Centres suggested that

> Centres tended to provide rural youth with a means to escape from the village: ex-trainees migrated to the town in search of employment, while even those who did return to the villages were seldom productively employed, and thus they did not utilise the training they received. (Reeves, cited by Crossley and Vulliamy, 1986:5)

Why were they not 'productively employed'? I suggest that it is in part because in the village context, youth are not in general expected to be 'productively employed' except on occasions as demanded by parents, leaders, and the seasonal cycle: house building, garden clearing, ceremonial occasions, fishing, and the like. A survey of Vocational trainees in the village after their marriage, would probably find a greater degree of productive activity and use of the skills they had learned at Vocational Centres.

There is a wide perception, and some evidence, that youths who return to the village immediately after schooling do not use their new skills in the village environment. At least, they do not use them in the ways hoped for by those who plan their training, although as will be evident later in this paper, it is plain that some skills *are* being utilised in the village.

If, as has been suggested for Manus (Weeks 1988), 70 percent to 80 percent of those who leave grade 10, under a policy of High School Education for all, are destined to return home; then there are serious implications for the home community. What do we expect these young people to do when they return home? Quietly slot back into the niche they emerged from ten years earlier? Act as change agents? Establish entrepreneurial ventures? Their ability to do any of these things depends in part on the individual, but also in great measure on parental and community expectations and attitudes. As Sheldon Weeks has noted, in a different context, about school,

> Curriculum initiatives can *contribute* to the process of attitude formation, but attitudes are largely formed by the community. (Weeks 1985:50)

We can summarise some aspects of village life and attitudes that are relevant to this discussion under three headings:

1. Egalitarianism/Participation/Sorcery Fears
2. The Status of Youth
3. New Skills and the Village Environment

Egalitarianism/Participation/Sorcery Fears

One perspective often forgotten by planners is that the individual who lives in the village is primarily a villager, and therefore required to participate in all the social, political, economic, and religious activities of the village: he or she is a member of the community, with all the obligations that are implicit in such membership. There are a number of implications we can take from this concerning participation in village affairs and the egalitarian ideology of Melanesian communities.

As I have noted elsewhere, the men or women who live in the village must play their full part in the community, or find themselves in some kind of difficulty. I know of an incident some thirty years ago where a man began spending most of his time fishing and selling his catch to the local freezer. A hardworking fisherman was able to make about $50 per week, which was good money in those days.

After a while, however, he began to find his nets slashed. It seems he quickly understood that his fellows were reminding him that, as a villager, he was obligated to attend meetings concerning village affairs, to assist in communal gardening activities, and to participate in other matters. His response was to abandon his fishing venture and return to full participation in village affairs (Monsell-Davis 1982, 1985; Kent Wilson 1968:64).

In this case, the individual had effectively withdrawn from village affairs in order to concentrate on making money. His fellows did not, apparently, practice sorcery against him, but did find an alternative means of forcing him back into community participation. We could cite many similar examples, such as the case of a man living for a long period in his garden house, rather than in the village, and finding one day that his garden house had been burned down. This was a way of forcing him to physically return to the village.

For a different kind of example, we can refer to one of my earlier tales: that of the man who had been very active in promoting the new village school, and whose sickness was diagnosed as the result of jealousy over his activities.

I could cite numerous similar examples of people who have withdrawn from leading roles in such communities because of fears of sorcery, or who have abandoned entrepreneurial ventures for the same reason, or who have never even attempted such initiatives because of these fears, which relate to the broad egalitarian ideology of Melanesian communities.

Sociologically we can argue that there is no true egalitarianism—women are not equal to men; uninitiated youths are not equal to adult men; hereditary leaders have better chances than those of commoner status, and so on. Nevertheless, there remains a broad ideology of egalitarianism at village level: individuals, or at least households, must be seen as having roughly equal access to resources of various kinds. Anyone perceived as having an unfair advantage was knocked down with sorcery—or feared being knocked down. Even the traditional big man or chief made sure that the fruits of his entrepreneurial skills were distributed among his followers.

The fact that people fear sorcery, or believe their ill fortune is caused by sorcery, does not prove the existence of sorcery in any scientific sense. But that is not the point. The point is the constraint that such beliefs imply for initiative at village level.

Carrier and Vulliamy discussed this at length in their article 'Sorcery and SSCEP',[3] and cited Chowning who commented that in most of Melanesia successful people 'are greatly inhibited by the fear of sorcery performed by those jealous of their achievements' (Chowning, cited by Carrier and Vulliamy 1985:22).

Weeks and Tawaiyole have responded to this by arguing that 'if the project is for a larger unit (clan business or youth or women's club) the fear of sorcery is largely eliminated' (1987:2). Unfortunately, my experience is that individuals are subject to the same pressures and fears even in these larger units. We have already observed the man who resigned from the school committee. In another example, a man who had almost completed a University degree withdrew from active participation in the successful revival of a village cooperative society, because he feared sorcery against his children. When I pointed out to him that his work for the cooperative society was benefiting the whole village, but that he himself was gaining nothing from it, he responded, 'Yes, I know, Mike, but when something is successful like this, those who are not directly involved themselves become jealous'.

Perhaps the point here relates to the egalitarian access to resources mentioned earlier: the ability to influence others can be seen as a resource, and someone who is successfully involved in a large project may be perceived as acquiring a greater share of influence than his fellow villagers.

There are events in the villages that might seem surprising to those who do not live there: in one village I am familiar with, the Health Department installed a solar-powered pump and a tank in the village. This saved the women a daily walk of over one kilometre carrying water. Yet the pipes were cut, and the women had to start walking

---

[3] SSCEP: Secondary Schools Community Extension Project. This was a project that aimed to incorporate practical, community-oriented skills into secondary schools while retaining the academic integrity of the core curriculum. In this way, secondary education was to acquire a new relevance to both the academic achiever and to those who returned to their villages (Crossley and Vulliamy, 1986).

again. The water was for everyone, equally, so who cut the pipes, and why? The culprit was never identified, but various villagers suggested that people at the furthest end of the village may have felt they were not getting an equal share, firstly because they had to walk a little further to carry water, and second because they were not always aware of when the lock was open on the tap, and sometimes came late. They therefore cut the pipes so that no one could get water.

These kinds of events are baffling and disheartening to planners and idealists, and if they occur too often can act wholly negatively on development plans.

Weeks and Tawaiyole have argued, correctly I think, that too much emphasis is placed on constraints in the village (1985). I believe it is also true, however, that we need to be aware of such constraints before we can effectively take account of them in planning. In the case of water supply, for example, with deeply buried pipes, outlets at several strategic points in the community and, preferably, no locks—as Weeks has pointed out in discussion.

Status of Youth

Another constraint that has long been recognized is the subordinate status of youth in the village environment. We do not need to belabour this point except to remind ourselves that it is a part of the issue: Young people are commonly not considered to be fully adult, and therefore fully responsible, until they are married and have children. This is a part of the question of transition from one status to another, and the conflicting expectations the community has concerning those undergoing the transition.

New Skills and the Village Environment

More serious is the question of the way in which newly acquired skills can be used in the village. The response to this may in part answer the earlier question of why Vocational graduates are not fully utilising their new skills. Carrier (1984) gives examples from Ponam of men with skills at repairing metal dishes and radio-cassette players. Both found there was considerable demand for their skills, but both found that the payment for their services was most likely to be fish, or garden food, or betel-nut, rather than cash. But the actual task of repairing dishes or radio cassettes required cash for spare parts, solder, batteries, kerosene for the lamp, and so on, with the result that the repairer was using his own money to repair other people's property. The consequence was that the two tradesmen found they could not continue, and withdrew their skills from the community. Dishes and radios are no longer repaired.

This does not mean that modern skills cannot be transferred to the village: Weeks and Tawaiyole point out that Carrier also shows how bread-baking skills have been successfully applied in the village (Carrier 1984:83–84; Weeks and Tawaiyole 1987:3). The important facts about baking skills, however, are first that it is understood in the community that baked goods are for sale only, therefore bakers have the continuing income to purchase the raw materials, unlike the dish-repairer. Secondly, the knowledge of baking is common in the community, thus the fruit of the knowledge, that is, a cash income, is available to a wide sector of the community. This is significant in the light of our earlier discussion of the broad egalitarian ideology of Melanesian communities: the bakers could not be perceived as possessing an unfair access to a resource (cash) because the potential is widely distributed, unlike the dish-repairer and radio-repairer, who were the only people with such skills.

DISCUSSION
Where does all this lead us? I began this discussion with consideration of the young people themselves and reference to the aspirations that youngsters have, and a reminder that the transition from youth to adult is a complex process. It can be a time of great confusion as a result of the conflicting demands being made on them. It is the age when they are bursting with energy and hope, but because of lack of experience they are most easily led off in false directions, to follow false heroes, and to go the way the crowd goes; it is the age when they are most easily disheartened when things go wrong; most easily crushed by the wrong kind of authority (Monsell-Davis 1986a).

It is the time when they need firm, clear guidelines for behaviour, and an anchor-point which should lie in the family and community.

Whether or not we educate everybody to grade 10, we have to consider what happens to young people back in the village. It is unrealistic to expect everyone to go home and start entrepreneurial ventures (how many people are ready at that age?). Even if we train young people with specific village-oriented skills, there are conflicting expectations over the role of youth, sorcery fears, and the lack of cash payment.

These are constraints, not impenetrable blockages. As Weeks and Tawaiyole pointed out, there may be some factors that act positively to reintegrate youngsters to the village, and to facilitate their use of their skills (1987).

While my own studies in the Bereina area of Central Province have highlighted the difficulties for people in initiating projects, it is also clear that some factors have in fact facilitated the integration of unemployed youth into the village: these factors include the opening of a road linking the village to town; changes in customary practices concerning such things as funeral rites, and the expected behaviour of youth; and villager perceptions that Moresby is a difficult place to live in. I have discussed these positive factors elsewhere (Monsell-Davis 1986b).

While young people can, then, go back to the village and feel at home there, they may have difficulty in implementing their new skills, except in relatively small ways. And, it is evident from the writing of Weeks, Yatu (1987), and others, that new skills *are* being utilized in the village. As Yatu says for the Bereina area, 'School leavers are applying SSCEP skills gained to modify existing projects, already established by their parents or wantoks...there is a mixture of SSCEP and traditional skills involved in project management' (1987:25). This, we could argue, is precisely what should be happening, and a vindication of SSCEP planners.

The problem, however, is that this is probably not enough. Despite the impediments we have discussed, the village, the parents, and the school leavers expect more, and unless they can discover legitimate ways to get more, we may see an increase in social problems.

It should not be assumed from this discussion that village society is conservative and against change. On the contrary, it is plain from the evidence of oral traditions, of archaeology, and of anthropology that Melanesian societies have always been willing to adapt and experiment with new ideas. There has been constant innovation. Most change, however, has taken place within the context of certain values such as egalitarianism and equal access to resources.

The history of colonial and postcolonial innovations in this country, however, has commonly been one of inflated expectations at village level—from Cooperative societies to SSCEP. When delivery has apparently failed, there has been disillusion, resentment, and withdrawal of support.

CONCLUSION

I believe that the issue at bottom is that of the kind of society we are trying to achieve. Presumably we are agreed that villagers should have equal access to good health, nutrition, literacy, and opportunities for a cash income. For this to take place fully raises the question of such things as rural electrification, rural telephones, clean water, wharves, roads, and other infrastructure facilities.

Successive governments since independence have placed varying emphasis on rural development. Over the years huge sums of money have been spent by national and provincial governments, and by village communities and individuals, on projects and capital goods that have collapsed and the money been lost—either through mismanagement or other factors.

I've briefly outlined in this discussion some of my experiences concerning the problems of initiative at village level—problems of management, jealousy and sorcery, vandalism, etc. A government-initiated seminar in Manus in July 1988 was plainly concerned, indirectly, with the same issue, that is, the village, because even though the subject was high school education for all, underneath the discussion lay evident concern about what would happen to those grade 10 leavers who did not continue to further training or jobs.

There can be little disagreement with the principle of high school education for all. We have heard the results of research that shows that the better educated the members of a community become, the more productive the society (Weeks 1988). However, if one does not provide the opportunities and infrastructure at the same time as the education, then we can also expect an increase in dissatisfaction and the resultant social problems.

In short, it is not simply a question of expanding opportunities for children to continue in high school up to grade 10. Rather, any changes at school need to be matched by full discussion at village level, educating leaders and parents as to the significance of educational changes.

Various proposals have been made for some kinds of learning and resource centres in villages, providing general information and facilities for continuing literacy (Sukwianomb 1988). I think this is an important proposal for encouraging new initiatives in the village environment. As a further aspect of this, we may think in terms of a programme of rural electrification, roads improvement, provision of solar telephones, banking agencies, and so on.

It is vitally important that any changes in the educational system are matched by educational and other initiatives at village level, including the provision of infrastructure. Without such a dual approach neither education nor rural development will have much meaning for most young people.

AFTERWARD

Reviewing this chapter in December 1996 for the purposes of this volume, I believe the material is as relevant now as it was eight years ago when I wrote the first version. It is possible to argue that conditions have deteriorated in many rural areas: feeder roads are inadequately maintained; schools, health posts, and other facilities are opened, closed, and reopened, depending on the availability of personnel, medicines, other supplies—and on the activities of *raskols,* who from time to time, harass and intimidate staff and burgle the premises; trade stores are closed and banking facilities withdrawn (O'Collins 1987; King *et al.* 1989). I have been disheartened at the very real fears of highway robbery expressed by people needing to travel on the Hiritano and Magi highways out of Port Moresby. On my last trip on the Hiritano highway in January 1996 the driver of my vehicle checked that his bush knife was close at hand, and insisted we travel in convoy with two other trucks, one of which carried a shotgun. A number of Papua New Guinean leaders, including Sir Julius Chan and Dr. Wari Iamo, have acknowledged the deteriorating conditions in rural areas (see for example, discussion on the 1993 Budget: EMTV 10 November 1993; *Post-Courier* 11 November 1993, p. 15).

Social changes are piling upon social changes at breathtaking speed and society's institutions are hard pressed to keep up. The legitimacy of various forms of leadership is increasingly under challenge—and this applies to quasi-traditional leadership (Monsell-Davis 1995) to church leadership and to parliamentary leadership about which villagers are becoming increasingly cynical.

It is important not to be wholly negative: people in the villages are getting on with their lives, planting, fishing, and harvesting according to the seasons. They are deeply concerned about events in the wider society, but they are still holding their ceremonies and hosting festivities. When I was in a Papuan village in the Bereina area for a few days in January 1996 we had a thoroughly enjoyable two days of canoe racing with neighbouring villages. But the concerns were there, in people's conversations, and for the first time in a thirty-year connection with that village, I felt that the youth lacked direction. And as new scourges such as HIV infection invade the rural areas, we are likely to see further destabilisation (Monsell-Davis 1995; United Nations 1996).

All of these factors make it imperative that we educate our youth to occupy themselves in constructive and imaginative ways. Throughout the Pacific there are more and more frequent calls to reinvent the school curriculum to cater for the growing problems of unemployment, violent crime, and urban homelessness (see, for example, the *Saturday Independent* 24 June 1995, p. E1; Robert 1996).

Michael Crossley's paper in this volume is an interesting and instructive discussion of the issues involved in the almost impossible task of building an education curriculum that reflects all the various needs and interest groups in society. He shows how, in both the colonial and independent state, approaches to formal education in Papua New Guinea have been influenced by two very broad, conflicting perspectives: one emphasising the importance of community and village life, the other stressing the need to educate people to cater for the cash economy, wage labour, and the needs of commercial organisations.

Neither perspective has been able to cater for the need both to reproduce viable rural communities *and* to create a worldly elite capable of dealing with the complex commercial and political realities of the world of the 1990s and beyond. I suggest that older, community-oriented curriculum initiatives reflected an idealized version of village 'communalism' that did not take account of some of the realities of life in the village: the jealousies, rivalries, enforced egalitarianism, and the expected roles of youth in a changing society.

This perhaps did not matter much until after 1945, when the Second World War had 'flushed [villagers] out of their ethnic backwater' (White 1967:137), and given them wholly new perspectives on colonial society. After this, community-oriented education did not seem to lead anywhere, either in the context of new aspirations, or in the context of an 'improved' village life. Although this chapter does not directly address curriculum issues, plainly its arguments lean towards a community perspective. I hope it does so in ways that will enable planners to take account of the realities of village life rather than the romance.

Plainly we need an education system that caters to the needs of both the international cash economy and the 'community' of the village—but it is a community that has already been incorporated into the cash economy. Politicians and policy makers need a community orientation in their thinking. Without it, as I suggest above, neither education nor rural development will have much meaning for most of our young people.

REFERENCES

Barber, K., 1993. *The Informal Sector and Household Reproduction in Papua New Guinea.* Discussion Paper No. 71. Port Moresby: National Research Unit.

Carrier, J. G., 1984. *Education & Society in a Manus Village.* ERU Report No. 47. Port Moresby: University of Papua New Guinea.

Crossley, M., and Vulliamy, G., 1986. *The Policy of SSCEP: Context & Development.* ERU Report No. 54. Port Moresby: University of Papua New Guinea.

Crossley, M., 1987. 'The transition from school: a case for coordinated support', in M. Crossley, J. Sukwianomb, and S. Weeks, eds., *Pacific Perspectives in Non-Formal Education.* Suva: Institute of Pacific Studies, USP, and Port Moresby: University of Papua New Guinea Press, pp. 51–59.

Hezel, F., 1977. 'Suicide epidemic among Micronesian youth'. *South Pacific Bulletin,* second quarter 1977. Noumea: South Pacific Commission.

King, D., Monsell-Davis, M., Miskaram, N., and Tapari, B., 1989. *Re-evaluation Study: Hiritano Highway Project in Papua New Guinea.* Impact Assessment and Data Collection. A Report prepared for the Asian Development Bank. Port Moresby: Departments of Geography and Extension Studies, UPNG.

MacPherson, C., and MacPherson, L., 1987. 'Towards an explanation of recent trends in suicide in Western Samoa', *Man,* 22(2):305–330.

Monsell-Davis, M., 1982. 'Nabuapaka: social change in a Roro community', unpublished doctoral dissertation, Macquarie University.

———, 1985. 'The village entrepreneur: businessman or villager?' Mimeo, University of Papua New Guinea.

———, 1986a. '"It's a man's game": identity, social role, social change and delinquency in Suva', in C. Griffin and M. Monsell-Davis, eds., *Fijians in Town.* Suva: Institute of Pacific Studies, USP, pp. 132–165.

———, 1986b. 'At home in the village: youth and community in Nabuapaka', in M. O'Collins, ed., *Youth and Society: Perspectives from Papua New Guinea.* Political and Social Change Monograph No. 5. Canberra: Australian National University.

———, 1995. 'Cultural factors and their influence on the transmission of HIV infection in the Pacific'. Working paper for UNDP, Suva, Fiji.

O'Collins, M., 1984. *Youth in Papua New Guinea.* Political and Social Change Monograph No. 3. Canberra: Australian National University.

———, ed., 1987. *Rapid Rural Appraisal: Case Studies of Small Farming Systems.* Port Moresby: Department of Anthropology and Sociology, UPNG.

Oliver, D., 1982. 'Coming to grips with the problem of youth suicide in Western Samoa', *Pacific Islands Monthly,* 54(11):15–17.

Preston, R., 1987. 'Youth programmes and their development: PNG and the South Pacific', in M. Crossley, J. Sukwianomb, and S. Weeks, eds., *Pacific Perspectives in Non-Formal Education.* Suva and Port Moresby. Suva: Institute of Pacific Studies, USP, and Port Moresby: University of Papua New Guinea Press, pp. 27–40.

Robert, K. G., 1996. *A Response to Crime in Papua New Guinea.* M.A. Thesis. Pacific Theological College, Suva, Fiji.

Sukwianomb, J., 1988. 'Alternatives to formal high school education'. Paper presented to seminar 'High School Education for all in Manus,' 11–13 July 1988, sponsored by the Manus Provincial Government and the Hanns Seidel Foundation.

United Nations, 1996. *Time to Act: The Pacific Response to HIV and AIDS.* Suva: United Nations.

Vulliamy, G., and Carrier, J., 1985. 'Sorcery and SSCEP: the cultural context of an educational innovation', *British Journal of Sociology of Education,* 6:1.

Weeks, S. G., ed., 1985. *Papua New Guinea National Inventory of Educational Innovations,* ERU Report No. 52. Port Moresby: University of Papua New Guinea.

Weeks, S. G., and Tawaiyole, P., 1987. 'Factors facilitating and blocking the involvement of grade 10 leavers in their villages', *Papua New Guinea Education Gazette,* 21(5/6):7-13.

Weeks, S. G., 1988. 'Education: Manus in the Papua New Guinea context'. Paper presented to seminar 'High School Education for all in Manus,' 11-13 July 1988, sponsored by the Manus Provincial Government and the Hanns Seidel Foundation.

White, O., 1967. *Parliament of a Thousand Tribes.* Melbourne: Heinemann.

Wilson, R. K., and Garnaut, R., 1968. *A Survey of Village Industries in Papua New Guinea.* New Guinea Research Bulletin No. 25. Canberra: Australian National University.

Yatu, J. K., 1987. 'Tracer study of grade 10 leavers of Bereina district, Mainohana High School'. Draft report, ERU, University of Papua New Guinea.

Acknowledgments

I would like to thank Michael Crossley, Sheldon Weeks, Barbara Hau'ofa, and anonymous reviewers for their very helpful comments on earlier drafts of this paper.

Sinclair Dinnen

LAW, ORDER, AND STATE

*L*AW AND ORDER ISSUES feature prominently in public debate in Papua New Guinea. Concerns centre around criminal violence and the limited effectiveness of state controls. High levels of interpersonal violence are apparent in the activities of criminal gangs, known locally as rascals, the tribal fighting occurring in parts of the Highlands as well as in everyday gender relations throughout the country. The continuing escalation of disorder in many areas is indicative of the limitations of state authority in PNG, as is most dramatically demonstrated in the bloody and unresolved secessionist conflict on Bougainville (May and Spriggs 1990; Spriggs and Denoon 1992). Burgeoning corruption among elements of the political and administrative elite provides another significant strand to current debate.

Addressing a National Crime Summit in Port Moresby in 1991, then–Prime Minister Rabbie Namaliu stated that law and order problems were the greatest threat facing PNG (*The Australian*, 12 February 1991). Almost five years later, the incumbent, Prime Minister Sir Julius Chan, declared 1996 to be 'the year of law enforcement', claiming that his government would lead Papua New Guinea out of its 'crime nightmare', reduce fear and violence, and invigorate public and investor confidence in the country (*Post-Courier*, 16 January 1996). Despite these bold pronouncements, 1996 ended with the imposition of a nationwide curfew following a series of violent and highly publicised crimes.

Popular concerns with personal security manifest themselves in the elaborate security precautions adopted by individuals, households, and businesses in daily life. National planners, on the other hand, have been preoccupied with the serious economic repercussions of law and order problems, notably their effects on investment confidence as well as their impact on PNG's fledgling tourist industry. In 1993 the Asian Development Bank bluntly warned that:

> Failure to secure an improvement in peace and order will have a major adverse impact on the performance of the economy over the next few years. (*The Saturday Independent*, 9 September, 1995)

This chapter outlines the principal law and order concerns in Papua New Guinea since independence in 1975 and the policies these have engendered. The first section looks at state responses, while the second examines specific areas of concern.

STATE RESPONSES

The macro setting for current concerns lies in the profound changes wrought by decolonisation, nation-building, and integration into the international economy over the past three decades. While numerous reports and reviews have been written on different aspects of the law and order situation, relatively few recommendations have been implemented. Even where legislative and institutional reforms have taken place, neither the level of concern nor lawlessness has noticeably decreased. Beyond the reassuring rhetoric of political leaders, most observers agree that lawlessness continues to increase, along with a corresponding diminution in the capacity of the PNG state to provide effective deterrence or control.

The two most comprehensive reports on law and order since independence have been the Morgan Report (Department of Provincial Affairs, 1983) and the Clifford Report (Clifford *et al.* 1984). There have also been a number of inquiries into particular kinds of crime. The Law Reform Commission, for example, has published a series of studies of domestic violence (LRC 1985a, 1985b, 1986a, 1986b, 1992). A study of the evolution of juvenile gangs in Port Moresby was produced in 1988 (Harris 1988). Criminal justice institutions have been the subject of separate investigations (Dinnen 1993a). Law and order issues have also generated a growing volume of academic articles as well as a small number of specialist books including *Crime in Papua New Guinea* (Biles 1976), *Law and Order in the New Guinea Highlands* (Gordon and Meggitt 1985), and *Law and Order in a Changing Society* (Morauta 1986). General books on PNG have also devoted increasing coverage to law and order issues (Dorney 1990:286–318; Turner 1990:162–180).

The instrumentalities of state charged with controlling crime—the police, courts, and prisons—have been progressively overwhelmed during the postindependence period through a combination of escalating demands and diminishing resources. In 1984 the Clifford Report warned that the PNG criminal justice system was 'in serious danger of losing the battle to manage and process, let alone constrain, the existing rates of crime' (Clifford *et al.* 1984:136). This situation has, if anything, worsened in the intervening period. A telling sign of the limited effectiveness of criminal justice is the massive growth in private policing that has taken place in recent years. Private security organisations now operate throughout the country. These range from large and sophisticated operations affiliated with international companies to small firms providing security services for households, commercial enterprises, and government departments. Concerns are often raised about the unregulated character of this major growth industry and the potential for human rights abuses on the part of its more cavalier members. Such concerns were accentuated by the recent murder of four youths at Dogura beach outside Port Moresby, allegedly by security employees carrying out a 'payback' on behalf of their employer (*Post-Courier*, 31 November 1996). For the majority of Papua New Guineans who cannot afford these services, security is provided by kin and *wantoks*[1], utilising a variety of self-help methods—some of which may themselves involve violence.

The inadequacies of state controls also provide the basis for the substantial amount of Australian aid directed at PNG's law and order sector. The single largest project is the Police Development Project which started in 1987 and is now approaching the end of its second five-year phase. Assistance is aimed at improving the administrative, managerial, operational, and technical capacities of the PNG police. A Correctional Services Project is also under way and seeks to strengthen the management and training capacity of the Corrective Institutions Service (CIS), improve prisoners' rehabilitation, and upgrade prison infrastructure.

The limited success of criminal justice in general, and policing in particular, has led to the supplementing of 'normal' criminal justice

---

[1] The term *wantok* in Melanesian Pidgin literally means someone who speaks the same language (i.e., one talk). In popular usage it refers to the relations of obligation binding relatives, members of the same clan or tribe, and people in looser forms of association.

processes with extraordinary measures such as curfews[2] and special policing operations. These have sought to restore order in designated areas through a combination of restrictions on movement, police raids, and orchestrated displays of militaristic strength. These public displays belie the actual capacity of PNG's security forces to control crime or disorder on any scale. In practice, police personnel are often joined by defence force soldiers and CIS employees. Such operations have attracted criticism from human rights and nongovernment organisations (NGOs) who complain about the 'militarisation of society' (*Post-Courier*, 7 August 1992). These critics claim that state responses amount to a 'normalisation of extreme emergency measures in the form of the Curfew Act'; the 'increasing use of military and CIS personnel in police duties'; and the 'increasing use of police mobile or riot squads in ordinary crime situations'.

While reactive responses of this kind usually have an immediate—albeit temporary—impact on lawlessness in the area affected, they also tend to have a number of distinctly counterproductive outcomes. Special policing operations conducted on their own, or under the auspices of a curfew, entail raids on villages or settlements in search of suspects or stolen goods. Raids are often followed by allegations of serious human rights abuses, including fatalities, rapes, assaults, destruction of property and livestock, and theft. The accountability of police for fatalities inflicted under these circumstances is diminished by the irregular holding of coronal inquiries, as well as the long delays involved (*Post-Courier*, 5 April 1995). Criticisms have also been levelled at the slow workings and closed character of the internal police complaints system (UNDP/ILO 1993). In 1990 police statistics indicated that investigations had been completed in only 13 percent of the total complaints made in that year (RPNGC 1990:41). An increasingly popular course of action is for citizens aggrieved as a result of such actions to initiate civil actions in the courts for substantial damages against the state. In August 1996, for example, the National Court reportedly awarded K103,800 to Wiliri and Awari people in Pangia, in the Southern Highlands, for personal injuries and damages inflicted during several police raids in early 1990 (*Post-Courier*, 14 August 1996).

---

[2] Prior to the Curfew Act 1987, curfews could only be imposed during a formally declared state of emergency. A state of emergency—which provides security forces with additional powers—was declared in the National Capital District in 1985 in response to an outbreak of violent crime in Port Moresby (Dinnen 1986).

Apart from the monetary cost to the state of large-scale militarised operations, including any damages awarded in subsequent civil actions, retributive policing contributes to high levels of mutual suspicion between police and local communities in many parts of PNG. This, in turn, undermines the trust and cooperation necessary for effective investigative police work. These hostile encounters tend to develop their own destructive momentum in practice, whereby lack of local cooperation is used to legitimate the use of aggressive police tactics, which leads to further local antagonism and so on.

Reactive policing can also inadvertently strengthen criminal organisation and commitment. Curfews and special policing operations, for example, often lead to the displacement of hardened criminals from one place to another, thereby contributing to the dispersal of criminal networks. Harris has also observed how Port Moresby gangs became more professional as a result of the restrictions imposed under the 1985 state of emergency (1988:34). Violent encounters with police have become an integral part of the rituals of rascal induction in the urban centres. Imprisonment, too, has been incorporated into the constitution of rascal identity, providing another means for achieving high criminal status.

Legislative responses to law and order problems have had mixed results. Judicial interpretation of the rights provisions in PNG's liberal Constitution has effectively put a brake on some of the more draconian statutes and restrictive provisions passed by Parliament. This was the case, for example, with the minimum penalties legislation (Dinnen 1992) and parts of the Inter-Group Fighting Act[3] and Internal Security Act (Dinnen 1993c). Other legal enactments, such as the controversial reintroduction of capital punishment for wilful murder in 1991, have yet to be given full effect.

CURRENT CONCERNS IN LAW AND ORDER DEBATE

According to Police Commissioner Bob Nenta, the major categories of crime in PNG today are those committed by rascal gangs, violence against women, tribal fighting, corruption, and white collar crime (Nenta 1996).

---

[3] Section 11(3) of the Inter-Group Fighting Act, for example, which reversed the burden of proof in respect of those suspected of participating in tribal fighting, was struck down as unconstitutional by the Supreme Court in *Constitutional Reference No. 3 of 1978; re Inter-Group Fighting Act 1977* (1978) PNGLR 421.

Gang Crime

The rascal gang remains the most potent symbol of PNG's law and order problems. From its relatively benign origins as a mechanism for enhancing self-esteem among young male migrants in Port Moresby in the 1960s (Harris 1988:4–10), rascalism has evolved into the most threatening face of contemporary lawlessness and has gradually spread to other towns as well as to many rural areas. Groups of predominantly young males engage in criminal activities ranging from shoplifting, bag-snatching, breaking and entering, to sophisticated armed robberies, rapes, and homicides. The organisation and *modus operandi* of these groups varies enormously between different parts of the country. In rural areas, rascal groups are likely to be ethnically homogenous, speaking the same local language, and often coming from the same village. The most common form of criminal activity is likely to be banditry, involving the holdup of vehicles travelling along the highways (*Post-Courier*, 26 July 1995). The incidence of offences will be episodic and affected by factors such as the need for cash (e.g. to pay school fees), the availability of suitable victims (e.g. coffee buyers), the presence of experienced criminals in the locality (e.g. prison escapees), the activities of law enforcement agencies, and so on.

The most lucrative opportunities for acquisitive crimes are in the towns and other areas of high development, such as around the vicinity of the large-scale mining operations scattered around the Highlands and Islands regions (*Business Review Weekly*, 14 August 1995). Well-organised gangs target payrolls, banks, business premises, and cash-in-transit. Urban groups are likely to be ethnically heterogeneous, reflecting the plural composition of the town population. Criminal participation will usually be more regular and group organisation correspondingly more sophisticated. The last available annual police report, published in 1990, confirms the concentration of criminal opportunities in urban areas. A total of 664 armed robberies occurred in the National Capital District (NCD) in 1990—that is, 42.4 percent of the national total of 1,566 reported robberies (RPNGC 1990:8). The same report stated that 27 percent of all reported breaking, entering, and stealing offences for that year were recorded in the NCD.

The use of modern firearms has greatly added to the menace of rascalism. Weapons include high-powered automatic rifles as well as assorted homemade guns. There have even been recent reports of rascal groups armed with grenades (*Post-Courier*, 22 August 1996). While generally carried to intimidate victims, weapons will be used in the case of resistance by victims or pursuit by police. The brazenness of criminal operations has become increasingly pronounced, with robberies being carried out in busy shopping areas in the middle of the day. Shoot-outs between criminals and police are regularly reported (*National*, 5 November 1996). The growing threat of criminal violence has, in turn, encouraged noncriminals to acquire, and occasionally use, firearms for self-defence. In 1995, for example, a foreign businessman, who was among a group of diners at a Port Moresby restaurant, reportedly shot dead four criminals involved in an attempted armed robbery (*The Bulletin*, 21 November 1995). During curfew operations between November 1996 and January 1997, the police allegedly recovered more than 45 factory-made pistols, shotguns, military and sporting automatic assault weapons and ammunition, as well as military-style fragmentation grenades (*National*, 22 January 1997).

There has been much speculation in recent years about the sources of the increasing number of illegal weapons in circulation in Papua New Guinea. A recurring claim is that consignments of marijuana, grown mainly in the Highlands, are being exported to Australia via the Torres Strait in return for firearms and ammunition. While conclusive evidence is hard to find, a joint operation between Australian and Papua New Guinea police in 1994 netted drugs worth an estimated street value of K3 million, along with eleven suspects (10 Australians and 1 Papua New Guinean). According to a confidential national intelligence brief published by the *Post-Courier* newspaper, the drugs-for-guns trade has become big business and fuels PNG's law and order problems (*Post-Courier*, 9–11 August 1996). A number of the weapons being used by criminals originate with the security forces themselves. In addition to weapons stolen by outsiders, certain security personnel appear prepared to sell or hire weapons in order to supplement modest wages. In November 1996, Prime Minister Sir Julius Chan ordered an urgent stocktake of defence force weapons amid concerns that such weapons were being used in serious crimes (*Weekend Australian*, 9–10 November 1996).

Violence Against Women

Violence against women, including domestic violence and gang rape, is a major area of concern in Papua New Guinea. The Law Reform Commission has documented the regularity of violence against women within marital and *de facto* relationships in urban and rural areas, as well as among both prosperous and relatively poor households (LRC *ibid.*). As with many of their counterparts elsewhere, law enforcement agencies in PNG have been reluctant to intervene in what is viewed as 'private' or 'domestic' matters. Serious sexual assaults and incidents of harassment are regularly reported throughout the country. Women's groups, the churches, and other NGOs have been at the forefront in publicising the growing level of violence against women (Zimmer 1990).

Available criminal justice data on this form of crime is generally of poor quality and has to be interpreted with care. Sexual offences are likely to be among the most underreported of all criminal offences in Papua New Guinea. Factors such as shame, fear of the perpetrators, apprehension about police questioning, and a scepticism about the likely effectiveness of police investigations contribute to this under-reporting. Rapes in PNG often involve multiple assailants—so-called 'pack rapes'. A premeditated rape may occur as 'payback' for a perceived slight on the part of the victim or those associated with her. Serious sexual assaults also appear to take place, as crimes of opportunity, during the commission of other offences, such as breaking and entering or armed holdups. One of the most disturbing features about these incidents is evidence of their increasingly sadistic and deliberately humiliating character. It is the degree of violence involved in assaults upon women today, as much as their frequency, that is a cause for such concern. Where violence occurs between women it is usually connected to marital matters. It is not uncommon for women to engage in violence as a result of adultery allegations. Polygamy, still practiced in many parts of PNG, provides another source of conflict and violence between women. In recent years there appears to have been a discernible increase in the number of women charged with murdering a co-wife within polygamous relationships.

Despite the existence of Constitutional rights and the prescriptions of the criminal law, many Papua New Guinean women and girls continue to experience high levels of personal insecurity on a daily basis. This insecurity translates into intolerable restrictions on their freedom of movement and expression in everyday life. Underresourced law enforcement agencies have had little success in reducing the level of violence against women. Police action in urban areas often consists of warning women that they should not visit certain parts of town, be out after dark, or wear 'provocative' clothing. Police personnel have themselves been subject to periodic allegations of having committed serious sexual assaults. Reported incidents have involved female suspects in police custody (*Post-Courier*, 16 May 1994), as well as women assaulted during police raids (*National*, 17 October 1994). A 1994 survey has also confirmed the extent to which domestic violence is pervasive within police families (*National*, 15–19 September 1994), as it is in the wider community.

The factors underlying current patterns of violence against women in PNG are complex. Changing household relations, high levels of societal tolerance of gender violence, alcohol abuse, the breakdown of traditional restraints, and the persistence of male dominance in all fields, all play a significant role. Many of the mechanisms designed to settle disputes at local levels reinforce gender inequalities in practice. Village courts, for example, often punish women accused of adultery more severely than their male counterparts. Institutions of polygamy and brideprice accentuate a view of women as the property of men. Human rights groups recently campaigned over the case of a young woman in the Western Highlands who had reportedly been offered as part of a compensation payment arising from the death of a man in a shoot-out with police. Relatives of the deceased were demanding payment of two young women, pigs, and K20,000 cash. The young woman in question was allegedly offered in settlement—against her will—along with twenty-four pigs (*Asia Pacific Network*, 21 May 1996).

Issues of gender and violence, then, are critical concerns in Papua New Guinea today. The quality of life for half the population, as well as their potential contribution to national development, remains seriously devalued as a result of male violence. Contrary to the impressions given in media reports, violence against women is by no means the preserve of rascal gangs, and is dispersed throughout all levels of PNG society.

Tribal Fighting

Although common to many Papua New Guinean societies prior to colonial intrusion, the incidence of so-called tribal fighting today is largely confined to parts of the Highlands, particularly in Enga, Western Highlands, and Simbu provinces. Tribal fighting is essentially a rural phenomenon and, in practice, often results in high casualties, extensive damage to property, and serious disruption to government services and commercial activities. The destruction of schools, aid posts, gardens, business premises, can have disastrous long-term effects upon development in the areas affected. The likelihood of fatalities and personal injuries has been greatly enhanced as warriors blend traditional methods with modern technology, including the use of high-powered firearms (Burton 1990). Between 1988 and 1996 fights in the Tsak-Wapenamanda area of Enga province alone reportedly claimed more than 300 lives (*National*, 23 January 1997). The increasingly costly outcomes of intergroup conflicts contribute directly to a cycle of retaliatory actions or 'payback' that becomes ever more difficult to break.

This phenomenon illustrates significant differences in the perception of conflict and conflict-resolution embodied in state law, on the one hand, and among large sections of the PNG population, on the other. Whereas state law views fighting as the problem—a clear challenge to its proclaimed monopoly over violence—participants tend to view the situation quite differently. For them, fighting is viewed as a legitimate strategy for resolving some underlying dispute between local groups over, for example, a piece of land or an earlier homicide. As the Clifford Report summarised it:

> Tribal fighting is a response to disorder, to a dispute or a breach of a norm and not a problem in itself. For participants the law and order problem is the offence or dispute, not the fighting. (Clifford *et al.* 1984:92)

Tribal fighting was effectively suppressed throughout much of the colonial period. The success of the colonial peace—*Pax Australiana*—was as much a consequence of the material and other positive inducements offered local communities under the colonial administration, as it was a result of the repressive impact of colonial controls. The revival of this practice in parts of the Highlands since the early 1970s broadly parallels the decline in government services, including official procedures of conflict resolution, during the postindependence period. In this sense, the reemergence of tribal fighting represents a growing withdrawal from state and reversion to older strategies of conflict resolution in the areas concerned.

State responses in the postindependence period have generally been of the familiar law and order variety, including the imposition of a state of emergency in 1979 and a succession of special policing operations. These responses have met with little lasting success. In the words of one observer:

> While police interventions in fights have temporarily halted them, ultimately they have prolonged battles, and possibly have made matters worse. (Mapusia 1986:68)

The strategies with the most positive impact in practice have often had little active state participation. These have involved local leaders, often acting through intermediary brokers, in prolonged negotiations and compensation settlements that seek to address the disputes underlying particular conflicts (*National*, 23 January 1997).

Corruption

The current governor-general, Sir Wiwa Korowi, stated in 1995 that corruption had become 'deeply rooted' in PNG (*Australian*, 14 June 1995). Former governor of the Bank of Papua New Guinea, Sir Mekere Morauta, has gone so far as to describe it as being 'systemic and systematic' (*The Press*, Christchurch, 3 July 1995). Respected parliamentarian, Sir John Momis, has also claimed that bribery and corruption have become an economic system in themselves and warned of dire political consequences if they are left unchecked (*Post-Courier*, 1 August 1996). Allegations of corrupt behaviour on the part of public figures have contributed to growing levels of popular disillusionment with political leadership and the integrity of government processes. They have also become a recurring theme in the legitimating rhetoric used by rascals to justify their own criminal activities (Dinnen 1993b).

Most incidents of corruption that become public knowledge do so as a result of formal inquiries or the deliberations of leadership tribunals. These tribunals are the mechanisms for investigating alleged breaches of the Leadership Code. The Code is administered by the Ombudsman Commission and applies to designated national leaders, including politicians and other public office holders. Under Section 27 of the Constitution, leaders are to conduct themselves in public or private life so as not to cause conflicts of interest, demean their office, bring their personal integrity into question, or diminish respect for the government. Moreover, leaders should not use their office for personal gain or to raise doubts about the discharge of their office.

The privileged access to state funds afforded politicians, often in the form of discretionary funds, and the limited effectiveness of existing controls has facilitated the spread of corrupt practices at the highest levels. Opportunities for corruption are greatest in the case of government ministers who wield considerable powers of patronage in practice. The processes of awarding licenses and lucrative government contracts have been particularly vulnerable to abuse on the part of unethical politicians and unscrupulous business leaders. Former Ombudsman Commissioner Sir Charles Maino has recently classified the four most common forms of economic crime in PNG as: the abuse of licensing regimes; the 'hands in the till' syndrome; political corruption and vote buying; and kickbacks and other improprieties in the decision-making process for government contracts (Maino 1994).

Between 1975 and 1991 a total of eighteen leaders and public office holders appeared before leadership tribunals. Apart from those who resigned before their hearings (thereby evading the jurisdiction of the tribunal), six of those who did appear were dismissed from office, one was suspended, another reprimanded, three were fined, and the rest found not guilty (*Post-Courier*, 30 September 1991). At a National Crime Summit in 1991, Prime Minister Namaliu revealed that the Ombudsman Commission was investigating allegations against 90 of the 109 members of the national parliament (*The Australian*, 12 February 1991). By 1995 the Commission had referred a total of nineteen members of parliament (including one prime minister) to leadership tribunals, as well as nine senior public servants (*Post-Courier*, 31 August 1995). A brief chronicle of some of the more significant cases follows.

The Ombudsman Commission Report about the so-called 'Diaries Affair' in the early 1980s recommended the prosecution of a number of senior public servants implicated in illegal dealings relating to the purchase of some 15,000 executive diaries from a Singaporean businessman (Ombudsman Commission 1982). In 1986 a Commission of Inquiry reported on the sale of the government's executive jet and the purchase of Israeli aircraft for the defence force (Report of the Commission of Inquiry 1986). Prime Minister Michael Somare and one of his senior ministers were among those investigated. No findings of illegal behaviour were established. Another inquiry was set up in 1986 to determine whether there had been any breaches of the Leadership Code involved in the purchase of shares after a float by Placer Pacific Party. Many prominent public figures, including then Minister of Finance Sir Julius Chan, made substantial profits out of their share acquisitions (Dinnen 1993b). The findings of this inquiry have never been officially released.

A Commission of Inquiry was established in May 1987 as a result of persistent rumors of ministerial misconduct, corruption, and transfer pricing in Papua New Guinea's forest industry. The commission, under the leadership of Judge Barnett, presented its final report to the prime minister in July 1989. The voluminous report documents endemic corruption and mismanagement in the forest industry. Among the long list of leaders implicated in the inquiry were former Prime Minister

Michael Somare and one-time Deputy Prime Minister Ted Diro. A leadership tribunal eventually found Diro to be in breach of the Leadership Code on eighty-three counts, mainly arising from what the Barnett inquiry had described as 'the reckless destruction of forests and a plan to systematically cheat (the landowners) of their rightful profits' (quoted in *The Saturday Independent*, 9 September 1995).

Other investigations of alleged abuses relating to the award of government contracts have included the Spring Garden Road/Poreporena Freeway Project in Port Moresby (Ombudsman Commission 1992) and the Disciplined Forces Institutional Project (Ombudsman Commission 1994). In both cases, the Ombudsman Commission highlighted 'the flagrant disregard of public tender procedures and numerous other breaches of laws dealing with the award of contracts for public works projects' (*ibid.*:96). Summing up the findings of the 1994 report, the Commission asked:

> When are the leaders of our country going to learn that the laws of Papua New Guinea must be respected and followed? (*ibid.*:96)

The most recent investigation examined the awarding of contracts for Upgrading of the Port Moresby Water Supply Project (Ombudsman Commission 1996). Among the findings, the report declared the selective tender process adopted by the local authority in question to be 'fundamentally flawed, unfair and prone to corruption' (*ibid.*:468).

The unstable, often volatile, character of national politics in PNG provides other opportunities for corruption on the part of individual politicians. An illustration appears in the findings of guilt delivered in the 1992 case of two former ministers, Peter Garong and Melchior Pep. Both had sought substantial sums from the prime minister's discretionary fund in the face of a proposed vote of no confidence in the government of the day. The clear implication was that their political loyalty could be guaranteed in return for these payments (Maino 1994). The provision of large discretionary funds to each of the 109 national parliamentarians for the development of their constituencies provides another obvious opportunity for corruption. At the beginning of 1995 each member was eligible for a K300,000 electoral development fund (EDF) and K200,000 in minor transport funds (Economist Intelligence Unit 1995:12). Such funds have commonly been used to buy votes, as well as to reward supporters after elections and consolidate local power bases through the strategic dispersal of a variety of development projects. They have also been increasingly used to build up the private wealth of individual politicians. Despite the existence of guidelines on how to spend and account for these funds, few politicians document their expenditure as required. Chief Ombudsman Commissioner Simon Pentanu has stated that only one member of parliament provided a full account of their EDF expenditure in 1994 and, moreover, that it was 'normal' for about 85 of the 109 members to fail to acquit funds charged in their care in any one year (*National*, 22 March 1995).

While the Ombudsman Commission continues to put up a valiant struggle against corrupt practices, its efforts are seriously affected in practice by an acute shortage of resources, as is faced by other government agencies (*Post-Courier*, 31 August 1995).

CONCLUSIONS

The range and gravity of law and order problems, alongside the weakness of state controls, provides the basis for the apocalyptic tone found in many recent commentaries on PNG. An implicit invocation of social disintegration pervades these commentaries. The poor performance of criminal justice agencies has been documented at length in the Clifford Report. That report recommended that greater use be made of community-based regulatory structures such as local government officials, village moots, churches, voluntary organizations, and in particular, the village courts. These informal mechanisms would be used to supplement the workings of formal state agencies.

Underlying the Clifford recommendations was the desire to diminish the perceived social gap that has developed between state and local-level institutions in recent years. One manifestation of this gap, according to the authors, lay in the widespread disrespect for state law. Such a view was expressed, somewhat simplistically, in terms of an implied dichotomy between state and community:

> Law and order in Papua New Guinea depends therefore on the government regaining its position and prestige with ordinary people and forging links that will build confidence and community. (Clifford *et al.* 1984, I/107)

The 'community revivalism' of the Clifford Report's non-state option also connects with nationalist critiques of western values and their adverse impact upon traditional values and social institutions. The critique of state law from this perspective reached its apotheosis in the rhetoric of decolonization at the time of independence. The appropriateness of institutions of colonial (viz. foreign) origin as instruments of social regulation in the distinctive and socially diverse PNG environment was questioned by many early national leaders (Kaputin 1975; Narokobi 1977). These views found strong expression in the Final Report of the Constitutional Planning Committee (CPC 1974), the Independence Constitution, and the early work of the Law Reform Commission (see, for example, Law Reform Commission Report No. 7, 1977). Law and order problems are viewed, in part, as a consequence of the failure of state law to accord with Melanesian perceptions of justice and, thereby, to secure the respect and allegiance of indigenous people (Narokobi 1988).

PNG's criminal justice system, as with other areas of state activities, is undoubtedly in need of capacity-building and institutional reform. There is also little doubt that the performance of the present system could be significantly enhanced through being given a more explicit community orientation. At the same time there is a need to recognise the inherent limitations of any system of criminal justice—no matter how well resourced or socially adapted. International experience provides ample testimony to these practical limitations. Indeed, many aspects of PNG's crisis of criminal justice—such as the patent failure of prison to deter or reform—are shared with other countries. Expectations of criminal justice also need to be modified in light of the broader context of rapid social and economic change that frames current patterns of lawlessness. Emergent marginalisations affecting particular social groups (such as urban youth), growing divisions in wealth between groups and regions, expanding criminal opportunities, rising material needs and expectations, rapid urbanisation, population growth, additional stresses on profoundly inequitable gender relations, the availability of firearms, and the abuse of alcohol, are among a host of factors at play in the current law and order environment. Just as there are no straightforward explanations of the current law and order situation, there are no simple solutions.

Change in PNG has not occurred in a social vacuum but within an environment made up of numerous small-scale societies, each with its own distinctive system of social ordering that has evolved over the course of thousands of years. The resilience of these older traditions in the face of the transformations of recent history provides one of the most distinctive features of the contemporary PNG social environment. Even among 'modern' urban rascals, we can discern the unmistakable influence of more enduring patterns of 'traditional' leadership, as well as the distributive practices upon which they are constituted (Goddard 1992 and 1995). The continuing subordination of women in all social contexts despite the equity provisions embodied in constitutional, statutory, and institutional frameworks provides further illustration. For the vast majority of Papua New Guineans, primary allegiances continue to reside in non-state social organisations, with local-level customary contexts exerting a greater regulatory impact upon the conduct of everyday life than state law. In practice, institutions and processes of relatively recent origin have blended in numerous complex ways with those they were intended to replace. Conflict and institutional dysfunctionality in modern PNG are more often than not the outcome of processes of cultural and institutional interpenetration, instead of being a product of the uniform processes of disintegration and collapse depicted in the more alarmist commentaries.

The growing reliance on militarised solutions to problems of order, noted earlier, can, at one level, be viewed as an attempt to disguise state weakness by relying upon its ostensibly strongest aspect. In practice, however, the violence employed by parts of the state is often indistinguishable from the wider problems of violence in PNG society. Growing levels of state violence have, in effect, promoted the legitimacy of violence as a political strategy among both state and non-state constituencies. In this respect, the conventional western distinction between legality and illegality fails to capture what is going on in both state and non-state coercive action. The question of a monopoly of violence neither characterises the PNG state nor legitimates its actions.

The postcolonial state in PNG has in many ways become the object of a process of upward colonization, whereby social forces emanating from the most local levels have penetrated even the commanding heights of the modern state. This is illustrated in the redistributive activities of political leaders, most apparent during elections. It is also evident in the growing entanglement between the obligations of kinship and those of public service that, in turn, underlies much of the behaviour currently designated as corruption. In the process, the boundaries between state and society have become increasingly blurred, and the state itself has become less coherent. This stands in contrast to the oversimplified polarisation between state and society underlying the analysis of the Clifford Report. Evidence suggests that it is not so much the gap separating state and society that underlies current problems of order in PNG, as the blurring between them.

REFERENCES

Biles, D., ed., 1976. *Crime in Papua New Guinea*. Canberra: Australian Institute of Criminology.

Burton, J., 1990. 'Tribal fighting—the scandal of inaction', *Research in Melanesia*, 14(1990):31-40.

Clifford, W., Morauta, L., and Stuart, B., 1984. *Law and Order in Papua New Guinea*. Port Moresby: Institute of National Affairs and Institute of Applied Social and Economic Research.

Commission of Inquiry, 1986. *Report of the Commission of Inquiry into Pelair and Other Matters*. Waigani: Government Printer.

Constitutional Planning Committee, 1974. *The Final Report*. Waigani: Government Printer.

Department of Provincial Affairs, 1983. *Report of the Committee to Review Policy and Administration on Crime, Law and Order* (Morgan Report).

Dinnen, S., 1986. 'Perspectives on law and order', in L. Morauta, ed., *Law and Order in a Changing Society*. Canberra: Department of Political and Social Change, Research School of Pacific Studies, Australian National University, pp. 76-89.

———, 1992. 'Criminal justice practice: conflict and interdependence in Papua New Guinea', in R. W. James and I. Fraser, eds., *Legal Issues in a Developing Society*. Port Moresby: Faculty of Law, University of Papua New Guinea, pp. 202-229.

———, 1993a. 'Causes for concern: control talk in Papua New Guinea', *TaimLain: A Journal of Contemporary Melanesian Studies*, 1(1):13-37.

———, 1993b. 'Big men, small men and invisible women—urban crime and inequality in Papua New Guinea', *Australian and New Zealand Journal of Criminology*, 26(March 1993):19-34.

———, 1993c. 'Internal security in Papua New Guinea', *Criminology Australia*, 5(2).

Dorney, S., 1990. *Papua New Guinea—People, Politics and History since 1975*. Milsons Point, NSW: Random House Australia.

Goddard, M., 1992. 'Big-man, thief: the social organization of gangs in Port Moresby', *Canberra Anthropology*, 15(1):20-34.

———, 1995. 'The Rascal Road: crime, prestige and development in Papua New Guinea', *The Contemporary Pacific: A Journal of Island Affairs*, 7(1):55-80.

Gordon, R. J., and Meggitt, M. J., 1985. *Law and Order in the New Guinea Highlands*. Hanover and London: University Press of New England.

Harris, B. M., 1988. 'The rise of rascalism—action and reaction in the evolution of rascal gangs'. Port Moresby: Institute of Applied Social and Economic Research.

Kaputin, J., 1975. 'The Law—a colonial fraud?' *New Guinea*, 10(1):4-15.

Law Reform Commission of Papua New Guinea (LRC), 1977. *The Role of Customary Law in the Legal System*. Port Moresby: Law Reform Commission.

———, 1985a. *Domestic Violence in Papua New Guinea*. Monograph No. 3. Port Moresby: Law Reform Commission.

———, 1985b. *Marriage and Domestic Violence in Rural Papua New Guinea*. Occasional Paper No. 18. Port Moresby: Law Reform Commission.

———, 1986a. *Domestic Violence in Urban Papua New Guinea*. Occasional Paper No. 19. Port Moresby: Law Reform Commission.

———, 1986b. *Marriage in Papua New Guinea*. Monograph No. 4. Port Moresby: Law Reform Commission.

———, 1992. *Final Report on Domestic Violence*. Port Moresby: Law Reform Commission.

Maino, C., 1994. 'Serious economic crime—a threat to us all'. Paper presented at the 12th International Symposium on Economic Crime, Jesus College, Cambridge University, September 1994.

Mapusia, M., 1986. 'Police policy towards tribal fighting in the Highlands', in L. Morauta, ed., *Law and Order in a Changing Society*. Canberra: Department of Political and Social Change, Research School of Pacific Studies, Australian National University, pp. 57-69.

May, R. J., and Spriggs, M., eds., 1990. *The Bougainville Crisis*. Bathurst: Crawford House Press.

Narokobi, B. M., 1977. 'Adaptation of Western law in Papua New Guinea', *Melanesian Law Journal* 5:52.

————, 1988 *Policy on Law and Order*. Waigani: Government Printer.

Nenta, R., 1996. 'Papua New Guinea: security and defence in the nineties and beyond 2000'. Conference Proceedings, Sydney, 28 June 1996.

Ombudsman Commission of Papua New Guinea, 1982. *Corruption in Government—A Case Study*. Port Moresby: Ombudsman Commission of Papua New Guinea.

————, 1992. *Report of an Investigation into the Spring Garden Road/Poreporena Project*. Port Moresby: Ombudsman Commission of Papua New Guinea.

————, 1996. *Report of an Investigation into the Disciplined Forces Institutional Housing Project*. Port Moresby: Ombudsman Commission of Papua New Guinea.

Royal Papua New Guinea Constabulary (RPNGC), 1990. *1990 Annual Report*. Port Moresby: Police Department.

Spriggs, M., and Denoon, D., eds., 1992. *The Bougainville Crisis—1991 Update*. Canberra: Department of Political and Social Change, Australian National University in association with Crawford House Press.

Turner, M., 1990. *Papua New Guinea: The Challenge of Independence*. Penguin Books Australia Ltd.

United Nations Development Programme/International Labour Organisation (UNDP/ILO), 1993. *Papua New Guinea: Challenges for Employment and Human Resource Development*. New Delhi: UNDP/ILO.

Zimmer, L. J., 1990. 'Sexual exploitation and male dominance in Papua New Guinea', *Point* 14 (Human Sexuality, Special Issue):250-267.

Christine Bradley

CHANGING A 'BAD OLD TRADITION'
Wife-Beating and the Work of the Papua
New Guinea Law Reform Commission

THERE ARE MANY WAYS in which the traditional customs and values of Papua New Guinea's diverse peoples conflict with the principles underlying the country's Constitution and introduced system of national laws. The most obvious way in which these two opposing conceptual systems clash is over the position of women. In particular, the question of whether or not husbands should be allowed to beat their wives has aroused much controversy in recent years.

Wife-beating is not exclusively a modern phenomenon. In most parts of Papua New Guinea, it was and is traditionally accepted that a husband may beat his wife if he thinks it necessary, provided he does not break bones or draw blood. Law Reform Commission research carried out in 1982–83 found that 65 percent of rural husbands and 55 percent of rural wives considered it acceptable for a husband to hit his wife (Ranck and Toft 1986:24).[1] Papua New Guinea's predominantly patrilineal cultures are strongly male-dominated, and the husband is expected to be the head or 'boss' of the family, with the right to enforce his will. In the minds of many Papua New Guineans, this expectation is directly linked to the system of paying 'brideprice', which can lead a husband and his relatives to feel that they 'own' the woman they have

---

[1] This figure is a national average which conceals a wide variation, ranging from over 90 percent for both sexes in parts of the Highlands, down to 17 percent for men and 7 percent for women in the New Ireland survey village (Bradley 1988:261).

'paid for'. [2] Christian missionary activity, for the most part critical of brideprice, has nevertheless tended (with recent exceptions) to reinforce the traditional dominance of the husband in the family.

By contrast, under the system of law introduced originally by the colonial powers and confirmed at independence in 1975, it is an offence, punishable by imprisonment, for any individual to use, or threaten to use, direct or indirect force on another person, whether or not injuries are caused.[3] The use of force by civilians may be lawfully justified only when used in self-defence, in response to provocation in certain limited circumstances, in the disciplining of children by parents or teachers, or where the victim consents, such as in the playing of sports involving bodily contact.[4] These laws cover everyone, whether male or female, rich or poor, single or married.

The Constitution, too, introduces a set of rights and duties which apply to all citizens equally. Section 55(1) of the Constitution states that 'all citizens have the same rights, privileges, obligations and duties irrespective of race, tribe, place of origin, political opinion, colour, creed, religion or sex'. There is no direct reference to wife-beating in the Constitution, but it is clear from section 55, and from the National Goals and Directive Principles laid out in the Preamble to the Constitution, that wife-beating is contrary to the spirit of the Constitution.

Goal No. 1 calls for each person to free himself or herself from every form of domination or oppression 'so that each man or woman will have the opportunity to develop as a whole person in relationship with others'. Goal No.2 affirms 'recognition of the principles that a complete relationship in marriage rests upon equality of rights and duties of the partners and that responsible parenthood is also based on that equality'. Section 36(1) provides that no person shall be submitted 'to treatment or punishment that is cruel or otherwise inhuman, or is inconsistent with respect for the dignity of the human person'.

Finally, the relationship of custom to the Constitution and the written law is set out in schedule 2 of the Constitution. Under schedule 2.1(1), customary law is adopted as the underlying law of Papua New Guinea. However, schedule 2.1(2) sets limits on the application of cus-

---

[2] There are many variants on how brideprice is perceived amongst Papua New Guinea's diverse cultures and there are circumstances in which brideprice operates to protect wives. The question of how brideprice affects wife-beating is a complex one which merits further discussion than space allows here.

[3] Section 243 of the *Criminal Code* and s.6 of the *Summary Offences Act*, chapters 262 and 264 respectively of the *Revised Laws of Papua New Guinea*.

[4] Sections 243, 266–271, and 278 of Papua New Guinea's *Criminal Code*.

tom, stating that a custom which is inconsistent with the Constitution, or with a statute (written law), or is 'repugnant to the general principles of humanity' shall not be applied or enforced. All three of these categories clearly apply in the case of wife-beating. In other words, wife-beating, like tribal fighting, is a custom which shall no longer be applied or enforced, and has no place in the kind of modern society for which the Constitution provides the framework.

When the Law Reform Commission came to consider what approach it should take to wife-beating, it faced something of a dilemma. The written law and the Constitution are firmly against wife-beating, yet one of the Commission's reasons for existence was to make the country's system of laws more compatible with Papua New Guinea's customary attitudes and practices.[5] As already noted, the Commission's own research had found that the majority of rural Papua New Guineans, especially of males, appeared to be in favour of wife-beating. As will be shown, the majority of husbands also practise it.

Clear though it was that women had every legal right to be protected from wife-beating, would it be appropriate for the Law Reform Commission to go against custom? And even if it were appropriate, would there be any point in recommending measures to reduce wife-beating if public opinion (whether at parliamentary or grassroots level) would prevent them from being implemented? Results from the Commission's urban surveys suggested that town dwellers (especially females) were much less in favour of wife-beating than were village dwellers.[6] Might attitudes in the villages also be in the process of changing in the same direction, and if so, how fast? How readily would rural husbands accept the modern notion that wives should not be beaten? These were among the questions considered by the Commission before the decision was made to take a stand against domestic violence in general and wife-beating in particular. The approach and methods the Commission subsequently adopted will now be described.

[5] See section 21.1(2) of the Constitution, chapter 1, *Revised Laws of Papua New Guinea*.

[6] In the survey of urban elites, 41 percent of husbands and 36 percent of wives approved of wife-beating, as compared to 65 percent of rural husbands and 55 percent of rural wives. In the urban low income survey, only 47 percent of husbands and 25 percent of wives said they agreed with wife-beating, a drop of 18 percent and 30 percent respectively from the corresponding rural figures (Ranck and Toft 1986:24).

THE LAW REFORM COMMISSION'S REFERENCE AND RESEARCH
It was in 1982 that a letter from the National Council of Women[7] to the minister for justice resulted in the Commission's being given a reference to work on domestic violence. The letter stated that violence by men against their wives or girlfriends had been a cause of increasing concern to the Council since its creation in 1975 and that women were not receiving adequate protection from the law. The minister then directed the Law Reform Commission to inquire into the nature and extent of domestic violence and to make recommendations for reducing the problem, on the grounds that 'domestic violence is contrary to the principles of our Constitution'.

The definition of domestic violence used by the Commission for its subsequent work needs some explanation. Domestic violence was defined as physical assault between husbands and wives, or between those living together as if they were husband and wife. This is the definition of domestic violence most commonly used by Law Reform Commissions and other legal agencies around the world, although 'marital violence' or 'spousal violence' would perhaps have been more accurate terms. Violence between other persons in a domestic setting, such as between co-wives of the same man, between relatives, or between in-laws did not come within the definition of domestic violence used by the Commission. Violence directed at children was also excluded, since this is normally dealt with under the separate topic of 'child abuse'. However, the many ways in which children suffer from violence between their parents were recognised in the Commission's research and recommendations.

In the absence of existing data on domestic violence in Papua New Guinea, the Commission undertook its own research. Studies were conducted in almost every province, in collaboration with staff and students at the Administrative College, with the Geography Department and the Law Faculty of the University of Papua New Guinea, and with individual researchers. Quantitative data were derived from three main questionnaire surveys: a rural survey covering 19 villages in 16 of Papua New Guinea's 19 provinces, a survey of low income earners and wives of low income earners in the capital, Port Moresby, and a postal survey of elites (defined for the purposes of the study as those employed in the Public Service at clerk class 10 and above, and their spouses). The same questions were put to male and female respondents, and efforts were

---

[7] The National Council of Women is the umbrella organisation for all of Papua New Guinea's women's groups.

made to ensure that each respondent was interviewed in privacy. The findings revealed a close match between the answers of males and females in each group, suggesting that respondents were answering honestly.

Other data were derived from a survey of two urban settlements, a hospital study, analyses of Local and District Court records in five provinces, of police records at three police stations, and of police attitudes in 15 provinces. More in-depth information was produced by case studies of beaten wives, five anthropological studies, interviews with magistrates and court officials, lawyers, public solicitors, police, welfare workers, church workers, community leaders, women's leaders, teachers, probation officers, and members of the public.

FINDINGS OF THE RESEARCH

As the results of the Law Reform Commission's research have been published in full elsewhere,[8] only the most relevant aspects will be mentioned here. The research showed conclusively that domestic violence is common in Papua New Guinea, and that its main form is wife-beating. Sixty-seven percent of rural wives interviewed said their husbands had hit them, and 66 percent of the rural husbands interviewed said that they had hit their wives. There was, however, a wide range across the country, with figures of up to 100 percent being reported from wives (and confirmed by husbands) in parts of the Highlands, and the lowest figure, of 49 percent, reported by wives in Oro Province.

As regards wives hitting husbands, 30 percent of rural husbands, 37 percent of urban low income husbands, and 50 percent of urban elite husbands said they had been hit by their wives. However, a comparison of violence against wives or against husbands merely in terms of numbers hit gives no indication of the real difference in seriousness between the two phenomena. If injuries caused and the involvement of the police are taken as indicatiors of seriousness, it becomes clear that wife-beating is a far more serious problem than is husband-beating. For example, a survey conducted at Lae's Angau Hospital showed that of all patients seeking treatment for domestic violence injuries during a ten-week period, 97 percent were women (Ekeroma 1985:78). Similarly, a study of police reports of domestic violence at three police stations in the National Capital District during three months in 1987 found that

---

[8] See Bradley 1987, 1988, 1990, and 1991; Law Reform Commission 1987 and 1992; Toft ed. 1985, 1986; Toft and Bonnell eds. 1986.

93.5 percent of complainants were women (Kaetovuhu and Tyrer 1987:7). Moreover, the Law Reform Commission's surveys found that the most frequent reason for wives to hit their husbands is self-defence (Ranck and Toft 1986:30). Clearly then, it is violence by husbands against wives which is by far the more significant problem, and it was this which became the main focus of the Commission's recommendations.

THE INTERIM REPORT

The Commission's initial recommendations were published in the *Interim Report on Domestic Violence* and presented to Parliament in March 1987. The members were not asked to vote on the *Interim Report,* nor on any of its recommendations. The Commission's intention was to test Parliament's reaction to the proposals and to generate discussion and feedback from amongst the general public. The second of these two aims was certainly achieved, since there was extensive media coverage of the *Interim Report* and of the Parliamentary debate. Copies of the *Interim Report* were also sent out for feedback from individuals and groups around the country. Many favourable comments and some criticisms were received, resulting in minor changes to some of the original recommendations. The result of the first aim, however, was disappointing.

Although there were speakers for and against the *Interim Report,* it was those against who dominated the Parliamentary debate and were the most widely reported. One member asserted forcefully that husbands will always be able to treat their wives however they like so long as the system of paying brideprice persists. Another was outraged that the nation's leaders were being asked to waste their valuable time discussing family quarrels, and another said he would like to tear up and burn the *Interim Report.* Disparaging remarks were passed about wives and jokes were made about women's failure to satisfy their husband's various requirements. Alarm was expressed that families would break up if husbands were prevented from beating their wives, and the Commission was accused of being biased towards women because it highlighted violence against wives. Despite warm support from a handful of members, it was clear that there was little hope that this Parliament would ever enact any of the Commission's recommendations on domestic violence.The Commission therefore decided to undertake its own public education programme on domestic violence before presenting its final report to Parliament. This campaign will be described shortly, but first a summary of the Commission's proposed approach to the problem of domestic violence will be given.

THE LAW REFORM COMMISSION'S PROPOSED STRATEGY TO REDUCE DOMESTIC VIOLENCE

The approach to domestic violence that the Law Reform Commission recommended in its *Interim Report* has two strands—the remedial and the preventive. All the remedial measures are intended to be applicable whether the wife or the husband is the victim. The preventive measures focus mainly on wife-beating, because this is by far the greater problem, and because customary attitudes have generally been supportive of wife-beating but not of husband-beating. Taking the remedial measures first, the Commission recommended a number of improvements in the way the courts and the police deal with cases of domestic violence.

Although the Local and District Courts have long had the power to issue Good Behaviour Bonds against husbands who assault their wives, magistrates were not making proper use of these provisions. Following consultations between the Law Reform Commission and the Magisterial Service, the Chief Magistrate issued an official circular to all magistrates laying down new guidelines to ensure the smooth and speedy hearing of applications for Good Behaviour Bonds in cases of domestic violence. As a result, many more beaten wives are successfully applying for Good Behaviour Bonds. There remain some difficulties with the existing legislation, and new legislation to allow for emergency and interim orders, with a more effective system of enforcement, was recommended and has since been prepared. The new legislation, if passed by Parliament, will improve the protection available to anyone at risk of violence, not just to marriage partners. It will also allow for a violent husband (or wife) to be barred from his (or her) own residence for up to three months.

However, the legal remedies available through the Local and District Courts can only help those people who can get to these town-based courts. Most village dwellers must rely on their Village Court. Village Courts do have the powers to punish for assault and to issue Preventive Orders against further violence or a breach of the peace, but most village magistrates do not realise that these powers also apply in cases of domestic violence. Village Courts normally follow local custom which, as has been shown, in most parts of Papua New Guinea allows a man to beat his wife within certain limits. Neverthless, schedule 2.1(2) of the Constitution states that custom cannot be applied where it is inconsistent with a written law, or with the Constitution itself.

Therefore the *Interim Report* recommended that the Village Courts Handbook be amended to make clear specific procedures for domestic violence, that the training of Village Court magistrates should cover these aspects, and that female magistrates should be recruited for village courts. Staff of the national Village Courts Secretariat and the Law Reform Commission have already begun to train Village Court magistrates on their powers and responsibilities as regards domestic violence, and plans are underway to implement the other two recommendations.

In relation to the police response to domestic assaults, the *Interim Report* recommended that the police should drop their former policy of nonintervention in domestic disputes and replace it with a policy of handling domestic assaults in the same way as nondomestic assaults. Within a short time of the release of the *Interim Report,* the Commissioner for Police acted on the recommendation and introduced new standing orders directing police to intervene and prosecute wherever sufficient evidence is available in cases of domestic violence. Sessions developed by the Law Reform Commission on the proper handling of domestic assaults are now included in police recruit training programmes and in in-service training programmes.

Two legislative changes are also recommended in the *Interim Report.* The first is to clarify police powers to enter private premises to investigate or prevent violence (whether domestic or nondomestic). The second is to ensure that wives cannot be forced by violent husbands or their relatives to withdraw charges against them once the case has been taken up by the police. As in the case of the Local and District Courts, significant improvements in the police response to domestic violence have already been achieved without the need to await Parliamentary approval for legislative changes.

The remedial measures so far described are important, not merely for the practical assistance they make available to victims of domestic violence, but also for their educational and symbolic value. Once it is seen that the State and its law enforcement agencies are taking action against domestic violence, the remedial measures will also have a preventive and deterrent effect. Thus they will contribute to the other, more direct preventive measures that the *Interim Report* recommends: for the provision of specialised domestic violence counselling, for training in communication skills for married couples, and for public education on the harm caused by domestic violence. In fact, the Commission believed that public education was so important that it decided to implement its own recommendation on this point, since it seemed in a better position to do this than any other organisation. By doing so, it also hoped to create a more favourable climate of opinion in Parliament as well as among the public, so that when the *Final Report on Domestic Violence* was finally presented to Parliament, its recommendations would have a better chance of being accepted.[9]

THE PUBLIC AWARENESS CAMPAIGN

The *Interim Report on Domestic Violence* recommended an extensive public awareness campaign to be directed at the public, at relevant professionals, and at young people through the formal education system. The intention was to educate people that domestic violence is criminal behaviour which has many harmful effects for the offender as well as for the victim, for the family and for society as a whole. The overall aim of the public awareness campaign was to help create a society that understands the dangers of domestic violence and that is supportive of victims' efforts to stop the violence in its earliest stages.

It is unlikely that Papua New Guinea will ever be able to afford the kinds of extensive support systems for victims that are provided by the State in more economically developed countries, even if this were desirable. In fact, the Commission believes it is infinitely preferable that the responsibility for dealing with domestic violence should remain as far as possible within local communities. If these communities become sufficiently motivated and responsive, most cases of domestic violence will be dealt with at the community level as soon as they arise and very few will escalate to the point where outside sources of help, such as the law enforcement agencies, or women's refuges, will need to be involved.

Shortage of funds was the main obstacle to the Commission's campaign, and to overcome this a nongovernmental voluntary body was formed, known as the Women and Law Committee. This committee was made up of representatives from the Law Reform Commission, the

---

[9] Since this paper was written, the *Final Report on Domestic Violence* was completed and presented to the minister for justice. It contains some modifications to recommendations in the *Interim Report* and some additions, mainly in the area of support services for victims. It was tabled in Parliament in 1992.

YWCA, the Department of Home Affairs and Youth, the media, and the legal profession. As a nongovernment body it was able to apply for funds from women's organisations and development agencies both in Papua New Guinea and abroad. Staff of the Law Reform Commission worked with the committee to prepare and distribute thousands of leaflets and posters carrying the message 'Wife-beating is a Crime', with supplementary information. All materials were printed in the three main languages of Papua New Guinea—*Tok Pisin,* English, and *Hiri Motu.*

The response from the public and from government and nongovernment bodies was, for the most part, extremely positive. The leaflets and posters were widely distributed by the Health Department to all aid posts, health centres, clinics, and hospitals throughout the country. The Education Department sent them to all educational establishments, from primary schools upwards. All youth groups, women's groups, welfare offices, District and Local Courts, Village Courts, police stations, Offices of the Public Solicitor,[10] probation offices, and Divisions of Primary Industry were supplied with leaflets and posters by their respective national headquarters, both for the use of their own workers and for distribution to the public. Other organisations which used or distributed the materials throughout the country were statutory bodies such as the Electricity Commission, the Post and Telecommunication Corporation, Air Niugini, many banks and business houses, and all the major churches.

Following the success of the leaflet and poster campaign, the Law Reform Commission and the Women and Law Committee undertook the production of a dramatised video in *Tok Pisin* and English to reach those people who could not read the written materials. Funding was provided by the Canadian High Commission (Canberra) and CUSO, a Canadian nongovernment development assistance organisation. The video incorporates sections suitable for use in the training of police, magistrates, welfare officers, probation officers, teachers, and social workers, and each section of the script was approved by the relevant authorities. It was filmed in the Eastern Highlands, but prior to filming the script was sent to women's groups in all provinces to be checked for cultural suitability and relevance in other parts of the country. Development and checking of the script took over a year.

---

[10] This is the arm of the Justice Department responsible for legal aid.

The video was launched publicly in February 1989, and it immediately aroused tremendous interest all over the country. Shortly after its public launch, the video was screened on national television, and a panel of prominent Papua New Guineans, including the prime minister and the governor general and their wives, also appeared on the programme to speak in support of the video and of the campaign to reduce wife-beating. Hundreds of copies of the video were made for distribution to schools, government departments and divisions, women's groups, youth groups, churches, and community groups throughout the country. This was the first time in Papua New Guinea that any locally produced video had been so widely distributed. However, the demand was far greater than expected, so hundreds more copies were made and distributed, with funding from UNICEF. The video has also been requested by groups in other Pacific and African countries, as well as by many Australian aboriginal groups and by Canadian native indians, who appreciate the video's nonconfrontational approach.

Other public education initiatives taken by the Law Reform Commission and/or the Women and Law Committee were the sponsoring of a community theatre group to tour provinces performing a wife-beating awareness play and working with local theatre groups to develop their own similar plays; the broadcasting of information programmes on national and provincial radio, and of a radio drama dealing with wife-beating; the production of a resource book on domestic violence for grades 11 and 12, and of a popular cartoon storybook about wife-beating called *Let's Talk it Over* for use with children in grades 5 and 6, distributed in class sets to all community schools in the country. The storybook, leaflet, and poster have been adapted for use with literacy projects. Social Science materials for grades 8 and 10 have also been revised to include discussion of domestic violence. As regards formal education for adults, information on domestic violence is now included in the training of police, magistrates, lawyers, law students, social workers, probation officers, community school teachers, health personnel, many church workers, and senior public servants.

Two other nongovernment organisations which have been most supportive of the public awareness campaign are the National Council of Women and the Catholic Church. A national policy on wife-beating was developed for the National Council of Women by the Law Reform Commission, and this is currently being implemented at national, provincial, and village level. Following submissions from the Law Reform Commission to the Catholic Bishops Council, the Catholic Church has also taken an active stand against domestic violence, by including discussion of the subject in their courses for married couples and young people, by requiring priests to point out specifically to every young couple preparing for marriage that payment of brideprice does not give a man the right to use force or violence on his wife, and by permitting beaten wives to apply for legal separation from their husbands. Other churches too have been stimulated to take their own initiatives against wife-beating as part of their pastoral work.

CONCLUSION

Since the introduction of the Law Reform Commission's public awareness campaign, the level of public interest in domestic violence has been high. Domestic violence, and in particular wife-beating, has become recognised as a social problem, at least among literate, town-oriented Papua New Guineans. That there has been a change in stated public attitudes among this small section of the population is undeniable. In 1987, when the *Interim Report* was being ridiculed in Parliament, the possibility that the prime minister and the governor general would one day publicly announce their support for the campaign against wife-beating seemed remote indeed.

However, it is impossible to assess at this stage what success has been achieved in real terms. Certainly it has become popular for many educated urbanised Papua New Guineans to proclaim themselves to be against wife-beating. Unfortunately there is no way of knowing whether this apparent change of attitude has been accompanied by a reduction in the rates of wife-beating or not, for the Law Reform Commission has neither the staff nor the resources to conduct follow-up surveys. An apparent increase in the number of wives taking action against their abusive husbands through District and Village Courts is almost certainly a result of women's greater awareness of their options, rather than an indicator of an increase in wife-beating.

It is even harder to assess the changes that are taking place in rural areas, where the majority of the population live. The Law Reform Commission and the Women and Law Committee have received hundreds of letters from men, women, and children in rural areas asking for awareness materials and legal information—an indication that what one Papua New Guinean journalist has called Papua New Guinea's 'bad old tradition' is at least being questioned.[11] For the moment, that is the best that can be said with any certainty.[12]

But this in itself is encouraging. Attitudes that have endured for centuries cannot be reversed in a year or two, particularly when the structures and belief systems that fostered them persist. Even in more developed countries, which have been wrestling for years with the problem of domestic violence, there are still many people who not only resort to domestic violence themselves but consider it normal, even desirable.[13] At least the Papua New Guinea Law Reform Commisison has started the ball rolling in the right direction. How far it continues to roll in the future will depend on how many Papua New Guineans recognise that the custom of beating wives is out of place in modern Papua New Guinea society. As the articles in this volume by Dinnen and Hammar testify, this issue is highly relevant to the security and health of the nation.

[11] Article by Frank Senge in the *Post-Courier* of 3 March 1989.

[12] A UNICEF-funded evaluation of the campaign carried out in 1992 found that 'The Campaign against Domestic Violence has generated more awareness, concern, action and education than any comparable social awareness or social justice campaign' (Cox 1992:1).

[13] According to Straus *et al.* (1980:47), one in three husbands and one in four wives in the United States believed that under certain circumstances, couples slapping each other was 'necessary, normal or good'.

REFERENCES

Bradley, S. C., 1987. 'Wife-beating—the Police Response to the Hidden Crime'. Paper presented to the Annual Provincial Police Commanders' Conference, February 1987. Port Moresby: Law Reform Commission.

———, 1988. 'Wife-beating in Papua New Guinea—Is It A Problem?' *Papua New Guinea Medical Journal*, 31(4):257-268.

———, 1990. 'Violence in Marriage in Urban Papua New Guinea: Some Suggestions for the Churches', *Catalyst, Journal of the Melanesian Institute*, 20(2).

Cox, E., 1992. 'Campaigning Against Domestic Violence: An Evaluation of the Papua New Guinea Women and Law Committee's Campaign Against Domestic Violence 1986-92'. Report prepared for UNICEF, Papua New Guinea.

Ekoroma, A., 1986. 'Spouse-beating: a hospital study', in S. Toft, ed., *Domestic Violence in Urban Papua New Guinea*. Occasional Paper No. 19. Port Moresby: Law Reform Commission of Papua New Guinea, pp. 76-100.

Kaetovuhu, E., and Tyrer, R., 1987. 'Domestic Violence in Papua New Guinea: the Reporting of Incidents to the Police'. Unpublished paper, Research and Planning Section, Department of Police, Konedobu.

Law Reform Commission, 1987. *Interim Report on Domestic Violence*.

———, 1992. *Final Report on Domestic Violence*. Report No. 14. Port Moresby: Law Reform Commission of Papua New Guinea.

Ranck, S., and Toft, S., 1986. 'Domestic Violence in an Urban Context, with Rural Comparisons', in S. Toft, ed., *Domestic Violence in Urban Papua New Guinea*. Occasional Paper No. 19. Port Moresby: Law Reform Commission of Papua New Guinea, pp. 3-51.

Straus, M., Gelles, R., and Steinmetz, S., 1980. *Behind Closed Doors: Violence in the American Family*. Garden City, N.Y.: Anchor Press/Doubleday.

Toft, S., ed., 1985. *Domestic Violence in Papua New Guinea*. Law Reform Commission Monograph No. 3. Port Moresby: Law Reform Commission of Papua New Guinea.

———, ed., 1986. *Domestic Violence in Urban Papua New Guinea*. Occasional Paper No. 19. Port Moresby: Law Reform Commission of Papua New Guinea.

Toft, S., and Bonnell, S., eds., 1985. *Marriage and Domestic Violence in Rural Papua New Guinea*. Occasional Paper No. 18. Port Moresby: Law Reform Commission of Papua New Guinea.

Philip J. Hughes and Marjorie E. Sullivan

ENVIRONMENTAL IMPACT ASSESSMENT, PLANNING, AND MANAGEMENT IN PAPUA NEW GUINEA

THE TRADITIONAL IMPORTANCE of the environment and its resources to Melanesian societies has been recognised in the Constitution of Papua New Guinea. The major piece of legislation covering environmental impact assessment, planning, and management is the Environmental Planning Act 1978, which requires that an environmental plan be submitted for any proposed development that may have significant effect on the environment. Under the Act 'environment' is broadly defined and includes the social and cultural as well as the biophysical environment. To date, this legislation has been widely used with project planning, but has not been applied on a regional scale.

The enactment of wide-ranging environmental planning legislation has had similar effects for resource management in Papua New Guinea, as did similar Acts in, for instance, Australia. In both cases it strengthened existing legislation, which was previously often difficult to enforce, by obliging developers to consider during the planning process likely impacts on natural and cultural resources.

The Environmental Planning Act is applied almost exclusively to new development projects, and of these, to date, only for the larger-scale mining, agriculture, forestry, and infrastructure projects have environmental plans been prepared. Existing operations or new, small-scale projects that have not been subject to the Environmental Planning

Act, but which use resources such as water and discharge wastes into the environment, can be regulated under the provisions of the Environmental Contaminants Act 1978 and the Water Resources Act 1982. These include a diverse range of activities such as small-scale alluvial mining, coffee processing factories, and the use of pesticides. The cumulative impact on the environment of these small-scale activities is arguably more extensive than that of large projects.

THE PHYSICAL AND SOCIAL SETTING

Papua New Guinea, which is situated within the humid tropics, consists of the eastern part of the main island of New Guinea and of several island groups (fig. 1). It has a total land area of about 463,000 square kilometres and is environmentally remarkably diverse (see e.g. Löffler 1977, Paijmans 1976). The interiors of all the main islands are mountainous, with the highest peak, Mount Wilhelm, rising to 4,500 metres. There are a large number of volcanoes, many of which are still active, especially in the seismically more active northern part of the country. The largest areas of lowlands occur along the south coast, and within these are extensive areas of freshwater swampland and intertidal mangrove communities.

Most of Papua New Guinea experiences a hot and wet climate with temperatures generally between 22° and 31° C. and an annual rainfall of more than 2,500 mm. Such areas support tropical rain forest. Other parts of the country, especially along the south coast, are also hot but have a much lower rainfall and a pronounced dry season; these areas support savanna and grassland vegetation. The highland areas, above about 1,200 metres, are cooler and experience a larger daily temperature range.

The present population of about 4 million is small compared with most other countries in the Asia-Pacific region. It is however growing at a moderately high rate of about 2.5 percent annually, and if this rate continues the population will double in the next thirty years. The average density of population, about eight per square kilometre, is low compared with neighbouring countries, but the population is unevenly spread with the highlands regions having the highest concentrations of people. Much of the population lives from subsistence agriculture and most of the land (97 percent) is held under customary tenure systems whereby ownership is vested in the group, clan, or village, not the individual (Eaton 1984:2-3).

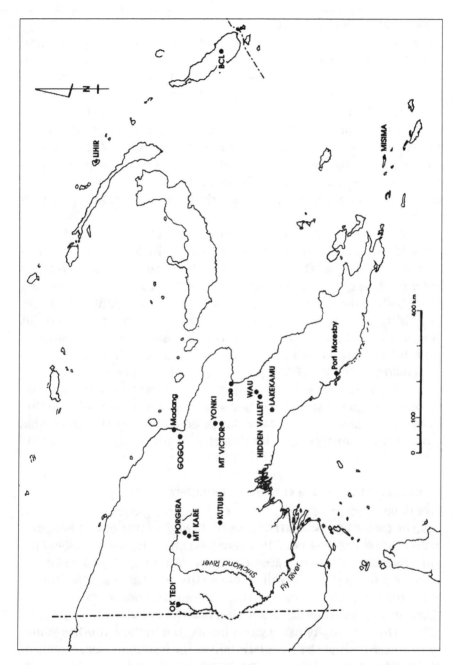

Fig. 1. Location of development projects, rivers, cities, and towns mentioned in the text. Map by Jonette Surridge, Cartography Laboratory, Department of Geography, University of Auckland.

The Economic Setting

Since Papua New Guinea gained independence in 1975, its population growth has kept pace with or outstripped economic growth, and commodity prices have generally been low. The closure of the Bougainville mine induced a marked downturn in the economy at the end of the 1980s and this has continued into the 1990s. Because of the still relatively small population there are no major land shortages at present and the country has abundant natural and agricultural resources. In planning for Papua New Guinea's future economic development, governments have placed a high priority on economic growth, especially in the agricultural sector, and have actively encouraged foreign investment.

The major exports are agricultural products, mainly coffee, tea, palm oil, cocoa, and copra; timber, mainly in the form of unprocessed logs; minerals, especially copper and gold; and, most recently, oil. The potential for expanding production and local processing in these and other industries such as fishing and oil and gas production is very promising. Although the long-term future of the country rests on its agricultural potential, there are excellent short- and medium-term prospects for minerals and petroleum. Papua New Guinea is rich in mineral resources, including gold, copper, oil, and gas. Exploitation of these resources, especially gold and oil, over the next decade is likely to provide a major boost to the nation's economy and it is predicted that by early next century Papua New Guinea could become the largest gold producer after the USSR and South Africa.

Benefits and Costs of Development

Like development projects in other developing countries, those in Papua New Guinea have attendant environmental and social impacts or costs as well as benefits. The brunt of such impacts is invariably felt most keenly by the local communities whose land will be alienated and whose traditional resources will be destroyed or degraded while the benefits are spread more widely throughout the country (Hughes and Sullivan 1988, 1989). In addition, associated processes such as in-migration, either to project camps and towns or to adjacent villages and squatter settlements, brings attendant social problems (see, for example, IASER 1986).

In planning for resource development projects, detailed consideration is theoretically given to the likely environmental and social costs as well as the economic and social benefits. Taking the mining industry as an example, all proposed mining projects are now subject to a comparatively rigorous analysis, as are to a lesser extent commercial agricultural projects. A detailed account of the likely benefits and costs of one such mining project, the Ok Tedi copper and gold mine, is given by Jackson (n.d.).

The major benefits from mining accrue to the national government and take the form of company and income taxes and profits from equity holdings. Provincial governments benefit mainly from their high share of the royalties. Local communities benefit from their share of the royalties, from compensation payments for loss of or damage to land and other resources, from wages, and from increased business opportunities. As pointed out above, these communities also bear the brunt of the negative impacts these projects inevitably have. Mining ventures require land—some areas of which are permanently lost, for example the site of the open cut pit, and others of which are radically transformed, like the sites of the rock waste dumps. Not only are there potential or actual land use conflicts, but other impacts occur, often far beyond the confines of the mine site, including pollution of rivers and the sea by mine wastes. An indication of the scale of operations of mines in Papua New Guinea, including the method of disposing of the tailings resulting from the processing of the ore, is shown in table 1 (see Hughes 1989a and 1989b for an overview of the environmental effects of mining at Misima and Pernetta in 1988 at Ok Tedi).

No environmental impact studies were carried out for Papua New Guinea's first mining project, the massive Bougainville Copper Ltd. (BCL) open cut mine (fig. 1), which began operation in 1971. While this mine has undoubtedly brought major economic benefits, the environmental costs have been considerable (Chambers 1985:179–81). In the 10-year period from 1975 BCL contributed about K660 million to the State, more than 20 percent of the country's internally generated revenue. In 1987 alone BCL paid more than K55 million in taxes to the State. In addition the State, which held 19 percent of the shares in the company, also received more than K17 million in dividends (BCL 1987).

Between 1973 and 1989, when the mine was forced to close, about one billion tonnes of ore and waste were processed. About half of this was deposited in rock waste dumps adjacent to the mine. The remainder, mostly tailings from ore processing, was discharged into the Jaba River valley. The coarser fraction of the tailings covered the floor of the thirty-five-km-long valley up to thirty m deep and one km wide, elevat-

Table 1

Characteristics of Mines in Papua New Guinea in 1991

Mine[a]	Tailings Tonnes/ Day	Mine Life	Work Force	Tailings Disposal Method
Bougainville	135,000	30	4,000	Into river.
Ok Tedi	80,000	30	2,500	Into river. >10,000 t/day of fine waste rock also enters river.
Misima	15,000	10	350	Deep ocean via submarine pipeline. 10,000 t/day of soft waste rock is dumped directly into ocean.
Lihir	13,250	30	1,300	Deep ocean via submarine pipeline. 75,000 t/day of soft waste rock will be dumped directly into ocean.
Hidden Valley[b]	10,000	10	300	Storage in tailings dam.
Porgera	9,000	18	900	Into river.
Mt. Kare[c]	3,000	3	200	Into river
Wau	1,400	9	280	Into river
Mt. Victor	400	2	100	Storage in sealed limestone sinkhole
Lakekamu[bc]	—	10	160	Virtually all rock wastes will be contained within the dredging area.

[a] Environmental plans (listed in the references) have been prepared for all these mines, except Bougainville and Ok Tedi.

[b] Hidden Valley and Lakekamu are still at the planning stage. The others have been or are operating mines.

[c] Lakekamu and Mt. Kare are alluvial or colluvial deposits. The others are all hard rock open cut mines, although a small part of the Porgera ore body is being mined by underground methods.

ing the river bed by as much as sixty m and transforming the single, sinuous channel into a straight, wide-braided stream. A delta about 700 ha in area accumulated at the mouth of the river. The fine fraction was carried in suspension to the sea and has accumulated on the floor of Empress Augusta Bay. These tailings were rich in copper (800–1000 ppm) and other chemicals. All aquatic life in the Jaba floodplain has been destroyed as a result of this physical and chemical pollution.

As Chambers 1985:181 pointed out, the project was commissioned with no regard for its impact on the environment, especially aquatic life, and it is unlikely that such a project would gain approval in Papua New Guinea today. For economic reasons BCL was in the process of altering its discharge system to pipe tailings directly to the shoreline of Empress Augusta Bay, bypassing the Jaba River at the time the mine closed. This proposed disposal scheme was being subjected to rigorous environmental planning controls, and BCL had commissioned several studies to evaluate various aspects of this current project. The new tailings disposal system would have had much less impact on the environment and would have allowed the partial environmental rehabilitation of much of the Jaba River floodplain.

In 1973 the first major forestry scheme in Papua New Guinea, the Gogol project in Madang Province (fig. 1), was commissioned without any prior environmental or feasibility studies to assess the suitability of the area or the project's economic viability (Chambers 1985: 183–184). The project involves large-scale clear felling of lowland tropical mixed hardwood forest, mainly for woodchipping, in a lease area originally covering 68,000 ha, but since extended. The original plan envisaged reafforestation and agricultural development of much of the logged land. In fact the rate of reafforestation has been slow and virtually none of the planned agricultural developments (rice, rubber, cattle, and agroforestry) have been implemented. Chambers concluded that there is no doubt that the Gogol project has been a disaster, at least for the local villagers. They have seen much of their natural environment destroyed, along with a great deal of their traditional way of life. Few of the expected benefits from employment, financial compensation for loss of land and resources, and reafforestation and agricultural schemes have eventuated and this has left the residents angry and bitter.

Unlike the generally good record the mining industry currently has for environmental and social planning, as well as economic performance, the forestry industry has been severely adversely affected by corrupt practices and economic and environmental mismanagement, as documented in the Commission of Enquiry into Aspects of the Forestry Industry in Papua New Guinea (Barnett 1989). Numerous forestry projects have been permitted since the environmental legislation described below was enacted in 1978, but with very few exceptions development approval has been given by the Department of Forests without regard to the requirements of the environmental legislation. Many of these projects were approved under the Forestry (Private Dealings) Act 1972 and 1974 which, as outlined below, did not specifically require environmental impact studies to be carried out. Where environmental plans have been prepared they have in most cases not fully addressed the likely environmental impacts. There have been occasional encouraging indications from some forestry environmental plans of a greater acceptance by the industry of the need for sound environmental planning and management (for example Saulei and Daur 1988), but no philosophy of aiming for excellence in environmental planning has yet been adopted by the forestry industry.

Successive governments have acknowledged the issues raised by the Barnett Enquiry and the World Bank–sponsored tropical forestry action plan review (World Bank 1990). The government committed itself to implementing in the early 1990s a new national forestry structure, forest policy, and legislation. The UNDP and other agencies are assisting with the development of a number of projects under the National Forestry and Conservation Action Programme (NFCAP), and in the finalisation of the new structures and legislation. Once fully implemented, it was envisaged that these measures would lead to a considerable improvement in environmental planning and management strategies and practices in the forestry sector. A forestry code of practice, approved by all stakeholders, was accepted by government in late 1996.

A major initial feature of the NFCAP was that it included an ambitious scheme to create an expanded network of Protected Areas, including World Heritage Areas (see King and Hughes, this volume). After 1993 the NFCAP focus was shifted from conservation management to the improvement of logging practices. Conservation management of forested areas became the focus of a United Nations–sponsored Global Environment Facility (GEF) integrated conservation and development (ICAD) project, and a diverse range of local and international non-government organisation (NGO)–sponsored regional plans.

The Environmental Legislation

The Fourth Goal and Directive Principle of the Papua New Guinea Constitution (1975) states: 'We declare our fourth goal to be for Papua New Guinea's natural resources and environment to be conserved and used for the collective benefit of us all, and to be replenished for the benefit of future generations.'

The Environmental Planning Act 1978 was enacted to give effect to the Fourth Goal and to protect the country's natural resources and environment, defined (sect. 2) as 'the total stock of physical, biological and social resources available to man and other species and the ecosystems of which they form a part.' The Guidelines to the Act (Sect. 5) recognise that environmental planning involves the consideration of eleven matters listed a–k, including (j) 'any permanent change in the physical, biological, social or cultural characteristics of the affected environment or in the possible future use of that environment' (Department of Environment and Conservation 1985).

Briefly, this Act requires a proponent of any development:

a)   to liaise with the Department of Environment and Conservation to determine if there is a need to prepare an environmental plan, and if necessary,

b)   to produce an environmental plan, which must be assessed before any decision concerning the development is finalised.

The plan must outline all aspects of the development project, including any changes in the social, cultural, physical, or biological characteristics; the use and discharge of contaminants; the costs and advantages of the project; the long- and short-term objectives; and any other matters considered necessary by the Secretary of the Department (Bargh n.d.:2).

Both the assessment and decision-making processes require consultation with local communities as well as the national and provincial governments. In addition to preparing a detailed plan the proponent must provide an executive summary of the proposal including its major benefits and disadvantages, and that summary must be produced in both English and either *Tok Pisin* or *Motu* as appropriate.

All government departments and authorities, as well as private developers, are bound by the Environmental Planning Act 1978. Fines of up to K500 are specified for several potential omissions or failures to respond appropriately to its requirements. A fine of up to K40,000 is payable for failure to observe the development conditions imposed under the Act, or for undertaking a project without government permission. During 1995 and 1996 wide-ranging consultations resulted in the development of regulations and codes of practice for some industries, and negotiations are proceeding with other industry groups.

Certain projects have been exempted from this Act and are instead covered by specific acts. To date these are: the Mining (Bougainville Copper Agreement) Act 1967, the Mining (Ok Tedi Agreement) Act 1976 and seven subsequent Supplemental Agreements, and the Petroleum (Gulf of Papua Agreements) Act 1976. Ok Tedi was, however, required to submit a detailed environmental plan under its enabling legislation and the BCL operation was subject to an environmental audit in 1976. In 1990 Chevron Niugini submitted an environmental plan for its Kutubu petroleum development project under the Environmental Planning Act.

In terms of the physical, biological, and social environment, a number of other acts are also important to the planning of resource development projects and associated infrastructure. These include the Environmental Contaminants Act 1978, the Water Resources Act 1982, as well as acts relating to town planning, public health, forestry, and mining (Eaton 1984).

Until mid-1992 forestry development was governed by two separate acts, the Forestry Act (Amalgamated) 1973 and 1975 and the Forestry (Private Dealings) Act 1972 and 1974. The former included a provision that the requirements of the Environmental Planning Act 1978 be adhered to. The Private Dealings Act, which was enacted to facilitate forestry agreements between villagers and prospective developers with minimal bureaucratic process, did not specifically refer to a need for environmental investigations. These two acts have been replaced by the Forestry Act 1991 which came into effect in 1992. Since 1992 the administration of forest policies and forestry management has undergone several major changes, and such changes are likely to continue. Currently the national Department of Forests formulates policy, and management is undertaken by regional and local forest authorities, with the advice of provincial forestry committees which include community representatives.

Other relevant legislation is the Conservation Areas Act 1978, which was enacted to conserve and manage sites and areas having particular biological, topographical, geological, historic, scientific, or social importance. This Act could theoretically be applied to the protection and management of elements of the cultural environment, and especially be applied to the management of any archaeological sites or places of traditional significance; however, it is not likely to be so in the foreseeable future given financial and staffing restrictions (Swadling 1983a:91). In Papua New Guinea the links between cultural issues and broader social issues (and likely impacts on both) are close. As a result there is frequently an overlap or commonality of interest between social and cultural impact assessments, an overlap which should be beneficial to the interests of cultural resource management.

The enactment of wide-ranging environmental planning legislation has had similar effects on natural and cultural resource management in Papua New Guinea as, for instance, the Environmental Planning and Assessment Act 1979 had in New South Wales. In both cases it strengthened existing legislation, which was difficult to enforce, by obliging developers to consider during the planning process likely impacts on natural and cultural resources (Sullivan and Hughes 1987).

The Department of Environment and Conservation (DEC) has acknowledged that it is unable to undertake environmental appraisals of even small-scale developments and has delegated this role, and that of preparing management plans, to project managers (including Department of Transport and Works officers) in the provinces.

An encouraging development in the late 1980s was the requirement of the aid agencies of foreign governments (e.g. Australia and the European Community) and the major lending institutions (e.g. the World bank and the Asian Development Bank) that environmental effects be considered at the feasibility stage for all development projects for which aid or loan funds are sought by the Papua New Guinea government. The practice of stringent environmental appraisal of such projects has now become well established.

Commenting on Papua New Guinea's environmental legislation soon after it had begun to be implemented, Spenceley (1980) noted that newly emerging independent nations such as Papua New Guinea were likely to be at an advantage over industrialised nations with regard to environmental legislation, since they could observe and avoid some of the problems which these nations had faced. After outlining the environmental legislation which Papua New Guinea had adopted, he pointed out that most of the country's population was still unaware of this legislation and that it would become effective only if people were educated to be aware of their own responsibilities, as well as those of large-scale developers. To a considerable extent the publicity surrounding environmental management problems such as those which beset the Ok Tedi and Bougainville mining projects and the Gogol timber project (Chambers 1985), and widespread media coverage of arguments about the practicability of building a tailings dam for the Porgera gold mine, have served to make the general Papua New Guinean population much more aware of the legislation than was the case in 1980, without the formal educative process which Spenceley saw as necessary. The public relations disaster which befell Ok Tedi in the mid-1990s (when landowners took legal action against the company) highlights the fact that landowner groups now have a well-developed awareness of their rights in relation to environmental issues.

A variety of nongovernmental organisations (NGOs) concerned with environmental issues are established in Papua New Guinea. These organisations have links with governments, political, and church organisations. Some are principally environmental organisations (e.g. the Friends of the Earth PNG, Melanesian Environment Foundation, and the Wau Ecology Institute), others developmental (e.g. the South Pacific Appropriate Technology Foundation and the Foundation for the Peoples of the South Pacific), and yet others are special interest groups (e.g. the PNG Bird Society). NGOs have been working in isolation from each other without much coordination and hence with reduced effect. Recognising this, the leading NGOs have formed the National Alliance of Non-Governmental Organisations (NANGO), one of whose major aims is to promote coordination of efforts in conservation and environmental protection. International NGOs, working with local counterpart organisations, have become increasingly active in conservation management in PNG during the 1990s.

Because of bureaucratic awareness that the Papua New Guinean population is generally poorly educated, government agencies have attempted to produce documents containing clear, simple advice to developers, made readily available through those agencies, provincial governments, and development authorities. These documents not only set out the practical requirements of the acts, but also advise consultation with all relevant government authorities. It is to be hoped that governments and NGOs (and indeed developers) work more closely together to disseminate a broad range of environmental educational materials to the community at large.

Implementation of Environmental Planning Legislation

Numerous environmental plans were submitted during the late 1980s in compliance with the Environmental Planning Act 1978. These include gold mining proposals (fig. 1) for:

- Misima Island in Milne Bay Province (Natural Systems Research [NSR] 1987a)
- Porgera (NSR 1988) and Mt. Kare (Mt. Kare Mining 1988) in Enga Province
- Mt. Victor in the Eastern Highlands Province (NSR 1987b)
- Wau (NSR 1985) and Hidden Valley in Morobe Province (Hidden Valley Gold 1989)
- Lakekamu in Gulf Province (Beca Gure 1988)
- Lihir Island in New Ireland Province (NSR 1989)

A plan was prepared for the Kutubu petroleum development project (NSR 1990), comprising field production facilities in Southern Highlands Province and an export pipeline to a marine terminal in the Gulf of Papua (in Gulf Province).

Environmental plans were also prepared for agricultural developments, especially oil palm and cocoa, for forestry, and for industry and infrastructure. Industrial and infrastructure environmental plans include those for a meat cannery at Madang, the Lae City garbage disposal site, the Joyce Bay sewerage scheme in Port Moresby, and stage two of the Ramu hydroelectric power generation scheme at Yonki in the Eastern Highlands. The Joyce Bay (Water Board of PNG 1987) and Yonki (Cameron McNamara Kramer 1985, 1986) reports especially give comprehensive accounts of a wide range of potential environmental problems and of measures that have been or will be implemented to mitigate them.

During the 1990s the rate of new development proposals, especially in mining and petroleum extraction, slowed and very few additional environmental plans were prepared.

Most plans for major agricultural development projects have been prepared by the proponents themselves, and they generally give very superficial accounts of the biophysical impacts and even less consideration to impacts on the cultural or social environment, especially the living conditions of the settlers brought in to service these developments and the adjacent local communities (see for example Cox 1987).

Nevertheless the projects have generally obtained government approval with few if any additional conditions being imposed.

Whereas biophysical aspects are always addressed in environmental plans, cultural and social resources are frequently not given proper consideration; recent draft environmental plans for some large-scale developments, particularly forestry, give at best a cursory consideration of impact on cultural resources, for example. This prompted the PNG National Museum and other concerned groups and individuals to comment forcefully on the lack of proper consideration of such impact. For instance, the Ok Tedi mining project environmental study report (Maunsell and Partners 1982) did not consider the likely impact that the project might have on archaeological sites. The results of a regional survey subsequently carried out by the PNG National Museum of the Ok Tedi impact area and its surroundings (fig. 1), demonstrated that in fact it contains a diverse range of archaeological, traditional, and material cultural resources (Swadling 1983b).

BROADER ENVIRONMENTAL CONSIDERATIONS

Despite financial, manpower, and other constraints, Papua New Guinea is legislatively well placed to ensure that biophysical, cultural, and social resources are properly considered in the environmental planning process, at least as it applies to new, generally large-scale developments. In 1994 an AusAID five-year institutional strengthening project commenced in DEC. This project has enabled DEC to develop regulations and industry agreements to strengthen its existing legislation. Judicious use of the provisions of the Environmental Contaminants Act and the Water Resources Act is resulting in more effective regulation of smaller-scale, ongoing activities not subject to the Environmental Planning Act. This included the import, distribution, use, and disposal of hazardous substances such as pesticides, and the use of water and the discharge of waste products by coffee and oil palm processing factories. Regulations for the import of pesticides and some other hazardous chemicals were gazetted in 1996.

The existing environmental planning and protection process copes reasonably well with project-by-project assessments. There is however already a need in some areas for environmental planning concepts to be applied on a regional basis. One such area is the Fly-Strickland river system which already carries the wastes from three mines; Ok Tedi, Porgera, and Mt. Kare, and which is likely to be affected by even more mines in the future (see Hughes and Sullivan 1989, Sullivan and Hughes 1988).

The existing bureaucracy and the environmental legislation it administers are not able to regulate the everyday activities of ordinary Papua New Guineans, activities which, as illustrated by the following three examples, can have considerable environmental impacts. In many cases it would be inappropriate, or even constitutionally impossible, for governments to intervene in such activities.

- The alluvial deposits along the Bulolo and Watut Rivers in the Morobe goldfield area have been extensively mined since the 1960s by Papua New Guineans using small-scale sluicing methods (Bowers 1985). These activities have continuously added at least as much suspended sediment to the river system as the tailings from the open cut mine at Wau, ensuring that the rivers remain constantly turbid. In recent years some of these small-scale miners have increased their scale of operation, and hence their impact on the environment, through the use of bulldozers and large bucket excavators.

- During the Mt. Kare gold rush in Enga Province, which at its peak in the late 1980s saw about 6,000 miners working the gold-rich colluvial deposits, the ground surface over an area of more than 200 ha was completely devegetated and the top few metres of colluvium over much of this area was completely worked over. As a result very large amounts of fine sediment were washed away and the river system remained permanently turbid for many kilometres downstream. Sanitary conditions in the shanty settlements in the forest around the goldfield were appalling and all streams draining the area were heavily polluted with human wastes. The forest was ravaged by people cutting timber for the construction of dwellings and other buildings, and for firewood.

- In a study by Unisearch PNG (1991) for the Papua New Guinea government it was estimated that in the late 1980s the annual rates of forest disturbance or destruction resulting from human activity were about 300,000 ha a year

(table 2). Subsistence agriculture, particularly shifting cultivation, has the greatest impact and while it is true that
much of the forest regenerates successfully, in areas where
increasing population densities result in a shortening of
fallow periods the forest may ultimately convert to secondary bush and then grassland. Other 'uncontrolled' activities such as firewood collection, resettlement, and urban
and village expansion are also degrading or destroying the
forest ecosystems.

Table 2
Annual Rates of Forest Disturbance and Destruction

Activity	Rate (ha/yr)	Type
Logging		
Clear-felling	6,000	Deforestation
Selective	70,000	Mainly disturbance
Agriculture		
Subsistence	200,000	Mainly disturbance
Commercial	10,000	Deforestation
Other Processes		
Mining	1,000	Mainly deforestation
Firewood	2,000	Mainly disturbance
Resettlement	5,000	Mainly deforestation
Infrastructure	2,000	Deforestation
TOTAL	296,000	

Source: Unisearch PNG, 1991, table 2.9.

CONCLUSIONS

While major developments such as mining and petroleum extraction
are subject to close evaluation of environmental impacts and to agreed
planning and developmental regulations this is still not the case with
resource industries such as agriculture and forestry. There are no mechanisms for regulating the effects of subsistence activities such as agriculture and small-scale mining. It is likely that such regulation will

only come about when and where local communities perceive that their activities are not sustainable in the long term, and that it will be effective only if the communities themselves are closely involved in its formulation and implementation.

REFERENCES

Bargh, B. J., n.d. *Environmental Handbook for Developers: A Guide to Environmental Approvals for Development Projects in Papua New Guinea.* Konedobu: Water Resources Bureau.

Barnett, T. E., 1989. *Commission of Enquiry into Aspects of Forestry in Papua New Guinea* (20 volumes). Port Moresby: The Ombudsman Commission.

BCL, 1987. *Annual Report 1987.* Bougainville Copper Ltd., Panguna, Papua New Guinea.

Beca Gure Pty. Ltd., 1988. *Lakekamu Gold Project Environmental Plan.* Lae: City Resources Ltd.

Cameron McNamara Kramer Pty. Ltd., 1985. *Yonki Dam Environmental Assessment: Physical Environment.* Boroko: PNG Electricity Commission.

———, 1986. *Yonki Dam Environmental Plan.* Boroko: PNG Electricity Commission.

Chambers, M. R., 1985. 'Environmental management problems in Papua New Guinea', *The Environmental Professional,* 7: 178–185.

Cox, E., 1987. 'Women in resettlement schemes: institutionalised gender bias and informal gender abuses', in S. Stratigos and P. J. Hughes, eds., *The Ethics of Development: Women as Unequal Partners in Development.* Port Moresby: University of Papua New Guinea Press, pp. 28–49.

Department of Environment and Conservation, 1985. *Environmental Planning Act: General Guidelines for the Preparation and Content of Environmental Plans.* Boroko, PNG.

Eaton, P., 1984. 'Institutional and legislative frameworks in the field of environment in Papua New Guinea'. *Country Monograph PNG.* Bangkok: UN Economic and Social Commission for Asia and the Pacific.

Hidden Valley Gold, 1989. *Hidden Valley Gold Project Final Environmental Plan.* South Melbourne: Hidden Valley Gold Pty. Ltd.

Hughes, P. J., 1989a. 'Mining and minerals processing', in R. A. Carpenter and J. C. Maragos, eds., *How to Assess Environmental Impacts on Tropical Islands and Coastal Areas.* Hawaii: Environment and Policy Institute, East-West Centre, pp. 175–186.

———, 1989b. 'The effects of mining on the environments of high islands: a case study of mining on Misima Island, Papua New Guinea'. *Environmental Case Studies: South Pacific Study No. 5.* Noumea: South Pacific Regional Environment Programme, South Pacific Commission.

Hughes, P. J., and Sullivan, M. E., 1988. 'Population, land use and gold mining in Papua New Guinea', *Yagl Ambu,* 15(2):40–60.

———, 1989. 'Environmental impact assessment in Papua New Guinea: lessons for the wider Pacific region', *Pacific Viewpoint,* 30(1):34–45.

IASER, 1986. *Social Impact Study of the Misima Gold Mine.* Port Moresby: Department of Minerals and Energy.

Jackson, R., n.d. *Ok Tedi: The Pot of Gold.* Port Moresby: University of Papua New Guinea Press.

Löffler, E., 1977. *Geomorphology of Papua New Guinea.* Canberra: Australian National University Press.

Maunsell and Partners, 1982. *Ok Tedi Environmental Study.* 7 volumes. Port Moresby: Ok Tedi Mining Ltd.

Mt. Kare Mining, 1988. *Mt. Kare Colluvial Gold Project Environmental Plan*. South Melbourne: Mt. Kare Mining Pty. Ltd.

Natural Research Systems Pty. Ltd., 1985. *Wau Mine Upgrading Environmental Plan*. Wau: NGG Holdings Ltd.

———, 1987a. *Misima Project Environmental Plan*. Port Moresby: Placer PNG Pty. Ltd.

———, 1987b. *Mt. Victor Project Environmental Plan*. Kainantu: Niugini Mining Ltd.

———, 1988. *Porgera Project Environmental Plan*. Port Moresby: Porgera Joint Venture.

———, 1989. *Lihir Project Draft Environmental Plan*. Port Moresby: Kennecott Exploration (Australia) Pty. Ltd. and Niugini Mining Ltd. Joint Venture.

Paijmans, K., ed. 1976. *New Guinea Vegetation*. Canberra: Australian National University Press.

Pernetta, J. C., ed., 1988. *Potential Impacts of Mining on the Fly River*. UNEP Regional Seas Reports and Studies No. 99.

Saulei, S. M., and Daur, P., 1988. *An environmental impact study on the development of Ioma Block 4 timber project, Oro Province*. Port Moresby: Dewai Resources Pty. Ltd.

Spenceley, A. P., 1980. 'Environmental legislation in Papua New Guinea', *Australian Geographer*, 14:371–373.

Sullivan, M. E., and Hughes, P. J., 1987. 'The application of environmental legislation to cultural resource management in Papua New Guinea', *Environmental Planning and Law Journal*, 4:272–279.

———, 1988. 'Environmental planning and applied geography in Papua New Guinea', *Erdkunde*, 42: 114–123.

Swadling, P., 1983a. 'Papua New Guinea,' in M. Bourke, M. Lewis, and B. Sani, eds., *Protecting the Past for the Future*. Canberra: Australian Government Publishing Service.

———, 1983b. 'How long have people been in the Ok Tedi impact region?' *PNG National Museum Record No. 8*, Boroko.

Unisearch PNG Pty. Ltd., 1991. *United Nations Conference on Environment and Development: Papua New Guinea National Report*. Port Moresby: Government of the Independent State of Papua New Guinea.

Water Board of PNG, 1987. *Environmental Plan: Joyce Bay Sewage Outfall Study*. 2 volumes, Port Moresby: Water Board of PNG.

World Bank, 1990. *Papua New Guinea. The forestry sector: a tropical forestry review*. A report prepared by the World Bank, Washington D.C., under the auspices of the Tropical Forestry Action Plan.

Acknowledgments

This paper was drafted in 1991 while the authors were on the staff of the University of Papua New Guinea and was completed later that year while one of us (PJH) was a University of Auckland Foundation Visitor in Environmental Science and Geography. Minor revisions were made in 1997 to take account of subsequent developments in this field in PNG. The figure was drawn by Jonette Surridge, Cartography Laboratory, Department of Geography, University of Auckland.

Betsy King and Philip J. Hughes

PROTECTED AREAS IN PAPUA NEW GUINEA

$\mathcal{P}$APUA NEW GUINEA, a continental island with surrounding volcanic and coral islands, encompasses in its 462,243 square kilometres enormous social, cultural, and biophysical diversity. Terrestrial habitats range from extensive lowlands with rain forest, savanna, grassland, and freshwater swamp to upland montane rain forests and alpine grassland (table 1). Its marine and aquatic environments, although little explored, appear equally diverse. There are more than 11,000 known species of flora, including 2,000 ferns alone, while the lowland rain forests have more than 1,200 tree species (World Bank 1990:iv). Much of this flora and its associated fauna is unique to Papua New Guinea, with large numbers of endemic species. An estimated 90 percent of angiosperm flora at the species level and 47 percent of breeding land bird species are not found elsewhere (Good 1974; Diamond 1984).

Papua New Guinea society and culture is also richly varied. People have lived in small numbers in lowland Papua New Guinea for at least 40,000 years (Groube *et al.* 1986) and in the highlands for more than 24,000 years (White and O'Connell 1982). With over 750 different linguistic groups, a wide variety of cultural responses to the environment has evolved. There is considerable spatial variation in population density, but of the 4 million inhabitants, 90 percent live in rural areas which are dominated by a subsistence economy. Shifting cultivation provides crops such as yams, sweet potatoes, taro, bananas, and a variety of greens, but hunting of pigs, wallabies, crocodiles, bandicoots, pigeons, echidna, and cassowaries, and collecting of bush plant foods,

383

Table 1
Vegetation and Habitat Cover in Papua New Guinea (after Beehler 1985).

Habitat	Area of Cover	Percent Cover
Undisturbed		
Lowland rain forest	110,615	33.76
Lower montane rain forest	76,180	23.26
Savanna	22,120	6.76
Palm swamp	21,010	6.39
Herbaceous swamp	19,535	5.97
Mangrove	4,800	1.49
Montane forest	4,695	1.43
Alpine	1,720	0.53
Swamp forest	710	0.22
Strand forest	205	0.06
	261,590	79.87%
Disturbed		
Grassland	27,180	8.30
Gardens	21,810	6.66
Degraded forest	15,910	4.80
Plantations	1,200	0.37
	66,100	20.13%

supplements this diet. Wildlife is also important for personal decoration, use on ceremonial occasions, and for its spiritual significance. Despite a long history of use of the environment, the low population densities have left 80 percent of the country still largely undisturbed. Papua New Guinea is therefore fortunate in having the highest remaining proportion of forestland of any tropical region in the world (Beehler 1985).

Traditional Papua New Guinea Societies and Conservation

It is claimed by many that traditional rural society in Papua New Guinea exists in balance with its surroundings. Indeed there are many examples of the ways in which the knowledge and practices of pre-contact Papua New Guinean societies have acted to conserve natural resources. About 98 percent of the total land area in Papua New Guinea is owned by individual clans or villages. Traditionally the owners have all rights to the use of resources, and rules and taboos are imposed to control overuse. Traditional land ownership patterns, for example, often restrict access to forest areas. Only certain groups are permitted to harvest forest products for medicine, magical or ritual purposes, and materials for religious buildings, thus restricting their exploitation. In some areas there are seasonal bans on hunting or fishing to allow stock recovery (Johannes 1982). The imposition of taboos or prohibitions has been used to protect sacred areas, for example burial places or the sites of old battlefields. Social taboos preventing certain sectors of the population from eating particular foods have helped reduce the total impact on those plants and animals. Fear of spirits in an area has also restricted use of parts of forests, caves, lakes, and mountain tops which are regarded as *ples masalai* (Bulmer 1982; Eaton 1985a and 1985b).

Many of the practices associated with gardening also allow sustainable resource use. Every agricultural society in Papua New Guinea has soil conservation techniques which vary according to local conditions. Ditching, mulching, mounding, composting, construction of soil-retaining fences, and mixed cropping help to prevent soil erosion at the same time as increasing fertility and crop yields (Wood and Humphreys 1982). There is also evidence for the tending and maintaining of wild plants and trees and the replanting of those harvested (Powell 1982).

Undeniably then, there are many traditional practices which appear to be conservationist and do result in the wise use of resources both in the short and the long term. On the other hand there is also ample evidence that widespread irreversible change, including forest clearance, took place long before colonial contact (Golson 1977). Archaeological evidence indicates the overhunting and local disappearance of animals such as dugong, megapodes, birds of paradise, tree kangaroos, and giant echidna (Swadling 1977; Pernetta and Hill 1984). It is difficult to argue that those actions which do appear conservationist are a result of a well-developed, conscious conservation ethic. Bulmer (1982) argues that traditional Papua New Guinea societies are concerned with short-term gain, short-term yields, and the minimisation of labour inputs. The immediate welfare of small groups of people is of greater concern to a villager than the benefit of future generations. This theme is reiterated by Allen (1988), who says that the management practices used by a group are determined by the need to compete in agricultural production with other social groups. Some practices have been conservationist while others, for example in the more densely populated highlands, have resulted in widespread land degradation and loss of fauna.

Today there is growing pressure on resources. Population size is increasing rapidly, with a marked decline in mortality but not associated decrease in fertility. Census data for 1970, 1980, and 1990 indicate that the average annual population growth rate has been between 2.1 and 2.5 percent. In the period 1971–1980 the total urban population increased at a rate of 3.4 percent per annum. With the influx of western ideas, traditional precontact land management practices are being replaced by those involving advanced technologies. As the monetary sector of the economy increases there have inevitably been increased ecosystem disturbances by agriculture, logging, mining, and other development projects. Conservation of the country's rich resources has therefore become a matter of national concern, and this concern has been translated into formal policy and legislation.

DEVELOPMENT OF THE PROTECTED AREAS SYSTEM

The first legislation allowing designation of protected areas in Papua New Guinea was the 1966 National Parks and Gardens Act, replaced in 1971 and then in 1982 by the National Parks Act. Inspiration came from the national parks concept pioneered in the United States by the establishment of the Yellowstone National Park in 1872. The initiative to set aside a protected area under the National Parks Act comes not from the landowners but principally from national and provincial governments. There is no provision in the Act for establishing conservation areas on privately owned land. Areas 'to provide for the preservation of the environment and of the national cultural inheritance' can be set aside on land which has been purchased, given as a gift, or leased from the landowner by the government. In the United States such acquisition of private land for national parks was possible in the nineteenth century because it was considered 'that wild areas suitable for conservation were unsuitable for sustaining the traditional economic pursuits of the

American Frontier' (Runte 1987). Similar sentiments applied in Australia. Papua New Guinean customary landowners, however, value all their land and are reluctant to sell it. Most land negotiations to date have therefore been on a lease basis or have concerned land already alienated. Usually more than one landowner is involved and protracted negotiations have held up the declaration of many reserves. Not until the land has been surveyed and the landowners have agreed upon and signed the lease can the area be declared in the National Gazette as 'committed to the care, control and management of the Director of National Parks'.

In 1991 there were only nine gazetted areas. Several more had been approved by the landowners involved but not gazetted and many were proposed but not yet fully processed and approved (table 2, fig. 1). Seven different categories of protected area have been identified, although these are not specifically mentioned in the National Parks Act. Just three of the gazetted areas have been designated as National Parks: McAdam, an area of *Araucaria* forest; Varirata with lowland rain forest and savanna; and Ruti in lowland and lower montane rain forest. These are small National Parks by international standards. The other six gazetted areas are even smaller, come under different classifications, and represent a variety of marine and terrestrial habitats as well as historical sites.

These protected areas are managed by a section of the Nature Conservation Division of the Department of Environment and Conservation. In 1988 the section employed twenty-three professional staff, mostly operating in the field from a provincial base with a core of four office-based staff in Port Moresby (table 3). Regulations pertaining to the areas are enforced by field staff, for example the prevention of shooting, trapping, fishing, damage to flora, and the collection of admission fees. Field staff are also responsible for liaison with local people, both during and after land negotiations, and for all the informal conservation education in their respective provinces. This is a massive task for which staff have little time available. In 1982 the Education Section of the Department of Environment and Conservation was disbanded because of lack of finance. Although one member of staff is responsible for provision of information, there is little assistance given to the provinces in this task.

The lack of precise definition of protected area categories in the Act has led to management difficulties, compounded by the fact that none of the areas gazetted has a working plan of management. Management

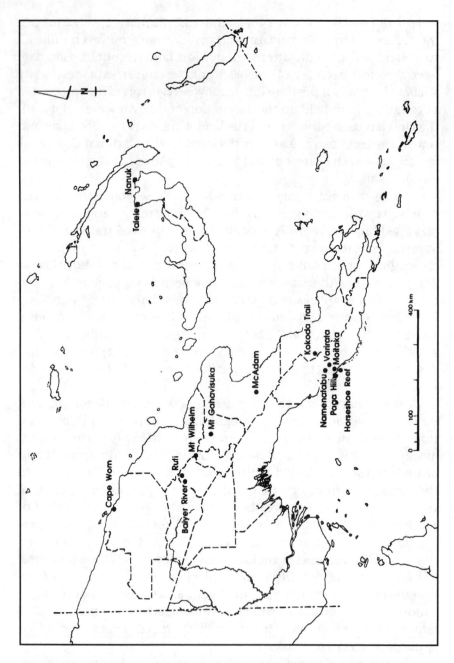

Fig. 1. Areas declared under the National Parks Act in Papua New Guinea (see table 2 for details). Map by Jonette Surridge, Cartography Laboratory, Department of Geography, University of Auckland.

Table 2
Areas Declared under the National Parks Act in Papua New Guinea

Classifica-tion	Function	Areas Gazetted or Approved by the Landown-ers[a]	Date of Gazettal	Area (ha)
National Park	1. Conservation of natural habitats	McAdam (Morobe)	1962	2,080
	2. Public use and under-standing	Varirata (Central)	1969	1,063
		Ruti (Western Highlands)	1986	4,180
	3. Education and research	Mt. Wilhelm (Simbu)	*	810
Provincial Park	1. Outdoor recreation	Mt. Gahavisuka (Eastern High-lands)	*	77
	2. Scenic importance	Paga Hill (NCD) (Scenic Reserve)	1986	13
Historical Reserve	1. Preservation of areas of historic significance	Cape Wom (East Sepik)	1969	105
	2. Public use and under-standing	Namenatabu (Central)	1979	27
Nature Reserve	1. Preservation of ecosys-tems and habitats	Talele (East New Britain)	1972	40
	2. Scientific research	Nanuk (East New Britain)	1973	14
National Walking Track	1. Provide for long distance walking in natural sur-roundings	Kokoda Trail (Central and Oro)	*	84
Sanctuary	1. Education and research about PNG Wildlife	Moitaka (Cen-tral)	*	43
		Baiyer River (Western High-lands)	1968	740

Table 2 (Continued)
Areas Declared under the National Parks Act in Papua New Guinea

Classifica-tion	Function	Areas Gazetted or Approved by the Landown-ers[a]	Date of Gazettal	Area (ha)
Marine Park	1. Conservation of marine habitats	Horseshoe Reef (Central)	*	396
	2. Research			
	3. Recreation			

Source: Department of Environment and Conservation Handbook 1988.

a Locations of these areas are shown in fig. 1.

Table 3
Field-Based Professional Staff, National Parks Section, 1988

Provincial Ranger		Ranger	
Central	1	Varirata	3
		Moitaka	1
Lae/Madang	1	McAdam	1
		Kokoda Trail	1
East/West Sepik	1	Cape Wom	2
Eastern Highlands/Simbu	1	Mt. Wilhelm	2
		Mt. Gahavisuka	1
Western Highlands	1	Baiyer River	2

plans are, unfortunately, not a statutory requirement. Recognising their importance, the National Parks Section produced their first Draft Management Plan for Mount Gahavisuka Provincial Park in the Eastern Highlands Province, in 1987. The two-year plan was produced after consultations with the local people, park rangers, and provincial and national government staff. It sets out short-, medium- and long-term management prescriptions which are prioritised according to available funds. Funding and suitable management are of course closely linked. As a Provincial Park, Mount Gahavisuka receives financial support from the Eastern Highlands Province. In other areas, however, funding all comes from a national source. Financial restraints imposed first by the

1982 national budget and reiterated in subsequent budgets have severely limited the management possibilities in these areas. Management plans can act as a useful funding tool and may assist the future development of protected areas if they become more widely available. They are also a means of fostering the understanding and valuable support of local people. With the present financial restrictions only areas which accrue revenue from recreational use (Varirata, Baiyer River, Cape Wom, and Mount Wilhelm) receive any substantial capital input, leaving less accessible areas without assistance. National Parks had an overall budget of just K460,000 (US$550,000) in 1988, reflecting the low priority given to conservation relative to projects which generate income. Lack of staff and resources has so far severely limited park management and provision for informal conservation education.

Gazetted areas are not always those areas most in need of protection, but merely those involving the least procedural difficulties. A total of a little more than 8,000 hectares have so far been gazetted, 0.02 percent of the total land area of Papua New Guinea. Ruti National Park, 4,180 hectares of lowland and lower montane rain forest in the Jimi Valley, Western Highlands, is the largest and most recently gazetted area. Gazettal was relatively easy as the land was already government owned. Ruti was deemed 'vacant government land with unassessable economic potential'. The surrounding land is sparsely populated and no land-use conflicts have yet arisen. But if future areas are to follow this same pattern, the 98 percent land area held under customary tenure will defy attempts at conservation under the National Parks Act. To attempt to overcome this problem, less conventional legislation was introduced by the government in 1966 and amended in 1979, the Fauna (Protection and Control) Act.

EMERGENCE OF A 'BOTTOM-UP' APPROACH

Landowners have had very little practical involvement with protected areas declared under the National Parks Act. A few local people may work as unskilled labourers in the parks, but in the main the continued traditional use of land is not emphasised. Under the Fauna (Protection and Control) Act it became possible for landowners to request that their land be reserved for their controlled use of wildlife and habitats. Wildlife Management Areas can be declared after consultation with the landowners and the Local Government Council. Sanctuaries, protecting all fauna unless specified by the minister, for safeguarding predetermined species can also be established under the Act. So far a total of twenty-one areas have been declared throughout Papua New Guinea (table 4, fig. 2), covering an area of about 97,000 hectares. Over a hun-

Table 4

Declared Wildlife Management Areas (w), Sanctuaries (s) and
Protected Areas (p) in Papua New Guinea (after Asigau 1989)

Protected Area[a]	Province	Area (ha)	Date
Tonda (w)	Western	590,000	1975
Baniara (p)	Milne Bay	100	1975
Pokili (w)	West New Britain	9,840	1975
Garu (w)	West New Britain	8,700	1975
Bagiai (w)	Madang	13,760	1977
Siwi Utame (w)	Southern Highlands	2,540	1977
Ranba (w)	Madang	41,922	1977
Long Island (s)	Madang	15,724	1977
Sawataetae (w)	Milne Bay	700	1977
Balek (s)	Madang	470	1977
Crown Island (s)	Madang	5,000	1977
Mojirau (w)	East Sepik	5,079	1978
Maza (w)	Western	184,230	1978
Lake Lavu (w)	Milne Bay	5,000	1981
Oia Mada Wa'a (w)	Milne Bay	22,840	1981
Zo-oimaga (w)	Central	1,510	1981
Ndrolowa (w)	Manus	5,850	1985
Nuserang (w)	Morobe	22	1986
Iomare (w)	Central	3,837	1987
Neiru (w)	Gulf	3,984	1987
Pirung (w)	North Solomons	44,240	1989

a Locations of these areas are shown in fig. 2.

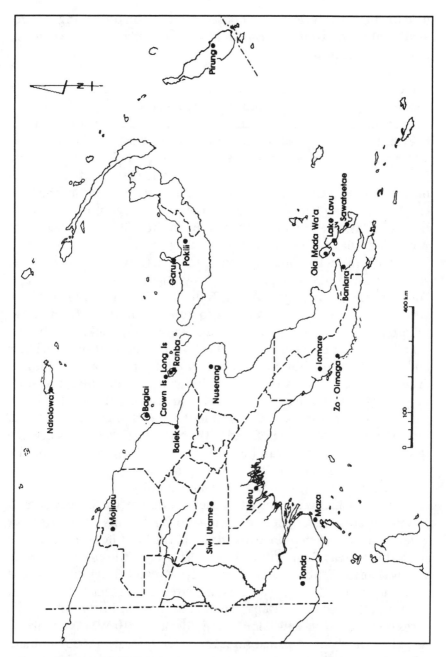

Fig. 2. Declared Wildlife Management Areas, Sanctuaries, and Protected Areas in Papua New Guinea (see table 4 for details). Map by Jonette Surridge, Cartography Laboratory, Department of Geography, University of Auckland.

dred further areas have been proposed, but work on processing the proposals has been extremely slow and most are unlikely to be gazetted in
the foreseeable future.

The initiative to establish a Wildlife Management Area (WMA)
comes usually from landowners worried about the decrease in wildlife
species considered locally important for food, exchange, or decoration.
Often there is a concern that traditional management rules and practices are being ignored or that the resources are being exploited by outsiders. After consultation with a member of staff from the Wildlife
Section of the Department of Environment and Conservation, a Wildlife Management Committee is formed and rules are made for the 'protection, propagation, encouragement, management, control,
harvesting and destruction of the fauna in the Wildlife Management
Area'. The rules are a means of combining good traditional management with modern conservation practices. They also allow for the
administration of licences, fees, and royalties to control wildlife use.
For example in the largest WMA, Tonda in Western Province, those
who do not hold customary rights to hunt in the area are obliged to
obtain a licence to kill a limited number of deer, duck, or fish. The
hunting area is restricted and use of fishing nets or hunting from boats
and vehicles is not allowed. Royalty is payable for each animal caught.
Fifty percent of the royalty is kept by individual landowners; the other
half is kept in a trust account for the development of the whole area. In
this way conservation and development are seen to go hand in hand.
Once the rules have been declared in the National Gazette they become
law and contravention can be punished by a fine of up to K20. The
Committee makes the rules, enforces them, and can change them
when the need arises, allowing for great flexibility.

Unless problems are voiced by the Committee, the Department of
Environment and Conservation has no further involvement after
gazettal. In 1988 there were two officials in the Wildlife Section dealing
with these areas. Initially Wildlife Officers in the provinces were
responsible for visiting management areas at regular intervals. After the
1982 budget cuts the officers were transferred to provincial government
services, attached to the Department of Primary Industry. Some provinces no longer have extension workers dealing with WMAs and many
areas have rarely been visited since their gazettal (Eaton 1986). In Maza
WMA, for example, the rules controlling fishing activities are not being
observed and the landowners are unable to enforce them (Moi and
Willie 1985). Full support from government is needed to maintain the

enthusiasm of landowners for the protection of their resources and to provide practical advice and assistance. Adequate conservation education is also required to ensure that management practices continue as a result of positive conservationist thinking as well as short-term experience (see also Moi 1988).

Wildlife Management Areas have provided a means by which landowners can register land and protect their wildlife from exploitation by outsiders and nontraditional methods. Unfortunately, in some areas increases in population have resulted in the overuse of certain species despite the use of traditional methods. There is no statutory provision for management plans for these areas and the Wildlife Section of the Department of Environment and Conservation has not sufficient staff available either to carry out an initial resource inventory or to write the plans. Without a management plan there is often no link made between the management of wildlife and the maintenance of wildlife habitats. Large undisturbed areas will be needed to protect the future of the many species of birds and mammals in Papua New Guinea which are restricted to forest habitats and are unable to survive the removal of the forest. Wildlife management by the people has proved an excellent means by which the ecological values of customary land can be conserved, but without guidance in modern conservation practice and long-term encouragement there is a danger that these areas will be being managed in name only.

In 1989 a team of senior students from the University of Papua New Guinea, led by Betsy King, visited the Pokili WMA in West New Britain to find out whether wildlife management by the people works in this particular part of Papua New Guinea (King 1990). The Pokili WMA had been established in 1975 in order to regulate the harvesting of megapode eggs and to safeguard the habitat of the megapodes. The team found that fifteen years later the WMA was still vigorously supported by the landowners because harvesting of the eggs brings in a much needed cash income. However, it has proved difficult for the Management Committee to enforce the rules and many of those questioned felt it would be easier for someone outside the community to enforce the rules; perhaps a ranger or warden and guards employed by the provincial government. This would require a financial and manpower commitment by the provincial government which is lacking at present.

It was evident that because the population of the local community was increasing rapidly, as was the need for cash, pressure to harvest the eggs at levels which are not sustainable will inevitably increase. Successful long-term management of the area requires more assistance from the national government through the Department of Environment and Conservation. The villagers do not have the expertise required to monitor changes in megapode numbers and to change their management practices accordingly. Many villagers would like to encourage tourism as an alternative source of income, but again this would require expertise and financial and manpower commitments from both the national and provincial governments. The team concluded that management by the people at Pokili can only work when the people have the necessary knowledge and skills. Neither the national nor the provincial governments have provided the necessary backup so far to ensure that this WMA will continue to work.

THE SYSTEM AT THE END OF THE 1980S: A SUMMARY

At independence in 1975 the National Goals and Directive Principles called in the Fourth Goal of the Constitution for 'Papua New Guinea's natural resources and environment to be conserved for the collective benefit of (us) all and be replenished for the benefit of future generations'. Legislation to achieve this goal with respect to nature conservation led eventually to two distinct styles of protection; the National Parks Act 1982 and the Fauna (Protection and Control) Act 1979. The designation of land under the National Parks Act given to, bought, or leased by the government from landowners for a National Park has progressed very slowly in Papua New Guinea because of land tenure problems. Landowners are reluctant to lose control over their resources for little economic gain. The few areas gazetted under this Act are therefore a very long way from being representative of the country's rich habitats. Because other proposed areas are mostly on customary land it is unlikely that they will be gazetted in the very near future. Those areas already gazetted face problems because there are insufficient staff and finance available to allow the necessary long-term management and extension work with local people.

Wildlife Management Areas declared under the Fauna (Protection and Control) Act have proved more successful with local landowners. Already there are more than fifteen WMAs, but over 100 more proposals are awaiting administrative action by the Department of Environment and Conservation. Although the areas actually or potentially covered by this network of WMAs is larger and more comprehensive than the system of National Parks, they do not yet constitute a representative sample of all the different ecosystems in Papua New Guinea (see also Dahl 1986).

Unless there is a greater commitment by governments in Papua New Guinea to nature conservation, a commitment translated into increased financial and manpower support for the Department of Environment and Conservation and the provincial departments responsible for nature conservation, the existing protected areas system will, at best, expand only very slowly. There are widespread indications that because of the lack of government support many of the protected areas now exist in name only as their natural resources are no longer being effectively managed. Landowners, whose cooperation is essential to the success of these areas, are becoming increasingly dispirited and are unable, or unwilling, to continue to control the exploitation of the areas' resources.

PROSPECTS IN THE 1990S

Throughout the 1980s there was a dramatic increase in global concern about the destruction of earth's remaining extensive natural areas. The tropics in general, and tropical rain forests in particular, have been the focus of special attention. Papua New Guinea's forests are particularly extensive and are well known for their outstanding biodiversity. The Tropical Forestry Action Plan (TFAP) is an international coordinating mechanism for halting the destruction of tropical forests and promoting their sustainable use for the economic and social benefit of people (World Bank 1990:iv). Recognising both the importance of the forest resource of Papua New Guinea and the gravity of the management problems it faces, the government requested the TFAP, through the World Bank, to review the forest sector and propose an action program for the future.

The World Bank (1990)–sponsored review placed considerable emphasis on the need to ensure a balance between forestry and conservation values. In Annex 6 of the report 27 areas warranting environmental protection were identified and very briefly described (table 5, fig. 3). A wide variety of ecosystems and landscapes were included in addition to rain forest: coral reefs, mangroves, savanna woodlands, grasslands, and wetlands. Every province (except Enga) and every major climatic and altitudinal zone was included. While the list of areas described was far from exhaustive it was certainly an excellent basis on which to develop a truly representative protected areas system.

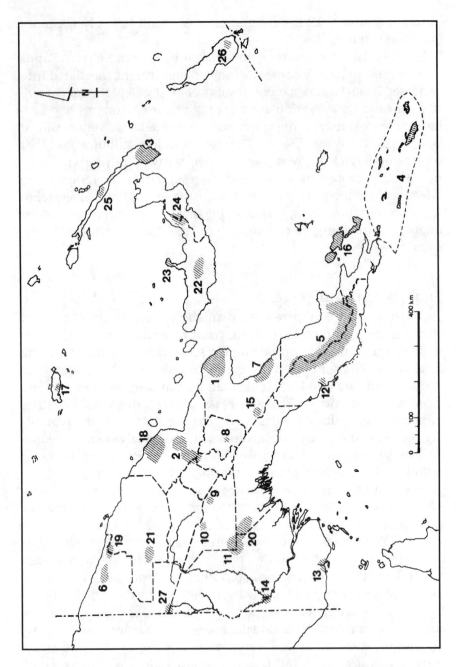

Fig. 3. Proposed new conservation areas in Papua New Guinea (see table 5 for details). Map by Jonette Surridge, Cartography Laboratory, Department of Geography, University of Auckland.

Table 5
Proposed New Conservation Areas (after World Bank 1990: Annex 6)

Area and Province[a]	Environmental Features
1. HUON PENINSULA Morobe	Lowland forest up through montane forest to alpine grassland. Uplifted coral terraces, coastal and glaciated terrain and 40,000-year-old archaeological sites.
2. BISMARK FALLS Madang, Simbu and Eastern Highlands	Lowland forest up through montane forest to alpine grassland. Glaciated terrain on the mountain summits, especially Mt. Wilhelm.
3. SOUTHERN NEW IRELAND New Ireland	Lowland and lower montane forest. Rugged limestone and volcanic landscapes with spectacular 'rift' valley. Highly varied coastal terrain.
4. LOUISIADE ARCHIPELAGO Milne Bay	Complex and extensive coral reefs and lagoons. Forests on islands rich in locally endemic species.
5. OWEN STANLEY RANGES Central, Oro and Milne Bay	The montane forests and alpine grasslands of the mountains of this range have exceptional floral and faunal biodiversity. Glaciated terrain on the mountain summits.
6. TORRICELLI RANGE West Sepik	Lowland and montane forest. Habitat of numerous endemic plant and animal species, including recently discovered tree kangaroo, *Dendrolagus scottae*.
7. MOROBE COAST AND RANGES Morobe	Complex and extremely beautiful coast. Hinterland with lowland and lower montane forest, notably unique forests on ultrabasic rocks.
8. OKAPA Eastern Highlands	Lower montane forest with extensive stands of *Araucaria*. The habitat of PNG's national emblem, *Paradisaea raggiana*.
9. MT. GILUWE Southern Highlands	A stratovolcano with montane forests characterised by extensive stands of *Nothofagus* and celery top pine. The most extensive area of alpine grassland and bogs in PNG. Varied volcanic and glacial landforms.
10. TARI GAP—DOMA PEAK Southern Highlands	A complex of volcanic peaks with montane forests and montane alpine grasslands. Very diverse flora and fauna, especially high altitude birds.
11. MT. BOSAVI Southern Highlands, Western and Gulf	An isolated volcano with lowland and lower montane forest. Many bird species and locally endemic plants. Should be combined with the adjacent Darai Hills (20) for increased diversity of landscapes and ecosystems.

Table 5 (Continued)
Proposed New Conservation Areas (after World Bank 1990: Annex 6)

Area and Province[a]	Environmental Features
12. GALLEY REACH Central	Extensive, diverse mangrove habitats and associated coastal and estuarine bird populations.
13. WASSI-KUSSA Western	A diverse savanna area with unique flora and fauna closely linked with Cape York to the south. Contains coastal and estuarine ecosystems as well.
14. LAKE DAVIUMBU Western	This lake and its associated Fly River plain wetlands support a great variety of water plants, some endemic, and a very rich bird fauna.
15. MENYAMYA ASEKI- Mt. Amungwiwa Morobe	Botanically diverse montane forest. Contains endemic genus *Piora* which is represented only by a single species.
16. GOODENOUGH, NORMANBY AND FERGUSSON ISLANDS Milne Bay	All areas of forest above 700m worthy of protection as there are many plants represented by local species at lower altitudes than on the mainland (Massenergebung effect). Very diverse bird fauna.
17. CENTRAL MANUS Manus	Lowland and lower montane forest from south coast to divide. Diverse flora and fauna.
18. ADELBERT RANGES Madang	Lowland and lower montane forest from the coast up to and including interior mountain ranges.
19. PRINCE ALEXANDRA RANGES East and West Sepik	Lowland and lower montane forest in the mountainous interior.
20. DARAI HILLS Gulf	Spectacular tower limestone terrain. Towers often 200–400m high, each with isolated capping of forest. Extreme scientific interest and diversity.
21. HUNSTEIN MOUNTAINS East Sepik	A biologically very diverse area of lowland and lower montane forest. Type locality for *Araucaria hunstenii*. Extensive stands of the endemic kauri species *Agathis labillardieri*.
22. WHITEMAN RANGES West New Britain	Lowland and lower montane forest on limestone and volcanic rocks. Biologically very diverse, especially the birds, many of which are endemic.
23. LAKE DAKATAUA West New Britain	An area of exceptional scenic beauty. The lake has a saltwater crocodile population, abundant bird and insect life, but no fish.

Table 5 (Continued)
Proposed New Conservation Areas (after World Bank 1990: Annex 6)

Area and Province[a]	Environmental Features
24. NAKANAI PLATEAU East and West New Britain	Lowland and lower and midmontane forest, the latter dominated by two species of *Nothofagus*. Forest is very diverse, with endemic species of *Asplenium*. Internationally renowned extensive cave systems in limestone.
25. LELET PLATEAU New Ireland	Lowland and lower- to midmontane forest of outstanding botanical diversity.
26. MT. TAKUAN North Solomons	Lowland and montane forest of great floral diversity with many Pacific elements. Mountain birds apparently show a high level of endemism.
27. STAR MOUNTAINS West Sepik and Western	A topographically and geologically complex mountainous area with diverse montane forest types with a rich and diverse fauna.

a Locations of these areas are shown in fig. 3.

At least six of the areas were considered to be of potential World Heritage status (World Bank 1990:56).

1. In Morobe Province, the summit of Mt. Bangeba, the terraces of the Huon Peninsula, and broad areas to the coast.
2. In the Madang, Eastern Highlands and Simbu Provinces, the Bismark Falls area, from the Ramu River to the summit regions of Mt. Wilhelm and Mt. Otto, and including the Gahavisuka Provincial Park northeast of Goroka.
3. In southern New Ireland Province, the area of the 'rift' valley and the ranges to the north and south.
4. In Milne Bay Province, the coral reefs and lagoons and islands of the Louisiade archipelago.
5. In Central, Oro, and Milne Bay Provinces, the Owen Stanley Ranges.
6. In West Sepik and East Sepik Provinces, the Torricelli Range.

The government established a National Forestry and Conservation Action Programme (NFCAP) Steering Committee to give effect to the recommendations of the World Bank report. Donor agencies indicated that once the government was in a position to implement specific proposals considerable funding was likely to be forthcoming. Particular interest was expressed in funding conservation initiatives, and many international NGOs, working with local NGOs, were keen to assist in their implementation. Indications were that more than K100 million might be forthcoming for conservation projects over the next decade or so. In mid-1991 six broad projects relating to conservation issues were proposed for implementation under the NFCAP. These projects, and progress in their implementation, are described below.

Strengthening the Department of Environment and Conservation

A project was designed to develop and enhance the management capacity and capability of the Department to adequately handle the requirements of environmentally sound and sustainable utilisation of the forests of Papua New Guinea. This included a review of existing environment and conservation legislation and of the Department's structure and manpower and resources requirements. Following that review a major five-year AusAID project to strengthen the Department commenced in 1994. A smaller-scale human resources development AusAID project was also implemented in the Department of Forests.

Rehabilitation of Existing Reserves

A review of existing reserves and a programme to strengthen management of these, and an upgrading of facilities was initiated by the World Wide Fund for Nature (WWF). The review was completed in 1992 and some key areas of forested land were 'adopted' by various international nongovernment organisations (NGOs) for upgrading management.

Biodiversity Studies

A project to collect information on biodiversity sufficient to determine and manage a series of reserves to conserve biodiversity was coordinated by Conservation International and resulted in a map and two-volume publication identifying areas of high conservation value. Some of the areas identified have been the subject of conservation management plans by various international NGOs, with a view to their gazettal as protected areas. These include highland and lowland forested areas, wetlands, and marine areas.

Conservation Areas/World Heritage Proposal

It was planned to acquire and to manage a comprehensive range of conservation reserves (including World Heritage areas) tentatively estimated to cover 20 percent of Papua New Guinea. There has been little progress with this endeavour to date.

Environmental Task Force

It was hoped to provide a mechanism for resolution of conflict between conservation and development as an interim measure prior to more permanent solutions through NFCAP programmes. Subsequent strengthening of the Department of Environment and Conservation's capacity has made this less urgent.

Landowner Awareness Project

The World Bank established a training and awareness information programme whereby mobile teams were trained to carry out extension activities with landowners. Awareness information was distributed to local community groups for discussion. The outcomes of this project have been disappointing, but there may be longer term benefits not yet perceived.

The ambitious programme envisaged in 1991 required a cooperative effort by national and provincial governments, landowners, and NGOs on an unprecedented scale. Because new conservation areas would be established almost entirely on customarily owned land, the Department of Environment and Conservation recognised that it would be necessary from the outset to involve the landowners in the planning process. In particular as landowners would have to forego potential revenue from economic activities such as large-scale commercial logging and plantation agriculture, activities which are incompatible with long-term conservation goals, incentive packages would have to be devised which would help the landowners to utilise the forest and other resources in an environmentally sound and sustainable manner.

It was envisaged that the incentive packages would vary between areas, and might include infrastructure and social services such as roads, schools, and health centres, and small business enterprises such as portable sawmills, orchid, and butterfly farming and tourism. These incentive packages would require considerable financial and technical support, particularly from the international donor community. The experience in the mining sector suggested that negotiations over land

and incentive packages would be very complex and lengthy and would need to be undertaken on an area-by-area basis.

Two such projects were commenced. One was an AusAID project to conserve the habitat of the Queen Alexandria butterfly, which is underway in Oro Province and which has established land use zones aimed at providing habitat protection. The other was an ambitious UN-supported Global Environment Facility (GEF) integrated conservation and development (ICAD) project initiated in New Ireland Province. Disappointingly, midway through that ICAD project local landowners allowed a forestry company to log the entire area proposed for conservation management. Smaller-scale forest management and rehabilitation projects have however met with some success in West New Britain and West Sepik Provinces.

The government still proposes to nominate some of these conservation areas for World Heritage listing under the World Heritage Fund administered by UNESCO. Papua New Guinea is not yet a member of the Fund. Should Papua New Guinea formally apply to join, this would convey to UNESCO and to the wider international community a clear signal that Papua New Guinea is prepared to commit itself to the programme of action set out in the NFCAP process.

REFERENCES

Allen, B. J., 1988. 'Environmental Ethics and Village Agriculture', in P. J. Hughes and C. Thirwall, eds., *Ethics and Development: Choices in Development Planning*. Port Moresby: University of Papua New Guinea.

Asigau, W., 1989. 'The Wildlife Management Area System in Papua New Guinea'. Paper presented at the Fourth South Pacific Conference on Nature Conservation and Protected Areas, Port Vila, Vanuatu, 4–12 September 1989.

Beehler, B., 1985. *Conservation of New Guinea Rainforest Birds*. ICBP Technical Publication No. 4:233–247.

Bulmer, R. N. H., 1982. 'Traditional Conservation Practices in Papua New Guinea', in L. Morauta, J. C. Pernetta, and W. Heaney, eds., *Traditional Conservation in Papua New Guinea: Implications for Today*. Port Moresby: Papua New Guinea Institute of Applied Social and Economic Research, 59–78.

Dahl, A. L., 1986. *Review of the Protected Areas System in Oceania*. Nairobi: UNEP/IUCN.

Department of Environment and Conservation, 1988. *1988 Handbook*. Papua New Guinea: Department of Environment and Conservation.

Diamond, J., 1984. 'Biogeographic Mosaics in the Pacific', in F. J. Radovsky, ed., *Biogeography of the Tropical Pacific*. Honolulu: B.P. Bishop Museum.

Eaton, P., 1985a. 'Tenure and Taboo: Customary Rights and Conservation in the South Pacific', in *Proceedings of the South Pacific National Parks and Reserves Conference*. Noumea: South Pacific Commission.

———, 1985b. *Land Tenure and Conservation: Protected Areas in the South Pacific*. SPREP Topic Review No. 17. Noumea: South Pacific Commission.

————, 1986. *Wildlife Management Areas in Papua New Guinea.* Land Studies Centre Report 86/1. Port Moresby: University of Papua New Guinea.

Good, R., 1974. *The Geography of Flowering Plants.* London: Longmans.

Golson, J., 1977. 'No Room at the Top: Agricultural Intensification in the New Guinea Highlands', in J. Allen, J. Golson, and R. Jones, eds., *Sunda and Sahul: Prehistoric Studies in South East Asia, Melanesia and Australia.* London: Academic Press, 601–638.

Groube, L., Chappell, J., Muke, J., and Price, D., 1986. 'A 40,000 year Occupation Site at Huon Peninsula, Papua New Guinea', *Nature,* 324:453–455.

Johannes, R. E., 1982. 'Implications of Traditional Marine Resources Use for Coastal Fisheries Development in Papua New Guinea', in L. Morauta, J. C. Pernetta, and W. Heaney, eds., *Traditional Conservation in Papua New Guinea: Implications for Today.* Papua New Guinea: Institute of Applied Social and Economic Research, 239–250.

King, B., 1990. 'Does wildlife management by the people work? A case study, Pokili Wildlife Management Area, West New Britain Province, Papua New Guinea'. *Tigerpaper: Regional Quarterly Bulletin on Wildlife and National Parks Management* 17(1), Bangkok: FAO Regional Office for Asia and the Pacific.

Moi, W., 1988. 'Recent Developments in Wildlife Management Areas in Papua New Guinea'. Papua New Guinea: Department of Environment and Conservation.

Moi, W., and Willie, T., 1985. 'Maza Wildlife Management Area: Report on the Problems of Management and the Law Enforcement of the Reserve'. Papua New Guinea: Department of Environment and Conservation.

Pernetta, J., and Hill, L., 1984. 'Traditional Use and Conservation of Resources in the South Pacific Basin', *Ambio,* 13(5–6):359–364.

Powell, J., 1982. 'Traditional Management and Conservation of Vegetation in Papua New Guinea', in L. Morauta, J. C. Pernetta, and W. Heaney, eds., *Traditional Conservation in Papua New Guinea: Implications for Today.* Papua New Guinea: Institute of Applied Social and Economic Research, 121–134.

Runte, A., 1987. *National Parks: The American Experience.* United States: University of Nebraska.

Swadling, P., 1977. 'Depletion of shellfish in the traditional gathering beds of Pari', in J. H. Winslow, ed., *The Melanesian Environment.* Canberra: Australian National University Press, 182–187.

White, J. P., and O'Connell, J. F., 1982. *Prehistory of Australia, New Guinea and Sahul.* Sydney: Academic Press.

Wood, A., and Humphreys, G., 1982. 'Traditional Soil Conservation in Papua New Guinea', in L. Morauta, J. C. Pernetta, and W. Heaney, eds., *Traditional Conservation in Papua New Guinea: Implications for Today.* Port Moresby: Papua New Guinea Institute of Applied Social and Economic Research, 93–114.

World Bank, 1990. *Papua New Guinea: The Tropical Forestry Sector: A tropical Forestry Action Plan Review.* A report prepared by the World Bank under the auspices of the Tropical Forestry Action Plan.

Acknowledgments

This paper was drafted while the authors were on the staff of the University of Papua New Guinea and was completed in late 1991 while one of us (PJH) was a University of Auckland Foundation Visitor in Environmental Science and Geography. In 1997 the section on 'prospects in the 1990s' was updated on the basis of information provided by Dr. Marjorie Sullivan. The figures were drawn by Jonette Surridge, Cartography Laboratory, Department of Geography, University of Auckland.

Contributors

CHRISTINE BRADLEY was Principal Project Officer of the Papua New Guinea Law Reform Commission, in charge of the Commission's work on domestic violence, from 1986 to 1990. She has a Ph.D. in Social Anthropology and worked in Papua New Guinea for over ten years. She currently lives in Canada and is an international consultant on domestic violence and other gender issues.

MICHAEL CROSSLEY is a Senior Lecturer at the University of Bristol, Graduate School of Education, U.K., where he currently coordinates the Research Student (Mphil/Ph.D.) Programme. Dr. Crossley was previously Associate Dean (Planning) in the Faculty of Education at the University of Papua New Guinea. He was Editor of the *Papua New Guinea Journal of Education* from 1985 to 1990; and is currently a member of the Editorial Board for *Comparative Education*, an Executive Editor for the *International Journal of Educational Development*, and a Corresponding Editor for the *International Review of Education*. Current research interests include studies of educational reform in Belize, Central America, and methodological work on the potential of qualitative research in the field of comparative and international education. Dr. Crossley has written widely on education and development, including editing a special issue of *Comparative Education* on education in the South Pacific (vol. 29, no. 3, 1993). With Graham Vulliamy (1997) he has recently published *Qualitative Educational Research in Developing Countries: Current Perspectives* (New York: Garland).

JEANETTE DICKERSON-PUTMAN is Associate Professor and Chair in the Department of Anthropology at Indiana University-Indianapolis where she has taught since 1989. She has done research in Papua New Guinea (1983–1984), the United States of America (1985–1986), the Republic of Ireland (1987–1988), and French Polynesia (1994). Her research interests include: age, gender, and the development process; the religious economy; the gendered life course; caregivers to the elderly; Oceanic cultures; and life history. The applied aspects of her work include her roles as consultant on the NSF-sponsored project 'Rural Tahitian Women and Capitalism' (1994) and on the NIA 'Project A.G.E.' (1988–89), and as Project Manager at the Philadelphia Geriatric Center (1985–1986). Recent honors include the Richard Kalish Innovative Publication Award, Behavioral and Social Science Section of the Gerontological Society of America for *The Aging Experience: Diversity and Commonality across Cultures* (1995) and

Indiana University Facet Teaching Award (1993). Dickerson-Putman is Guest Editor of a Special Issue of *Pacific Studies: Women, Age, and Power: The Politics of Age Difference among Women in Papua New Guinea and Australia* (1996), which includes her paper, 'From Pollution to Empowerment: Women, Age, and Power among the Bena Bena of the Eastern Highlands'.

SINCLAIR DINNEN lectured in the Law Faculty of the University of Papua New Guinea between 1984 and 1988. From 1991 to 1994 he was Head of Crime Studies at the National Research Institute, Port Moresby. He has written extensively on issues of crime and criminal justice in Papua New Guinea and has recently completed a doctoral thesis based on his criminological research in PNG. He is presently a full-time researcher on the State, Society and Governance in Melanesia Project in the Department of Political and Social Change at the Research School of Pacific and Asian Studies, the Australian National University. This work involves an investigation of issues of violence and social control in the context of changing state/society relations in the Melanesian countries.

COLIN FILER taught sociology and anthropology at Glasgow University from 1975 to 1982, and at the University of Papua New Guinea from 1983 to 1994. In 1991 he was appointed as the Projects Manager of the UPNG consultancy company, Unisearch PNG Pty. Ltd. Since 1995 Filer has been Head of the Social and Cultural Studies Division at the Papua New Guinea National Research Institute (formerly IASER). Filer's early fieldwork was in the Sepik region of Papua New Guinea. He has since focused on the social impact of the mining industry and the social context of forest policy, and has recently edited a volume entitled *The Political Economy of Forest Management in Papua New Guinea*.

LAWRENCE HAMMAR'S ethnographic fieldwork on Daru island, capital of Papua New Guinea's Western Province, 1990–92, focused on sexual transactions and sexually transmitted diseases, AIDS knowledge, and the political economy of sex. He received in 1996 his Ph.D. in Anthropology from the Graduate School and University Center of the City University of New York. His publications on these topics can be found in *Genders, Research in Melanesia, Anthropology and Humanism*, and in *Transforming Anthropology* (forthcoming). He is currently interested in the changing relations of space and time in early colonial Papua. Other research interests include history of venereology, AIDS/HIV issues, medical anthropology, gender and sexuality, and prostitution studies. He has taught at, among other institutions, Lewis and Clark College (Portland, Oregon) and the University of Oregon (Eugene, Oregon).

PHILIP J. HUGHES is a Canberra-based consulting environment and heritage specialist. He has been involved in numerous research and consulting environmental and heritage projects in PNG since 1974. Between 1985 and 1991 he was Associate Professor and Coordinator, Environmental Science, at the University of Papua New Guinea. In 1990 and 1991 he was also Pro Vice-Chancellor (Consulting) and foundation Manager, Unisearch PNG Pty Ltd. While with Unisearch PNG he was responsible for all consulting work undertaken by the University, including projects associated with assessment of the environmental and social impact of major development and infrastructure projects in PNG. Hughes has authored or co-authored more than 70 articles in refereed journals and monographs and has co-edited seven monographs on a wide range of environmental and social issues relating to PNG and the wider South Pacific region. He has also written more than 20 reports on environmental consultancies carried out in many different parts of PNG.

TIM T. KAN received his Ph.D. in Fisheries and Wildlife from Oregon State University in 1975. He has research experience through works in Taiwan, Canada, U.S.A. and, especially, the South Pacific. His areas of specialization include all aspects (science and technology, production, management, socioeconomics, and marketing) of fisheries and aquaculture systems. During the past twenty years, he taught at the PNG University of Technology and the University of Papua New Guinea, and was the President of Overseas Fisheries Development Council of the Republic of China (Taiwan). Currently, he is Vice Chairman and CEO of Niugini Fishing Co. Pty. Ltd., a Port Moresby–based purse seiners company.

BETSY KING was Senior Tutor in Geography at the University of Papua New Guinea between 1986 and 1990 where she was particularly concerned with issues of conservation and environmental awareness. She is currently Executive Director of the Scottish Environmental Education Council based at the University of Stirling.

DAVID KING is Senior Lecturer in Geography at the School of Tropical Environment Studies and Geography at James Cook University in North Queensland. He taught geography at the University of Papua New Guinea during the 1980s, where he was also active in promoting field research among UPNG students, accompanying and supervising hundreds of Papua New Guinean students during their first field experiences.

OSKAR KURER is Professor and Head of the Institute of Political Economy, University of Erlangen-Nuremberg, Germany. His past positions, in economics, were at London School of Economics, University of Papua New Guinea, and Queensland University of Technology in Brisbane, Australia. His major publications include *The Political Foundations of Development Policies* (1996) and *J. S. Mill: The Politics of Progress* (1991), as well as journal articles: 'J. S. Mill and the Wages Fund Doctrine', *Journal of the History of Economic Thought* (forthcoming 1998), 'Political Foundations of Development Policies', *Journal of Development Studies* (1996), 'Clientelism, Corruption, and the Allocation of Resources', *Public Choice* (1993), 'J. S. Mill and Utopian Socialism', *Economic Record* (1992), 'J. S. Mill and the Welfare State', *History of Political Economy* (1991), and 'J. S. Mill's Theory of Government Intervention', *History of Political Thought* (1989).

PETER LARMOUR is Director of Graduate Studies in Development Administration at the National Centre for Development Studies at the Australian National University in Canberra, Australia. He previously taught at the University of Tasmania and the University of Papua New Guinea. He is currently researching 'governance' issues, and recent books include (as coeditor) *New Politics in the South Pacific* (University of South Pacific, Suva, Fiji 1995), and (as coauthor) *Market Bureaucracy and Community: A Students' Guide to Organisation* (London: Pluto, 1993). Larmour's contribution to this volume originally appeared in *Pacific Economic Bulletin,* 10(1) (July 1995).

MARTHA MACINTYRE is a Senior Lecturer in Anthropology at La Trobe University in Melbourne, Australia. She completed her postgraduate studies in Anthropology at Cambridge University in England and The Australian National University, Canberra. Since 1979 she has undertaken field research in Milne Bay Province, on Tubetube and Misima islands, and more recently in New Ireland Province on Lihir, the site of a large gold mining project. Her research on Misima and Lihir included specific examination of the social impact of mining on family life and women's roles during the dramatic transition to industrialisation on these islands. She has published numerous articles on gender issues in Melanesia and co-edited (with Margaret Jolly) *Family and Gender in the Pacific: Domestic Contradictions and the Colonial Impact* (1989, Cambridge University Press).

NORRIE MACQUEEN was Lecturer, then Senior Lecturer, in the Department of Political and Administrative Studies at the University of Papua New Guinea between 1986 and 1990 where his research was concerned mainly with Papua New Guinea foreign policy and regional organization in the island Pacific. He is currently Senior Lecturer in Political Science at the University of Dundee in Scotland. His latest book is *The Decolonization of Portuguese Africa* (1997, Longman).

SCOTT MACWILLIAM is employed by Curtin University of Technology in Perth, Western Australia. He researches and writes on Papua New Guinea, Kenya, and Australia. MacWilliam currently is working on the third volume of the history of Burns Philp, which deals with the activities of this major South Pacific firm from 1946 to 1979. Between 1983 and 1985 he was senior lecturer in public administration at the University of Papua New Guinea, and has subsequently published extensively on the late colonial and postcolonial political economy of the country. He is a visiting fellow in the Department of Political and Social Change, School of Pacific and Asian Studies at the Australian National University during 1997–98, completing research for a monograph on agriculture's role in development in post–Second World War Papua New Guinea.

MICHAEL MONSELL-DAVIS first went to Papua New Guinea in 1964 where he completed teacher training in Rabaul and taught in vocational schools in Mt. Hagen and Kairuku (Yule Island). He graduated with a B.A. from the University of Papua New Guinea in 1971, and later undertook his Ph.D. through Macquarie University. His dissertation, *Nabuapaka: Social Change in a Roro Community* (1981), is an ethnography concerned with the traditional leadership and religion of the Roro people, and with local entrepreneurship as villagers attempt to take advantage of the opportunities of the cash economy. Monsell-Davis has taught at the University of the South Pacific, in Fiji, where he researched issues concerning street kids in Suva, and later co-edited a book with Chris Griffin: *Fijians in Town* (1986). After two years in Niue as acting Director of the USP Centre, he returned to PNG in 1984. He spent five years in the Extension Studies Department as Coordinator of Centres, and a further five years lecturing in the Department of Anthropology and Sociology. Currently he is back at USP as Senior Lecturer in the Department of Sociology. He has retained his interests in education, youth, and crime, and in rural entrepreneurs. He has written on distance education; youth, community, and crime in rural and urban areas; village entrepreneurs; the socioeconomic impact of roads and causeways (in PNG and Kiribati); culture and the spread of HIV infection; and is currently trying to find the time to prepare a book on social change in the Pacific, and other monographs that have been in his head for some years.

FRED L. OLSON, after receiving a Ph.D. in Agricultural Economics from the University of Minnesota, worked with several state and federal agencies for more than three decades. He retired from the National Marine Fisheries Service as a Chief Economist and subsequently took up an appointment as Visiting Professor at the University of Papua New Guinea 1988–90. He has since been associated with the Hawaii-based Global Ocean Consultants, Inc., as a senior partner in fisheries planning and development.

PAMELA ROSI received her Ph.D. in anthropology from Bryn Mawr College in 1994. Since conducting research at the Papua New Guinea National Arts School in 1986, she has curated exhibitions of contemporary Papua New Guinea art at Monmouth University (1987; reviewed in *Art in America,* March 1988), Bryn Mawr College (1989), and Bridgewater State College (1989). Her publications include 'Papua New Guinea's New Parliament House: A Contested National Symbol', *The Contemporary Pacific* 1991, 3:2:289–323; 'Larry Santana', *Paradise* 1991, 87:31–34; and (with Laura Zimmer-Tamakoshi) 'Love and Marriage among the Educated Elite in Port Moresby', in *The Business of Marriage: Transformations in Oceanic Matrimony*, ed. R. Marksbury, Pittsburgh: University of Pittsburgh Press 1993. She is currently organizing a new exhibition of contemporary PNG art at Pine Manor College, and working on a book on the role of the Papua New Guinea National Arts School in the creation of national culture and identity.

MARJORIE E. SULLIVAN is a Canberra-based consulting environmental scientist working mainly in PNG, South East Asia, and the South Pacific. She has undertaken numerous research and consulting environmental and heritage projects in PNG since 1974. Between 1985 and 1991 she was Associate Professor, then Professor in the Department of Geography at the University of Papua New Guinea, where she taught several physical geography courses. Sullivan has authored or co-authored more than 120 articles in journals and monographs, and has written more than 30 environmental consulting reports from throughout PNG and numerous others from elsewhere in the Pacific. Recently she has worked with the Departments of Conservation and Environment and Works to develop environmental impact assessment and management planning guidelines for infrastructure projects in PNG.

LAURA ZIMMER-TAMAKOSHI has conducted research in Papua New Guinea since 1982, most recently in 1994—studying a Papua New Guinea business woman—and in 1995 as a mining consultant at the Ramu (Kurumbukare) prospect in Madang Province. She was a Lecturer in Anthropology at the University of Papua New Guinea from 1986 through 1989. In 1990 and 1991 she taught anthropology at Bryn Mawr College and the University of Pennsylvania and was a participant in an NEH Seminar on The Politics of Culture in the Pacific, held at the East-West Center in Honolulu in the summer of 1991. Since 1991 she has taught in the Social Science Division at Truman State University (formerly Northeast Missouri State), where she is now Associate Professor of Anthropology and author and co-producer of the award-winning website, *The Anthropologist in the Field* which focuses on her research among the Gende in Madang Province (http://www.truman.edu/academics/ss/faculty/tamakoshi/index.html). Zimmer-Tamakoshi's most recent professional appointments include Media Review Editor for *Pacific Studies,* board member of the Association for Social Anthropology in Oceania (ASAO), and secretary-treasurer of Central States Anthropology Society (CSAS).

Index